# Europ of Japanese Philosophy

CHISOKUDŌ

The *European Journal of Japanese Philosophy*, the official academic organ of the European Network of Japanese Philosophy, is a peer-reviewed journal published annually in the fall. Its aim is to provide a forum for critical articles and translations related to Japanese philosophy. Contributions are welcome in English, French, German, Italian, Portuguese, Romanian, Spanish, and Japanese.

> Individual printed copies are priced at approximately $15 US (or its equivalent in euros) and may be ordered directly on-line from Amazon.com.

Submissions should be addressed to ejjp.submissions@gmail.com.
Books submitted for review should be sent to the address given below.

Cover design by Claudio Bado

Copyright © 2017 by European Network of Japanese Philosophy, ENOJP

*All rights reserved. No part of this publication may be reproduced, distributed, or transmitted in any form or by any means, including photocopying, recording, or other electronic or mechanical methods, without the prior written permission of the publisher, except in the case of brief quotations embodied in critical reviews and certain other noncommercial uses permitted by copyright law. For permission requests, write to the publisher, addressed "Attention: Permissions Coordinator," at the address below.*

> The European Network of Japanese Philosophy, ENOJP
> Universität Hildesheim, Institut für Philosophie
> Kulturwissenschaften und ästhetische Kommunikation
> Universitätsplatz 1, 31141 Hildesheim, Germany
> www.enojp.org

ISBN 978-1976080289
ISSN 2367-3095

Designed and typeset at the Nanzan Institute for Religion & Culture, Nagoya, Japan
Published in collaboration with Chisokudō Publications

ISSN 2367-3095

# European Journal of Japanese Philosophy

Number 2 · 2017

Editors' Introduction    5

## Articles

Philosophy and Japanese Philosophy in the World
John W. Krummel    9

An Apology for Philosophical Transgressions
James W. Heisig    43

Sacred Appellations
Secular Zen, New Materialism, and D. T. Suzuki's *Soku-hi* Logic
Rossa Ó Muireartaigh    69

The Dialectic of Hegel and Nishida
How to Deal with Modernity
Osaki Harumi    85

La temporalidad metanoética
Sobre Tanabe, Heidegger y Shinran
Rebeca Maldonado    113

Kuki Shūzō
Contingence et temps
Marc Peeters    145

Le statut du végétal dans *Fūdo* de Watsuji
Quentin Hiernaux    159

Leibliches Üben als Teil einer philosophischen Lebenskunst
Die Verkörperung von Kata in den japanischen Wegkünsten

Leon Krings    179

Watsuji's Ethics from the Perspective of *Kata*
as a Technology of the Self

Jordančo Sekulovski    199

Lieu de médiation
Nishida, Tanabe, Simondon

Kuroda Akinobu    209

Reading Hiromatsu's Theory of the Fourfold Structure

Katsumori Makoto    229

## Translations

Andō Shōeki: "Parabola păsărilor"

Roman Paşca    263

Nishida Kitarō: "Über die Philosophie des Lebens"

Ralf Müller    295

## Reviews

J. W. Heisig, T. P. Kasulis, J. C. Maraldo y Raquel Bouso García, eds.
*La filosofía japonesa en sus textos.*

Jordi Vallverdú    317

板橋勇仁,『底なき意志の系譜』

Imono Mika    320

山崎庸男,『安藤昌益の実像:近代的視点を超えて』

Roman Paşca    323

竹村牧男,『ブッディスト・エコロジー:共生・環境・いのちの思想学』

Inutsuka Yū    327

Oleg Benesch
*Inventing the Way of the Samurai:*
*Nationalism, Internationalism, and Bushido in Modern Japan*

Thomas P. KASULIS   329

Yuho Hisayama
*Erfahrungen des ki. Leibessphäre, Atmosphäre, Pansphäre*

Leon KRINGS   333

CONTRIBUTORS   337

# Editor's Introduction

The value of insight in philosophy, as in many other fields, is determined by two things: (1) an intuitive moment that confronts us with the possibility of shifting paradigms in our modes of thought, and (2) the subsequent unnamed, often uncredited, and yet equally important work of concretizing the significance of that turning point. The American philosopher Robert Wood provides a good image of this process in a lecture on "The Liberal Arts and the City" delivered at the University of Dallas in 2011.[1] As history books tells us, the Wright brothers' first powered flights in 1903 completely changed human discourse in terms of our relation to the sky. Current appreciation of the significance of their invention—often devoid of any knowledge of advanced physics or engineering—is expressed unwittingly each time we take a flight. But even when the image of the Wright brother comes to mind, it is accompanied by gross forgetfulness. We hardly ever pay attention to the series of incredible inventions and breathtaking ingenuity that followed and surpassed the miracle of those famous inventors. Nevertheless, the unnamed achievements that carried forward the "immense coordination process"[2] that led us to where we are today are crucial to an account of the full discourse on aviation that ultimately came to define the meaning of that first flight more than a hundred years ago.

With no less ambition, the editors of this journal were among a small group of colleagues to form the European Network of Japanese Philosophy

---

1. https://www.youtube.com/watch?v=CHtMVaj7xmg#t=26m36s
2. https://www.youtube.com/watch?v=CHtMVaj7xmg#t=45m46s. Wood talks about how Liberal Arts Education enables us to appreciate the immensely complex invention of the institutions that grounded the "coming to be" of human civilization. Here we are using his example in a much more restricted sense to refer to the "coming to be" of our own academic network.

in 2014. At the time, we had no doubt that we would leave a mark on the philosophical map. After all, the wind was at our backs and things were moving more quickly than any of us could have anticipated. In the intervening years since its inauguration, the ENOJP organized two international conferences on Japanese philosophy, the first at the Universitat Pompeu Fabra in Barcelona (2015) and the second at the Université Libre de Bruxelles (2016). These two events combined to draw over 150 participants from across the world to make presentations on their work. Discussions on the intellectual history of Japan in general and on a wide variety of engagements with particular Japanese philosophical texts fueled our intellectual enthusiasm and broadened the horizons of our initial dream. It seemed only natural for the ENOJP to direct its energies towards the launch of its own academic journal. In summer of 2016 the *European Journal of Japanese Philosophy* was born.

Perhaps the time has come to think about directing our efforts toward the second part of philosophical insight. The first volume of the *EJJP* was a kind of the euphoric first flight. The sheer excitement of having the finished journal in our hands, after so much preparation and the help of so many collaborators, was its own reward. The warm encouragement that reached us from so many quarters helped keep that exhuberance alive, and with it the dream that what began as a small coterie of scholars working at the fringes of academia was destined to outgrow its origins. The preparation of the second volume of the journal has had a sobering effect as the challenge of keeping up the pace and the standards we had set ourselves began to sink in. The ideal of harnessing the selfless dedication and unacknowledged cooperation of young academics from so many different language groups was bound to run head-on into the increasing demands that their own careers pile on them. Happily, at this critical juncture new faces stepped up to lend a hand and carry us over from the resounding overture into the more measured advance of an annual publication.

Many members of the ENOJP members hold this volume in their hands for the first time at the 3rd ENOJP Conference scheduled to be held in Paris from 2 to 4 November at INALCO and Université Paris I Panthéon-Sorbonne. Many of us imagined it would take a decade and more for Sorbonne to open its doors to a major conference on comparative and non-western philosophy. But here we are, *EJJP* in hand, preparing to hold discussions with representatives from the French capital of continental philosophy.

Others will join me in the surprise that our maiden flight has lasted this long, certainly longer than any of us could have anticipated. Perhaps it is that more and more philosophers and their students in France are ready to embrace the plurality of philosophical thinking reaching the halls of traditional Western academia from around the world. Whatever the reason, the hard truth remains that without the orchestra in the wings, the dancing on stage would quickly come to a halt.

For the journal to continue its course and for the network to gain a foothold in academia, we will have to count on a consistent number of volunteers from our ranks—established scholars as well as those still in the bud—keeping their heads down and shoulders to the wheel. Editorial work like this may go by and large unacknowledged, but for many of us it is an essential part of what it means to live out one's philosophical vocation in collaboration with other scholars. Without the kind of conviviality that has kept us going so far, not only future issues of the journal but future conferences of the ENOJP will simply not be possible. And, to return to where we began, the value of our whole project has drifted away from its initial inspirations and now rests in the hands of those who can enhance it by making it concrete.

In closing, the editors are pleased to announce that with this second issue we are now in a position to begin submitting the *EJJP* to scholarly search engines (like the Philosopher's Index) and online distribution services (like J-Stor and Pro-Quest). We have no doubt that there is much in these pages that merit the attention of a wider audience. As always, your support and encouragement in spreading the work of the Network and the ideas of the journal have our gratitude.

Jan Gerrit Strala<br>Takeshi Morisato

John W. Krummel
*Hobart and William Smith Colleges*

# Philosophy and Japanese Philosophy in the World

In tackling the question of what is Japanese philosophy, the paper discusses: (1) philosophy in general, (2) the issue of Japanese philosophy, and (3) the relevance of both philosophy and Japanese philosophy in our present age of globalization. Examining the definitions of philosophy provided by Kant, Hegel, and Heidegger, and looking at the philosophies of Nishida and Nishitani among others, I argue the source of philosophy—its originary and universal motivation—to be the question of meaning of existence. Japanese philosophy is no exception. I then discuss whether there is something unique to Japanese philosophy in particular and look into the question of the essence of Japanese philosophy. Furthermore, I argue that in order to be true to the original motivation of philosophy, the study of Japanese philosophy, if it is itself to be considered philosophy, cannot be reduced to biography, history, or philology. It must be relevant to our life. I then conclude with a discussion of the relevance of Japanese philosophy and the philosophical study of Japanese philosophy to our life today.

KEYWORDS: Philosophy—Japanese philosophy—Nishida Kitarō—Nishitani Keiji—Kant—Hegel—Heidegger—Miki Kiyoshi—Nakamura Hajime—Nakamura Yūjirō—globalization—Ueda Shizuteru—Karatani Kōjin—*tetsugaku*—*nihon tetsugaku*

We are here to discuss the question of Japanese philosophy. What is Japanese philosophy? Is there such a thing? But more fundamental is the question of What is philosophy? In order to examine what Japanese philosophy is, we need to inquire into the general meaning of philosophy itself and in addition examine what the adjective "Japanese" entails. It is certainly not an easy task to define once and for all what philosophy is. It has meant different things to different thinkers throughout the ages. And we cannot ignore the linguistic, socio-cultural, and historical conditions of particular traditions that inevitably influence how philosophy is understood. Japanese philosophy is no exception here. Its definition depends on a variety of factors that make it difficult to pinpoint exactly what it is. As Uehara Mayuko 上原麻有子, the head editor of the *Journal of Japanese Philosophy*, remarked in her introduction to vol. 1 of the journal, the definitions of both "philosophy" and "Japanese philosophy" need to be reconsidered all the time.[1] In the following I would like to tackle first this preliminary question of philosophy itself. Following this, I will discuss in light of the first question, the issue of Japanese philosophy. I will then conclude with their relevance—of both philosophy and Japanese philosophy—today. Throughout this process I will be making references to, and discussing the positions of, a number of philosophers and scholars from past and present, Japan and the West. But in tackling both these questions of philosophy in general and Japanese philosophy in particular, I want to stress the very philosophical import or relevance of Japanese philosophy and moreover the study of Japanese philosophy.

1. Uehara 2013, 1.

## What is Philosophy?

What is philosophy? Contemporary Japanese philosopher Nakamura Yūjirō 中村 雄二郎 has defined philosophy (哲学) as an exercise of the mind, whereby we ground our ideas or way of living.[2] Similarly comparative and Asian philosophy scholars H. Gene Blocker and Christopher Starling have taken philosophy in its narrow sense as a "critical, reflective, rational, and systematic approach to questions of very general interest."[3] Since not everything is conveniently placed before one's eyes, philosophy with a critical spirit attempts to cast out the arbitrary despite the fact that in this very attempt there nevertheless often results a proliferation of different competing philosophical views that in turn feed endless and lively debates and arguments, continually engendering philosophical discourse.[4] For example, philosophy has often historically arisen within religious traditions that have writing, and when it does so we might distinguish the philosophical component from the rest of the religion as "the attempt to intellectually explain and systematize problems that arise in interpreting and defending religious texts."[5] Blocker and Starling argue that in that sense we can recognize at least three independent original traditions of thought that qualify as philosophy: Greek, Indian, and Chinese.[6] That is not to say that we can ignore the historical origins or etymological significance of the word *philosophy*. In our attempt to understand what philosophy is, it would also be helpful to see how philosophy has been understood and defined through the ages.

As most students of philosophy know, the word *philosophy* comes from the Greek word *philosophia* (φιλοσοφία) meaning literally the "love of wisdom." Pythagoras was said to have coined the Greek word *philosophos* (φιλόσοφος)—"lover of wisdom"—by combining *philos* (φίλος) ("friend") and *philein* (φιλειν) ("to love") with *sophos* (σοφός) or *sophia* (σοφία) ("wise," "wisdom," etc.). Despite its originally ethico-religious sense in Pythagoras and noticeable still in Plato's *Phaedo*, Aristotle equated *philosophia* with *epistēmē* (ἐπιστήμη) for "rational knowledge" or "science" in general.

---

2. Nakamura Y. 1967, 173.
3. Blocker and Starling 2001, 16.
4. See Blocker and Starling 2001, 16; Nakamura Y. 1967, 194.
5. Blocker and Starling 2001, 21.
6. See ibid., 16.

Immanuel Kant in his attempt to critique reason considers what such "rational knowledge" would be and connects it with the interests or ends of reason. He provided two definitions for philosophy in terms of its ideal and the concrete attempt to actualize it : (1) "a mere idea of a possible science, which nowhere exists *in concreto*"; and (2) the exercising of "the talent of reason, in accordance with its universal principles, in certain actually existing attempts at philosophy."[7] More specifically that ideal of philosophy (the first definition) would be "the science of the relation of all knowledge to the essential ends of human reason"[8] or the science "…in which everyone necessarily has an interest."[9] In other words, for Kant, the field of philosophy is inseparable from the interests of reason. This leads us to the question of what those interests of reason are. And if the interests of reason themselves shift—although that certainly was not Kant's belief—or the possible modes for attempting to realize them shift according to historical conditions, we are led to the question even more fundamentally of: What are the conditions of human existence that guide such interests of reason?

In the attempt to understand what philosophy is, we certainly cannot ignore the historical development of philosophy itself. If ways of thinking can differ on the basis of the socio-cultural environments, they may also change when those conditions change. G. W. F. Hegel provides a certain understanding of philosophy on the basis of its historical development. His brief definition of philosophy was that it is the "thinking study of things."[10] Philosophy thinks about the concerns of other disciplines of knowledge, their presuppositions, their justifications, etc., at a higher and more systematic level. In other words, it involves not only thinking directly about the objects of these other disciplines but also about their thinking of these objects. But the concrete attempt to engage in philosophy as such has led to its historical development and plurality of competing claims to philosophy.[11] For Hegel these many philosophies complement each other and their

---

7. A838/B66 in Kant's first Critique: Kant 1993, 753; and Kant 1965, 657.
8. A839/B867 in Kant's first Critique: Kant 1993, 753; and Kant 1965, 657.
9. A840/B868 in Kant's first Critique: Kant 1993, 754 and note; and Kant 1965, 658 and note a.
10. Hegel 1975, §2, 4.
11. See Hegel 1975, §13, 18–19.

inconsistencies or incoherences are resolved only through their transition to another higher level philosophy that would sublate the lower ones, embodying the very principles each of the competing philosophies hold in opposition to one another. The implicit claim is that it is Hegel's own philosophy as universal philosophy that embraces what is true in all earlier philosophies by reflecting on them. Yet philosophy, and especially universal philosophy, as such can appear only when the main business of life is done, that is, only when we no longer have to worry about the basic concerns of life. Heidegger provides another view to philosophy that rejects that claim.

From Martin Heidegger's perspective, the very interests of reason that would guide philosophy for Kant presuppose certain fundamental facts of human existence, our essential situatedness or "(t)here" (*Da*) of our existence in the world, such as our concern for being in the face of death, that is, our mortality, as it becomes explicated in the late 1920s. We might generalize this to mean our concern for the meaning or the value of existence, being, in the face of its annihilation or nothingness, that is, the pointlessness or meaninglessness of existence. Heidegger early on (1926–1927) speaks of philosophy as a science of being (*Sein*) rather than of *a* being (*Seiendes*).[12] It digs beneath the sciences of particular sorts of beings and particular views of the world in order to look at being (*Sein*) as such. But it can do so only by investigating what makes these particular sciences and perspectives possible, our "being-(t)here" (*Dasein*) that shapes our preconceptual understanding of being. In other words, the questions of philosophy, as the queen of the sciences, are questions in which the philosopher herself is *already* entangled rather than being questions of an abstract and impersonal academic exercise. In his attempt to revitalize philosophy as a *practice*, Heidegger, from his early years, wanted to emphasize philosophy's connection to "life."[13] Hence in a 1921 letter to Karl Löwith, Heidegger writes, "I work concretely and factically out of my 'I am,' out of my intellectual and wholly factic origin, milieu, life-contexts, and whatever is available to me from these as a vital experience in which I live...."[14] For Heidegger in *Sein und Zeit* (*Being and*

---

12. Heidegger 2004, 6ff; 1997, 17; and 1988, 13.
13. On this see Malpas 2006, 40.
14. Letter of August 19, 1921 in Pappenfuss and Pöggeler 1990, 27–32, 29. For the English see Kisiel 1993, 78.

*Time*, 1927) it is precisely our mortality, our comportment to death, that shapes our understanding of being and accordingly our being-in-the-world (*In-der-Welt-sein*). Philosophical inquiry in investigating our understanding of being is disconcerting because it is motivated by unsettling moods like anxiety, which frees us from our day-to-day concerns to face being *as such* in its irreducible abyss. Such moods set us on the path to philosophize, to inquire after being *as such*. Even a few years later (1930) when Heidegger is no longer particularly concerned with our being-towards-death (*Sein-zum-Tode*), he maintains that philosophy remains disconcerting in that it questions into the whole (*Ganze*) of being[15] in which we ourselves are implicated.[16] In 1936 he states this to mean also an inquiry into the "ground of beings": "With this question it had its inception, in this question it will find its end...."[17] In 1929 Heidegger expressed that question as: Why are there beings at all instead of nothing?[18] We might add then that philosophy in that sense makes explicit the abyssal depths of being—for the whole cannot be conceptually or intellectually fathomed in the context of that environing nothing. In that respect it is *also* transformative by putting the very being of the questioner into question. Even if Heidegger in his later years, post-1930, begins to distance himself from "philosophy," identified with the metaphysical tendencies of the Western tradition that he wants to overcome, replacing it with "thinking" (*Denken*) which he associates with poetry, we might still accept Heidegger's earlier understanding of philosophy as something broader and deeper than mere metaphysics taken narrowly as one occluding direction philosophy might fall into. That is, it looks into the depths of being in general including our very own existence in the face of an abyss

---

15. HEIDEGGER 1994, 141.

16. Later, however, Heidegger comes to identify philosophy with metaphysics itself in its onto-theological constitution that originates the *forgetfulness* of being and *leads to* (rather than springs from) nihilism under the reign of technology. Thus, the later Heidegger poses "thinking" itself that attempts to commemorate the address of being as an alternative to this pejorative sense of philosophy.

17. HEIDEGGER 1983, 26; and 2000, 26. It is good to keep in mind here that *Grund* for "ground" here can also be translated as "reason," and hence can signify the *why*, the purpose or meaning of things.

18. HEIDEGGER 1976, 121.

that metaphysical solutions—claiming universal or eternal solutions—tend to cover over.

It has often been stated that the original motivation for philosophy—the "love of wisdom"—ultimately springs from a sense of wonder, amazement or bewilderment—what the Greeks called *thaumazein* (θαυμάζειν). When Socrates was overcome by thoughts to be thrown into prolonged states of motionless and speechless shocked wonder, the content of his absorption, according to Hannah Arendt, was untranslatable into words. Plato and Aristotle agreed that *thaumazein* as such is the beginning of philosophy.[19] Plato stated, "For this is an experience which is characteristic of a philosopher, this wondering: this is where philosophy begins and nowhere else" (*Theaetetus* 155d)[20] and Aristotle wrote, "For it is owing to their wonder that men both now begin and at first began to philosophize" (*Metaphysics* 982b12ff).[21] And what is it that we wonder at or are amazed by? Taking off from our discussion of Heidegger above, the wonder would be in facing being *as such*, in its abyss, that is, its precariousness or absurdity, or perhaps what the Kyoto School philosophers called "nothing" (無). Heidegger in his works from the 1920s often referred to Max Scheler's notion of nothingness. Scheler proposed that what grounds philosophical activity is the insight "that *there is anything at all*... that '*there is not nothing*' (whereby the word 'nothing'... means *absolute nothing*...)."[22] In this proposal, Scheler emphasized the positive nature of this insight that "there is not nothing," prompting philosophical wonderment, which is precisely what the Greeks seems to have meant by *thaumazein*. Philosophy is driven by the existential question concerning being in the face of nothingness, which also means meaning in the face of meaninglessness. The wonder that there is... (x) rather than nothing, that I exist rather than not, or that there are beings when there may just as well be nothing, or that we find (x) meaningful when we find no reasons why—a wonder that can be provoked by confrontations with death, the sublime, the absurd, or senses of boredom, uncertainty, contingency,

---

19. Arendt also adds here that for them some such state of speechless wonder is also its end. ARENDT 1998, 302 and note 67.

20. PLATO 1997, 173.

21. ARISTOTLE 1941, 692.

22. SCHELER 1954, 93: "die evidente Einsicht... daß überhaupt Etwas sei... daß '*nicht Nichts sei*' (wobei das Wort Nichts... *absolutes Nichts* bedeutet...)."

nihilistic despair—initiates the activity of philosophy. What are we to make of our existence when a secure ground seems to be lacking, when *is* could just as well be *not*? What is its meaning despite the contingencies and failures of our various projects or when there is no ground, reason, guarantee to support it? That seems to me to be the ultimate concern of philosophy. This cannot be merely an intellectual or academic issue, for it has existential implications. But at the same time philosophy aims to systematically articulate and respond to these concerns.

The lives of both Nishida Kitarō 西田幾多郎 and Nishitani Keiji 西谷啓治 may serve to illustrate my point despite Nishida's own contrasting of his view from the ancient Greek postulation of wonder or *thaumazein* (驚き) as the beginning of philosophy. Nishida in 『無の自覚的限定』[Determination of the nothing in self-awareness, 1932] instead identifies the starting point of philosophy to be "the facticity of the self-contradiction of our self" (我々の自己の自己矛盾の事実) and its motive to be "the deep sorrow of human life" (深い人生の悲哀),[23] that is, the pain of living as man. And in his 「生の哲学について」[On the philosophy of life] of the same period, Nishida writes that "What has been called philosophy since ancient times in some sense has always been founded upon the deepest demands of life. How can there be philosophy without the issue of human life?"[24] Those familiar with Nishida's life know how much his life abounded in tragedy. As a young man he lived through the failure of his father's business and the family's loss of land and inherited estates. In his adult life he endured a series of deaths in his family, not only his parents, but including the passing of his first wife, four daughters, and a son—that is, five of his eight children plus his wife—from a variety of diseases, in some cases after long periods of being bedridden. Tanabe Hajime 田辺元 allegedly noticed the resemblance of Nishida's life to that of Job from the Old Testament.[25] Already in his preface to 『善の研究』[Inquiry into the good, 1911], Nishida implies the issue of human life to be the basis of philosophical inquiry,[26] and two years previous to this, in a preface written for Fujioka Sakutarō 藤岡作太郎 who had published his

23. Nishida 2002, 92.
24. Ibid., 335.
25. See Kosaka 2003, 29.
26. Nishida 2003, 6; and 1990, xxx.

book in memory of his deceased daughter, Nishida who had also lost his daughter in the same year, states:

> …the spiritual life of man cannot be meaningless but must have some deep significance. To solve the issue of death is the greatest matter of human life. In the face of death, life is like a bubble. Only by solving the issue of death will we awaken to the true meaning of life.[27]

Gōdo Wakako 神戸和佳子 argues that with the passing of his daughter, Nishida could not bear the possibility of life's meaninglessness and as a consequence began his philosophical inquiry. Here the deep sorrow of losing people he loved served to motivate his philosophizing.[28] So it is likely that this sentiment was behind Nishida's repetitions throughout his later years that "the motivation behind philosophy is the consciousness of pathos [or sorrow] (悲哀)."[29]

But we also know that the starting point for Nishida's early philosophy was what he called "pure experience" (純粋経験). Ueda Shizuteru 上田閑照 thus focuses on what he considers to be the "call" of pure experience and its unfolding descent and—in the reverse direction—the ascending climb out of philosophical concern back towards that source, and their alternating currents and interpenetration.[30] For it is in pure experience that we first encounter the above-mentioned contradiction of the self, the sorrow or pathos of living life, and from which fundamental philosophical questions emerge about the real world—both the life-world and the world of history—in which we are born, act, and die. Ueda, looking at the same passage we pointed to above in Nishida's *Determination of the Nothing in Self-awareness*, likewise notices that what is questioned in this world of actuality (現実の世界) tied to the being of one's self is the "facticity of the self-contradiction of our self." He interprets this to be the fissure that runs through the world wherein we are born, whereby the world is a "world of anxiety and unrest" (不安動揺の世界).[31] According to Ueda, Nishida's response to

---

27. Preface to 『古文学史講話』 [Lectures on the history of classical Japanese literature] in NISHIDA 2003, 332–3.
28. See GŌDO 2013, 97–8, 100.
29. See KOSAKA 2003, 13.
30. See UEDA 1991, 86–7.
31. Ibid., 359–60.

that fissure or crack entering into everyday life, the acuteness of the "sorrow/pathos of life," is in its very concrete experience: "My way of thinking, ever since the idea of pure experience has been to start off from the most immediate concrete reality."[32] For Nishida, "we need to grasp most deeply what our most ordinary everyday life is…" but we do this by plumbing into its depths through that very fissure as passage. If the fissure in the immediacy of everyday life is the start of philosophy, its solution also lies deep within, just as spring water gushes forth from the depths of the underground.[33]

Nishitani describes what initiates the philosophical enterprise to be specifically nihilistic despair that pulls the rug from under one's feet. What moved him to begin his study of philosophy was a "pre-philosophical nihilism" (哲学以前のニヒリズム).[34] When he was sixteen his father died from tuberculosis and he himself then became ill with tuberculosis. Such experiences sparked a certain "existential doubt" about his own existence, whereby he fell into a state of despair or nihilism that he describes as the mood of "nihility" (虚無).[35] He thus came to feel as if life itself is nothing but suffering,[36] and it was such anomie that led him to the enterprise of philosophy.[37] For Nishitani nihilism then is the starting point of philosophy, as well as the beginning of the religious quest that poses the question, "For what purpose, why, do I exist?"[38] And he claims that its overcoming is "the single greatest issue facing philosophy and religion in our times."[39] Here Nishitani understands the religious quest as man's search for "true reality" and the avenue of that "self-realization" (自己実現) or "self-awareness of reality" (実在の自覚)—a quest that arises from a profound personal existential crisis at the limits of one's existence, where the meaningfulness of day-to-day living is negated.[40] In this sense, a religious significance is discovered here in the practice of philosophy.

---

32. Nishida 1989, 138 cited in Ueda 1991, 360.
33. Ueda 1991, 360–1.
34. Nishitani 1990a, 186.
35. See ibid., 178ff, 180, 186, 193–5.
36. Ibid., 175–6.
37. See Nishitani 1993, v; and 1990b, xxxiii.
38. Nishitani 1987, 5–6; and 1982, 2–3.
39. Nishitani 1987, 54; and 1982, 47.
40. Nishitani 1987, 8–9; and 1982, 5–6.

Now despite their differences there seems to be a common ground here among these distinct postulations of the source of philosophy—what Heidegger and the Greeks called wonder, what Nishida called the deep sorrow of life, and Nishitani's nihilistic despair. The sorrow of life is its "self-contradiction," most acutely felt in the face of death, the annihilation of existence. The wonder of being for Heidegger comes out explicitly in its contrast to nothing—"Why are there beings rather than nothing?" Death looms large also in Nishitani's nihilistic despair. Epicurus also seemed to regard anxiety stemming from an unacknowledged fear of death as the cause of philosophy. If Socrates was often found in motionless states of shocked wonder, Nishida, at least once, was found analogously motionless gazing into the sea for a long time. Nishitani Keiji recalls a story of how when an old woman, noticing Nishida staring into the sea, asked him what he was thinking, Nishida replied, "I'm thinking about the world. The world is indeed mysterious."[41] Nishida had also written in his 「鎌倉雑詠」 [Kamakura poems], "I love the sea, it seems to me that something unlimited is moving there."[42] All of these apparently distinct starting points of philosophy—wonder, sorrow, anxiety, despair—involve an experience of contingency, indeterminacy, uncertainty in regard to life or existence that calls into question the very meaningfulness of things. It points to an *excess* or *other* that exceeds, is irreducible to, and disrupts or disturbs the pre-given framework of meaning.[43] Even if it evokes anxiety or sorrow, it also evokes awe and wonder. Nishida's experience of the sea seems indicative of this. Some might also describe this as the experience of the sublime in Kant's sense or what Rudolf Otto called the experience of *mysterium tremendum et fascinans*.[44] They are all cases in which the presumed world, the framework of intelligibility, ordinarily taken for granted, has crumbled or threatens to crumble. And they point to an *otherness* lying beyond the horizon of the familiar that shakes its framework—an ungrounding—opening up its indeterminacy or contingency. As the meaningfulness of existence is called into question, we

---

41. NISHITANI 1951 cited in UEDA 1991, 393–394. An English translation is available in NISHITANI 1991, 19. My translation differs slightly.

42. Cited in UEDA 1991, 394. The poems have been published in NISHIDA 2004.

43. For a discussion of the occurrence of the other or alien that can motivate philosophy, see WALDENFELS 2011, 81.

44. Although Otto (in his *Das Heilige*) takes this to be the origin of religion. See OTTO 1958.

can either resign or despair, even engage in nihilistic self-destruction—as in the suicide of the character Matsuko at the end of Ōshima Nagisa's 大島渚 1966 film *Violence at Noon* (『白昼の通り魔』) with the crumbling of her ideal world informed by love and humanism—on the one hand, or partake in an investigative quest for, or reconstruction of, meaning on the other. Philosophy is one such course. I am not so sure if that means that philosophy in itself is an attempt to "escape" the meaninglessness of life.[45] I think it is instead an attempt to come to terms with that shaking of the foundation and to positively deal with it.

But furthermore because that undoing of the horizon often happens in the interstices between cultural communities, that is, between horizons, in the fragile space of exchange and circulation between them—fragile in the sense that the space lacks any positive communal identity or grounding—Karatani Kōjin 柄谷行人 suggests how philosophy as such, emerging from that interstitial space—a "space of sheer difference" that is insubstantial and amorphous—is homeless.[46] Socrates' philosophizing challenged—and hence displaced him from—the very communal framework of Athens. The source of René Descartes' doubt that led him on his search for certainty was precisely his "multicultural" experience through his travels that one's own tradition is not necessarily better than what appears to one as the "eccentric" traditions of others, "others" who may not necessarily be barbarians or savages but rather may be possessed of reason, just as much as or even more than those of one's kin.[47] This homelessness of philosophy will indeed be relevant in the next sections when we look into the question of Japanese philosophy and its place in the world.

In any case, to the extent that philosophy is motivated by that question thrust upon the meaningfulness of our existence or life, it can neither be simply an intellectual or academic exercise nor can it be reduced to mere biography, historiology, or philology. Of course historical knowledge as well as biographical or philological knowledge can contribute to philo-

---

45. As Gōdo seems to suggest. Or at least she says it was an attempt in the case of Nishida to escape the fear that life is meaningless (see Gōdo 2013, 99). "Escape" seems to connote a sense of inauthenticity which would be antithetical to the purpose of philosophy.

46. See Karatani 2005, 81–2, 98, 134. Also see Žižek 2004, 266–7.

47. See Descartes 1994, pt. 2, §4, 32, 33.

sophical understanding. Nevertheless every work that claims to be philosophical ought to keep in mind the original motivation for philosophizing and make itself relevant to our lives. And to the extent that we can never treat the matter of this concern as an object standing outside of ourselves—since it implicates our very own existence—Heidegger states that all great philosophers "think the same." To this Miki Kiyoshi 三木清 adds that philosophy is an expression of life itself (生のひとつの現はれ), an existential necessity of a process proceeding from *within* life itself (生の裡から発生する過程の存在論的必然性), whereby one questions the very world wherein one lives along with one's own existence for—as we saw above—the nature of life itself is insecure.[48] In that sense every thinker is him/herself implicated in the very activity of philosophizing as it emerges from his/her own life. And yet because that "same" is so rich and saturated in its abyssal excess of potential meaning, no individual thinker can ever exhaust it.[49] In this connection we are led to the question of how philosophy as such, in its attempt to think and give shape to that excess, manifests in other historical epochs and cultural regions that have provided distinct preconceptual horizons for thought.

Nakamura Hajime 中村元, for example, looked for the root of philosophical enterprise in what he called "ways of thinking" or "thought" (思想), as expressed in the popular sayings, proverbs, songs, myths, and folklore of a people as opposed to the self-conscious systems of thought that would be "philosophy" (哲学) proper.[50] He found thought as such to be a cultural phenomenon (文化現象), involving socio-historical, psychological, aesthetic, and linguistic phenomena, etc.[51] Nakamura suggests that thought as such is the cultural-historical site of concrete issues encountered in everyday life which then provides a foundation indispensable to the growth of philosophy.[52] Philosophy thus becomes manifest in different ways according to its cultural or regional setting—its socio-cultural environ-

---

48. MIKI 1966, 36. For the English translation, see MIKI 1998, 309–10.
49. HEIDEGGER 1961, 46; and 1979, 36; Cf. also HEIDEGGER 2007, 198; and 1984, 156.
50. See NAKAMURA H. 1964, 5, 10.
51. See the forward by Arthur Frederick Wright in ibid., vii-viii; and the editor's preface by Philip P. Wiener in ibid., xi.
52. See ibid., 9.

ment—and changes as those environing conditions change. The definition of philosophy itself is thus bound up with the very "practice of philosophizing within distinctive cultures"—as the editors of the *Japanese Philosophy: A Sourcebook* (James Heisig, Thomas Kasulis, and John Maraldo) have argued.[53] But as cultures change, philosophy has a history. Philosophy thus gives voice to the universal concern of man—the issue of being, existence, meaning, life—within the perimeters of its setting, which however are not permanent and may perhaps be challenged. This returns us to the definition of philosophy as a "critical, reflective, rational, and systematic approach to questions" Blocker and Starling provide that we saw at the beginning of our discussion. On the other hand, Heidegger had claimed that the only philosophy is Western European philosophy.[54] This leads us to our next question: Japanese philosophy, is there such a thing?

### Japanese Philosophy?

The concept of "philosophy" as known in the West was first imported to Japan during the Meiji (明治) period (1868–1911/1912) and enthusiastically pursued by the intellectual milieu. It was a time when a generation of scholars were devoted to importing Western intellectual culture as a whole, including a variety of academic fields from the West. In 1874 the Japanese term *tetsugaku* (哲学) was introduced when Nishi Amane 西周 (1829–1897) neologized the term *kitetsugaku* (希哲学), "the science of seeking clarity," to translate the Western concept and then shortened it to *tetsugaku*. At the time philosophy or *tetsugaku* was conceived by the Japanese as exclusively Western in origin and distinct from the traditional forms of intellectual pursuit originating in East Asia. The general belief was that in order to compete with Western powers and avoid being colonized, they ought to embrace the variety of Western sciences, including philosophy.

---

53. Heisig, Kasulis, and Maraldo 2011, 17.
54. See Heidegger 2002, 228; and 1968, 224. We ought to remember here however that this statement is connected to Heidegger's critique of the Western tradition as metaphysics as shaped by Platonic dualism, which he attempts to overcome with what he calls "thinking" (*Denken*).

Even today in Japan the distinction is often made between on the one hand *tetsugaku* as referring to Western philosophy and modern and contemporary Japanese philosophy that had been engendered through the adoption of Western philosophical methods and approaches, and on the other hand *shisō* (thought, thinking) referring to pre-Meiji intellectual practices and traditions. For example, Uehara Mayuko has defined *tetsugaku* in Japan as designating the scholarly domain (学問領域) opened through the introduction of Western philosophy during Japan's modernization process that began in the Meiji period.[55] "Thought" or *shisō* however points to the rich intellectual history of Japan that encompasses the sort of literature that in other non-Western regions—such as in India and China—has become classified as "philosophy." Through contact with the modern West, Indians have borrowed the Western concept of "philosophy" to call their own ancient thought, "Indian philosophy." Likewise the Chinese, after learning of Western philosophy, from the 1920s have appropriated the Japanese neologism for philosophy to call their own ancient intellectual traditions, "Chinese philosophy" (*zhōng guó zhé xué* 中国哲学).[56] By contrast, Japanese intellectuals for the most part have regarded their own native intellectual traditions as precisely *not* philosophical for the reason that it is not logical, analytical, abstract in the same way Western philosophy is. Even Nakamura Hajime suggests that the more sensual, integrative, or aesthetic aspects of Japanese thought traditions, in distinction from the more intellectual elements imported from China and thus from Chinese or Indian philosophy in general, precludes them from being philosophy.[57]

Meiji thinker Nakae Chōmin 中江兆民 famously declared in 1901 that "from ancient times to the present, there has never been any philosophy [*tetsugaku*] in Japan."[58] He not only refused to call the thought of National Learning ("Nativist" thought), Confucianism, and Buddhism philosophy, but also to regard as philosophy what his Westernized intellectual contemporaries were doing for lack of sufficient originality.[59] Many contemporary

55. UEHARA 2008, 65.
56. On this, see BLOCKER and STARLING 2001, 3–4; and Davis 2015, 6.
57. See BLOCKER and STARLING 2001, 8.
58. NAKAE 1975, 8.
59. See BLOCKER and STARLING 2001, 1; NAKAMURA Y. 1967, 174.

Japanese intellectuals are sympathetic to this view. What at first appears here to be a rather narrow view that refuses to recognize the finer points of traditional Japanese thought, in Nakamura Yūjirō's reading of Chōmin's statement, was in fact for the sake of freeing thought and enlivening what ought to be enlivened by carefully considering what "philosophy" is without being shackled by traditional Eastern thought but also without becoming an absolute devotee of "Western thought."[60] Nakamura suggests that what was lacking in traditional thought is an objectification or thematization of the subject of study—whether "nature," "self," or "norms"—modeled on rationality as opposed to the "emotive naturalism" (感情的自然主義) prevalent in Japanese intellectual life that assumes the self-evident and ordinary to be what is natural and which culminated in the traditional "family system" and "emperor system."[61] Miki Kiyoshi, while studying abroad in Germany towards the end of the Taishō (大正) period (1912–1926), also wrote a piece for a local German newspaper in which he discusses the lack of any recognition for history in the traditional Japanese worldview and the lack of objective historical research. Miki's target here is what he calls "Buddhistic naturalist pantheism" (仏教的、自然主義的汎神論) and Nakamura identifies this with what he calls "emotive naturalism."[62] We might object that simply objectifying one's own origins or milieu, the self-evident or what is assumed as natural, cannot be the end-all of philosophy. If the very act of philosophizing itself implicates one's own subjective being, one cannot deny the hermeneutics involved in philosophizing. Nakamura's point however is that to simply take for granted what seems natural is arbitrary and antithetical to philosophy, the task of which is to repel the arbitrary. His point is that such "emotive naturalism" has been the spiritual milieu of Japan, thus making it difficult for philosophy to be realized in that setting.[63] Nakamura thinks that it is only through the work of Nishida Kitarō, with the 1911 publication of his *Inquiry into the Good*, that one could speak of a philosophy in Japan, suggesting that only with this work was Chōmin's judgment dis-

60. Nakamura Y. 1967, 181, n. 1.
61. See ibid., 186, 190–1.
62. Ibid., 192, n. 3.
63. See ibid., 193–5.

proven.[64] Nakamura Yūjirō however adds to this that even today, despite the passing of over half a century since Chōmin's critique, he has felt the same sort of lack in the Japanese intellectual milieu, for example, that there are no thoroughgoing debates in politics between distinct intellectual positions or ideological stances that move beyond mere compromise.[65] The observation Nakamura makes here about the general intellectual climate of contemporary Japan, of course, does not necessarily pertain to the exercise of philosophy within the academic setting nor mean an outright denial of the existence of a "Japanese philosophy."

Some decades after writing the above-mentioned German newspaper article, Miki also wrote in a piece aptly titled, "There is no Philosophy in Japan" (「哲学のない日本」) that Nishi Amane, who came up with the very term *tetsugaku* as we discussed above, may have been of a similar opinion as Chōmin, but *also* that this all depends on what we understand by "philosophy" (*tetsugaku*). Miki refers to Ikuta Chōkō 生田長江, a critic, who remarked that if we simply accept the concept of *tetsugaku* as imported from the West and try to fit everything into that category, indeed, we would not find anything corresponding to that idea in Japan of the past. Nevertheless Ikuta also could not help but eventually concede that one cannot find any great "scholars" (学者) nor "scholarship" (学問) in the history of Japan. Miki thus concludes that the statement, "There is no philosophy in Japan," really refers to philosophy as "scholarship" or a "scholarly discipline."[66] In other words, there has been no philosophy in Japan as a scholarly or academic discipline, that is, the kind of scholarly discipline that developed in the West as "philosophy." The pre-Meiji intellectual schools were not scholarly enough to be counted as such.

On the other hand, the editors of *Japanese Philosophy: A Sourcebook*— James Heisig, John Maraldo, and Thomas Kasulis—have argued that if philosophy means "the critical investigation of deeply perplexing questions," there is no a priori reason to limit it to the way it has been construed and conducted within a particular cultural context, i.e., the Greco-European tra-

64. NAKAMURA Y. 1995, 80.
65. See NAKAMURA Y. 1967, 176.
66. MIKI 1968, 153–154. For an English translation, see MIKI 2016.

dition.⁶⁷ Their claim is that there was already in Japan prior to the mid-nineteenth century coining of *tetsugaku*, "a solid philosophical tradition rooted in an intellectual history that provided it with resources comparable to but very different from those that have sustained Western philosophy."⁶⁸

In his own study, "Defining Philosophy in the Making," John Maraldo⁶⁹ has isolated four senses in which the notion of "Japanese philosophy" has been used: (1) Western philosophy as it happens to be practiced by Japanese scholars; (2) traditional Japanese thought (Confucian, Nativist, Buddhist, etc.) as it was formulated prior to the introduction of Western philosophy; (3) a form of inquiry with methods and themes that are Western in origin, but that can be applied to pre-modern, pre-Westernized, Japanese thinking; and (4) a kind of reverse Orientalism that asserts the superiority of specifically Japanese ways of thinking. With some modifications, this four-fold sense of Japanese philosophy was adopted by the editors of *Japanese Philosophy: A Sourcebook*, of which Maraldo was a part, in their discussion of the topic.⁷⁰ Let us examine these four senses.

In correspondence with the first sense of Japanese philosophy, it was Meiji-era critics who denied Japan had its own philosophy and who applied the term *tetsugaku* to describe what the scholars who imported European philosophy were doing. But as we saw above, the prevailing view in Japan even up to the present has been that philosophy is a scholarly discipline that developed in the West and that if there is a Japanese philosophy (日本哲学), it is only as a discipline first made possible by the importation of, and consequent appropriation of, Western philosophy since Meiji times. Yet many others feel that this places too severe a limit to the meaning of *tetsugaku*⁷¹ and question whether pre-Meiji *shisō* (thought) might be regarded as "*tetsugaku*" or not.

The most intriguing of the four senses, in my view, are the second and the third. On the opposite end of the spectrum from the first sense is the second sense that would claim classical Japanese thought to be philosophy

---

67. Heisig, Kasulis, and Maraldo 2011, 17–18.
68. Ibid., 17.
69. Maraldo 2004, 238–42.
70. See Heisig, Kasulis, and Maraldo 2011, 19–21.
71. See ibid., 19.

insofar as it deals with ultimate reality and general principles, for example as Inoue Tetsujirō 井上哲次郎 asserted concerning premodern Japanese Confucianism. Bret Davis makes the point that even if "philosophy" as a scholarly discipline arose in the West, it aims at a universal truth that transcends cultural linguistic horizons, and that likewise pre-Meiji Japanese thinkers of Buddhist and Confucian schools—Kūkai 空海, Dōgen 道元, Hayashi Razan 林羅山, Ogyū Sorai 荻生徂徠, and so on—pursued universal truths that transcend the Japanese cultural context. Insofar as they were *also* inquiring into truths about life and existence that would be universally valid or applicable, can we not include their claims and arguments into philosophical discourse?[72] Blocker and Starling also assert that there is no question that pre-Meiji Japanese thinkers have been deeply engaged in certain issues in a way we can characterize as philosophical and that there is a large body of Japanese literature even before the Meiji period that is sufficiently philosophical *and* sufficiently Japanese even if deriving from the Chinese tradition that we can regard as "Japanese philosophy," in addition to the Japanese philosophy influenced by and contributing to the Western tradition of philosophy since the Meiji period.[73] This issue of whether the pre-modern Japanese intellectual traditions are philosophical or not in the sense of being sufficiently rational or analytic is certainly not an easy question to solve but analogous sorts of questions also arise concerning certain figures in the margins of the Western tradition—e.g., Presocratics like Heraclitus, medieval mystics like Meister Eckhart, or even moderns like Nietzsche or Dostoevsky or contemporaries like Emil Cioran—that is, whether they can be regarded as part of "philosophy" or not. Some within the West regard them as philosophers and some do not. But even if we cannot accept pre-Meiji thinking just as it is as "philosophy," as Davis asserts,[74] we certainly cannot deny that it is one source for us who engage in philosophy today. At the same time, however, any philosophical discussion of these premodern Japanese intellectual currents needs to be cognizant of its own *reconstructive* nature, its use of a *more* methodologically aware philosophical thought, informed by

---

72. See DAVIS 2015, 6.
73. BLOCKER and STARLING 2001, 11.
74. DAVIS 2015, 6.

the contemporary world including the modern West, as a lens for viewing premodern thought[75]—a lens not previously available.

This leads to the third sense of Japanese philosophy that intentionally takes such methods and themes borrowed from Western philosophy and applies them to premodern, pre-Westernized, Japanese thinking, engaging premodern thought intentionally under the light of modern philosophical terms and methods, for example the philosophical explication, analysis, or critique of key concepts appearing in Native Studies, Confucian thought, or Buddhist thought. At the same time, however, premodern thinking might also illuminate contemporary Western philosophical issues by proposing alternative solutions. So critique here can run in both directions to contribute to the broader tradition of philosophy that continues to grow and unfold in the contemporary global context.[76] In this regard, Kyoto School (京都学派) philosophy in particular may be regarded as a prime exemplar of this sense of Japanese philosophy. For example, Uehara adds to her definition of *tetsugaku* we saw above that seemed to limit philosophy in Japan to post-Meiji developments, that "Japanese philosophy" (*nihon tetsugaku*), even while rooted in the modern introduction of Western philosophy to Japan was established on the basis of an intellectual history which *also* inherits the traditions of Japanese and Eastern thought.[77] I would also say that while we can point to Nishidian philosophy as the prime example, we probably should not however to restrict Japanese philosophy to a particular school of thought—Kyoto School—stemming from Nishida and his colleague, Tanabe, and we might find the same sort of inter-epochal examination and development of pre-modern thought as philosophy among other modern and contemporary intellectual currents in Japan.

Maraldo in his own work argues for the superior viability of the third of these four senses for it pays due hermeneutical attention to the Greek origins of the philosophical methods and themes that have been inherited. But at the same time he stresses that these methods and themes, enriched by the plurality of perspectives brought by different times and cultures, are essentially always "in the making," and that the production of "Japanese phi-

---

75. On this see HEISIG, KASULIS, and MARALDO 2011, 20.
76. See ibid., 20.
77. UEHARA 2008, 65.

losophy" will have to "strike a balance between reading (pre-defined) philosophy into the texts [of the pre-modern Japanese tradition] and reading alternatives out of them, constructing contrasts to that [pre-defined] philosophy [of the West]."[78] In other words, this third sense can lead to the critical *reexamination* of the very meaning of philosophy and hence participate in the ongoing historical hermeneutic of philosophy's self-understanding. Davis makes the point that *shūkyō* (宗教) for "religion," like *tetsugaku*, was also a Meiji era neologism that has been used to apply to pre-modern Japanese practices and modes of thought. In the same way that an investigation into purported "religions" like Buddhism forces us to redefine the concept of "religion," our application of the term "philosophy" for pre-Meiji thought may contribute to the ongoing hermeneutical discussion and reexamination of the meaning of philosophy itself. This is not to deny the complex political implications and dangers of applying a term coming from one cultural sphere to practices and traditions belonging to another—a topic that Leah Kalmanson has been examining in her work on Japanese philosophy.[79] Davis[80] reminds us in his discussion of this topic that in the history of Western philosophy, "philosophy" itself has been redefined from time to time. And even today philosophers from different schools of thought are continuing the discussion of "What is philosophy?" So the question arises: Why not include pre-modern Japan into these discussions? Especially considering the fact that the harshest skeptics in regard to considering pre-modern Japanese thought as philosophy have been the Japanese themselves and that it has been comparativist philosophers and scholars of the West who have been willing to concede the possibility that pre-modern Japanese thought could be philosophy, a cross-cultural discussion on this issue could contribute to the ongoing unfolding of philosophy and a fuller comprehension of its nature.

And yet we also cannot deny the very Japanese cultural context from out of which such a contribution to philosophy as such would emerge. For even if philosophy aims at a universal truth, a philosopher cannot ignore his/her own cultural-linguistic-contextual horizon that shapes his/her own intellect.

---

78. MARALDO 2004, 244. See also HEISIG, KASULIS, and MARALDO 2011, 17.
79. See KALMANSON 2015, 205–6.
80. See DAVIS 2015, 6.

This relates to the issue or question of whether there is an *essentially* Japanese form of philosophy, that is, a *Japanese* philosophy as distinct from simply philosophy *in Japan*. As Davis explains, while there certainly are those in Japan who research, comment upon, interpret, criticize, and develop Greek philosophy or German philosophy, only when that becomes developed in an original way that reflects Japanese linguistic and cultural characteristics and the traditional modes of thinking of Japan, can it be called "Japanese philosophy."[81] For example Nakamura Yūjirō, as we saw earlier, pointed to the character of "emotive naturalism" belonging to Japanese intellectual life. If philosophy begins with "self-cognition," it cannot be utterly unconnected to its own spiritual milieu. Nakamura thus argues that even if philosophy *ought* to be universal, its *material* must be rooted in its immediately given actuality. In the case of Japan, this means the "emotions" and "nature" of the Japanese people. The Japanese philosopher cannot ignore the conditions of her being Japanese, the "emotive naturalism" of her intellectual cultural milieu that Nakamura had argued to be precisely un-philosophical. Nakamura therefore argues that a Japanese philosophy would have to take such "emotions" and "nature" as its *objects* of a thorough investigation—even if their *complete* objectification or thematization may be impossible—rather than simply taking them for granted from the very beginning.[82] And this is where a specifically *Japanese* philosophy, Nakamura seems to suggest, would differ from pre-philosophical Japanese thought. Moreover, Nakamura also acknowledges that Japanese "emotive naturalism" had birthed a pre-modern tradition of "aesthetic sense" or "aesthetic consciousness" (美意識) that has functioned in a way somewhat similar to philosophical thinking, which we may be able to enliven and grasp within the bounds of philosophy.[83] Blocker and Starling as well argue that not only the European origin in Meiji times onwards of philosophy in Japan but the Chinese influence in pre-Meiji times would not preclude the emergence of a distinctively Japanese philosophy deriving from those origins just as we can argue for the existence of an American or German philosophy that developed from Greek origins. It is an inevitable result of the process of acculturation that transforms, modi-

---

81. Ibid., 6.
82. See Nakamura Y. 1967, 195–8.
83. See ibid., 199.

fies, and adapts an imported philosophy originating from elsewhere so that it comes to express local ideas and values and in its modified form becomes a tradition in its own right.[84] Undeniably, an example of such *nihon tetsugaku* would be Kyoto School philosophy stemming from Nishidian philosophy that while working within the intellectual perimeters of the academic discipline of philosophy imported from the West, has also inherited the traditions of Japanese and Eastern thought. But Blocker's (and Starling's) point is that these inherited pre-modern traditions in themselves can be considered Japanese philosophy insofar as they are "philosophical" and are "Japanese."

However, even if there is such a thing as "Japanese philosophy" that unfolds from the linguistic and cultural horizon and intellectual traditions of Japan, Davis reminds us that insofar as it is "philosophy," that is, something that aims for universal validity, it ought not to preclude the participation of non-Japanese people. In other words, Japanese philosophy ought not to be a monopoly of Japanese people. Just as Japanese intellectuals and philosophers participate in discussions and arguments concerning Western philosophy, Westerners and other non-Japanese can likewise participate in discussions and arguments concerning Japanese philosophy to contribute to its ongoing development.[85] And at the same time we need to always keep in mind that what is meant by "Japanese" here is a contingent and multisided ever-changing complex with historical origins and that the identity of individual persons—Japanese or otherwise—is never a simple issue.

And this brings us to the fourth and final sense of Japanese philosophy for which I have reservations. For it tends toward an inverted Orientalism that stereotypes or essentializes qualities or characteristics identified as uniquely Japanese. It is possible to "generalize certain fundamental orientations as commonly or typically 'Japanese'" as the *Japanese Philosophy: A Sourcebook* editors remark[86] and as Nakamura Yūjirō suggests with his talk of "emotive naturalism." Nevertheless we should heed Nakamura Hajime's warning concerning common stereotypes—whether it is Orientalist essentialism or the East-West dichotomy—that might accompany the attempt to discover what

---

84. See BLOCKER and STARLING 2001, 9, 11.
85. See DAVIS 2015, 6–7.
86. HEISIG, KASULIS, and MARALDO 2011, 21.

is unique to Japanese thought.[87] Concerning "Eastern thought" (東洋思想) Nakamura Hajime concluded that we are "incapable of isolating a definite trait which can be singled out for contrast with the West," and that "there exists no single 'Eastern' feature…,"[88] and therefore that commonly repeated clichés, such as those concerning East and West, are conceptually inadequate and need to be reexamined.[89] But if there is no Eastern essence, what about the essence of Japanese thought? Nakamura Hajime's analyses show the contingency of thought to linguistic and socio-cultural conditions. Certainly differences in language, culture, and tradition determine the direction of philosophical thought.[90] And this can lead to the development of a certain kind of philosophy distinct to a certain region, such as Japanese philosophy, as Blocker and Starling, and Davis, all suggest. Those cultural and linguistic conditions that characterize our ways of thinking or philosophizing, however, are not easily reducible to a single and eternal essence. While there are recognizable trends, tendencies, and orientations, they are not set in stone. They are certainly not unalterable, unbreakable or eternal for the environing conditions themselves change. What we call "essences" are themselves contingent to time and space, allowing for fluidity and diversification, rather than being monolithic eternities. If we trace the origination of such "essences," we find that it always occurs at the margins of pre-existent horizons where they meet other horizons—an interstitial space, as mentioned above, or inter-horizonal chiasma—whereby the origin, to borrow Reiner Schürmann's term, is an-archic.[91] In the end I think every philosopher ought to keep in mind that the perpetuation of intellectual customs and stereotypes is not the aim of philosophy, although it is also important and necessary to recognize them.

---

87. Nakamura's target here however is the essentializing of "the Orient" rather than Japanese thought *per se*. See NAKAMURA H. 1976, 205–12; and 1964, 3–4, 12ff. For example, without naming Watsuji Tetsurō's 和辻哲郎 name, Nakamura points out the difficulty in his theory of summing up the characteristics of the whole of what Watsuji called "the monsoon zone" (India, China, and Japan) and labeling it as "Asiatic." See NAKAMURA H. 1964, 18–19.

88. Ibid., 21.

89. NAKAMURA H. 1963, 59; and 1992, 4.

90. See UEHARA 2013, 1.

91. Schürmann develops this idea throughout his major works. See for example, SCHÜRMANN 1987 and 2003.

I myself am most sympathetic to the second and third senses of Japanese philosophy with a slight preference for the third. But the third sense as we saw above, in a certain sense, can also lead to the second sense in its reevaluation of the premodern and hermeneutical reexamination of what constitutes philosophy. The line between the second and third senses can thus be blurred or at least allow for crossing over. But in addition, in regard to that third sense that Maraldo argued to be the most viable, I would also emphasize that a philosophical discussion of premodern thought should not be mere intellectual history. That is, the discussion ought to speak to contemporary philosophical concerns. While philosophy cannot ignore its history, that encounter with the past—if it is to be *philosophical*—cannot be mere historiology or philology. Hegel, Nietzsche, and Heidegger, for example, all emphasized how thinking itself involves engagement with the history preceding and conditioning one's own thinking.[92] But the point here is not to simply duplicate what has already been said but to make it philosophically relevant to our own concerns through appropriation, which is what Hegel, Nietzsche, and Heidegger all attempted to do in different ways. Philosophy in confronting its past—or its other—cannot remain at a safe distance from its subject matter but must engage it in a thoughtful manner that implicates its very own identity as well as that of the philosopher.

We need therefore to be aware of the danger that philosophical inquiry become nothing more than philology or intellectual history. The practice of philosophy itself always involves translation and transmission and continued assimilation by succeeding generations of the material inherited from prior generations.[93] This is an ongoing dialogical process, requiring linguistic and historical expertise. Philosophy can certainly employ philology, historiology, or biography as tools for its analyses. But at the same time philosophy engages in living questions and confronts issues that are alive or real to us. For to philosophize is to take part in a conversation crossing not only individuals, texts, and traditions, but also generations. When philosophically examining the ideas of previous philosophers, we ourselves must philosophize, otherwise our work is not philosophy. We must take their content and place it into our own context to make it a living and meaningful

---

92. See JACOBS 1999, 5, and see 11 on the following.
93. See HEISIG, KASULIS, and MARALDO 2011, 22.

issue. Simply parroting Nishida's ideas would not constitute philosophy. A philosophical analysis of his thought must confront, engage in, and appropriate it in a way that is meaningful to us, or relevant to our concerns. The philosophical examination of previous thought in that sense involves a critical hermeneutic. And this goes for the philosophical examination of premodern Japanese thought as well. Here we ought to bear in mind Nakamura Hajime's critique of the fields of Chinese philosophy and Indian philosophy in Japanese academia. His criticism was aimed at the predominantly philological approach taken in those fields and their lack of any critical spirit willing to tackle philosophical issues that matter to us.[94] His point was that these ancient philosophies have contemporary relevance with implications for our lives. Hence their study ought to make their *philosophical* relevance, transcending region and period, evident within today's global context despite their historical-cultural particularities. In that respect the historical hermeneutic involved in the philosophical examination of previous thought not only leads to the reexamination of what philosophy is but should also contribute in some way to our own self-understanding, which is the topic of our next and final section.

### Conclusion: Philosophy and Japanese Philosophy, Their Relevance:

Through investigation and critique philosophy opens up a space for dialogue that can cross borders and reshape constellations of difference. Such a space is crucial if humanity is to survive this current trend of globalization. Philosophy has universal relevance and Miki Kiyoshi, even while expressing skepticism concerning the existence of a Japanese philosophy prior to modernization—that is, philosophy at least as an academic or scholarly discipline—believed that Japan *needs* philosophy especially in order to face world scale conflicts, including the ideological and class wars of his time.[95] And philosophy continues to be relevant for us today in the post-WWII and post-Cold War world. But to realize this potential, philosophy itself must mature beyond its Eurocentric pubescence and open its horizons

---

94. Nakamura H. 1976, 233–5, 299.
95. Miki 1968, 154–5.

to the diversity of perspectives having their source in other cultural regions of the world. There is the necessity to critically regard the restrictions and preconceptions stemming from one's own cultural, linguistic, or traditional starting point *and at the same time* to investigate its actual or potentially universal significance stored within that starting point but without taking that universality simply for granted.[96] And this goes for both Western and Japanese philosophy. Nakamura Hajime's critique of the narrow approach of what Japanese academicians called "pure philosophy" (純粋哲学) that only recognized Western philosophy while ignoring Asian thought[97] was related to his belief that the study of Indian and Buddhist thought, for example, belong within a *philosophically* broader perspective than mere philological studies and can be placed within a global context that could make their relevance evident. He believed philosophical claims and ideas possess value and meaning for the entire human race despite the particularities of their historical-cultural context.[98] At least they can be considered in light of our current concerns and possess a storehouse of ideas that might be made relevant. We can say the same for Japanese philosophy in both its pre-modern and contemporary guises even if Nakamura Hajime himself seemed reluctant to consider pre-modern Japanese thought as philosophy. Whether or not there is universal philosophical significance in something culturally particular as in Japanese thinking—whether pre- or post-Meiji—ultimately can only be decided through *philosophical* dialogue, argument, and discussion, and Japanese thought/philosophy ought to be included in that dialogue. Hence we have to cast serious doubt on any attitude that would maintain the superiority or predominance of Western philosophy over non-Western philosophy and intellectual currents and/or refuses to acknowledge the latter's existence or relevance.

The Japanese intellectual tradition—whether one regards it as philosophy or as thought—harbors the influence of a multiplicity of cultural and religious traditions coming from India, Central Asia, China, and Korea.

---

96. See Davis 2015, 6. Davis gives the examples of how the idea of "democracy" that arose in ancient Greece and developed in the modern West has come to hold universal significance today, and how the notion of "emptiness" that developed within the Buddhist tradition likewise also has universal significance.
97. Nakamura H. 1976, 233–5, 299.
98. See ibid., 304–5.

And Japan after the Meiji period as well has served as an intense juncture for the meeting of Western and Eastern cultures. Ueda Shizuteru thus sees the "place" of Japan as a rich reservoir of ideas that can contribute to the formation of a world philosophy. As one example of an exceptional individual philosopher who placed himself in this fertile ground into which diverse intellectual currents were flowing, Ueda mentions Nishida Kitarō.[99] The result was the formation of the Kyoto School of philosophy, which as many acknowledge and as we have already mentioned serves as a prime example of Japanese philosophy but with global significance. It is an example of Japanese philosophy unfolding in a global setting with relevance, not just for Japan, but of global proportions. But this is just one example, and there are other non-Kyoto School strands of Japanese philosophy developing today that should be able to make significant contributions to philosophy as a whole. The global significance of philosophical movements like the Kyoto School is especially pertinent when we realize that we ourselves, Japanese or non-Japanese, Westerner and Easterner, today are placed—whether we like it or not—within the interstices of different cultural communities as a result of so-called globalization. Moreover it is precisely in the fragile interstitial space *between* communities that, as Karatani suggested with the example of Descartes' "multicultural" experience,[100] true philosophy as that which questions and critiques the natural and obvious emerges. Philosophy thus in its constitutive "homelessness"[101] emerges to challenge any positive identity that is simply to be assumed *as is*. Japanese philosophy thus emerging out of that space where identities are both constructed and deconstructed can thus contribute today to the ongoing discourse concerning philosophy's *own* identity and its resulting unfolding. It permits us to reexamine *who* we are—as Japanese, Westerners, human beings, and so on—and *what* we are doing when philosophizing.

And this forces me to return to a point I have been making throughout this paper. When we today engage and examine Japanese philosophy or thought—pre-Meiji, modern, or contemporary—and/or engage in a comparative philosophical examination of such Japanese philosophy with any

---

99. UEDA 2011, 22.
100. See KARATANI 2005, 81–2, 98, 134.
101. ŽIŽEK 2004, 267.

non-Japanese philosophical thought, we must not forget the philosophical relevance of what we are doing. Even the study of previous philosophy, if the study is itself to be regarded as philosophy, cannot end with mere intellectual history or philology, it must be philosophical. Philosophy implicates us, must be relevant to our lives, as it looks into the very depths and grounding of our existence. And so as Wilhelm Halbfass says, "comparative philosophy" cannot just be the comparison of *philosophies*. As philosophy it aims at self-understanding and must be prepared to self-referentially bring into its comparative analysis its own standpoint and horizonal conditions of comparison.[102] In our engagements with Japanese philosophy, some of us are historians, some linguists or philologists, some sociologists, etc. But insofar as we are doing philosophy or claim to be doing philosophy, we cannot forget the importance of a *philosophical* engagement with Japanese philosophy that brings Japanese philosophy into *philosophical* conversation with philosophy in the rest of the world, making it relevant to our own philosophical concerns in our current and immediate context. We need to bring what we study into philosophical dialogue with the world at large, including Western philosophy, in a way meaningful and relevant not just to Asianists or those in Japanese Studies or even comparativists but to *philosophers* in general. The hope is, for example, that someday Nishida can be discussed, not just as a *Japanese* philosopher or even as an *Asian* philosopher, but as a *philosopher* alongside Kant, Hegel, Schopenhauer, or Heidegger, standing on equal ground with them.

In conclusion I believe that the study of Japanese philosophy will contribute to this opening of the philosophical horizon as well as to intercultural dialogue that is much needed today when the sense of belonging to a single globe has been intensified to the degree that it can no longer be ignored. And in this process Japanese philosophy will contribute to the ongoing unfolding of its own definition as well as of philosophy in general. If philosophy must presuppose the very conditions of life in which it (or the philosopher) is situated, the context of one's factical implacement—as both Heidegger and Nishida suggest—then it cannot ignore the contemporary broadening and/or disruption of our horizons, whether we like it or not, wherein we face a multiplicity of competing truth claims, imaginaries,

---

102. Halbfass 1988, 433.

and world views. This is especially so when the present situation—along with the origination of Japanese philosophy as its prime example—indeed presents what one might argue has always been the case for the origin of philosophy in general—its homelessness of emerging out of an interstitial space between horizons or their margins. That is, while we cannot ignore the locality of its and our origins, we also cannot ignore the *dislocation*—the very *dislocated location*—of/in that very *origination*, *both* of philosophy and of ourselves. In philosophizing, along with philosophy itself, our own being is thus also implicated, questioned, deconstructed and reconstructed, and transformed vis-à-vis those contexts and horizons.

## References

Arendt, Hannah
    1998    *The Human Condition*. Chicago: University of Chicago Press.

Aristotle
    1941    Metaphysics. In *The Basic Works of Aristotle*. Edited by Richard McKeon. New York: Random House, 689–926.

Blocker, H. Gene and Christopher I. Starling
    2001    *Japanese Philosophy*. Albany, NY: SUNY Press.

Davis, Bret
    2015    「〈日本哲学〉の定義について」[On the definition of "Japanese philosophy"], 『西田哲学会会報』[Nishida Philosophy Association bulletin] 13: 6–7.

Descartes, René
    1994    *Discours de la méthode/Discourse on Method*. Bilingual edition, translated by George Heffernan. Notre Dame: University of Notre Dame Press.

Gōdo Wakako 神戸和佳子
    2013    "Motives for Philosophy: Examination of the First Works of Nishida Kitarō and Miki Kiyoshi." In *Papers from the 2012 University of Tokyo–University of Hawai'i Summer Residential Institute in Comparative Philosophy*. Roger Ames, Masato Ishida, Takahiro Nakajima, Shinji Kajitani, eds. Tokyo: University of Tokyo Center for Philosophy, 91–101.

Halbfass, Wilhelm
    1988    *India and Europe: An Essay in Understanding*. Albany: SUNY Press.

Hegel, G. W. F.
    1975    *Hegel's Logic: Being Part One of the Encyclopaedia of the Philosophical Sci-*

*ences.* Translated by J. N. Findlay. Oxford: Clarendon Press/Oxford University Press.

HEIDEGGER, Martin
- 1961 *Nietzsche* vol. 1. Pfullingen: Neske.
- 1968 *What is Called Thinking?* J. Translated by Glenn Gray. New York: Harper & Row.
- 1976 *Was ist Metaphysik?* In *Gesamtausgabe Band* 9: *Wegmarken*. Frankfurt: Vittorio Klostermann, 103–22.
- 1979 *Nietzsche* vol. 1: *The Will to Power as Art*. Translated by David Farrell Krell, San Francisco: Harper & Row.
- 1983 *Gesamtausgabe Band* 40: *Einführung in die Metaphysik*. Frankfurt: Vittorio Klostermann.
- 1984 *The Metaphysical Foundations of Logic*. Translated by Michael Heim. Bloomington: Indiana University Press.
- 1988 *The Basic Problems of Phenomenology*. Translated by Albert Hofstadter. Bloomington: Indiana University Press.
- 1994 *Gesamtausgabe Band* 31: *Vom Wesen der menschlichen Freiheit: Einleitung in die Philosophie*. Frankfurt: Vittorio Klostermann.
- 1997 *Gesamtausgabe Band* 24: *Die Grundprobleme der Phänomenologie*. Frankfurt: Vittorio Klostermann.
- 2000 *Introduction to Metaphysics*. Translated by Gregory Fried and Richard Polt. New Haven, CN: Yale University Press.
- 2002 *Gesamtausgabe Band* 8: *Was heißt Denken?* Frankfurt: Vittorio Klostermann.
- 2004 *Gesamtausgabe Band* 22: *Die Grundbegriffe der antiken Philosophie*. Frankfurt: Vittorio Klostermann.
- 2007 *Gesamtausgabe Band* 26: *Metaphysische Anfangsgründe der Logik im Ausgang von Leibniz*. Frankfurt: Vittorio Klostermann.

HEISIG, James W., Thomas P. KASULIS, and John C. MARALDO, eds.
- 2011 *Japanese Philosophy: A Sourcebook*. Honolulu: University of Hawai'i Press.

JACOBS, David C.
- 1999 "Introduction: Heidegger, the History of Being, the Presocratics." In *The Presocratics after Heidegger*. Edited by David C. Jabos. Albany, NY: SUNY Press, 1–24.

KALMANSON, Leah
- 2015 "If You Show Me Yours: Reading all 'Difference' as 'Colonial Difference' in Comparative Philosophy," *Comparative and Continental Philosophy* 7/2: 201–13.

KANT, Immanuel
- 1965 *Critique of Pure Reason*. Translated by Norman Kemp Smith. New York: St. Martin's Press.

1993 *Kritik der reinen Vernunf.* Hamburg: Felix Meiner.

Karatani Kojin 柄谷行人
　2005　*Transcritique: On Kant and Marx.* Translated by Sabu Kohso Cambridge, ma: mit Press.

Kisiel, Theodore
　1993　*The Genesis of Heidegger's "Being and Time."* Berkely: University of California Press.

Kosaka Kunitsugu 小坂国継
　2003　『西田幾多郎の思想』[The thought of Nishida Kitarō]. Tokyo: Kōdansha.

Malpas, Jeff
　2006　*Heidegger's Topology: Being, Place, World.* Cambridge: mit Press.

Maraldo, John
　2004　"Defining Philosophy in the Making." In *Japanese Philosophy Abroad.* Edited by James W. Heisig. Nagoya: Nanzan Institute for Religion and Culture, 220–45.

Miki Kiyoshi 三木 清
　1966　「パスカルに於ける人間の研究」[The study of man in Pascal]. In 『三木清全集』[Complete works of Miki Kiyoshi]. Tokyo: Iwanami Shoten, 1: 1–191.
　1968　「哲学のない日本」[Japan with no philosophy], in *Complete Works of Miki Kiyoshi.* Tokyo: Iwanami Shoten, 16: 153–5.
　1998　"An Analysis of Man." In *Sourcebook for Modern Japanese Philosophy: Selected Documents.* Translated and edited by David Dilworth and Valdo Viglielmo, with Agustín Jacinto Zavala. Wesport: Greenwood Press, 298–315.
　2016　"There is no Philosophy in Japan." Translated by Takeshi Morisato. https://www.academia.edu/8143921/Miki_Kiyoshi_There_is_No_Philosophy_in_Japan_Miki_Kiyoshi_Zensh%C5%AB_16_153_54.

Nakae Chōmin 中江兆民
　1975　「一年有半」[One year and a half]. In 『中江兆民、大杉栄、河上肇集：現代日本文学全集』[Collection of writings by Nakae Chōmin, Ōsugi Sakae, Kawakami Hajime: Contemporary Japanese literature collection] vol. 3. Tokyo: Chikuma Shobō, 5–44.

Nakamura Hajime 中村元
　1963　"Comparative Study of the Notion of History in China, India and Japan," *Diongenes* 42: 44–59.
　1964　*Ways of Thinking of Eastern Peoples: India-China-Tibet-Japan.* Honolulu: East-West Center Press.
　1976　『比較思想論』[On comparative thought]. Tokyo: Iwanami Shoten.
　1992　*A Comparative History of Ideas.* Delhi: Motilal Banarsidass.

NAKAMURA Yūjirō 中村雄二郎
- 1967 『哲学入門』[Introduction to philosophy]. Tokyo: Chūōkōronsha.
- 1995 "Une philosophie japonaise est-elle possible?", *Ebisu* 8: 77–102,

NISHIDA Kitarō 西田幾多郎
- 1989 『西田幾多郎全集』[Complete works of Nishida Kitarō], vol. 13. Tokyo: Iwanami Shoten.
- 1990 *An Inquiry into the Good*. Translated by Masao Abe and Christopher Ives. New Haven: Yale University Press.
- 2002 『無の自覚的限定』[Determination of the nothing in self-awareness]. *Complete Works of Nishida Kitarō*, vol. 5.
- 2003 『善の研究』[Inquiry into the Good]. *Complete Works of Nishida Kitarō*, vol. 1.
- 2004 『西田幾多郎随筆集』[Miscellaneous works of Nishida Kitarō]. Edited by Ueda Shizuteru. Tokyo: Iwanami Shoten.

NISHITANI Keiji 西谷啓治
- 1951 「わが師西田幾多郎を語る」[Talking about my teacher Nishida Kitarō]. In 『わが師を語る』[Talking about my teacher]. Tokyo: Shakai Shisō Kenkyūkai.
- 1982 *Religion and Nothingness*. Translated by Jan Van Bragt. Berkeley, CA: University of California Press.
- 1987 『宗教とは何か』[What is religion?]. In 『西谷啓治著作集』[Works of Nishitani Keiji]. Tokyo: Sōbunsha, vol. 10.
- 1990a *Works of Nishitani Keiji*, vol. 20.
- 1990b *The Self-Overcoming of Nihilism*. Translated by Graham Parkes. Albany, NY: SUNY Press.
- 1991 *Nishida Kitarō*. Translated by Yamamoto Seisaku and James Heisig. Berkeley: University of California Press.
- 1993 『ニヒリズム』[*Nihilism*]. In 『西谷啓治著作集』[*Works of Nishitani Keiji*], vol. 8. Tokyo: Sōbunsha.

OTTO, Rudolf
- 1958 *The Idea of the Holy*. Oxford: Oxford University Press.

PAPPENFUSS, Dietrich and Otto PÖGGELER, eds.
- 1990 *Zur philosophischen Aktualität Martin Heideggers*, vol. 2, *Im Gespräch der Zeit*. Frankfurt: Klostermann.

PLATO
- 1997 *Theaetetus* in *Plato: Complete Works*. Edited by John M. Cooper. Indianapolis: Hackett Pub. Co., 155–234.

SCHELER, Max
- 1954 "Vom Wesen der Philosophie und der moralischen Bedingung des philosophischen Erkennens." In *Vom Ewigen im Menschen* (*Gessamelte Werke* vol. 5). Bern: Francke Verlag, 61–99.

SCHÜRMANN, Reiner
 1987 *Heidegger on Being and Acting: From Principles to Anarchy.* Bloomington: Indiana University Press.
 2003 *Broken Hegemonies.* Bloomington: Indiana University Press.

UEDA Shizuteru 上田閑照
 1991 『西田幾多郎を読む』[Reading Nishida Kitarō]. Tokyo: Iwanami Shoten.
 2011 "Contributions to Dialogue with the Kyoto School." In *Japanese and Continental Philosophy: Conversations with the Kyoto School.* Bret Davis, Brian Schroeder, and Jason Wirth, eds. Bloomington: Indiana University Press, 19–32.

UEHARA Mayuko 上原麻有子
 2008 「西田幾多郎の〈場所〉に見る〈形なきものの形〉」[The "form of the formless" as seen in "place" in Nishida Kitarō], 『明星大学研究紀要』[Meisei University research bulletin] 16: 54–78.
 2013 "Introduction," *Journal of Japanese Philosophy* 1: 1–3.

WALDENFELS, Bernhard
 2011 *Phenomenology of the Alien: Basic Concepts.* Translated by Alexander Kozin and Tanja Stähler. Evanston: Northwestern University Press.

ŽIŽEK, Slavoj
 2004 "The Parallax View: Toward a New Reading of Kant," *Epoché* 8/2: 255–69.

James W. Heisig
*Nanzan Institute for Religion & Culture*

## An Apology for Philosophical Transgressions

The essay that follows is, in substance, a lecture delivered in Brussels on 7 December 2016 to the 2nd International Conference of the European Network of Japanese Philosophy. In it I argue that the strategy of qualifying nothingness as an "absolute," which was adopted by Kyoto School thinkers as a way to come to grips with fundamental problems of Western philosophy, is inherently ambiguous and ultimately weakens the notion of nothingness itself. In its place, a proposal is made to define nothingness in terms of "connectedness." The discussion is bound on both ends by an apology for transgressing established academic boundaries. On one end, I open with a brief digression on a common ground for philosophies East and West as a *mestizaje* to which no tradition can claim dominance. On the other, I close with an appeal for restoring respect for the role of mythical narration as a way to bridge the connection between theory and practice without having to revert to moral absolutes, particularly as it relates to safeguarding this fragile planet of ours from the ongoing sepsis of economic "progress."

KEYWORDS: Nothingness—absolute—Kyoto School—Nishida—Nishitani—connectedness—myth—universal—metaiconography

The strategy of drawing on western philosophical resources to bring a fresh perspective to problems rooted in Asian intellectual history has a history that reaches back at least four hundred and fifty years to Matteo Ricci's discussions with Confucian scholars. To many critics of modernity, it is a history so badly scarred with the same hubris and triumphalism which fed the colonial and militaristic ambitions of the West that any sympathy for the spirit of philosophical adventure behind it has all but evaporated. Meantime, the complementary strategy of drawing on Asian philosophical resources to shed new light on perennial questions of the western philosophical tradition has had to contend with the general academic bias against incursions by quasi-religious, pop-philosophical, half-baked ideas from the East. Like many of you here, I have marinated too long in the philosophical stew of Japan to take any of this seriously.

### A PHILOSOPHICAL *MESTIZAJE*

Applying the tools of conceptual analysis and historical deconstruction to the idea of engaging philosophies "East" and "West" in dialogue has led to criticism that such talk is at best naïve and at worst morally unacceptable or even violent. The same holds for the notion of a "Japanese philosophy," which is said to endorse similarly subtle tyrannies of racial isolationism and cultural imperialism, if not to be just so much logical silliness. As long as the critique remains at a level once removed from what those terms describe to those who actually use them, there is no hope that a simply change of vocabulary would make the criticisms go away, and even less hope of finding a common ground on which to refute them. The only victory that could possibly satisfy such attacks would be one where the vanquished would join forces in turning the very tools that were their undoing against other ideologically and irrationally tainted conventions infecting philosophical thought.

The caricature I have just drawn would be laughable were it not such an attractive and simple way for so many to refuse a place in philosophical history to intellectual traditions not nurtured in the Mediterranean basin. I do not see there is much to gain in refining those criticisms in order to tangle with them any further. I much prefer to offer an apology for having spent my life crossing established borders and then to lay out, as clearly and succinctly as I can, an apology for questioning a central tenet of Kyoto school philosophy.

I approached the study of Japanese philosophy much the same as I had approached western philosophy. On the advice of the older and wiser Jan Van Bragt, I first read selected essays of the three pillars of the Kyoto School, Nishitani, Tanabe, and Nishida. In time, as I found my way around more and more of their books, I came to realize that I knew far too little of the resources they were drawing on. The western authors whose names surfaced here and there were for the most part known to me. But there were other springs flowing in and out of their writings, many of them from underground, of which I knew all too little. At times it was an unfamiliar name; at others, an unknown textual reference; and at still others, no more than an odd turn of phrase. Not every trail led somewhere, but over the years I tried to train myself to a workable feel for what the Kyoto School philosophers knew from their cultural surroundings, from their formal education and upbringing, from their appreciation of the Japanese language, and from their intangible native sensibilities.

I remember how Whitehead, the first philosopher whose complete works I had read as a young man, had driven me back to Plato and Leibniz; how Hegel's *Phenomenology* and *Logic* had made me read Kant and Schelling again; how Heidegger and Jaspers only began to make sense when I went back to read Aristotle and Nietzsche more closely. And so it was that in the case of Japan's philosophical tradition, I traced a few obscure, peculiar threads through the weave until I eventually found myself standing in front of a vast, but increasingly less exotic and surprisingly more familiar, tapestry.

As the range of resources opened to me broadened, the framing of philosophical questions changed radically. A border transgressed is never the same border, and the more frequent the transgressions, the less likely one is ever to feel completely at home on either side again. I remember thinking about this the first time I stood on the shores of the upper Amazon in Manaus, where the black waters of the Rio Negro and the muddy waters of the Rio Solimões flow along side by side, at different speeds, for more than three miles until further downstream they merge into one another and lose their distinct identities.

Assuming there is nothing out of the ordinary in this process, I have marveled time after time, conference after conference, why, with such a rich mine of resources at their disposal, so many philosophers stand still on the shore upstream, writing treatises comparing one philosopher to another or one idea to another when they could use the confluence of their offsetting modes of thought to rewrite the philosophical map and recode fundamental questions.

It is not scholars of Eastern philosophers discussing with their counterparts in western philosophy who will release philosophy from its bondage to the thought systems that originated in the Mediterranean basin. It is not the textual exegetes or historians of ideas who have had the greatest dialogical impact, but those *mestizos* who have already begun to philosophize using resources from both to pry western philosophy open.

As William James remarked, if philosophy, as Plato and Aristotle said, begins in wonder, it

> is able to fancy everything different from what it is. It sees the familiar as if it were strange, and the strange as if it were familiar. It can take things up and lay them down again. It rouses us from our native dogmatic slumber and breaks up our caked prejudices.[1]

It would be wrong to think that this is the privilege of established senior professors. The work in which James wrote these words, *Some Problems of Philosophy* bears the subtitle *A Beginning of an Introduction to Philosophy*. Exactly. From the start and at any point after that, postponing, sacrificing, or diluting wonder is the death of philosophy. The world that lies between the lines of Japan's philosophical texts is too startling to be domesticated by pulling out one or the other idea, comparing it to a similar idea from west-

---

1. *Some Problems of Philosophy: A Beginning of an Introduction to Philosophy* (New York: Longmans, Green, and Co., 1921), 7.

ern philosophy, and then closing the book. Unless one takes into account the confluent state of mind in which their ideas took shape, there is little to wonder at in any coincidence of ideas.

It is one thing to use words like "East and West" and "Japanese philosophy" to denote fixed blocs of reality that can be contrasted, compared, and brought into contact as such. It is another thing to use them as temporary markers that lose much of their usefulness and dependability in a confluence of philosophical worlds. Accusations of a subversive agenda at work behind the scenes may still be made, but they are no reasonable grounds to honor them with a response—unless, of course, one wishes to take on the radical campaign of holding every distinction made in the history of philosophy suspect to the charge of treason.

In-depth study of Eastern philosophers and comparative studies of individual philosophers or currents of thought seem to have found their place as acceptable forms of East-West philosophical dialogue. Broadening the base of who is included in the history of philosophy can be an important first step in that direction, but it is just as likely to distract attention from the more radical step of including the resources of another tradition in philosophical thinking proper. If there is any chance of bringing philosophers East and West into dialogue, it will not take place in an encounter between recognized representatives of each side. If western philosophies are to open up to other philosophies in anything approaching the measure in which they have themselves been received around the world, it will not take place only in dialogue among specialists with their counterparts in other traditions or in comparative studies. Rather, western philosophers need to talk seriously with the philosophical *mestizos* who have already taken steps to do their thinking with a greater wealth of materials than those of their own tradition and many of whom can no longer say with confidence which tradition they belong to. This *mestizaje* is a hidden treasure within our reach, and it is hard to understand how it can still be systematically ignored, because without it, western philosophy's ambitions to "world philosophy" will remain embarrassed by its attachment to pedigree.

I am afraid if I ramble on any further, I will begin to give the impression of a tantrum thrown by a neglected child. For my part, I believe that openness to philosophical funds from the East is an irreversible insight for a younger generation of students drawn to philosophical thinking, and that they will be the ones, through their teaching and writing, to break down the walls of the echo chamber in which so much of philosophy continues to justify itself.

There are many ways to employ the resources of Japanese philosophy, but the most difficult of them—and also, I believe, the most philosophical—is to look at the world through a lens ground to the measure of different presuppositions, to examine the refraction critically, and then to adjust one's own worldview accordingly. It is just this kind of *mestizaje* I mean to bear the brunt of my apology here for transgressions into Japanese philosophy.

## Dissolving the absolute

I begin with a deep slash of Ocham's razor aimed at the idea of the absolute dominant in Kyoto school philosophy. For the pivotal thinkers of the school, Nishida Kitarō, Tanabe Hajime, and Nishitani Keiji, allusions to "the absolute" and to certain ideas and philosophical tools as "absolute" are so frequent and so centrally positioned that their respective worldviews would appear to totter without them.

The immediate stimulus for making nothingness into an absolute may have come from Hegel, who established the absolute as a philosophical concept into western philosophy, but it would not have taken the hold it did, had it not also struck a chord in the Buddhist sensitivities of the Kyoto philosophers. The slow, dialectical ascent of mind through its relative conditioning to the final freedom of pure self-consciousness and absolute knowledge where subject and object have been transcended was a natural fit for making the ideal of enlightenment philosophically reasonable. For all their criticisms of Hegel in the particulars, the general modes of thought Hegel opened up for them were crucial in shaping their ideas. Never mind that Hegel's stature in an intellectual tradition that had only recently come into contact with western philosophy was too great to ignore, the way the Kyoto School philosophers adopted the dialectical method and sanctified the notion of the absolute was far from unambiguously Hegelian. Yet even taking into account the sum total of their criticisms, I am persuaded that the adoption was misguided.[2] In fact, aside from its use as a marker for criti-

---

2. In his book, *The Kyoto School's Takeover of Hegel: Nishida, Nishitani, and Tanabe Remake the Philosophy of Spirit* (Lanham, MD: Lexington Books, 2011), Peter Suares has taken a first

cisms against the absolute of being, the notion of an absolute of nothingness is only of limited use to them. I have come to believe that Kyoto School philosophies of nothingness would be better off dispensing altogether with the notion of an absolute and returning the notion of the relative from its exile at the fringes to the center of the field of vision. The dispensation is not as difficult as the verbal tangles would lead one to believe.

To begin with, the use of the word *absolute* in Kyoto School philosophy is not univocal. To be clear about what I am proposing, let me lay out three distinct meanings of the term *absolute* from their texts. As important as the distinctions are, they rarely rise to the surface and it is not uncommon to see overlaps of meaning in the same sentence, leaving it to the reader to sort out the muddle or—which is more often the case—ignore it altogether.

In a first and *literal* sense, the absolute refers to a reality that by nature completely transcends the reality of the world, cut off from dependence on anything else, dislocated from any wider environment, unaffected by time and history. Second, there is a *revised literal* sense in which all the qualities of the literal absolute are not given originally but achieved as the culmination of an extended interaction with the world. Here absoluteness is the final stage of a process which may or may not entail a self-emanation of reality that eventually recovers its primordial identity by being poured out of itself and then flowing back into itself through time. Finally, there is a *metaphorical* use of the absolute which is only marginally related to one or the other literal or revised literal meanings and is meant to describe something or some event as complete, utter, consummate, unsurpassed, unqualified, or simply as infinite. Its usage is more or less rhetorical, depending on the context, but in no way is it obliged to either of the first two meanings.

By tying the absolute to the dialectic—affirmations generated by negating negations and subsuming contradictions—the absolute forfeits the kind of literal meaning it has, for example, in dualistic theism, and takes on a revised sense. The identity that Nishida claimed for "the absolute" is in fact dependent on its relationship to that which it is not in the sense that it subsumes into itself that negation of itself and thereby negates its own separa-

---

step towards sorting out and evaluating Kyoto School readings of Hegel. The suspicions I am raising here run deeper to question the extent of their engagement as a distraction.

tion from what it is not. Nishida is clear on this point, as one passage in his final essay advises:

> The true absolute does not simply cut itself off from opposition. If it did, it would be no more than absolute negation and could not avoid being relativized. The true absolute must be something that faces its own absolute negation in itself and includes it in itself…, something that mediates itself through absolute negation.[3]

Now it might warm the heart of a Hegelian to talk of the absoluteness of the absolute as a negation of its own absoluteness, but I find myself cringing at the reliance on dialectical logic to decide what is a "true" absolute and what is not. I will have more to say of this later, but for now it is enough to note that taking the term *absolute* to mean something like a radical internalization of relatedness itself unfairly expropriates the term *relative* and dilutes its original meaning. For one thing, there may be something seriously wrong with the absolute-relative distinction itself. For another, not even the totally transcendent, *totaliter aliter* deity of the scholastic metaphysics could qualify as absolute without discarding biblical language, not to mention living forms of theistic faith and centuries of the Christological imagination. The idea of making nothingness into an absolute by contrasting it with the absolute God of being was a misleading strategy and I am persuaded Kyoto School philosophy would have been better off without it. In any event, when supremacy is transferred from God to nothingness, God is in effect made relative to the *absolute of nothingness*. Whatever sentiments of ultimate dependency, whatever hopes and aspirations the idea of a supreme Being may stir in the soul, in the end it is relative to nothingness; as a literal absolute, it can only register as a failed attempt of reason to awaken to the true reality of the absolute.

When it comes to talk of the absolute, Kyoto school prose is disconcerting. One has the sense that it hangs together logically, but rarely the sense that much of any consequence hangs on it. To see the matter at hand through their eyes, to stand where they stood when they wrote what they wrote requires more than mastering the technical vocabulary they are using. Beginning with "absolute nothingness," many of their terms were not

---

3. 『西田幾多郎全集』(Tokyo: Iwanami Shoten, 2004), 10: 333.

predefined but worked out in the employment. For another, mastering a philosophical lexicon does not allow one to generate new ideas or criticize previous formulations unless one is also caught up in some version of the questions that prompted it. Obviously, none of this can be done by proxy. Either you wrestle with the ideas firsthand or you submit to them and spend your time parsing and paraphrasing the texts just as they are. All I can do here is outline the conclusions to which my own limited reading of the Kyoto school have driven me.

Just what kind of an absolute, then, is absolute nothingness? Despite disclaimers of comparison to the absolute God of being, the literal, strict sense of the absolute is at times an entirely fitting attribute of nothingness. If the absolute is said to denote unconditional release from anything that can claim a hold on it or stand vis-à-vis to it, if it is said to be absolved of all attachments, obligations, conditions, qualities, and even other modes of reality, it comes close to a dualistic view of reality. If the absolute of nothingness cannot be a thing among other things, let alone the sum of all things in the world, then even if the world as we know it is ultimately a mental illusion, it is still set up as one false, imperfect reality transcended by another, truer reality. For absolute nothingness to coincide with reality as it truly is, it must lie beyond the separation of mind and matter in a supreme and unchallenged self-identity, dependent on nothing, needing nothing, wanting nothing apart from itself. In this sense, the "self-awareness of absolute nothingness" is the negation of the experienced, phenomenal world and the affirmation of another world beyond experience and appearance.

To follow this line of reasoning would make philosophy meaningless, or at least reduce it to a radical negation of everything we think we know about the world and ourselves in it. The only way out is to de-absolutize the absolute and somehow restore true reality to the world. This is precisely what the Kyoto school philosophers had to find a way to do.

If you permit me a quick aside, I find their quandary similar to the one that the God of scholastic metaphysics posed to Cusanus. In *De docta ignorantia* he attempted to skirt the ethereal theological speculation of the day by introducing a distinction between God as the *maximum absolutum*,[4] and the rest of creation is a *minimum absolutum*. The terms "absolute highest"

---

4. *De docta ignorantia*, Book 1.2.

and "absolute lowest" would seem to represent the polar extremes of reality, a *ne plus ultra* and a *ne plus infra*, but in fact they are meant to depict a perfect coincidence of divinity and creation. The world and everything that makes it up are seen as a *contraction* of the divinity, leading Cusanus to cite the pseudo-Hermetic *Liber XXIV philosophorum*, "God is a circle whose circumference is nowhere and whose center is everywhere." In practice, God is completely and utterly related to everything and everything to God—the exact opposite of a literal absolute.

Quite apart from any association with the God of Judeo-Christian faith, Cusanus' God can be shown to fulfill the general requirements of a first principle in Greek philosophy. Taking a lead from Pythagoras' idea of a "seminal point" from which all of existence sprung, the Stoics posited a single principle in which reason and reality coincide so perfectly that the *logoi spermatikoi* that burst forth from it flower naturally into the multitude of things that make up the world.[5] Were it not for the cause-and-effect duality set up between a creative one and a created many, the long Platonic tradition of the unity of the rational and the real represented in the Stoic model might have found itself at home in the rich Buddhist tradition of imaginative thinking on the nonduality of principle and fact. As it was, when Augustine transported this idea of seminal reason to the Middle Ages, he made the primordial unity of reason and reality subservient to an otherworldly, divine providence. Cusanus took a modest step back in the direction of the primordial unity the Platonists envisioned, and hence of the primordial unity of God and world that had hidden itself from the scholastic mainstream in mystical and hermetic literature.

I have pulled out one thread from the enormous tapestry into which metaphysical notions of a first principle or "absolute" have been variously woven, but only to isolate the problem the Kyoto philosophers faced: how to adopt the idea of the absolute without allowing it to be controlled by the idea of an absolute otherworldly God. As their familiarity with the western philosophical tradition broadened, they came upon thinkers sympathetic to many of their own reservations and closer to the nondual worldview they

---

5. For a helpful review of the question, see Hiro Hirai, "*Logoi Spermatikoi* and the Concept of Seeds in the Mineralogy and Cosmogony of Paracelsus," *Revue d'histoire des sciences* 61/2 (2008): 245–64.

wanted at all costs to preserve. Throughout it all, only the God of the philosophers interested them. The personal God of Abraham, Isaac, and Jacob was left aside and did not even merit a refutation. In contrast, the idea of God's self-emptying in the kenosis of the incarnation was an image they found sympathetic precisely because it served to negate the idea of a supreme, transcendent being by defining it as essentially self-negating.

The Kyoto school thinkers ventured into these waters not out of a sense of obligation to any particular western philosophical tradition but because they wanted to position the idea of nothingness at the center of reality. To do that, they had to relegate being and the God of being to a lower status and to elevate nothingness to an absolute that would render all being relative to it. Standing on its own, the glyph 無 that we have come to render as "nothingness" was too ambiguous for philosophical argument. Adding the qualifier "absolute"—a kind of *ignotium per ignotius*—made the transition easier but only as an expedient means. Hegel's conception of the absolute, which travelled in the same direction as Cusanus' but in the open and at full speed, was the one the Kyoto school philosophers adapted to insert nothingness into the discussion and, finally, to de-absolutize the literal absolute of Western philosophy.[6] Their revised absolute shared two fundamental traits with Hegel's logic. First, it defined an ultimate universal encompassing all other universals and rendering them relative. Second, it introduced an evolutionary process by which the relative finds its way to union with the absolute. When Nishida depicted his logic of *basho* as an ascent of the self-aware mind to absolute nothingness, he did so with a series of concentric circles, the very thing that Hegel had done in describing all of philosophy as an "a circle of circles," an image whose etymology figures in his choice of a term to designate his system as a whole: *Encyclopedia*. Incidentally, I am surprised never to have found a reference in Nishida or his commentators to this fact.[7]

---

6. In Tendai Buddhism 相待 was used to describe things understood in relation to or comparison with something else, and its opposite 絶待 was used to describe something supreme that cannot be described in terms of anything else. This pair of terms existed for a time but seems to have given way from the last nineteenth century to 相対 and 絶対 and were used to translate Hegel.

7. "Each part of philosophy is a philosophical whole, a self-contained circle, in which the Idea appears in its element as a particular determination. Each individual circle, imbued with a

Before we go any further, I should add a word about the third, metaphorical use of the word *absolute*, a rhetorical emphatic that stands opposed to the de-emphasizing attribute *relative*, which describes a thing or action as partial or limited. Absolute negation, absolute mediation, absolute dialectic, absolute love, absolute time, absolute death, absolutely unlimited, absolute irrational, absolute disruption of reason, absolute contradiction—all of these expressions and more familiar to readers of Kyoto school philosophy are examples of this metaphorical use of the term. It would make no sense to describe death or love or dialectic or contradiction as *the* absolute, even in a revised sense, but this does not mean that the usage is simply hyperbole and that the literal sense is entirely absent from the connotation. Quite the contrary, the quality of absoluteness is attributed precisely to show that something of absolute nothingness has rubbed off on the idea in question. They all serve as markers of the absolute without themselves qualifying as absolute in the same sense in which it is applied to "nothingness." In other words, we are not speaking of something absolute in itself but something *relative* to that which is absolute in itself. Linguistically this is reflected in the way in which "the absolute of nothingness" is used as a synonym for "absolute nothingness" but not for any of other term described as absolute.

It seems to me that for Kyoto school philosophy, seen from inside or out, the adoption of nothingness as a metaphysical absolute in any sense, is superfluous, logically confusing, and philosophically distracting. If we take it as a synonym for the unity of reality, the One of which it is said that all things taken together make up, such a One would have to be relative to the many because it would have no meaning apart from the sum total of the many. Reality would be absolute only in the sense that it is a final tally and that there is nothing outside of it that can be called real. The word absolute adds nothing to the One that the many does not at once take away—unless, of course, you assume that there is some place in the world you can stand and see the One all at once. This is so even if you were to subscribe to a

---

drive to totality, breaks through the barriers of its element to set the stage for a wider circle. In this way the whole presents itself as a circle of circles, each circle comprising a part so that the organization of the various elements constitutes the Idea as a whole at the same time as the Idea appears in each one of them." *Encyclopädie*, § 15. Replace *Idea* with *self-awareness*, and the passage reads as a condensed version of Nishida's logic of *basho*.

monistic worldview in which the totality of reality is ultimately nothingness and not being.

The revised sense of the absolute as the culmination of full self-awareness towards which relative beings are evolving has to contend with a number of objections. First among them is reliance on the dialectic as a producer of insight into a "true absolute." The problem with dialectical logic, as Bergson would say, is not that it is too rational but that it is too *intellectual* and not rational enough. If, as Christian piety understands all too well, a transcendent absolute of being, be it the orthodoxy of the scholastics or the panentheism of Spinoza, keeps us foreigners from God, an absolute of nothingness wedded to a dialectics of negation, as students of the Kyoto school should know just as well, obstructs our intimacy with the world. The reduction of meaning to a moment of eternity in time dispels history and is a clear sign that something is wrong.

Aside from the general pattern of the dialectic in which negations and negations of negations propel the mind toward loftier and loftier affirmations, the main thing the Kyoto philosophers took over from the Hegelian scheme was what they called "self-awareness of absolute nothingness." Given their commitment to overcoming the subjective self that we usually associate with consciousness and the objective reality that we usually associate with the world, Hegel's objective consciousness with its culmination in absolute knowledge did not seem to them a true absolute. The ambiguity of the phrase occasionally suggests, and we said as much above, that absolute nothingness is somehow aware of itself, but it is normally meant to imply that it is that to which the mind awakens at its highest level of performance. This presents the idea with a predicament. On the one hand, making the fully awakened mind an ontological absolute is out of the question, either as the mind of individual subjects or as some cosmic mind like Hegel's. On the other, to talk of mind at all is to talk of something that really exists, which disqualifies it as a nothingness.

The long and short of it is that if nothingness is absolute, it is unaffected by the fact that minds are aware of it, or at least infer it by seeing through the relativity of everything around them. The only way it could be "cut off" from the relative is if it were no more than an infinite void like Plato's *chōra*. The reason for bothering to enhance awareness is not that it somehow secures final unity with the void of nothingness, since there is literally and without qualification *nothing* to unify with.

As Hegel realized, our attempts to be reasonable are part of reality, but the dialectical bridge from abstract logic and its necessities to actual life cannot bear the weight of ordinary experience. Assume that human consciousness is the highest form of mental activity in the universe if you will, to make its path to perfection into an absolute with no wider environment to embrace it is an offense to the long history out of which our consciousness evolved. Nothing real is without its environment, and I see no good reason that claims of absoluteness for nothingness should suggest otherwise. I do not see that the Kyoto school's revised notion of the absolute escaped from Hegel's faith in truth as eternal, objective, necessary, and one, and his view of the world as one in which only what *must be* are real, can withstand the moral and aesthetic demands of living in a world in which the most we can say most of the time is how things *may be*. To say that only that which has no environment, no *basho*, is ultimately true defies our every attempt to be reasonable in practice, however much it satisfies the contemplative intellect. The idea of absolute nothingness is a soap bubble that refracts the whole of the world for a brief moment, only to dissolve at the slightest breeze of change.

I am afraid I have oversimplified, but only enough to show that the nothingness of the Kyoto School philosophers cannot amount to an absolute in any but a metaphorical sense. It may seem that I have plucked too many feathers from the idea of absolute nothingness to leave it any hope of flight. But if we eliminate talk of a literal absolute from the discussion of nothingness, Nishida's claim cited above implies that the historical world of being and becoming argues against the absoluteness of the absolute, and that absolute nothingness is only truly absolute when it is *not* absolutely cut off from the world of relative beings but directly related to it. In short, the only way to preserve the true nature of the absolute is that it *not* be seen as absolute in any literal sense at all.

Think of it. If there is no greater enveloping presence or power to which nothingness can be called "relative," then it would seem to merit the name "absolute." If nothingness is the absolute other of being, and being the relative other of nothingness, then there is a sense in which an absolute of nothingness could subsume all relative being into itself and retain its absolute character. But if the absolute has no being to embrace, if there are no circles within its circle, if it can no longer be called a universal of universals, then there would be no point to even using the term *absolute*. If, on the contrary, it is in the nature of the absolute to encircle what is relative, it still fails to merit the name "absolute." If the absolute is only absolute vis-a-vis the relative, any literal sense of independence falls away.

Referring to nothingness as an absolute reality is a half-truth, but the reason for suggesting we eliminate it altogether is that the part of it that is true tends to distract us from the part that is not. The vast emptiness that Nishida imagined to reach beyond the final circle of being without itself being encircled either will have to be reimagined so that the world of being and becoming can be held in the embrace of emptiness, or it will have to be reduced to nothing more than a critique of other pretenders to the throne of the absolute.

### Re-imagining nothingness

There are other, more pressing reasons why the Kyoto school's idea of nothingness can no longer feed on the empty husks of dialectical logic in its pursuit of the status of an absolute. I do not mean to ignore philosophy's efforts to make reality as a whole, somehow or other, reasonable. I just think that the notion of nothingness as an absolute frustrates that end. In the attempt to highlight the logical confusion in the way Kyoto School philosophers talk of the absolute, I have kept things on much the same high level of abstraction as their own texts. There is almost no indication in their writings of what practical difference it makes to the human community to think of reality as nothingness rather than as being. I happen to think it does, and I offer that practical reason as an apologia for trampling on their notion of the absolute.

Perhaps promoting the self-awareness of nothingness would make for a kinder view of society than promoting the struggle for power or wealth. But that promotion would make a mockery of critical thinking if it did not include the bigger question: What practical difference can it make to see reality in its full embrace of everything and everyone as an empty nothingness rather than as, say, the sum total of all beings? If there are no reasonable, practical consequences, what reason have we to embrace nothingness and forsake the many traditional paths at hand for arriving at radical skepticism, pessimism, and the despair of making any sense of the world?

While the literal sense of *the absolute* in Japanese—dis-connection, 対を絶する—captures the philosophical meaning of the word, it contradicts the whole point of grounding a philosophy in nothingness. I see no reason to compromise. Let nothingness be understood in its most extreme, uncompromising sense and not diminished to an apophatic tactic aimed at dogmatic descriptions of reality. Let it be nothingness pure and simple. Let it, too, be a philosophical ground, a fundamental, all-encompassing fact of reality. As we have hinted, nothingness would be unknowable, and thus meaningless, if it did not actually embrace anything. The world of interconnected, relative beings is the only manifestation of nothingness we have. To understand the world surface and depth is our only path to awakening to the nothingness of reality. Nothingness must be radically—or metaphorically put, absolutely—relative to this world in which we exist. The search for the unqualified and indefinite is not a search for the unrelated but for the supremely related—that which is related immediately to everything, always and everywhere. This is how I understand the Kyoto philosophers' maxim, 無即有、有即無: nothingness is only real in being, and being is only real in nothingness.

For these reasons, I am convinced that a heavier dose of the classical Buddhist conception of the inalienable reliance of ultimate truth on conventional truth would better serve the logic of a "self-awareness of nothingness" than associating it with a dialectical logic of the absolute. I fail to see any cause for eliminating the mind and the ordinary reality of the world as pure fictions. I am in sympathy with Kawabata Yasunari when he spoke in his Nobel Prize speech of "losing the self and entering into the realm of nothingness…, an emptiness in which everything communicates freely with everything, transcending bounds, limitless," but in which one remains "master of one's own thoughts."[8] Far from having Kyoto School philosophy redefine itself as some kind of romantic transcendentalism or get lost in postmodern criticisms of the absolute, the self-awareness of nothingness seems to me a highly original but practical way of steering philosophy towards what seems to me its most momentous but largely neglected task today.

---

8. *Japan the Beautiful and Myself* (Tokyo: Kōdansha, 1969), 56.

What I have in mind is this: The concept of nothingness and our awareness of it should not be defined primarily as abstract concepts, as reactions against western ontology, or even ways to describe the experience of "enlightenment." These are derivative functions that can be justified only by the light they shed on a more basic problem: the search for an understanding of our relationship to the earth that can inspire us to put an end to the systematic havoc that civilization is inflicting on the natural world. Without a healthy planet, sooner or later human existence will be reduced to a caricature of itself. We have watched philosophy become marginalized throughout the twentieth century by the subservience of academics around the world to the economic and political order. The erosion of the teaching of philosophy to comply with the progress of education in a globally competitive world is not something for those with a philosophical vocation simply to monitor and criticize from the sidelines—or to do so to the extent that it does not jeopardize one's career or status within the philosophical establishment. To ignore the earth is matricidal. We cannot afford to send young students with these concerns back to the texts on the assumption that everything has been said somewhere before. The question sears the conscience precisely because it has been so slow to find its proper place in philosophical discussions. This is not a problem a dialectical logic of absolute nothingness can handle any more than that logic has been able to contribute to scientific research. I admit there is a bit of mischief in what I am about to propose, but my only regret is that I did not ask it sooner and more forcefully in the philosophical circles of Japan where Kyoto school thought is studied so fervently.

The notion of absolute nothingness circulating among Kyoto School scholars is not only irrelevant to the crisis of the planet; it is, at least indirectly, an argument against its relevance. The best way to demonstrate this is to try to give it an expression responsive to the crisis that faces us. By that I mean, redefine it in such a way that it speaks directly to our experience, locates that experience in a broader tradition of thought, and opens up into an awareness of what is morally acceptable for the advance of human society on this fragile commons we call our earth.

Raising this question, I am struck by the way the concept of nothingness changed shape in the short history of Kyoto school philosophy. Nishida's absolute nothingness was through and through speculative. It managed to introduce the *concept* of the historical world without actually engaging that world as it is lived. Tanabe took exception to this, but in his attempt to see absolute nothingness as a historically regulative principle rather than a metaphysically constitutive principle, he, too, failed to bring it from its rarefied heights down to the level of concrete moral choice. Nishitani, in contrast, was rich in concrete examples of how we experience nothingness from the watered down nihilities of life's frustrations to its full, radical sense. Others, like Mutai Risaku and Shimomura Toratarō labored to draw the broader human community and the problems of modern science into the picture without upsetting the foundations that Nishida had laid. In the process, however, the idea of absolute nothingness became diluted or at least pushed to one side. The next step, it seems to me, is to de-absolutize nothingness, *pace* Nishida, and reexamine it in a way that honors the story of its development while admitting that it has become stale and out of touch with a growing awareness of the primacy of the earth.

It may seem an exaggeration to accuse absolute nothingness of blinding us to the devastation of the natural world. But the mere fact that it has *not* generated discussions of its own, that it has had to be bracketed for that discussion to begin, suggests otherwise. The problem, in fact, is not with nothingness (or with being, for the matter), but with two other matters that apply as much to philosophies of being as to those of nothingness.

First is the imagined transcendence of the subject, one of those ideas that have deep and stubborn roots in modern philosophy since Descartes. The dominant idea of mind among Kyoto School thinkers is the very idea that we find Sartre criticizing for being detached from the world for failing to see ego as a temporary constellation of the social milieu.[9] The transition from Kant's transcendental categories of thought to a self-awareness liberated from the subject-object dichotomy assumes that, in the liberation, subjectivity can function in an elemental state without interference by the impediments of innate a priori or experiential a posteriori conditioning. It is from this state of mind that the compassionate return to the human historical world takes its start and defines its goal, namely, the spread of the same state of selfless action. In this sense, it is not surprising that care for the natural

---

9. I am referring, of course, to his *La transcendence de l'ego*, a dense but important essay in which he argues against the phenomenological assumption that the ego can be defined apart from the concrete situation in which it finds itself.

world is made subservient to the enhancement of mind in its natural journey to the self-awareness of nothingness.

Second is the imagined unity of reality which, combined with the transcendent subject, creates a distance between the individual and the vastness of the cosmos. One can lose oneself in the *All-Einheit* without actually relating to it responsibly. To surrender oneself to the cosmos may bring the self to an ultimate stage of transcendence, but may also anesthetize it against its obligations to its immediate surroundings. This is the self-awareness of nothingness at its most romantic. There seems little to gain by regrounding oneself in the world once the self has already lost itself in the groundless void of the all or absolute nothingness.

Structurally, the tendency to marginalize responsibility to the natural world in order to maximize the purification of the subject is not so different from the hope of an afterlife whose quality depends on regulations set down by an otherworldly transcendent being. This does not mean that the purification of mind as such is irrelevant to the health of the planet, only that insofar as it obstructs awareness of the problem it needs to be developed further. This is hardly a matter of irrelevance or secondary concern to a philosophical worldview committed to the real world we live in. This further development begins with defining the notion of nothingness in such a way that self-awareness includes the natural world as an essential component. In effect, where the relationship to the earth is considered in terms of a self that relates itself to an absolutely transcendent, supreme being whose judgment it must survive to attain life beyond the grave, it is no different from the self that loses itself in an awareness of absolute nothingness. In both cases, there is a transcendence—divine or human—that needs to be relativized to the primacy of the earth.

It will help if we elevate the notion of the relative to the status that had been reserved for the absolute. To begin with, the *relative* need not be seen as the opposite of *absolute*. The opposite of the absolute is a radical pluralism that abstains from asserting a principle of unity at work in reality. The absolute, one way or the other, always implies a principle of oneness to reality, even if experience at its soberest and most enlightened tells us that the actual world is a moving picture that surrounds us on all sides and looks differently from different perspectives. No matter how many small connections we can register, they do not add up to an assertion of absolute unity. Even so, radical connectedness as such does not entail a denial of that unity, only a denial of its metaphysical supremacy. Absolute nothingness, in contrast, is inextricable from a monism in which the self becomes selfless and being is awakened to as a manifestation of an all-encompassing emptiness. The radical relativization of nothingness makes no such demands on our view of reality. Nor, for that matter, does it require notions of absolute space and time that shaped the dominant metaphors by which nothingness was distinguished from the world of being and becoming.

Let me be clear. The idea of a pluralistic reality seems to me a better fit for the idea of nothingness than a monistic view, but it is not required for a radical realtivization of the idea. The important thing is a positive notion of nothingness that preserves the essential Buddhist insight of the Kyoto School philosophers that nothingness is only real in being, and being is only real in nothingness. If we take the accumulated experience of the physical sciences along with our own human experience as a foundation, the idea of the radical connectedness of reality allows for such a positive view of nothingness. Connectedness does not exist as such but is only manifest in the actual connections that make things real as what they are. To see nothingness as connectedness means that nothing can be real and at the same time be disconnected from the rest of reality. Put the other way around, the idea of absolute disconnects, like that of absolute unity, are possible only in the speculative human imagination.

If everything in the world of being and becoming is, directly or indirectly, connected to everything else, it follows that the actual connections themselves are temporary and constantly being redrawn, rerouted, and misconnected in a way that the mind experiences as disconnection. In fact, nothing has been disconnected. Everything that is, always is *with* something else, but there is nothing that includes everything. No transcendent unifier or principle of unity is needed to hold this pluralistic reality in existence. To repeat the a thirteenth-century pseudo-hermetic text cited earlier, connectedness is the nothingness of a circle whose center is everywhere and whose circumference is nowhere.

The idea of nothingness as connectedness is of course a metaphysical abstraction. As in the construction of a rock garden, one first sets the master rock and then proceeds to set the other rocks in accord with its request. Connectedness is not an absolute ground but a foothold in relativity, nothing more. There is nothing novel about this image of reality. It is as old as Buddhist philosophy and as new as astrophysics. Versions of it are scattered across the entire intellectual and religious history of humanity. Its first function in philosophy is to clarify the foundational form of the forms of things that make up the real world, but that is not the end of it. On the contrary—and this too is a very old, if often neglected idea—it needs to be accompanied by a new image of metapraxis, the form of the forms of moral action. As we have been saying, even if we can imagine what seem to be disconnections, the sum of our experience does not allow us to imagine a disconnected world. All disconnects in the end turn out to be redirections of connectivity. New technologies and their accompanying modes of production and distribution, for example, are often experienced as a human disconnect from the natural world. On balance, the benefits too often outweigh the disadvantages, which are easily dismissed as a romantic desire to return to a simpler life that keeps us in touch with the world. This way of thinking needs to be looked at more closely. What we experience as a disconnect is in fact a loss of direct connection. This is not only true of our personal histories but of the tools we rely on for social life. Technologies and industries do not disconnect anything. Their immediacy and utility merely oblige us to take detours—longer and more labyrinthine detours as the process advances—to reconnect with the natural world. The way we imagine the connections among the things that make up our life changes as a result. It is these detours, these undesirable irrelevancies, that need to be looked at, but that is only possible if we first recognize them as such.

This is where Ocham's razor performs its most sensitive cut: to eliminate the absolute from our moral ideals. Insofar as an idea of nothingness or of another world disconnected from our own informs a praxis that deliberately sidelines the natural world and our responsibilities to it, metapraxis in an interconnected world is in peril of being reduced to the private realm or absorbed in the general ideological agendum of society. Nishitani, you will recall, describes the standpoint of emptiness as seeing the world in a kind of double-exposure in which the transiency of the world displays itself to imagination and liberates us from attachment to immediate desires and satisfactions. At the same time, he insists that the world is more than an occasion for refining personal awareness of the illusions that infect the mind. It is only *really* the world for us when we allow it to be what it is and not what we imagine it to be for our own purposes. To actually do this, we need to go further than Nishitani did. That is, we need not only to *see through* our image of the world but to *walk through* the detours that have distracted our imagination from our own conspiracy in the overconsumption and devastation of the planet. Self-awareness is incomplete without an exposure of the habits of thought and action that we have come to take for granted. The demands of daily life are so tangled up in a nonsense that passes for common sense that we no longer find it reasonable to demand fresh water, fresh food, and fresh air—or even pay attention to those whose enjoyments of these basic rights are being taken away from them in the name of technological progress. In a word, we have come into the habit of making do with a polluted savoring of the things of life that reconnect us more and more indirectly to the natural world. We experience the planet ambiguously, through technological misconnections that have turned it into a virtual reality, resigning ourselves to the idea that direct connection is no more than romantic pining for a bygone era.

Awareness of the form of the forms of thinking and the form of the forms of acting does not easily translate into a change of habits. Metaphysics and metapraxis alone do not provide the impulse to do so. Something more is needed to bridge the self-awareness of nothingness to the natural world, namely, an impulse to a living sympathy with the aboriginal, unknown and uncontrollable miracle of connectedness. Unless we can see our brief and fragile existence as part of a greater story, our metaphysical and metapractical speculations risk declining into moral indifference. I am convinced it is time to restore trust in the big stories that philosophy and science have collaborated to demythify out of rational thinking.

I recall some years ago standing in the Piazza del Duomo in Milan with a small circle of friends, one among many such circles there, engaged in animated discussion of our philosophical worldviews. I had just come from the quarters of Cardinal Martini and was full of questions and doubts that arose over conversation at dinner. When our circle dispersed, I wandered into the magnificent medieval cathedral at the head of the piazza. At once, the row of towering pillars transported my gaze up into the vast expanse that arched overhead. I felt, as anyone who steps into that space must, lifted up, my lungs filling up deeply and irresistibly with a sense of awe. As many times as I have known that feeling, I have never been able to contain myself, let alone understand it. At such moments, it is as if one has seen the place where great stories of heaven and earth breath the air they need to speak of things more than words can tell.

These stories—many of them from traditional religious cosmologies, more and more of them inspired by scientific cosmologies—can help cast a bridge from philosophical speculation about our habits of thought and action to actual practice. No one is moved by all of them and not everyone is moved by any of them. Then, too, enough of them get distorted into literal or dogmatic verities which tear them down and built them up again as walls to cut off the faithful from the unbelievers. To reconstruct these stories as if they were the seepage of a higher truth from another world into our feeble and porous minds is to deprive them of their power to move. Literalism disempowers them, and a philosophy satisfied with a critique of literalisms is as much at fault as a hermeneutics that scales them down to apophatic expression. Where these great stories are at their best, they serve to transform the chilly, rationalized ideas of the piazza into living but incomplete symbols that cry out for concrete investiture in action. Without such symbols, the hope of reconnecting to this sick and ailing planet of ours is seriously discouraged. To put this philosophically, metaphysics and metapraxis need the complement of a metaiconography that includes more than the demystifying and comparative study of mythologies. We coat these big stories with sugar or dust at our own peril. How very much we still have to learn from religions and cosmologies grounded in the natural world but marginalized by a rationalism that does not understand their unique reasonableness.

Simply put, I do not see how we can manage our nearest neighbor, the earth, without inspiration from a story of the cosmos. Whether our philosophical lenses are ground to the measure of nothingness or that of being, without these nonphilosophical stories, our philosophies cannot avoid contributing to shortsightedness that the earth pays for day by day to satisfy the suicidal gluttony of civilization.

## Concluding remarks

The argument can be made that the creativity of the Kyoto school has spent itself and that its only remaining influence is in the world of historical scholarship. Sure enough, that scholarship has raised a few eyebrows and generated discussions about the western control of philosophy. I agree that to incorporate them into a new *mestizaje* is not to deculturalize philosophy but to interculturalize it. These thinkers remind us, too, that transcendence can be restored to philosophy in the form of transcending the limits of the everyday, self-deluded ego. But if their writings are to survive as more than arcana from the East, we need to find a place for the transcendence of the earth and to include its story, immeasurably longer than human reason, into their vision. Kyoto school philosophy has to understand that the great cosmic stories of creation and the exploits of the gods are not, as Tanabe once suggested, mere "myths to be washed away and transformed radically into dialectical symbols."[10] They are the cathedrals of the mind without which our relationship to the natural world is greatly impoverished. In the image of Rabbi Ovadia Ben Adar of Izmir, they are "the cradle between words and deeds, the place where our breath perceives the infinite, after which our mouth falls open with admiration and we cannot but smile."[11]

The idea of an absolute of nothingness is showing signs of ageing. Its final refutation, as I have been trying to say, comes from its moral consequences. It is far from obvious what kind of things an absolute nothingness would make morally unacceptable that we are not already sufficiently aware of. To ask that question, I suggested the notion of a "connectedness" that is our permanent environment but is not an absolute. Whatever lies beyond the nothingness we see manifest in the world of being and becoming is beyond the reach of our poor reason and the tools of our sciences and technologies. To allow the absolute of nothingness to define moral judgment is to devalue the world that lies within our reach as no more than a beguiling fantasy. Absolute nothingness is an upper-floor abstraction at the end of a steep and spiraling staircase. The way that leads to moral responsibility is down the stairs to the ground and out the door.

At the same time, there is every reason to endorse the efforts of the Kyoto school philosophers to find a proper place for religion in a philosophy of self-awareness rather than dismiss it as a scientific embarrassment. As Jacques Lacan once remarked, "If science works at it, the real will expand

---

10. THZ 10:31.
11. Mario Satz, *La palmera transparente. Parábolas, historias y enseñanzas de la Kábala* (Madrid: Editorial EDAF, 2000), 200.

and religion will thereby have still more reason to soothe people's hearts."[12] It is not only the all-merciful being of a deity that can soothe the heart; so can an absolute nothingness in which individual and universal melt into a dialectical identity of contradictory opposites, to use Nishida's phrase. But here again, I have to insist: the soothing of our hearts and mystical union with the One are ultimately pointless if they render us insensitive to the irritations and the injustices imposed on the much, much older world around us. As much as we need our cathedrals of the mind for personal comfort, the earth needs them more.

François Jullien has helped us appreciate the basic ambiguity of the philosophical quest of the universal—and I mean to include Kyoto School philosophy here—by distinguishing between the uniform and the common.[13] Any universal that is not grounded in the radical pluriformity of reality is as much a perversion of the term as the economic and political pressure for globalization. The truer universal is a commons which is the property of everyone, every culture, every great story by being the possession of none. And what truer example of a commons can there be than the earth itself? And what better way to honor the writings of the Kyoto school philosophers than to draw their ideas out of the precincts in which they have been enshrined and into that commons to face the questions that the sufferings of the natural world are putting to them?

---

12. Jacques Lacan, *The Triumph of Religion* (Cambridge: Polity Press, 2013), 64.

13. François Jullien, *On the Universal: The Uniform, the Common, and Dialogue between Cultures* (Cambridge: Polity Press, 2014).

Rossa Ó Muireartaigh
*Aichi Prefectural University*

# Sacred Appellations
Secular Zen, New Materialism, and D. T. Suzuki's *Soku-hi* Logic

The logic of *soku-hi* is presented as an articulation of a post-Kantian view of reality that embraces the truths of science with the assumption of the transcendental subject. As such, *soku-hi* represents the philosophical posture of both the secular Zen of the Kyoto School and the new materialists of contemporary continental philosophy. It describes how material reality is not all even though there is nothing else.

KEYWORDS: D. T. Suzuki—secular Zen—*soku-hi* logic—new materialism—Slavoj Žižek—Louis Althusser—Nishida Kitarō

Science can never be defeated. It points at what is actually there and nothing other, and will keep pointing regardless of how much we may wish away what we see before our eyes. There is no argument against direct empirical pointing. The myths, the magic, the mystical mysterious that point at the unseen are no match for the hard wallop of the indisputably visible. But if it is the case that only the empirical, what is "actually" there can be claimed to be true, where is there "space" for religion or God? Is the triumph of science absolute and total? Has the meta-hypothesis of science removed Him from our cosmologies, making atheism the only rational description possible?[1] I seek here to demonstrate through an exploration of D. T. Suzuki's *soku-hi* logic how secular Zen, that Kyoto School creation, has embraced the non-scientific and non-rational, the space where religion and God can still lurk, whilst agreeing with the basic claims of scientific and empirical enquiry. In doing so, secular Zen has followed much of what contemporary continental philosophy, in the guise of new materialism, has to say, albeit with important moments of divergence.

---

1. Nishitani Keiji has also posed this question, stating that the standpoint of modern atheism seeks to ground itself from start to finish in actual being. This is related to the denial of God, in that full engagement of the self in actual being requires a denial of having already been determined within the world-order established by God, as well as a denial of having been fitted out in advance with an orientation to God in one's very soul. Both standpoints stress the importance of not becoming detached from the locus in which one 'actually' is, of remaining firmly grounded in one's actual socio-historical situation, or more fundamentally, in actual 'time' and 'space.' But do these standpoints [of modern atheism] really engage actual being to the full? (NISHITANI 1990, 189–90)

## Religion and science

From the earliest moments of his intellectual career, D. T. Suzuki was concerned about the relationship between science and religion. He believed that religion should not deny the claims of science. Rather, religion should embrace science to purify itself of its own superstitions and pointless rituals.[2] However, Suzuki felt that science and, indeed, philosophy (which he saw as involving exclusively dualistic rational thinking) could only go so far in explaining the truths of human existence. Science and rational thinking ("philosophy" in Suzuki's terminology) are based on a dualistic and linear mode of enquiry, forever moving forward with new data and information. In other words, science is not structurally designed to ever grasp the full truth of human life. Truth is always deferred to the future, awaiting one final piece of confirming data that never comes. Religion, though, is circular where science is linear.[3] It grasps the unity that is now. But to say that religion is circular and non-differentiating where science is linear and (dualistically) differentiating, and at the same time to acknowledge the compatibility between both positions (Suzuki never rejects science, we must remember) involves embracing a frame of mind that clearly acknowledges and conforms to the absolute contradictions of this posture. Suzuki's *soku-hi* logic was one clear articulation of this posture, and it was an articulation that has been echoed elsewhere, explicitly in the Kyoto School, but also, I hope to demonstrate, implicitly in large swathes of contemporary continental philosophy.

Science and religion are, of course, both slippery concepts and we must be mindful that both camps and each philosopher within may have different understandings of what each concept means. However, the important point is that both groups see science as a form of knowledge about the world that constantly effaces its own grounds for its own operation. Science is "done" by people who must effectively pretend that it is not they that are "doing" it, that it is just happening, it is just done. For instance, Nishitani comments: "Science is not something separate from the people who engage in it, and that engagement, in turn, represents only one aspect of human knowledge."[4]

2. Suzuki, 2001a.
3. This circularity versus linearity theory was also present in the thinking of Suzuki's mentor Imakita Kōsen (see Suzuki 2001b).
4. Nishitani 1982, 46.

In a similar vein, Althusser embraces the philosopher of science, Gaston Bachelard, with the result that, as Pfieffer points out:

> Because for both Althusser and Bachelard, science and scientific knowledge are products of the practices that science engages in, there is no "external" check on that knowledge that proves that it is "objective." In other words, science and scientific knowledge—even insofar as it is able to overcome the Bachelardian "web of beliefs"—is produced solely within the realm of a given set of scientific practices and concepts.[5]

Similarly religion is seen by both groups as not so much the practices and rituals out there in the world as the beliefs within the mind of the believer. Religion is foremost ideological, a belief system that asserts that the material is not all, that there is a beyond, a realm of knowledge, whether true, and hence believed, or simply felt, and hence false, that science cannot touch on.

## Secular Zen and New Materialism

To gather up in one bumpy bundle the pile of gravelly concepts that is Suzuki's Zen philosophy, I will use the term "secular Zen."[6] It can be defined as seeking religious certainty prior to religious affiliation, where said religious certainty does not wholly reject the paradigm of what can be described as the scientific, empiricist, naturalist, or materialist standpoint. (Of course "Zen" itself is a religious affiliation but this paradox is part of its pleasure.) I will be contrasting secular Zen with a group of contemporary continental philosophers dubbed the "new materialists" by Geoff Pfeifer, namely Louis Althusser, Alain Badiou, and Slavoj Žižek.[7] I will chart how

---

5. Pfeifer 2015, 20.

6. A 1916 work by D. T. Suzuki, entitled 『禅の第一義』 (2011) has been republished with the subheading "The Primary Purpose of Western Zen" emblazed on its front cover. The book is in Japanese but this subheading is written in English with no translation. We can behold here a semiotic move that would take a whole army of cultural studies scholars to decode. However, my quick, spontaneous interpretation of this book cover title is to see it is as a way of distancing Suzuki from the orthodoxy of Zen as institutionally practiced in Japan, whilst paying homage to Suzuki's intellectual validity and creativity. I will follow this example and see Suzuki as the articulation of a new tradition of "secular" (i.e., "Western") Zen, without worrying too much about issues of institutional legitimacy or heterodoxy.

7. Pfeifer 2015.

*soku-hi* logic encapsulates the secular Zen standpoint, while at the same time, articulating core sections of the new materialist position. Both follow a common trajectory but with a final and vital split emerging at the end.

## Soku-hi

D. T. Suzuki introduces his concept of *soku-hi* in this form[8]:

AはAだというのは、
AはAでない、
ゆえに、AはAである

We can translate it as "A is A implies A is not A, therefore A is A."[9] Suzuki asserts that this is the form of argumentation the Diamond Sutra engages in, asserting something, then negating it, then reasserting it on the basis of that negation.[10] For instance, the sutra states, as translated by Suzuki in *A Manual of Zen Buddhism*: "all these many particles of dust are no-particles of dust and therefore that they are called particles of dust."[11]

Suzuki claims that his *soku-hi* logic is a description of *prajña*-intuition, a core concept in Mahayana Buddhism.

### A is A

Let us look at the first step in this logical formulation: A is A. This is a

---

8. Suzuki, 2001c.

9. Another possible translation, as presented by Wayne S. Yokoyama, is "For A to be affirmed as A, A has to be non-A; therefore, it is A." Yokoyama 2011, 216.

10. Suzuki's translation of this aspect of the Diamond Sutra has been disputed and seen as inaccurate by some. For instance, Tachikawa has commented on

> the paradoxical expression that "A is non-A. Therefore it is called A" that repeatedly appears in the Diamond Sutra means "A is non-existent. Therefore, it is worded as A." The domain of discourse of the proposition "A is non-A" is not the whole, but A. Therefore, the phrase "A is non-A" should be interpreted to mean that "the being that is considered to exist in the name of A is in reality non-existent," not that "A is all the things other than A." In line with this argument, we have no reason to assume that an unconventional logic governs the Diamond Sutra. (Tachikawa 2002, 209–10.)

The fact that a possible mistranslation has helped in the expression and conceptual development of secular Zen demonstrates the creative and dialogic nature of translation in the development of religion and philosophy in human history. Indeed, I have myself penned a humble monograph which ruminates on this very subject. See Ó Muireartaigh 2015.

11. Suzuki 1960, 44.

description of the world that is very much in keeping with that of core scientism, naturalism, paleo-materialism, empiricism, or any such ideology which sees the world of nature, and our representation of it, as stable and coherent. In this view, objects have their own coherence apart from humans. An apple is an apple and can be "seen" as an apple even without humans. A is A is where every object and every event in the universe can be labelled and related to the whole, the collection of all other objectively identifiable objects and events in the world. There is nothing else going on but this world, and the things ("A"s) in it. It is the world being as it is in its "actuality."

## A is not A

Why would A not be A? Most generally, in the continental philosophical tradition, the assertion of A's non-A-ness can be derived from the idea of the Kantian transcendental (rather than transcendent) subject (which the condition of A being A is dependent upon), and the family of concepts and positions that have derived from this assumption ever since.[12] To argue why A is not A, when we include the transcendental subject, we can follow a number of commonly trod steps that have been taken, with alternate terminologies, by those in the secular Zen and new materialism traditions.

### *The notion of a filtered world*

This here is the idea that the conscious self existing in the world cannot be one more object in the world. What this means in effect is that A being A is a subjective imposition or filtering without which there would be no world of A is A, but only a cosmic mush of eternal non-differentiated A-ness. We exist in the world but filter that world which means: (1) As filters, we are outside the set of all that is being filtered. We cannot be included in the world. To repeat, we are not one more object in the world. Atman is anatman, self is

---

12. As Slavoj Žižek explains:

When I misperceive some object in my phenomenal reality, when I mistake it for a different object, what is wrong is not that I am unaware of how things "really are in themselves" but of how they really appear to me. One cannot overestimate the importance of this Kantian move. Ultimately, philosophy as such is Kantian and it should be read from the vantage point of the Kantian revolution, namely, not as a naïve attempt at "absolute knowledge" as a total description of the entirety of realty, but as the work of deploying the horizon of preunderstanding presupposed in every engagement with entities in the world." (Žižek 2003, 44–5)

no-self. The filtering atman of self cannot be ascribed positive existence since this would put it on the other side, as in that which is being filtered and not the filter itself. (2) Our filters cannot be absolute truth. We sift truth, break it down into bits, destroy its essential totality, and leave out the truth of its utter interpenetration. We see only the partial truths we have constructed with our filters. The world looks coherent to us not because that is how it really is but because we have made it so.

*Difference first*

The next step is to recognize that difference, not object, is primordial in our world. (This is how filters work, they "make" objects through their prior differentiating function.) One clear way of expressing this idea is the Derridean notion of *différance*. This is how Geoffrey Bennington explains it:

> Identities in general (of whatever kind, at whatever level) arise out of difference, but difference is not itself any thing at all. It is not that there are first things, and then differences and relations between them: the "things" emerge only from the differences and relations, which have an absolute priority, and that emergence is never complete. It's that insight that led to the neologism *différance*.[13]

While neither secular Zen nor new materialism explicitly use the term *différance*, the posture it expresses ("difference is not itself any thing at all") can be traced and delineated in both. *Différance* is found in much of Kyoto School thought in the idea that the world is not about constant separate "A"s emerging in nature but how these "A"s, as the products of difference and relations, are masking how their own supposed absolute differentiation is the outcome of a prior undifferentiatedness.[14] This prior undifferentiatedness cannot be one more A (as in the mass of all "A"s together) in the world, so it is emptiness (空). In other words, any view that embraces difference to be primordial must also acknowledge the unifying realm from which this difference is to emerge, and also understand that this realm is not a prior step in a chain of differentiation but the immanent grounding and place of the differentiation. As Nishitani describes it, "that all things are severally what

---

13. BENNINGTON, 2016.
14. For a detailed description of the resonance of *différance* with Kyoto School thinking, see KOPF 2011.

they are in themselves directly implies that they are all collected together. Such is the field of emptiness."[15] The point being that when we see A as A we are seeing the outcome of that prior realm of absolute emptiness. This is not the interplay of A turning into non-A, or A emerging from where there was the emptiness of non-A, nor is it the sum of all amounting to zero through pluses and minuses, but is the very condition of A when the self as non-self is to be accounted for. This mirrors the comments by Slavoj Žižek regarding difference between "everything is matter" and "there is nothing which is not matter." For Žižek, the difference "that a truly radical materialism is by definition nonreductionist: far from claiming that 'everything is matter,' it confers upon 'immaterial' phenomena a specific positive nonbeing." Žižek is reacting against the crude materialism where A is A (to borrow Suzuki's description), and emptiness has no positive value. Žižek writes, "when we imagine the Whole of reality, there is no longer any place for consciousness (and subjectivity). There are two options here: either subjectivity is an illusion, or reality is *in itself* (not only epistemologically) not-All."[16]

*Overdeterminism*

"A is A" as the world of discreet stable identities is also the world of identifiable and discreet causes and effects. If we picture a world at one instance, we see a world where all is divided synchronically into its unit components. If we picture the world then at the very next moment in time, there is still a division of the world into discreet units, but this division has changed somewhat. There are now different units, new units have replaced old ones. In other words, there has been a movement in the world, and units in the prior instant have caused, and can be linked to, all the new units that have appeared in the current present world.

However, when "A is A and is not A," the act of delineating what is moving and what has moved between any two instances of time becomes an act of arbitrary heuristics. Which causes are necessary and which are contingent is a judgment, not a measurable quantity. In fact, when A is not A, it is the everything that is causing the all to change between any two instances of time. There is not a chain of being, but ruptures of events which can never

---

15. Nishitani 1981, 192.
16. Žižek 2006, 168.

be fully explained except through fictions of cause and effect relations edited from the sum of all. In this vision of Althusserian overdetermination or Buddist *pratītyasamutpāda* (co-dependent arising) there are still possible rankings of causes, between the contingent and the necessary, the *hetu* and the *pratyaya*, but necessities are distinguished from contingencies in an ultimately contingent way since the only necessity is the all, or rather the emptiness of all.[17]

*Ideology*

To briefly recap, I have followed a chain of argument that posits the transcendental self, and sees this self as filtering or imposing the identification that makes A to be A. This act of imposition makes difference primordial to the object that is defined as A, and when all is put in motion and A changes into what it is not, this is on account of causal relations that are non-linear, over-determined and which can only be implied in a partial sense since any final account of causality would be total and hence neither descriptive nor useful. This lack of fit between the world out there and the world as we are imposing it can be referred to as ideology. Ideology is our most basic experience of truth, as in A is A, the reality that is there in its "actuality." However, it is ideology that is making A to be A. In other words, there is a contingency, an imposition on a site or field where A is not A. That is to say, A is not absolutely A, nor either is it anything else (like "B"). It is a site of infinite other possible configurations.

The contingency of A is A works when it is experienced as absolute. Yet, as an absolute, this A is A masks the fact that A is not A. Why does ideology do this? Because in our reading of the world ("A"s being "A"s) we cannot take into account (structurally) the position of the reader (which should be one more "A"). The eye sees by not seeing itself. Similarly, consciousness qua ide-

---

17. For example Louis Althusser states: "instead of thinking contingency as a modality of necessity, or an exception to it, we must think necessity as the becoming necessary of the encounter of contingencies." Quoted in PFEIFER 2015, 6.
Similarly, Imakita Kōsen (D. T. Suzuki's sensei) explained that the Buddhist distinction between direct and indirect cause (*hetu* and *pratyaya*) should be seen in unison in a world where, due to absolute interpenetration, the myriad things do not come or disappear, increase or decrease (不生不滅不增不減). SUZUKI 2001b, 219.

ological action works by effacing itself. This notion is expressed in Suzuki's account of *vijñāna* (in contrast to *prajña*).

> *Vijñāna* is not the creator of the logical law, but it works by means of the law. *Vijñāna* takes it as something given and not provable by any means devised by *vinjana*, for *vijñāna* itself is conditioned by it. The eye cannot see itself; to do this a mirror is needed, but what it sees is not itself, only its reflection. *Vijñāna* may devise some means to recognize itself, but the recognition turns out to be conceptual, as something postulated.[18]

And so both new materialism and secular Zen follow the same story in their crushing of positivist A is A-ism. However, both face the same problem where A is A meaning A is not A can descend into relativist incoherence or even deeper ideologically masked fantasies of certitude, as in the self-validating, but ultimately self-deluding, notion that one sees the true fluidity of the world in a way that nobody else does.

## Therefore A is A

However, both new materialism and secular Zen go one step further to assert that "therefore A is A," the fact is that A can only ever be A. There is no place where A is not A can happen. There is no transcendence from the world of positive existence. We are stuck in our world of "A"s. There is no escaping this. Similarly there is no escaping ideology. There is no no-ideology, no no-samsara. The idea that one can remove the false view that A is A and see the world as it really is, is itself an ideological fantasy. In other words, the metaphor is not about taking off the rosy distorting glasses of false delusion and seeing the true world out there, but rather the metaphor is about the eye being able to see itself seeing. This is of course impossible, as is any escape from ideology. This impossibility then, and the aporia, antinomy, and parallax that expresses it, is necessary and structural. Taking away this impossibility would mean indulging in the ultimate ideological blindness.

The solution is not to try and overcome or transcend the impossibility but to embrace it. What is to be embraced and what this embracing involves can be better understood if we take into consideration the two acts of "seeing" we are discussing here. The first type of seeing is simply the case of you

18. Suzuki 1955, 120–21.

seeing the world and objects and events in it. The second type of seeing is you seeing the impossibility of seeing "seeing" itself. This second type of seeing involves pure freedom in that this act can never be automatic. Only you can consciously decide to engage in this act of seeing. It cannot be done for you. It is that part of human consciousness that, for instance, AI (where AI is designed in a mechanical, computational, and modularly composite way) will never reach or replicate.

The aporia has consequently deepened in that not only do we face the impossibility of ever seeing ourselves seeing (when in fact seeing ourselves seeing is our deepest moment of self-conscious certitude), but now we also face the fact that we are both absolutely determined and absolutely free. We are absolutely determined in that our act of "seeing" the world is biologically derived. We are one more object in the world and as such utterly embedded in the events of the world as much as any other part of nature. But we are also absolutely free in that we can choose to break out of this act of seeing the world and decide to see ourselves seeing the world (with the impossibilities of this seeing being ultimately what it is that is seen). This second type of seeing cannot be ultimately linked to physical causation. It is not part of the great chain of being but is something that erupts from pure self-will. Thus, freedom and determinism both equally describe our condition. *Jiriki* (自力) and *tariki* (他力) are one and the same.

But let me go further and assert that it is from this ability to see oneself seeing that arises the social and the religious. When we see ourselves seeing the world, the idea that the world sees us back arises. This is not necessarily a logical conclusion but rather a potent and inadvertent intuition. The eyes of the other is felt to be endowed with the same pure freedom that we experience within ourselves. When another looks at you, you know they know you are there. However, tied in with this social sense of being, there is also a sense that the world itself *en masse* is looking at you and knowing you. There is what we can describe as an uber-consciousness out there. A personality in and beyond the world that sees you and knows you. There is a big Other, a God. Again, this is not a logical conclusion but something that we seem to be primed to sense from the most primordial beginnings of our conscious life.

So far, then, secular Zen and new materialism are still together and in accord. But it is at this point that the two diverge. In the concluding remarks to his book on the new materialists, Pfieffer makes an interesting link between the new materialists and the sociologist Emile Durkheim. Basically, the connection is the fact that Durkheim saw the existence of the social not as the sum of all individual minds in a given society, but as a collective consciousness out there, beyond, but only ever to be experienced by individuals. It is this social that is the source of the sacred in the world. It is consciousness, it is out there beyond the self, but is only really ever in the self, and as such, it is never transcendent of the world. It is imminent in the material. Pfieffer observes:

> We might argue that, for both Badiou and Zizek, what is new in their materialism is the newness found in the rebirth of the old claim to universalism, but here encountered in a new form—as appearing within existence (and not as external to it). Here again the Durkheimian conception of the "sacred" is relevant, as whatever is "sacred," and hence collective, *appears* materially in effervescent moments, and it becomes a matter of figuring out how to sustain those moments. As Badiou puts it at the end of *Logics of Worlds*, "But I need neither God, nor the divine. I believe that it is here and now that we arouse or resurrect ourselves as Immortals."[19]

However, whereas the new materialists see the social in the sacred, the secular Zen tradition sees the sacred in the social. The fundamentally Durkheimian idea is that when humans group together and engage in rituals, these rituals, although of sacred meaning, are ultimately about group solidarity. By contrast, secular Zen sees group solidarity and the love of neighbor it implies, as emanating from a deeper "field," to borrow Nishitani's term, that is of a religious (i.e., beyond the material) nature.[20] The case in point being Nishida who, speaking for secular Zen, sees the God of the social other as, indeed, God. The other is the space where God emerges. There is no other place for God to be. God coemerges with the self. Nishida writes:

> Our self is established as the affirmation of the absolute self-negation of God, and… this is real creation. The absolute does not merely transcend the relative. If that were so, it would be merely negative, while in actuality it is relative. The true absolute faces its own absolute self-negation and embraces absolute negation within itself: it mediates itself in an absolutely contradi-

---

19. Pfeifer 2015, 137.
20. Nishitani 1982, 284–85.

catorily self-identical way through absolute negation—as the logic of *soku-hi* as the Diamond Sutra has it. Our self is established through God's absolutely negating self-mediation; it exists at the outer limit of the self-negation of the absolute one into the individual many. Therein our self, the self-projecting point of the absolute one, is the image of God and absolutely volitional.[21]

Unpacking this statement, we can see that Nishida is asserting God as that which co-emerges with the self. This assertion can be grounded on the fact that the absolute, that which includes all, cannot have a positive value, be one more thing in the world, nor can it be the whole world added up either (such an adding up would remove the self). It can only be understood as the contradictory condition of the existence of the self in the world, the fact that the world is not where the self is but is not not there as that place where the self exists as itself. To put it in other terms, the big Other will stand in opposition to us at that moment our consciousness is generated from and as our self. The world out there where the big Other lurks is identified as being everything that is not one's self, despite being utterly depended on one's self for its identification. There is no other means by which to resolve this innate contradiction of the self in the world than to see it as the very site of consciousness and meaning in the world. The self and the other creating each other by not being each other but never coherently separating on account of this act of absolute self-mediation that unites through the very act of separation points to a deeper non-differentiating, or rather pre-differentiating consciousness wherein lurks the religious. Let us follow Suzuki in calling this *prajña*. As Suzuki explains:

> *Prajña*, however, is the eye that can turn itself within and see itself, because it is the law of identity itself. It is due to *prajña* that subject and object become identifiable, and this is done without mediation of any kind. *Vijñāna* always needs mediation as it moves on from one concept to another—this is in the very nature of *vijñāna*. Therefore, it swings the staff; sometimes it asserts; sometimes it negates, and declares that "A is not-A and therefore A is A." This is the "logic" of *prajña*-intuition.[22]

---

21. Nishida 1987, 85–6.
22. Suzuki 1955, 121.

Conclusion

Both new materialism and secular Zen agree that the existence of the self in the world creates an inherent structural contradiction that generates identity and meaning but is undermining of that meaning in its very operation. There is a gap in the cosmos, and here can lurk the space for God. Is it a case of the oft-spoken *gap of the God*, that fantasy we use to plug in the gaps in our knowledge, or the *God of the gap*, that which emerges because the meaning out there in the world, the sense of the Other beyond but with us, is meant to be known. There is meaning in the world because the world is meaningful. Where Lacanians may see the big Other as God that emerges with the development of consciousness as fantasy, Nishida sees it as a "real creation." No science will ever resolve this issue. It is the logic of *soku-hi*, the very fabric of reality.

References

Bennington Geoffrey
    2016    "Embarrassing Ourselves," *Los Angeles Review of Books*, March 20, 2016, accessed April 27, 2017, https://lareviewofbooks.org/article/embarrassing-ourselves.

Kopf, Gereon
    2011    "Language Games, Selflessness, and the Death of God: A/Theology in Contemporary Zen Philosophy and Deconstruction." *Japanese and Continental Philosophy*. Edited by Bret W. Davis, Brian Schroeder, and Jason M. Wirth, 160–78. Bloomington: Indiana University Press, 160–78.

Nishida Kitarō 西田幾多郎
    1987    "Logic of Topos and the Religious Worldview." Translated by, Michiko Yusa. *The Eastern Buddhist* 20–1: 81–119.

Nishitani Keiji 西谷啓治
    1982    *Religion and Nothingness*. Translated by Jan Van Bragt. Berkeley: University of California Press.
    1990    *The Self-Overcoming of Nihilism*. Translated by Graham Parkes and Setsuko Aihara. Albany: State University of New York Press.

Ó Muireartaigh, Rossa
    2015    *Begotten, Not Made: Explorations in the Philosophy and Sociology of Religious Translation*. New York and Dresden: Atropos Press.

Pfeifer, Geoff
    2015    *The New Materialism: Althusser, Badiou, and Zizek*. New York: Routledge.

Suzuki, D. T. 鈴木大拙
- 1955　*Studies in Zen*. New York: A Delta Book.
- 1960　*Manual of Zen Buddhism*. New York: Grove Press.
- 2001a　「新宗教論」『鈴木大拙全集第23巻』. Tokyo: Iwanami Shoten.
- 2001b　『今北洪川』. Tokyo: Shunjūsha.
- 2001c　『金剛経の禅・禅への道』. Tokyo: Shunjūsha.
- 2011　『禅の第一義』. Tokyo: Heibonsha.

Tachikawa Musashi
- 2002　"Logic Seen in the Diamond Sutra," *Indologica Taurinensia* 28, accessed April 27, 2017, http://www.indologica.com/volumes/vol28/vol28_art10_tachikawa.pdf.

Yokoyama Wayne S., trans.
- 2011　Introduction to "The Logic of Affirmation-in-Negation." *Japanese Philosophy: A Sourcebook*. Eds., James W. Heisig, Thomas P. Kasulis, John C. Marlando. Honolulu: University of Hawai'i Press.

Žižek, Slavoj
- 2003　*Organs without Bodies*. New York: Routledge.
- 2006　*The Parallax View*. Cambridge, MA: MIT Press.

Ōsaki Harumi
*McGill University*

# The Dialectic of Hegel and Nishida
## How to Deal with Modernity

This essay discerns in Nishida's later work lines of thought that could constitute a project of overcoming modernity, and explores its potentials and problems. My guiding thread is a comparison between Nishida's philosophy and that of Hegel, who, according to Habermas, first developed a clear concept of modernity through his idea of dialectic. Nishida perceived the Hegelian dialectic as conceptually endorsing Western colonialism, one of the ill effects of modernity. I argue Nishida's philosophy, which puts forward another dialectic based on absolute nothingness, had the potential to undermine the justification of colonialism and propose a worldview in which different peoples could coexist free from subjugation. I also argue that Nishida nevertheless ruined this very potential by essentializing his own nation as the privileged embodiment of absolute nothingness. This essay thus emphasizes the necessity to tackle ethnocentrism that lurks in philosophical thinking and sabotages its creativity.

KEYWORDS: Nishida—Hegel—Habermas—dialectic—modernity—overcoming modernity—absolute nothingness—colonialism—cultural essentialism—national subjectivity

In contrast to the conception of Western modernity, which has often been taken as *the* sole form of modernity, postcolonial discourses offer alternative perceptions that argue modernity can have different origins or take different shapes in diverse locations. As such, these discourses view the modernization of non-Western regions not as merely an imitation of Western modernity or subjugation to Western hegemony, but as the product of their own powers and possibilities. Thus, postcolonial discourses do not speak of one "modernity," but rather consider a plurality of "modernities." While accepting the strength of this position, however, Timothy Mitchell notes its weakness as well: "the language of alternative modernities can imply an almost infinite play of possibilities, with no rigorous sense of what, if anything, gives imperial modernity its phenomenal power of replication and expansion."[1] Even though there can be infinite forms of modernity, they may sometimes reproduce imperial power relations similar to those of Western modernity. Nevertheless, the alleged "alternativeness" of non-Western modernities can prevent investigations into such relations inherent in these modernities. In this case, they would no longer be "alternative," as they conserve within themselves the negative legacies of Western imperial modernity.

A case in point is a symposium titled "Overcoming Modernity," organized by prominent Japanese intellectuals in 1942, soon after the beginning of the Asia-Pacific War. From the Meiji period onward, Japan had embarked on modernization by importing Western culture; modernization, here, was equal to Westernization. Therefore, when it launched the war against Western countries, Japan's urgent task, as perceived by the Japanese people, was not only to surpass the West, but also to overcome the modernity equated with

---

1. MITCHELL 2000, xii.

the West. The symposium's slogan, "Overcoming Modernity," effectively outlined the public opinion of the country at the time. Many Japanese intellectuals also took this slogan, which epitomized the reasons for Japan's fight against Western imperialism, as a justification for Japan's colonial aggression in Asia. Harry Harootunian famously notes that the arguments of this symposium were in fact "overcome by modernity," as they practically reaffirmed the ideologies of Western modernity that they had professed to surmount.

While the participants of the symposium included four members of the Kyoto School, the school's founder, Nishida Kitarō, did not take part. Still, historical situations cast a shadow upon his thought: several years before the symposium, in his 1937 lecture, "The Scholarly Method," he described the task of Japanese scholars as, "creat[ing] a new global culture from Eastern cultural backgrounds that have fostered us for thousands of years,"[2] while working in Western disciplines in which Eurocentric ways of thinking still dominated. Despite his absence during the 1942 symposium, it can be argued that Nishida was also engaged in a philosophical project to overcome Western modernity.

Thus, the objective of this essay is to explore Nishida's work on modernity and his philosophies on how Japan could overcome it. My guiding thread is a comparison between his philosophy and that of Hegel, who, according to Habermas, was "the first philosopher to develop a clear concept of modernity."[3] My strategy is to analyze Nishida's confrontation with Hegelianism, and discern the lines of thought Nishida put forward to tackle Western modernity and its ill effects. As such, my attempt is a retrospective interpretation. Although this approach cannot completely avoid the projection of external schema, it can enable one to cast fresh light upon the potentials buried in a past philosophy. At the same time, if we look at its potential, we should turn our eyes to its limits as well. By considering both its strengths and limitations, this essay will reveal how Nishida's philosophy proves that, although they may appeal to the postcolonial vision of numerous "modernities," non-Westerners' challenges to Western modernity do not necessarily guarantee their success in overcoming it. My point is not that non-Western modernities are doomed to imitate and submit to Western modernity;

2. NKZ 7: 385. Unless otherwise indicates, translations of Japanese texts are my own.
3. HABERMAS 1987, 4.

instead, I argue that closer attention needs to be paid to whether different modernities can really be considered "alternative." Otherwise, much like "overcoming modernity," the term "alternative modernities" risks becoming a mere slogan—a deceptive slogan that distracts our eyes from the persistence of the same old problems.

To clarify what is at issue here and why it should be dealt with, this essay begins by addressing the formulation of modernity Habermas finds in the Hegelian dialectic. Based on this interpretation, I will explicate the ill effects of modernity in reference to the critical insights into modernity offered by contemporary scholars, Peter Osborne and James Tully. I will then discuss Nishida's criticisms of the Hegelian dialectic and worldview based on his evaluations of these ill effects of modernity. I will thus demonstrate how Nishida's project to overcome modernity is present in his work on surmounting the defects he saw in Hegelianism. Subsequently, I will examine a further dialectic and worldview Nishida presented, which he intended to be free from the defects of Hegelianism he perceived, and thus present the potential of his project to overcome modernity. Finally, I will critically examine his work in terms of its consistency and show that Nishida's reasoning ended up contradicting the goals of his project, and ruined its potential of "overcoming modernity."

## Modernity in its emancipatory and oppressive aspects

According to Habermas, the essence of the historical consciousness of modernity is the tendency to distinguish itself as the most recent stage of advancement in relation to the past, or even from the modern.[4] Modernity thus understood consists of the distinct differentiating movement from old to new. However, since the most recent quickly becomes less new over time, for modernity to sustain itself, it must continue to differentiate itself from itself. This generates what Habermas refers to as "a *continual renewal*."[5] This untiring urge towards incessant progress is for Habermas the principle of modernity.

4. Ibid., 6.
5. Ibid., 7.

Habermas remarks that if Hegel could conceptualize the principle of modernity as such, it is by his concept of "an absolute that… retains as unconditional only the infinite processing of the relation-to-self that swallows up everything finite within itself."[6] The absolute mentioned here is absolute spirit as Hegel conceives of it, namely, the substance that posits itself as the subject, while at once making its object diverge from it. Hegel describes this substance as "the doubling which sets up opposition, and then again the negation of this indifferent diversity and of its antithesis." That is, absolute spirit, after positing itself as the subject and making its object diverge from it, negates the opposition between the two by cognizing the object. Hegel alludes to the "*self-restoring* sameness"[7] of this spirit, by which he means absolute spirit, through this synthesis, restores its sameness as the subject, while enriching itself by incorporating the object. Habermas describes this movement of spirit as the "processing of the relation-to-self," or, more precisely, the relating of itself to itself through the mediation of its other that is to be integrated into the self. The logic operative in this movement, posing the opposites and resolving their contradiction through their synthesis, is the so-called "dialectic." Absolute spirit infinitely repeats this movement so that it creates all the things that constitute the entire world and its history, and sees itself realized in them. Habermas therefore describes "the infinite processing of the relation-to-self" as "swallow[ing] up everything finite within itself."

Spirit's self-cognition thus carried out is not only the realization of rationality, but also that of freedom, in the actual world. While the spirit in developing its self-cognition repeats bifurcation and integration, humans having different positions face and surmount their oppositions or conflicts, so as to attain greater truth and freedom. Hegel believed the dialectical movement of the spirit that goes towards this goal moves the world and carries history forward: "World history is the necessary development, out of the Notion of spirit's freedom alone, of the moments of reason and so of the self-consciousness and freedom of spirit. This development is the interpretation and realization of the universal spirit."[8] Although the phrase that world history

---

6. Ibid., 36.
7. HEGEL 1977, 10.
8. HEGEL 1952, 216; translation modified with reference to HW 7: 504. For consistency in the

develops "out of the Notion of spirit's freedom" may sound odd, it has its reason in Hegel's view: for him, it is not that an object comes first and then is grasped by the Notion. Instead, it is the Notion that precedes the object and makes it emerge so it is recognized by the Notion, and thus accomplishes it. Hegel writes: "The Notion is what truly comes first, and things are what they are through the activity of the Notion that dwells in them and reveals itself in them."[9] This view, which seemingly turns things upside-down, becomes understandable if we take into account Hegel's equation between the Notion and absolute spirit itself: "It is essentially only spirit that can comprehend the Notion as Notion; for this is not merely the property of spirit but spirit's pure self."[10] By positing its objects, absolute spirit creates everything; by cognizing them, it identifies them with itself. While thus continually diverging from and returning to itself, absolute spirit realizes and comprehends itself through itself, and also enriches itself and its self-knowledge. Then, absolute spirit is equal to the Notion that it has of itself, or the Notion that reflects itself by itself, and multiplies itself. As such, the Notion has a power to realize what it conceives. That world history develops "out of the Notion of spirit's freedom" means absolute spirit, through understanding itself as freedom, leads humans to work on realizing it in the actual world. Through this process of realization, world history is created.

When Habermas finds the principle of modernity in the movement of absolute spirit conceived by Hegel, what is at stake is not only the incessant innovation articulated by this movement, but also the advancement of the human knowledge and spirit, and the acquisition of freedom, all of which should occur concomitantly. For Hegel, various manifestations of absolute spirit through this movement culminate in the concretizations of reason as the highest human faculty in social and historical reality. Certainly, Habermas does not entirely agree with Hegel's idea of absolute spirit. Still, Habermas shares with Hegel the belief that the gradual actualization of reason corresponds to the progress of humans and the achievement of

---

translation of technical terms, I replace "concept" with "notion" to translate *Begriff*. As for the translation of *Geist*, I replace "mind" with "spirit." I also replace "actualization" with "realization" for the translation of *Verwirklichung*.

9. HEGEL 1991, 241; translation modified with reference to HW 8: 313.
10. HEGEL 1969, 618.

freedom. Hence, Habermas' qualification of modernity, the project of Enlightenment, is an eternally unfinished project that should be pursued endlessly towards ever-further improvement of human conditions. Looking on the bright side of Habermas' project, Bernard Stevens optimistically remarks that, "Modernity in the political sense is the still-incomplete effort to emancipate humanity from what oppresses it, including Western imperialism," and as such is "a project that… has yet to be achieved either in the West or in the East."[11]

This, however, is not so simple. The complexity resides in the inseparability of the emancipatory aspect of modernity and its oppressive aspect that implicitly endorses Western imperialism. When Peter Osborne claims, "modernity is a Western concept, inextricably linked to the history of European colonialism," he draws our attention to the inextricability of modernity from the socio-political conditions of its emergence. In his view, the sources of the time-consciousness of continual renewal are "the temporalities of capital accumulation and its social and political consequences,"[12] generated against the backdrop of incessant concentration of wealth at the expense of the exploitation of others. As an act that propels this concentration of wealth, Western imperialism is a crucial factor to the formation of Western modernity. Western imperialist ideologies cast a shadow upon the time-consciousness of Western modernity, especially upon the characteristic manner by which this consciousness deals with its others. The time-consciousness of Western modernity, which consists in differentiating itself as the "newest," cannot but regard non-Western others who live elsewhere as corresponding to different moments in its past, simply because they are different. Osborne describes this operation as follows:

> The results of synchronic comparisons are ordered diachronically to produce a scale of development which defines "progress" in terms of the projection of certain people's presents as other people's futures, at the level of the development of history as a whole.[13]

The others of Western modernity, regarded as its pasts, are meant to arrive at

---

11. STEVENS 2011, 235.
12. OSBORNE, 1995, 13.
13. Ibid., 17.

its stage in the future. Here, they are regarded as different stages of development simply integrated into one and the same historical process—into the universal history whose forefront and standard are Western modernity. The West's consciousness of the "backwardness" of non-Western others, attained in view of this alleged universal history, provides pretext for the West's domination over them, often in the name of enlightenment and rescuing them from their "backwardness." Thus, Western modernity's time-consciousness, in an encounter with non-Western others, turns into a mechanism of hierarchically subjugating them. This, in turn, lends itself to the justification of Western imperialism. What complicates this is that the logic that formulates continual renewal and supposedly promises progress and liberation of all the humans at the same time contributes to legitimating certain people's oppression of others, thus breaking this promise.

We can find this mechanism of subjugation already operative in Hegelianism, in which the first formulation of Western modernity was given. Hegel believed that different peoples are situated on different stages of the single universal history of the development of absolute spirit:

> For that history is the exhibition of the divine, absolute development of Spirit in its highest forms—that gradation by which it attains its truth and consciousness of itself. The forms which these grades of progress assume are the characteristic "National Spirits" of World History; the peculiar tenor of their ethical life, of their Government, their Art, Religion, and Science.[14]

Hegel here asserts that the development of absolute spirit proceeds through stages, and the form in which this spirit appears as a human spirit at each stage corresponds to each national spirit. In doing so, he reduces the difference between various nations in the world to the degrees of variation in the progress of human spirit, and establishes a hierarchy among these nations while integrating them into the single universal history.

Hegel's sense of hierarchy manifests itself more bluntly when he refers to the concrete others of Europe. For example, he states that Africa "is no historical part of the World; it has no movement or development to exhibit."[15]

---

14. Hegel 1956, 53; translation modified with reference to HW 12: 73. I added the word "World" to the phrase, "'National Spirits' of History" to better reflect the original term, *die welthistorischen Volksgeister*. I also replaced "moral" with "ethical" to translate *sittlich*.

15. Ibid., 99.

Excluding certain regions or peoples from history in this way means refusing them the possibility of progress, which he himself claims should reside in all human beings. Looking down upon them works to regard them as not a part of humanity proper. He also states, "Europe is absolutely the end of History, Asia the beginning."[16] In his view, Europe is at the forefront of progress, and Asia is the least advanced, or at the starting point of progress. Then he declares, "It is the necessary fate of Asiatic Empires to be subjected to Europeans."[17] Strictly speaking, Hegel sees the most advanced stage of human spirit in his own nation: "The German Spirit is the Spirit of the new World. Its aim is the realization of absolute Truth as the unlimited self-determination of Freedom."[18] Naturally, theorizations of a hierarchy among different regions or peoples can easily lead toward rationalizing the allegedly superior should wield power over the allegedly inferior. When one professes certain people correspond to the most advanced stage of the development of absolute subject, this could mislead them into believing that their treatment of others who are allegedly at less advanced stages as mere "objects" is authorized.

As Habermas criticizes the solipsism and dogmatism of the traditionally conceived rational subject, including that found in Hegelianism, one may expect the modernity he reformulates would be free from Eurocentrism. Habermas decenters the subject through his idea of communicative rationality, namely, the rationality to be realized in the communication between plural subjects, rather than in the self-referential monologue of the solipsistic or dogmatic subject. He reconceives modernity as the movement of such decentered subjects of communication. However, even in Habermas' reformulation, the fact remains that the emancipatory aspect of modernity involves another oppressive aspect that implicitly endorses Western imperialism. By contradicting Habermas from the perspective of Michel Foucault, James Tully draws our attention to the problem inherent in the common argument about Western modernity, which Habermas also shares, namely that world history is the linear progressive path of humans' individual and social development.

16. Ibid., 103.
17. Ibid., 142.
18. Ibid., 341.

These ambiguous logic-of-development arguments aim to show that individual and social evolution moves through progressive stages of development, the stages can be ranked hierarchically by neutral criteria, and the decentered worldview Habermas associates with modernity represents the highest stage. These kinds of developmental argument have been used since the late seventeenth century to try to establish the superiority and universal significance of European ways and they have often been employed to legitimise European imperialism.[19]

Tully's point is that even though Habermas invokes the ideas of the decentered subject and worldview, insofar as such modes of subject and world are put at the highest stage of unilinear development, they are taken as the norms for this development and used to situate other modes of subject and world at lower stages in a hierarchy. As such, Tully insists, "Habermas' theory is of the same general kind as other subject-centered philosophies." In this theory, "a form of the subject… is taken for granted at the outset and protected from, rather than opened to criticism."[20] The subject-centeredness mentioned here is, paradoxically, the centeredness of the decentered subject, which is still based on the model of European modernity. When Habermas takes this subject as the ideal interlocutor of communication, he practically disqualifies other kinds of subjects from proper communication: "An interlocutor who questions using the decentered worldview as the standard against which to judge forms of reasoning that anthropologists describe in other cultures, for example, is characterised as an irrational relativist."[21] Nevertheless, the alleged "decenteredness" of the subject guarantees its status as the standard, and gives this exclusion the appearance of legitimacy. What is going on here is not so different from Hegel's endorsement of European imperialism. Here again, certain people's dominance over others is approved on the pretext of the former's alleged advancement and the latter's alleged backwardness, judged according to the norm of the single subject, or at least the single type of subject, at the forefront of the universal history of progress.

Looking at Hegel and Habermas through the eyes of Osborne and Tully, it seems that what underpins the oppressive aspect of modernity are three

---

19. TULLY 1999, 106.
20. Ibid., 112.
21. Ibid., 111.

elements closely associated with each other: (1) the idea of a unilinear history of progress with modernity at the forefront, which entails the hierarchical ordering of the degrees of this progress; (2) the centeredness of the single (type of) subject as the agent or norm of this progress; and (3) the equation of a certain human group with the privileged personification of this subject, accompanied by the subordination of other peoples situated at lower stages of progress. Even though Habermas' conception of modernity might be more sophisticated than the concept of modernity discerned in Hegel's philosophy, it retains these elements and incorporates the oppressive aspect of modernity. Given this, when exploring ways of dealing with the ill effects of modernity, it is not a pointless move to return to Hegel's philosophy, in which the concept of modernity, with its double aspect, found its first formulation. This is especially significant regarding his ideas of absolute spirit and dialectic as the logic of its movement, given that they are crucial constituents of his concept of modernity. Keeping this in mind, this essay will now turn to Nishida's criticisms of Hegel, in order to trace in them a line of thought that could challenge the modernity formulated by Hegelianism.

### Nishida's attack on the Hegelian dialectic as the logic of modernity

If we look into Nishida's later works in which he ponders history, the state and the world, we can discover that his criticisms of Hegelianism address the aforementioned three elements of the oppressive aspect of Western modernity. While Nishida deals with these separately, his thought also connects them logically.

In "The Problems of Japanese Culture," published in 1940 based on his lectures in 1938, Nishida critically mentions the Eurocentric idea of the universal history of progress in which the East is situated at a less advanced stage compared to the West. This corresponds exactly with first element of the oppressive aspect of Western modernity, namely the idea of a unilinear history of progress with Western modernity at the forefront:

> As a consequence of the conflicts and frictions among various cultures for thousands of years [in Europe], a theoretical archetype [of European culture] was formed. [European people] regard it as the single cultural archetype. According to this archetype, they conceive of the stages of cultural forms and

situate Oriental culture at an undeveloped stage. They believe that Oriental culture, if it develops, should necessarily become the same as their culture. Even such a great thinker as Hegel had a similar thought. I think here is the problem.[22]

According to Nishida, the "theoretical archetype" of European culture, taken for granted by Europeans, is itself a product of history, formed at a certain point in time as a result of a particular course of events. He describes this as "conflicts and frictions among various cultures." Nevertheless, once it is formed, people come to mistake such an "archetype" as the single cultural archetype, which then becomes the standard according to which they judge other cultures as undeveloped and inferior. Hegel's aforementioned idea of universal history—in which Asia is situated at the beginning, Europe at the end, and from which Africa is excluded—comes from the imposition of a similar single standard of progress upon regions other than Europe. This imposition allowed him to one-sidedly judge cultural others as less advanced. Nishida believes this mentality of assuming the single standard and imposing it upon others is not specific of Hegel, but common to contemporary Europeans. Naturally, a philosopher's thought cannot but reflect the collective consciousness of his time and place, more or less.

Furthermore, for Nishida, Hegelianism is not just one example among many to express this consciousness, but rather its very epitome. Along this line, Nishida perceives Hegelianism's affinity with European imperialism, which was a dominant and accepted ideology in Europe during Hegel's time. Nishida also sees overlaps between the problems of Hegelianism and those of the dogma that advocates European imperialism. Nishida criticizes Hegelianism for being complicit with this dogma based on its subject-centered ways of thinking originating from Hegel's concept of absolute spirit. In "The Problems of Japanese Culture," he presents his opinion that, when "people came to think that the center of human action is in the subject" in Europe, "the imperialistic human form in the nineteenth century" appeared.[23] He continues:

---

22. NKZ 12, 284.
23. Ibid., 376.

> Hegel's ethical philosophy would express the morality of such a time. Behind the historical subject as he conceived of it was absolute spirit.... However, absolute spirit conceived by Hegel was still subjective [主体的], to put in my own terms, in the category of the grammatical subject [主語的]. It could be said that thinking the world to be environmentally one is the culmination of a way of thinking characteristic of Western culture, a way of thinking in which the world is taken to be subjectively one.[24]

In Hegel's philosophy, since absolute spirit is the permanent subject of world history, there is ultimately only one world corresponding to this single subject that produces, cognizes, and identifies with that world, and thus carries history forward. Absolute spirit as this ultimate subject expands itself so as to swallow the whole world far beyond being the center of it. In this concept, Nishida sees the culmination of the subject-centered way of thinking, and takes this extremity of subject-centeredness as coordinated with "the imperialistic human form" at Hegel's time. Thus, Nishida connects the acceptance of the dogma of Western imperialism with the extremity of subject-centeredness in Hegelianism. In doing so, he makes a direct link between European imperialism and the idea of the centeredness of the single subject as the agent or norm of progress, the second element of the oppressive aspect of Western modernity.

In Nishida's view, this subject-centrism also permeates Hegel's dialectic formulating the movement of absolute spirit. In the note to "The Hegelian Dialectic from My Standpoint," published in 1931, Nishida draws out this point:

> If you ask me, the Hegelian dialectic is still subjective [主語的] and noematic. At least, I cannot help but say that it puts stress on that direction. On the contrary, however, I think that true dialectic must emerge where we break away from such a standpoint."[25]

"Noematic" is the adjective form of "noema," which is the object or the objective aspect of thought. As such, this is something that can be the grammatical subject (主語) to be predicated in the proposition. Given the Hegelian dialectic characterizes the movement of absolute spirit

---

24. Ibid., 376–7.
25. Ibid., 84, n.

positing the object and integrating it into itself, this dialectic cannot but be understood with regard to the object that is grasped by absolute spirit. Hence, Nishida's qualification of this dialectic as noematic, which he theorizes is the movement of the permanent subject (主体) of consciousness grasping the object and making it the grammatical subject (主語) of the proposition. Whereas Hegel believes the production of reality consists in this noematic movement, for Nishida being noematic means not only falling into the category of the grammatical subject (主語的), but also being subjective (主観的) in the sense of depending on and solely deriving from the subject of consciousness.

This noematic character has manifested itself in Hegel's view of world history that results from the Notion qua absolute spirit through its dialectical movement. While absolute spirit is the permanent subject (主体), the Notion is its objective aspect to be made into the grammatical subject of the proposition (主語). To the extent that the world history as Hegel conceives of it develops through the continual opposition and synthesis of these two kinds of subjects, it can also be qualified as noematic in Nishida's sense.

Elsewhere, in "The Problems of Japanese Culture," Nishida further discusses the problem of the dialectic thus conceived: "There is no absolute negation. Insofar as the subject remains, still [this logic] consists in thinking from the subject."[26] Although Nishida refers merely to Hegelian logic, we can see the criticism he raises here as also applicable to the Hegelian dialectic. In fact, negation, whose lack in this logic Nishida deplores, is an essential constituent of the Hegelian dialectic. This dialectic is commonly formulated as "the negation of the negation," in which the subject is first negated by the object, this subject negates the opposition between the subject and the object, and this subject finally affirms both in their synthesis. In this process, negation is supposed to enable subject and object to transform themselves so they can be synthesized beyond opposition, to create something new. However, in Nishida's view, since absolute spirit persists throughout the entire process of this dialectic as its permanent subject, the subject is not really negated. He criticizes this state of affairs as the lack of absolute negation. Here, the synthesis between the subject and the object, which is supposed to be the affirmation achieved by the negation of this negation, is

---

26. Ibid., 362.

not truly the synthesis of the opposites. Rather, it is simply the enlargement of this permanent subject and enrichment of its self-knowledge through the integration of the object.

If universal history is conceived of on the basis of this dialectic, it cannot be modeled after the self-expansion of this single permanent subject that does not undergo true negation. Naturally, the path of the history thus conceived would be the course of linear, gradual and unceasing development of this subject at the expense of the subjugation of its others as "objects." Viewed from this perspective, ultimately, it is the Hegelian dialectic's lack of true negation as a necessary consequence of the extremity of subject-centeredness that made Hegelianism complicit with the dogma of European imperialism. As a result, the Hegelian dialectic not only articulates the single subject's impulse for expansion and domination over others, but also endorses, or even celebrates, the uninterrupted run of this impulse.

In relation to this lack of negation resulting from the noematic nature of the Notion, Nishida raises another important point on the defects of the Hegelian dialectic in "The World as Dialectical Universal," published in 1934:

> Hegel's "Notion" [概念] also did not avoid being an organic unity. Even if it returned to itself by its own self-negation, it still did not avoid being a universal, or, if not that, a singular individual. This is the reason why the Hegelian dialectic cannot be thought to be a dialectic of true absolute negation.[27]

In addition to the lack of true negation in the Hegelian dialectic, Nishida here implies the Notion or absolute spirit, which is the single permanent subject of this dialectic and allegedly the most universal among all entities, is merely "a singular individual" alongside many others. Hegel asserts the universal, including absolute spirit, is "the ground and soil, the root and

---

27. Nishida 1970, 167; translation modified to reflect NKZ 7, 313. I replaced "concept" with "notion" to translate 概念, a Japanese word corresponding to the German *Begriff*. This was done to keep the consistency in the translation of technical terms and to show the relevance of Nishida's statement here to Hegel's argument about *Begriff*. I also replaced "a singular entity" with "a singular individual" to translate 唯一の個物. *Kobutsu* (個物) is a key term in Nishida's philosophy and is usually translated as "individual." The term "entity" obscures Nishida's reference to the arguments in logic, including those of Hegel, concerning the relation among the universal, the particular, and the individual.

substance of the individual,"²⁸ and as such "permeates all the particulars and embraces them within itself."²⁹ Therefore, for him, there is nothing wrong with the universal's subsuming all individuals under it, given that they are included in it in the first place. However, even though Hegel qualifies it as absolute, for Nishida, absolute spirit is merely an individual entity far from being such a universal. When a particular individual is wrongly professed to be such a universal, it ineluctably ends up imposing its own particularity onto others in the name of universality. In Nishida's view, this is what happens in the Hegelian dialectic and the world history conceived based on it. In a prior statement, Nishida alludes to this risk:

> Even if, on the contrary, a dialectical process is conceived as an infinite dynamic unity, as long as a dynamic unity is conceived as spirit or as matter, it cannot avoid being one thing. It cannot avoid the monistic viewpoint.³⁰

This universalization of an individual entity named "absolute spirit" is not only analogous to the universalization of the archetype of European culture as the standard to be applicable to all cultures,³¹ which Nishida discerns in the collective consciousness of Europeans at Hegel's time. Remember that Hegel in a similar vein justified the subjugation of Asia and Africa to Europe, while finding in Germany the most advanced realization of absolute spirit, and situating neighboring European countries on similarly advanced stages. The universalization of a single particular type of culture or human group in a way that justifies the subordination of others is supported and reinforced by the assertion that this very culture or group exclusively embodies absolute spirit as the most universal, par excellence. However, this assertion would contradict itself if the universal really were what Hegel describes it as, namely, "the ground and soil" that "permeates all the particulars and embraces them within itself." This means the universal invoked in

28. HEGEL 1991, 253; translation modified to reflect HW 8: 327. I changed "of the single instance" with "of the individual" to translate *des Einzelnen*.
29. Ibid.
30. Nishida 1970, 167; translation modified with reference to NKZ 7: 312. I replaced "infinitely" with "infinite" to be true to Nishida's phrase 無限なる動の統一, because "infinite" qualifies "unity."
31. Naoki Sakai, in his insight into the self-consciousness of the West, illustrates how a particular, called "the West," universalizes itself and subjugates others as particulars (SAKAI 1989, 95).

the above assertion is not truly universal in this sense, but itself a particular individual entity. That is why it can be easily projected onto another similar entity. Nishida here discloses the falsehood of the alleged universality of absolute spirit. In doing so, he indirectly undermines the third element of the oppressive aspect of Western modernity, namely the equation of a certain human group with the privileged personification of the single (type of) subject as the norm or agent of human progress.

Nishida's criticisms of Hegelianism address the three elements of the oppressive aspect of Western modernity. This suggests his thought, developed around such criticisms, tends not only towards resolving the problems of Hegelianism, but also towards surmounting the ill effects of Western modernity formulated by Hegelianism. It is to this extent that we can discuss Nishida's project to overcome modernity. As we have seen, Nishida's criticisms of Hegelianism mainly target Hegel's ideas of absolute spirit and the dialectic. Thus, there is an expectation that exploring Nishida's ideas of the ground for all reality and of the dialectic will enable us to illuminate what is at stake in his project. Concretely speaking, this investigation can illuminate the kind of logic or worldview, alternative to those that characterize Western modernity, that Nishida's project can lead to. This exploration and illumination will be our next task.

## Nishida's alternative dialectic and worldview

Nishida regarded absolute nothingness as the ultimate ground for all beings and created his own dialectic based upon it. Although it is well known that his recourse to nothingness was inspired by his religious Zen experiences, it also has a philosophical significance. In his view, Western philosophy has mainly grounded itself on Being, and developed in the center of it, while regarding all beings as derivative of or dependent on it. Seen from this viewpoint, creating a philosophy grounded in absolute nothingness can be an objection to the premise of Western philosophy, or at least of its dominant tendency.[32] As such, Nishida's dialectic of nothingness was not merely

---

32. It is worth noting that, as Heisig warns, "It is a mistake—alas, a common mistake—to confuse western philosophy with Nishida's generalizations about western philosophy" (2001, 39).

intended to rival the Hegelian dialectic. Still, given his critical comments on this dialectic, it is undeniable that one of Nishida's motives for creating his own dialectic was to surmount the defects he saw in the Hegelian dialectic. His criticism of the Hegelian dialectic for assuming the subsistence of absolute spirit can be regarded as a manifestation of his critical attitude towards Western philosophy's tendency to ground itself on Being.

The question of how Nishida conceives his own dialectic as distinguished from Hegel's in order to solve its problems remains. As Nishida states "the true dialectical movement begins with nothingness' becoming beings."[33] The true dialectic for him is the process that starts from nothingness, which is the radical negation of all beings. In this process, nothingness, through the negation of itself as the most fundamental negation, creates beings and reaches the affirmation of beings. Nishida believes true dialectic is only possible in this way, in the literal sense of the synthesis of the opposites and the affirmation through the negation of negation. Here, if nothingness is the ground for all beings, it is only insofar as it negates itself as the ground. As such, it is the groundless ground, so to speak. In the process in which nothingness turns into beings through self-negation, and this negation turns into affirmation, "the equation between nothingness and being" holds and "self-affirmation is immediately self-negation, and self-negation is immediately self-affirmation."[34] This state illustrates what Nishida formulates as absolute contradictory self-identity.

A brief summary of Nishida's dialectic is enough to show he intended it to surmount the defects he found in Hegel's dialectic, even though this may not have been the only thing at stake. First, Nishida's dialectic, by taking absolute nothingness as the ground for all beings, challenges the Hegelian dialectic's assumption of the subsistence of absolute spirit as the permanent subject and saves dialectic from subject-centeredness. Secondly, Nishida's dialectic, by basing itself upon the most fundamental negation and going through the negation of this negation, introduces true negation, which the Hegelian dialectic lacks, because of its subject-centeredness. This restores to dialectic its dynamics to synthesize the opposites through this true negation.

In creating his own dialectic, Nishida neither simply denies the Hegelian

33. NKZ 12: 74.
34. Ibid., 81.

dialectic, nor invokes nothingness out of nowhere. Rather, he inquires into the Hegelian dialectic's presupposition and introduces the idea of nothingness in a way that complements the deficiency of this presupposition. In a classical tradition of Western philosophy, which Hegel also follows, the essence of knowledge has been sought in the unity between the knowing subject and the known object. Thus conceived, knowledge is not so different from the subject's self-awareness. Given the unbridgeable gap between subject and object as discrete entities, their unity, supposed that it is possible, would be conceivable only if the subject imposes its unity upon the object. Then the subject, by cognizing the object, only recognizes itself projected upon it. This concept of knowledge fits Hegel's noematic dialectic that proceeds through the subject's cognition and incorporation of the object. However, for Nishida, knowledge or even self-awareness is not possible in this subject-centered way:

> Against the conventional idea that self-awareness is the unity between the knowing and the known, I take self-awareness as seeing the self in the self…. The self's seeing the self in the above sense of self-awareness must mean the self's becoming nothingness, the self's becoming what determines itself while itself being nothingness. Insofar as the self sees itself in conformity with the object, in other words, insofar as it is conscious of itself, it cannot be said that the self is truly aware of itself. The self of which it is conscious is not the true self.[35]

For Nishida, knowledge is not the unity between the knowing subject and the known object, nor is self-awareness the awareness of the sameness of the knowing self and the known self. Rather, if the self can know the object—whether it is this very self or something else—it is because the self has emptied itself so it can envelop the object as it is. In other words, both knowledge and self-awareness are possible because the self has already become nothingness. Only by being nothingness can the self determine the object as such, while at once determining oneself as the subject knowing it, of which the self is conscious as another object. What Nishida calls "the true self" is not the subject that is itself a known object, but the nothingness that underlies both this noematic subject and all its objects. To this

---

35. Ibid., 66–7.

extent, true self-awareness is the self-awareness of nothingness; this awareness undergirds the self-awareness in the usual sense, as that of the subject's knowing itself as the object. Thus, self-awareness and knowledge are not possible in subject-centered ways through the confirmation of the subject's self-sameness, nor through the imposition of the subject's unity upon the object. Instead, they become possible by virtue of nothingness, which is absolutely different from beings, including subject and object, through its enveloping them and enabling their determination while negating itself in this determination. Here again, the dialectic of nothingness is working, while echoing the logic that presides over the ontological dimension in the epistemological: nothingness, through its self-negation, achieves the affirmation of beings. Hence Nishida's following statement:

> I think that what is regarded as the Hegelian dialectic can be also understood by putting at its beginning what I call the self-awareness of nothingness. What is regarded as true dialectic must genuinely signify the self-aware determination of nothingness.[36]

For Nishida, the Hegelian dialectic, which he qualified as subjective and noematic, should be grounded in his dialectic of nothingness. As such, he sees drawing upon the latter dialectic as allowing us to correct the errors of the former and see things in more comprehensive ways.

Nishida's "The World as Dialectical Universal" discusses what kind of new worldview he believed would be opened from the standpoint of this dialectic of nothingness. He often describes absolute nothingness as the "universal of all universals" in the sense of the most universal. In fact, as shown by his statement in this book, "When the universal truly negates itself, it must become a world of individuals,"[37] he thinks that when nothingness negates itself and creates beings, it becomes itself a world that envelops them as individuals. The title, "The World as Dialectical Universal," indicates that the book thematizes the world that nothingness becomes dialectically. It is thus reasonable to read into this work an expression of Nishida's worldview based on his dialectic of nothingness, even though what is included in this worldview is in fact not limited to one such "world."

36. Ibid., 76.
37. Nishida 1970, 167.

It is noteworthy that Nishida also calls this world as dialectical universal the concrete universal, using the same term Hegel used to describe the state, which for him is an exemplary concretization of absolute spirit as the most universal. This appellation suggests that Nishida's idea of the world that nothingness becomes through its dialectical movement is also meant to present a view of the state different from Hegel's.

Now let us turn to how Nishida conceives such a world. He qualifies it as "particular" and explains the self-determination of this particular world as the self-determination of place. The place is that which is in itself nothing, and therefore that in which anything can be placed. Thus, Nishida's equation between place and nothingness follows. Self-determination of place means that nothingness determines itself by becoming the world as the concrete universal in which things are placed, while these things recognize it as their own concrete place. Strictly speaking, what thus becomes is necessarily plural: "The self-determination of the particular is conversely the self-determination of place. The self-determining particular always possesses the other in the determination of place."[38] If the most universal is not Being, but nothingness, it cannot impose its own unity upon the beings it encapsulates. Besides, if nothingness is one, what becomes of it through self-negation should be multiple. Consequently, what thus becomes must be multiple concrete universals that are not unified by, or integrated into, the single higher universal. This is why the self-determination of absolute nothingness cannot but lead to the self-determination of the particular, insofar as the particular designates that which possesses other particulars and is distinguished from them by its genuine difference. The self-determination of absolute nothingness as the most universal necessarily leads to the self-determination of multiple particular places, whose particularities are determined by their different locations. Thus, the worldview that results from Nishida's dialectic of nothingness is that in which plural particular worlds, as many concrete universals, coexist: "In the determination of place as the self-determination of the dialectical universal, innumerable worlds are possible."[39] Considering the Hegelian equation between the concrete universal and the state, what Nishida presents here is the worldview in which different states, with their

---

38. Ibid., 229; translation modified with reference to NKZ 7: 419.
39. Ibid., 229–30; translation modified with reference to NKZ 7: 419.

respective particularities, are affirmed as they are, freed from unification or integration. That nothingness allows for different worlds or states is echoed by each particular world's enveloping beings as individuals, or, concretely speaking, each state's comprising its members with respect for their individuality.

In Nishida's philosophy, this relation between different states also applies to different national spirits, due to the inseparability between the state and national spirit. He mentions this inseparability in the second appendix to the supplement to his *Philosophical Essays* vol. 4, presumably written between 1943 and 1945[40]:

> When a national spirit is formed by the heroic efforts of a certain ethnic group at a certain point of time and place, a state is established. National spirit is nothing but a historical and corporeal formative force formed as the reciprocal determination between subject and environment. The form thus forming itself is the structure of the state.[41]

In Nishida's view, a state is established when a human society, formed in the interaction between subject and environment, attains the power of self-formation beyond the extent of this interaction. For this to happen, the people living in this society must form themselves into one collective subject that determines itself by itself. Nishida defines national spirit as the force of this self-formation, the formation of the state with its own sovereignty, and the mentality peculiarly ascribed to these people as the result of such formations. Then, the relation between states resulting from the dialectic of nothingness is the same as the relation between the national spirits as their formative forces. This is why different national spirits, formed in different locations and characterized by respective particularities, are affirmed as they are. They are not hierarchically ordered according to the alleged degrees of

---

40. The supplement and first appendix were written and published in 1944. The third appendix was written and mimeographed in 1943, and the second appendix was discovered later and added to the old version of NKZ 12. For the summary of the courses in which these texts were written and published/mimeographed, see the afterword by Shimomura Toratarō, one of the editors of the older version of Nishida's *Complete Works* and a member of the Kyoto School, NKZ 12: 470–3.

41. Ibid., 420.

progress that correspond to the unilinear course of the gradual realization of absolute spirit, as is the case with Hegelianism.

Nishida not only contrasted his own dialectic with Hegel's, but also differentiated his worldview based on it. If Nishida meant his dialectic to be more fundamental than the Hegelian dialectic, the same would be true of his worldview resulting from this dialectic. The message implied in this worldview would be that, even if a certain group of people or states rule over others in the status quo, the state of affairs in which the diversity of states or nations is respected without unification or hierarchization, or in which many different worlds coexist, is more fundamental. This is true to the authentic reality of the absolute ground for all beings.

### The collapse of Nishida's project to overcome modernity

In presenting alternatives to the Hegelian dialectic as the logic of modernity and the Hegelian worldview that endorse Western imperialism, Nishida's philosophy seems to tackle the first and second elements of the oppressive aspect of modernity, namely the hierarchical ordering of different states allegedly corresponding to the degrees of progress in unilinear universal history, and the centeredness of the single subject as the agent or norm of this progress. However, with regard to the third element, that is, the equation of a certain human group with the privileged personification of such a subject, Nishida's stance is ambiguous, or indeed, problematic. One may question whether it is possible that Nishida still equated certain people with the personification of such a subject, despite being so opposed to Hegel's assumption of the absolute spirit as the single permanent subject of a universal history of progress. Strictly speaking, the problem is precisely that Nishida equated a certain group of people with the privileged personification of absolute nothingness. In doing so, he did not only substantialize and subjectify nothingness, but also introduced a hierarchical ordering of diverse states that, while differently conceived than Hegel's, worked against Nishida's supposed goal of eliminating such hierarchies. Here, Nishida is unfaithful to his own criticisms of Hegelianism.

In "The Problems of Japanese Culture," Nishida sees the particularity of Japanese culture in the attitude of "thoroughly negating oneself and becoming the thing," or "emptying oneself and seeing a thing, immersing oneself in the thing." He equates this attitude with the quintessence of Japanese spirit: "The quintessence of Japanese spirit must consist in being united into the thing or matter. To do so means to become one where there was neither the self, nor someone else in the first place."[42] In thus discerning the quintessence of Japanese spirit in the attitude of negating and emptying oneself, Nishida practically claims that Japanese spirit embodies absolute nothingness par excellence. This claim does not seem not so different from Hegel's idea that the national spirit of Germany is the highest realization of absolute spirit.

Although Nishida argues that Oriental culture in general has a tendency in which "the subject negates itself and becomes environmental, becomes the thing,"[43] he asserts that two major Oriental cultures—Chinese and Indian—"lacked the spirit of going towards truth to the end, and therefore were stiffened and fixed."[44] Japanese spirit, he states, pursued this direction to the end. Nishida here simplistically reduces the difference between national spirits to the difference in the degrees to which they embody nothingness. Nishida once criticized Hegel and his contemporaries for setting up the single archetype of European culture as the standard to judge other cultures as undeveloped and inferior. Yet, Nishida here does the same thing, judging other cultures according to the archetype he invented based on the model of Japanese culture.

Nishida's advocacy of Japanese spirit is not merely a matter of genuinely encouraging the morality of self-negation or annihilation. Given the inseparability between the state and national spirit as its formative force, promoting the value of Japanese spirit is promoting the value of the Japanese state, or indeed its structure that makes it as such—that is, the form formed by this spirit, as attested by Nishida's following statement in the appendix to "The Problems of Japanese Culture":

> Today we should not only be proud of the particularity of the structure of our state, but also have an eye to the global profundity of this structure

42. Ibid., 346.
43. Ibid., 345.
44. Ibid., 280.

and illuminate it, and then promulgate it in the world in both theory and practice.

Later, he writes: "Then, consequently, a new world order will be constituted based on this form."[45] This passage makes it obvious that Nishida recommends the promulgation of the structure of the Japanese state, which entails constructing a world order based on this structure. While it is not stated outright, doing so ostensibly requires this state to gain global hegemony strong enough to make this happen.

If we leave aside this claim's affinity with wartime expansionist propaganda, for which some scholars argue Nishida was forced to express his support, what remains problematic is his assertion that a certain nation—indeed, his own—personifies the absolute ground for all beings par excellence.[46] This assertion permits him to situate Japan at the most advanced stage of the embodiment of nothingness and make it the privileged agent and norm of this embodiment, which other states, one-sidedly judged as less advanced, should follow or model themselves after. Consequently, this assertion ruins the worldview he presented based on the dialectic of nothingness—the worldview in which different states coexist with their diversity affirmed, freed from unification and hierarchization. Moreover, by granting Japan the status of this privileged agent and norm, this assertion permits not only strong subjectivity to be attributed to Japan, but also substantializes and subjectifies nothingness. If a single state that embodies nothingness par excellence is granted strong subjectivity, the nothingness thus embodied is not really nothingness, but the single incomparable absolute subject, comparable to absolute spirit.

Concerning Japan's subjectivity, Nishida's following statement is frequently invoked as attesting to his refusal to make Japan a subject: "What we should above all caution ourselves against is making Japan a subject." Strangely enough, another statement made shortly after this tends to be disregarded: "That we demonstrate the principle of world formation lying at the basis of our [Japanese] history does not mean that Japan stops being a

---

45. Ibid., 410–11.
46. Curiously enough, this assertion is largely accepted as a decent formulation of "Japanese cultural uniqueness," even today.

historical subject."[47] That is to say, if Japan is to demonstrate the dialectic of nothingness that has cultivated Japanese spirit in Japanese history, Japan need not stop being a subject. Nishida's claim expressed by these two seemingly opposite statements is that Japan can be a subject insofar as it negates itself as a self-centered subject, and realizes the morality of self-annihilation grounded in absolute nothingness. Some scholars may read this claim as Nishida's secret resistance to the wartime regime, remonstrating against its egoistic military expansionism. However, combined with his prior claim that Japanese spirit embodies nothingness par excellence, more likely this claim implies that Japan has realized this morality of annihilation in its history, is an essentially moral state, and therefore is already worthy of subjectivity. Whether Nishida supported the wartime regime from the bottom of his heart or not, this dogmatic conviction of the superiority of one's own state and its subjectivity was a basic tenet of wartime ideologies. Besides, one trick of such ideologies was to use moral ideals to embellish and justify brutal acts of colonial aggression. Nishida's assumption of the essential morality of his own state and assertion of its selfless subjectivity would never remonstrate against such acts, but rather practically justify them under the banner of the moral state and its selfless subjectivity.

Nishida, in view of surmounting the defects of Hegelianism, presented alternative ideas of the ultimate ground for reality, the dialectic and the world. In doing so, he undercut the centeredness of the single absolute subject, equated by Hegel with such a ground, and the hierarchical ordering of states, modeled after the unilinear course of this subject's dialectical movement. However, Nishida equated his own state with the privileged personification of the alternative ground for reality. In doing so, he allowed room for making this ground another single absolute subject and reintroducing another hierarchical ordering of states in the name of this subject. As Nishida gave new life to the third element of the oppressive aspect of modernity—the equation of a certain group with the privileged personification of the subject—he essentially nullified the positive outcomes of his efforts to tackle the first and second elements. Thus, the project of overcoming Western modernity discerned in Nishida's philosophy collapses because

---

47. Ibid., 341.

of its own inconsistency. It fails to be true to itself and interrupts the very lines of thought it pursues.

Hegel's and Nishida's philosophies provide a comparative case in which the professed emancipatory potential of a philosophy is undermined by the philosopher's ethnocentric assumptions. When some scholars nonchalantly celebrate Nishida's philosophy as heralding an alternative modernity, surpassing modernity, or even postmodernity, the ethnocentric pitfall into which his philosophy fell is largely ignored. However, given that Nishida's fallacy ruined any positive outcomes of his project of overcoming modernity, we need to take this failure seriously and make efforts to search for ways to tackle this problem, rather than disregard it and highlight only the bright side of things. Otherwise, we risk repeating the same mistakes, possibly without even realizing it, while indulging in the illusion that we have overcome them.

## Bibliography

*Abbreviations*

NKZ 『西田幾多郎全集』 [Complete works of Nishida Kitarō]. Tokyo: Iwanami Shoten, 1965–1966, 19 volumes.

HW Georg W. F. Hegel, *Werke*. Edited by Eva Moldenhauer, and Karl M. Michel. Frankfurt: Suhrkamp, 1969–1971.

*Sources cited*

Habermas, Jürgen
    1987 *The Philosophical Discourse of Modernity: Twelve Lectures*. Translated by Larry Kert. Cambridge: Polity in association with Basil Blackwell.

Hegel, Georg W. F.
    1952 *Philosophy of Right*. Translated by T. M. Knox. Oxford: At the Clarendon Press.
    1956 *The Philosophy of History*. Translated by J Sibree. 1899. Reprint, New York: Dover.
    1969 *Science of Logic*. Translated by A. V. Miller. New York: Humanity Books,.
    1977 *Phenomenology of Spirit*. Translated by Arnold V. Miller. Oxford: Oxford University Press
    1991 *The Encyclopaedia Logic with the Zusätze*. Translated by Théodore. F. Geraets, W. A. Suchting, and H. S. Harris. Indianapolis: Hackett.

HEISIG, James W.
: 2001 *Philosophers of Nothingness: An Essay on the Kyoto School*. Honolulu: University of Hawaiʻi Press.

MITCHELL, Timothy.
: 2000 "Introduction." In *Questions of Modernity*. Edited by Timothy Mitchell. Minneapolis: University of Minnesota Press, xi–xxvii.

NISHIDA Kitarō
: 1970 "The World as Dialectical Universal." In *Fundamental Problems of Philosophy: The World of Action and the Dialectical World*. Translated by David A. Dilworth. Tokyo: Sophia University, 163–235.

OSBORNE, Peter
: 1995 *The Politics of Time: Modernity and Avant-Garde*. London: Verso.

SAKAI Naoki
: 1989 "Modernity and its Critique: The Problem of Universalism and Particularism." In *Postmodernism and Japan*, 93–122. Edited by Miyoshi Masao and Harry D. Harootunian. Durham: Duke University Press.

STEVENS, Bernard
: 2011 "Overcoming Modernity: A Critical Response to the Kyoto School." In *Japanese and Continental Philosophy: Conversation with the Kyoto School*, 229–46. Edited by Bret W. Davis, Brian Schroeder and Jason M. Wirth. Bloomington: Indiana University Press.

TULLY, James
: 1999 "To Think and Act Differently: Foucault's Four Reciprocal Objections to Habermas' Theory." In *Foucault contra Habermas: Recasting the Dialogue between Genealogy and Critical Theory*. Edited by Samantha Ashenden and David Owen. London, Thousand Oaks and New Delhi: SAGE Publications, 90–142.

Rebeca Maldonado
*Universidad Nacional Autónoma de México*

# La temporalidad metanoética
## Sobre Tanabe, Heidegger y Shinran

In Tanabe's reading of time in the work of Heidegger and, through Shinran's interpretation, of the seventh-century Chinese philosopher Shandao (J. Zendō), one can see that both Heidegger's and Zendō's viewpoints do not go beyond the ethical standpoint of self-power. Tanabe distances himself from any view that strays from the eternal present as it is witnessed in the practice of metanoesis, in which one attempts to live the continuous practice, not as if one were dead, but by effectively being so, that is, by practicing and witnessing the breaking through of the self, which in turn is the only thing that can foster the eternal present of naturalness. This is definitively Shinran's viewpoint.

KEYWORDS: *Jinen hōni*—self-power—other-power—eternal present—resolution—three minds—sincere mind—deep mind—mind of aspiring for birth—faith

En este artículo presento la apuesta temporal que entraña *Filosofía como metanoética* de Tanabe Hajime. Dicha obra se dirige al «eterno presente», ya sea en su confrontación con Heidegger o en su lectura de las tres mentes de Zendō siguiendo las señas de Shinran y Soga Ryōjin. En ambas lecturas se presenta una crítica a la conciencia autoidéntica basada en el propio poder (*jiriki*). Así en relación con Heidegger, Tanabe elabora una crítica a la subjetividad que desde la resolución intente despertar al sí mismo desde la caída (*Verfallen*) en el uno. Con respecto a Zendō, Tanabe lanza una crítica a la subjetividad que desde su determinación ética intente salvarse a sí a través de actos buenos y meritorios, como sucede en la interpretación del pensador chino de las tres mentes consideradas necesarias para el nacimiento en la Tierra Pura y que aparecen en el *Sutra de la meditación*. Ambas interpretaciones se encontrarían en un nivel ético que es un punto de vista atravesado por el propio poder. Ambas lecturas de Tanabe intentan mostrar su distancia con respecto a cualquier posición que se aleje del presente eterno testimoniado desde la práctica de la metanoesis. En dicha práctica se trata de vivir continuamente no como si uno estuviera muerto, sino efectivamente siéndolo, esto es, efectivamente realizando la práctica y testimonio de atravesamiento del yo que es lo único propiciatorio del eterno presente. El salto de la ética a la religión y la concepción de una filosofía de la historia religiosa buscan pensar la posibilidad de renovación y renacimiento continuo de las sociedades en el presente eterno.

¿No es de llamar nuestra atención que Hajime Tanabe haya recurrido a Kierkegaard y a Shinran, justo a dos pensadores marcados por la experiencia religiosa profunda, para transformar su arrojamiento en la historia en el instante como «átomo de eternidad» o en la «naturalidad» (*jinen hōni*) que produce el abandono de sí? En definitiva el átomo de eternidad en Tanabe lleva el sello de la naturalidad y de la práctica que, como veremos en el texto, no solo nos disuelve a nosotros mismos sino que además disuelve lo fijado, e incluso lo más preciado de la tradición que, al disolverse continuamente, invita a crearlo de nuevo abriendo en general espacio al porvenir desde la práctica del abandono o del morir a sí continuamente. Lo fijado al des-endurecerse se transforma en renovación constante.

Después de leer *Filosofía como metanoética*, se advierte que uno de los cometidos más importantes de su autor fue producir una subversión de la temporalidad, mucho más importante que la lograda por Nietzsche con su idea del eterno retorno, para quien la transformación del tiempo era también asunto de la voluntad. Él pretendía subvertir la temporalidad desde la voluntad redentora que dice «así lo quise, así lo quiero y así lo querré». Al leer a Tanabe uno está ante otra cosa, uno tiene la impresión de leer a un filósofo que se encuentra con las fuentes del tiempo. ¿Qué puertas al tiempo se abren cuando no es cuestión de voluntad, ni de resolución de nacer en la Tierra Pura, ni de hacer posible el poder ser más propio? No tenemos otro camino para entender la subversión del tiempo que realiza Tanabe que la «vía larga», esto es, acompañar a Tanabe en su lectura de Heidegger y de las tres mentes de Zendō siguiendo los guiños de Shinran-Soga con respecto al tiempo.

Un lector que no tenga noticia alguna de las tres mentes puede ser tomado desprevenidamente, y podría preguntar por lo que ellas son. Desde la lectura de Tanabe las tres mentes es la propuesta budista de temporalidad más honda, pues el núcleo de estas como mente profunda es la metanoesis. Así tenemos a la conciencia de haber actuado, pensado y hablado interna y externamente con pureza de mente, tal es la mente sincera. La mente profunda es «una doble mente» como conciencia de nadar en el mar del nacimiento y de muerte desde un pasado sin fin y, al mismo tiempo, fe profunda en la compasión infinita de Amida Buda. Por último, el deseo de nacer en la Tierra Pura por la trasferencia de méritos, tal es la aspiración al nacimiento. Estas tres mentes para Tanabe son susceptibles de ser interpretadas temporalmente desde la metanoética. Tanabe declara:

> La cuestión de las tres mentes es una cuestión de importancia filosófica en el sentido que corresponde al análisis fenomenológico de la estructura existencial de la conciencia del tiempo en la filosofía occidental, cuyos orígenes datan desde Agustín y que podemos decir que ha alcanzado la cumbre de su desarrollo en la filosofía existencial reciente. Más aún, el concepto de las tres

mentes profundiza más que los intentos de la filosofía occidental porque está en contacto con una dialéctica más profunda[1].

Al leer en unidad estas perspectivas, uno tiene la impresión de que Tanabe ha realizado una auténtica confrontación entre Heidegger y Shinran, donde la búsqueda del poder ser propio choca con la naturalidad sin esfuerzo (*jinen hōni*), y al hacerlo, Occidente y Oriente realizan una coalición aún mayor. Pero también, Tanabe, al traer a cuento problemas que la filosofía occidental desde antiguo ha trabajado, como es el problema del tiempo, se enfrenta a la interpretación esencial del tiempo budista que entiende al hombre perdido en un mar de sufrimiento, a la caída. Hajime Tanabe en cuanto *Existenz* padece esa caída, ese arrojo, ese endurecimiento del ser, y no tiene otro camino que arar el tiempo desde ahí.

## La confrontación con Heidegger

¿Cuál es el modo de ser de esa transformación que va transformando aflicción y culpa en serenidad de vivir como alguien que ha muerto y de la cual *Filosofía como metanoética* es mostración de esa experiencia? ¿En qué consiste el constante paso entre contingencia y libertad? Tal pregunta tortura a Tanabe y modela en todos sus tonos y acordes *Filosofía como metanoética*. ¿Cómo podemos olvidar que el militarismo y el nacionalismo japonés fueron acontecimientos que marcaron el origen de esta obra fundamental, según la propia confesión de Tanabe? ¿Cómo podemos olvidar que Tanabe, como él lo confiesa, no se opuso al militarismo, grave omisión que significó contribuir al sufrimiento y miseria del pueblo japonés? Tanabe experimenta *zange* (vergüenza y arrepentimiento) y hace filosofía como camino del arrepentimiento (*zangedō*). En dicho camino el ser humano arrojado en la contingencia y en el *ser dado* experimenta conversión (*metanoesis*). Para Tanabe no hay manera de escapar de su propia responsabilidad, esa historia colectiva forma parte de su propio pasado, sin dejar de pensar que esa historia forma parte del pasado de cada uno de los miembros de esa sociedad participante de dicha tragedia colectiva. Sin dualismos de por medio, para Tanabe todos somos responsables[2]. Para Hajime Tanabe la historia es algo

---

1. Tanabe 2014, 329.
2. En este sentido, Tanabe llega a declarar en su impresionante prefacio a *Filosofía como*

que nos determina, y, sin embargo, gracias a la contingencia se alcanza la libertad. Sin contingencia no habría libertad. Pero insisto ¿cómo es que este libro transforma contingencia en libertad y tras su lectura lo sigue haciendo? y aún ¿cómo los tres tiempos son reacuñados y son ellos también despertados a su unidad? Para Tanabe la historia tiene que ver con la contingencia, no con un hecho natural, que se repite siempre, y el opuesto dialéctico de la historia es la libertad. Los hechos de la historia en tanto que marcados por la contingencia «son así porque son así» y pudieron no haber existido[3]. Así los hechos de la historia no son algo que se puedan conocer deductivamente, ni son algo que se encuentre determinado por leyes. Pero, ¿cómo y de qué manera se transforma contingencia en libertad? Para Tanabe la única forma de liberación que abre futuro desde la contingencia es la metanoesis:

> Metanoesis (*zange*) significa arrepentimiento por los errores cometidos, acompañado por el tormento de saber que no hay manera de reparar mis faltas. Significa también vergüenza por la impotencia e incapacidad que me condujeron a la desesperación y a la claudicación[4].

Tanabe, en el tener que habérselas con su propio pasado y con el de su propio pueblo, se lanza a una apasionante aventura filosófica que le permitirá dar cuenta de las posibilidades de la metanoesis como método filosófico y, por lo tanto, de la transformación de metanoesis en metanoética. La metanoesis, en cuanto experiencia de conversión y transformación que abraza pensamiento y acción desde la vergüenza y el arrepentimiento (*zange*), restablece de una nueva forma las relaciones entre pasado y futuro. Para Tanabe, abrir futuro desde el arrojamiento en la contingencia tiene que ver en lo profundo con la onda expansiva de la metanoesis transformadora de pasado y creadora de futuro desde el presente absoluto. Esclarecer esto obliga a escribir este trabajo. Tanabe sondea en la metanoesis en todas sus dimensiones en *Filosofía como metanoética*, no sin antes problematizar en el pensamiento de Martin

---

*metanoética*: «[...] siempre estamos obligados a practicar metanoesis mientras seamos conscientes de nuestra responsabilidad colectiva en cada acontecimiento que tenga lugar en nuestra sociedad» (ibid., 67). Más adelante señala: «[...] estoy profundamente convencido del hecho de que cada uno es responsable colectivamente por los asuntos sociales» (ibid).

3. «Esta contingencia primordial —el hecho de que exista lo que pudo no haber existid— es una de las cosas principales que distingue la historia de la naturaleza» (ibid., 145).

4. Ibid., 63.

Heidegger de *Ser y tiempo* en lo que respecta a las ideas de arrojamiento o condición de arrojado (*Geworfenheit*) y proyecto (*Entwurf*) y su propuesta del temple de ánimo de la angustia[5].

No debemos olvidar que *Ser y tiempo* ofrece una filosofía del despertar de la conciencia desde el arrojamiento y la caída, hasta la resolución (*Entscholessenheit*) de abrazar el poder ser más propio que consiste en ser desde el mismo fundamento de la nihilidad *culpable*.

### Arrojamiento y proyecto en el contexto de filosofía como metanoética

Si nosotros queremos entender cómo interpreta Tanabe los conceptos de arrojamiento y proyecto, tendremos que comprender primero que en el planteamiento de Martin Heidegger la condición de arrojado (*Geworfenheit*) tiene que ver con «como uno está y cómo a uno le va», esto es, con el temple de ánimo (*Befindlichkeit*), porque a la luz de esos temples de ánimo se revela que el Dasein se encuentra abierto para sí mismo, es decir, «*que es*», pero sin poder advertir «de dónde y adónde». Ello muestra que uno simplemente está arrojado o lanzado, pues se ha de recordar que lanzar o arrojar es en alemán *werfen*, así que de dónde y a dónde permanecen en la oscuridad. La condición de arrojado revela «la facticidad de la entrega a sí mismo»[6]. En la condición de arrojado se revela que el Dasein «en cuanto mío y en cuanto éste [concretísimo], ya está cada vez en un determinado mundo y en un determinado círculo de determinados entes intramundanos. La aperturidad es esencialmente fáctica»[7]. Tanabe se permitirá interpretar la condición de arrojado (*Geworfenheit*) en términos de contingencia. Dice Tanabe:

> La filosofía existencialista contemporánea habla de la contingencia de los hechos históricos como nuestro arrojamiento (*Geworfenheit*), un término utilizado para expresar el pasado del Dasein. Debemos aceptar los hechos actuales por su contingencia y su incapacidad de fundamentarse en la razón; son simplemente algo en medio de lo cual estamos «arrojados». El pasado nos es dado y, por lo tanto, es contingente. No es algo que podamos determi-

---

5. Cfr. Heidegger 2003a, 158 &29
6. Ibid., 159 &29.
7. Ibid., 241 &44.

nar a voluntad; estamos arrojados en la historia y no tenemos otra alternativa que aceptarla como es[8].

Ahondando en Heidegger, Tanabe entiende que sin la mediación del pasado no habría manera de alcanzar la autenticidad, ya que el carácter determinante del pasado, que está fuera de nuestro control y comprensión, nos mueve a comprenderlo, de modo que el pasado media nuestra existencia para que el yo, mediante la libre decisión, llegue a ser auténtico. Así, Tanabe da un paso más. Además de *asimilar* el arrojamiento al pasado, hace lo mismo con su contraparte, el proyecto, es decir, entenderlo como futuro:

> [...] el ser del yo libre, consciente de la mediación de la contingencia del pasado, puede cristalizar la intención en práctica y acción: el aspecto de futuro al cual se refiere la filosofía contemporánea como proyecto (*Entwurf*)[9].

Con respecto al proyecto (*Entwurf*), este revela el lanzar. Somos algo previamente lanzado y, a la vez, un lanzar, somos algo proyectado y, simultáneamente, algo proyectante, por lo que el proyecto es en realidad un proyecto arrojado (*geworfener Entwurf*). En el ahondamiento del planteamiento de Heidegger, Tanabe piensa que la historia transforma contingencia en acción y la libertad transforma contingencia en decisión determinante. Sin embargo, ¿la contingencia tiene principio determinante o carece de él y es «completa ausencia de subjetividad»?

### La lectura ontológica del tiempo: la dialéctica entre pasado y futuro

En la lectura de Tanabe, la relación entre arrojamiento (o condición de arrojado) y proyecto es dialéctica. Si es que sin contingencia no habría libertad, es porque solo desde la contingencia se experimenta el ser lo opuesto a lo que es y, a la inversa, si es que sin libertad no habría contingencia es porque solo el proyecto libre revela la contingencia a la conciencia. Así, contingencia y libertad coexisten y determinan nuestra conciencia del tiempo. Es decir, no puede haber arrojamiento sin un sujeto que se proyecte

---

8. Tanabe 2014, 146.
9. Ibid., 147.

libremente a sí mismo hacia el futuro. Para Tanabe, pasado y futuro, libertad y contingencia guardan una relación de unidad:

> Hablando dinámicamente, los opuestos son siempre correlativos, uno solo puede existir porque su opuesto también existe. La oposición dinámica está marcada por el hecho de que aun cuando —o precisamente porque- los opuestos son contradictorios e incompatibles. Se necesitan entre sí[10].

Pero ¿por qué el conflicto y la unidad se necesitan entre sí? Esto no tiene respuesta. Es, digámoslo de este modo, constitutivo del ser de la realidad, es ontológico. Y lo que podemos hacer es despertar a la comprensión de que en la contradicción hay una unidad, sin dejar de ser contradictorios, y en la unidad hay contradicción absoluta, sin dejar de ser unidad. Para Tanabe, la referencia mutua y unitaria y, sin embargo, contradictoria entre opuestos, además de ser constitutiva de la realidad, como habíamos mencionado, determina la estructura del tiempo y es dicha estructura la fuente de la existencia del yo. Pensar algo para Tanabe ha de hacerse conforme a ese principio. ¿Cómo es que aparece este principio en Agustín, en esta obra que es referente fundamental en la comprensión occidental del tiempo? Para Tanabe, incluso en Agustín la oposición y unidad entre pasado y futuro establecen la unidad del tiempo y estos, al oponerse no existiendo en el presente, hacen que su no existencia en el presente sea su afirmación. Así, el ser existe en su propia negación. El lugar del presente es que este se muestra como el momento mediador de la nada absoluta[11]. Entonces la unidad entre pasado y futuro acontece en el eterno presente absoluto. Tenemos aquí entonces la aproximación ontológica al presente absoluto, que como vemos es insuficiente. El problema de Agustín es que si la existencia de la inexistencia logra la presencia del pasado y la presencia del futuro en la presencia del presente, el tiempo se vuelve espacio, disolviéndose realmente la diferencia que guardan entre sí en un «ahora eterno». Si pasado y futuro se vuelven simétricos, coexistiendo en el presente, lo que se disolvería finalmente es el tiempo, o «se

---

10. Ibid., 149.

11. «El pasado y el futuro se oponen entre sí como contradictorios: son iguales, en el sentido de que ninguno existe en el presente. Sin embargo, en la medida en que son capaces de establecer la unidad del tiempo, no basta con hacer hincapié en su inexistencia. Debe verse también que la negación —su inexistencia en el presente- ejerce la función mediadora de fundamentar la afirmación de que ellos «existen» en el presente, en el verdadero sentido de la palabra» (ibid., 150).

detendría su flujo» tornándose el tiempo en espacio[12]. Por eso, para Tanabe, es necesario transitar desde la lectura ontológica del tiempo a la fenomenología, lo que supone el giro al ser del yo o el giro al ser del autodespertar de la conciencia.

### La lectura fenomenológica del tiempo y la crítica al poder-ser de Heidegger

Tanabe piensa la estructura del tiempo dialécticamente y, sin embargo, requiere de otra interpretación. Se hace necesario una fenomenología y no solo una ontología, porque como se mencionó anteriormente el concepto de tiempo solo viene a la conciencia cuando se lo ve desde la postura del yo, perteneciendo el tiempo al ser del autodespertar[13]. La gran propuesta de Heidegger es haber podido explicar en su obra la estructura esencial del tiempo atendiendo la estructura del autodespertar manifiesto en el gran asunto de la resolución (*Entschlossenheit*), la cual el filósofo alemán interpreta como el despertar al más propio poder ser del yo, esto es, despertar al ser culpable al hacerse cargo del fundamento de la nihilidad que él es[14]. Con lo cual se abre una gran diferencia entre Heidegger y la metanoética. Si para Heidegger el autodespertar es «una actividad basada en el propio-poder», para la metanoética «el autodespertar debe ser una transformación basada en la gran actividad del Otro-poder»[15]. En Heidegger la conversión acontece por la afirmación negativa del ser arrojado y eso para Tanabe delata un insondable autocentramiento y una permanencia en el reino del ser. Así que por mucho que Heidegger señale que ninguna dialéctica aunque se refugie en la negación, puede determinar el no como problema[16], para Tanabe

12. Cf. Ibid.
13. Cf. Ibid., 151.
14. Heidegger dice: «la resolución es el proyectarse hacia el más propio ser del Dasein» o, leemos también en Ser y tiempo: «Resuelto, el Dasein se hace cargo propiamente, en su existencia, del hecho de que él es el fundamento negativo de la nihilidad. [...] Sólo la resolución precursora comprende en forma propia e íntegra, es decir, originaria, el poder ser culpable» (Heidegger 2003a, 325)
15. Tanabe 2014, 152.
16. Dice Heidegger: «La ontología se encontró con el no, e hizo uso de él. ¿Pero es tan evidente que todo «no» sea un *negativum*, en el sentido de una deficiencia? ¿Queda agotada su posibilidad en ser constitutivo del «paso» [dialéctico]? ¿Por qué toda dialéctica se refugia en

«ninguna expresión que permanezca dentro del reino del ser puede describir lo que acontece en la transformación de la nada»[17]. Es decir, si bien Heidegger no permanece en el reino del ser al punto en el que permaneció Agustín al pensar el ahora eterno, y pasó a pensar el tiempo desde el punto de vista del autodespertar, el filósofo alemán sigue estando en el punto de vista del ser al pensar el propio poder ser.

Siguiendo con nuestra lectura, para Heidegger el horizonte del tiempo es extático, lo cual significa superar un yo previamente determinado en una transformación continua de lo determinado en lo determinante. Para Heidegger el sujeto práctico, aun cuando esté determinado por el pasado, puede superar estas determinaciones y posee una apertura infinita orientada hacia el futuro que hace que lo determinado sea ahora determinante[18]. Sin embargo para Tanabe, el horizonte del tiempo no puede ser algo que expanda sus límites cada vez más o como algo que expandiendo sus límites elimina todo límite de una vez y para siempre. Tanabe piensa que la transformación de lo determinado en lo determinante, ha de pensarse «como una apertura hacia la nada»[19]. Para Tanabe necesitamos en lugar de una estructura extática, que siempre va más allá y más allá, una «dialéctica concreta que está operando en la transformación de la nada»[20]. Así, la transformación de la nada es ese movimiento en el cual el yo, al ser continuamente negado, se mueve continuamente hacia fuera y regresa continuamente a su unidad. Se trata de un movimiento absoluto. Escribe Tanabe:

---

la negación sin fundamentarla a ella misma dialécticamente, e incluso sin poderla siquiera determinar *como problema*? ¿Se ha problematizado siquiera alguna vez el *origen ontológico* de la negatividad (*Nichtheit*) o buscado *previamente las condiciones* que permiten plantear el problema del no y de su negatividad y de su posibilidad?» (Heidegger 2004, 304 &58)

17. Tanabe 2014, 155.

18. Porvenir-haber-sido-y presentación para Heidegger no son un ente, sino una unidad extática que consistente en estar vuelto *hacia sí, de vuelta a y hacer comparecer* algo manifiestan la temporeidad como el original fuera de sí y por lo tanto extático por excelencia: por eso los fenómenos de futuro, haber sido y presente ya caracterizados, los llama éxtasis de la temporeidad. Solo desde la temporización es posible la unidad de los éxtasis, y no una secuencia de ahoras. Aquí tenemos que prestar toda nuestra atención, porque para Heidegger: «El fenómeno primario de la temporeidad originaria y propia es el futuro» (Heidegger 2003., 346 & 65).

19. Tanabe 2014, 155.

20. Ibid.

[...] el autodespertar no se hace consciente del yo como ser, sino como nada. Se hace consciente del yo no como autoidéntico, sino como contradictorio. Es decir, que el autodespertar de esta circularidad no establece al yo como algo quieto, sino que lo pone en la acción y en la práctica como flujo de actividad. El yo se afirma no como un sujeto autoidéntico que actúa, sino siempre e invariablemente como algo que es negado[21].

Para Tanabe, no hay un despertar al poder ser más propio, sino un despertar a la nada, una transformación en nada. Por eso comenta Tanabe: «Es imposible transformar los términos espaciales del ser en lo símbolos temporales de la nada»[22]. Así, acción significa que la nada absoluta emerge para operar de manera que el ser se convierte en nada y la nada en ser. Acción es puro movimiento sin sustrato. Es conversión incesante. Es discontinuidad. Es aniquilación y transformación incesante de ser en nada y nada en ser. El autodespertar no es continuidad de algo que sigue existiendo, es aniquilación, es disrupción: «[...] no hay algo autoidéntico que subyazca más allá y fuera de este transformador proceso de la acción que pueda dar unidad auténtica a la acción»[23].

A Tanabe no le queda claro cómo acontece la transformación de pasado en futuro en Heidegger sin tomar el camino de la dialéctica y concluye que, por no hacerlo, este se enfanga en un aristotelismo, que puede verse en los conceptos de facticidad y poder ser[24]. Para Tanabe, la lógica de la autoidentidad prevalece en el pensamiento de Heidegger, al no alcanzar a barruntar el «autodespertar de la nada absoluta, en la cual la acción de la mediación [de la nada absoluta] puede transformar verdaderamente el arrojamiento en proyecto»[25]. En la metanoética, esta continua transformación de ser en nada y de nada en ser hace que el yo sea abandonado, sin que reste algún yo que pueda actuar. Así, el yo «solo es restaurado como un eje temporal de transformación absoluta cuando coopera en la realización de la realidad absoluta (historia) y sirve de mediador de la nada absoluta»[26]. El

---

21. Ibid., 156.
22. Ibid., 155.
23. Ibid., 157.
24. Ibid., 159.
25. Ibid., 160.
26. Ibid., 124.

autodespertar de la acción de la nada no puede ser intuido, el autodespertar es «afirmación del desapego del yo y abandono de lo que pueda ser llamado mío»[27]. El proyecto en la metanoética es la conversión en eje temporal de transformación absoluta.

Esto nos permitiría entender el nuevo abismo que se abre entre Tanabe y Heidegger: mientras que Tanabe piensa un despertar basado en la acción del morir a cada momento a sí mismo, para el filósofo alemán el Dasein es fundamento de una nihilidad que ha de asumir y despertar al ser culpable. Para Tanabe, ese tipo de aserciones pertenecen al reino de la interpretación, permiten ver que Heidegger no se ha dado cuenta «cómo la nada absoluta, en cuanto principio de transformación absoluta, funciona como fundamento»[28]. En la metanoética, la nada no es algo que posibilite ser, la nada es más bien la ininterrumpida transformación de nada en ser y de ser en nada en una circularidad interminable, deviniendo la acción, la acción de la nada absoluta y el yo en mediador de la nada absoluta en el presente. La acción no es el llamado de la conciencia al propio poder ser culpable, ni la resolución a despertar al más propio poder ser. Por lo que, junto con Kant, Heidegger alcanza en *Ser y tiempo* un punto de vista en el cual se «mantiene al yo como el sujeto de la autoconciencia e interpreta al ser desde ese punto de vista». En Heidegger, la nada es un supuesto del yo, su fundamento, pero aún no es mediador de la nada. Para Tanabe la nada no es inmanente al yo, ni es un postulado del yo, sino que el yo es el mediador de la nada y es manifestación de la nada. Para Tanabe, dado que Heidegger no tiene la idea del yo como mediador de la nada absoluta (ni de una inmanencia de la trascendencia como principio de existencia), no puede ofrecer «una base adecuada para la temporalidad»[29].

En Heidegger la resolución es un dejar comparecer sin distorsiones aquello que dicha resolución toma entre manos. Como Heidegger mismo señala, el fenómeno de la temporeidad originaria y propia es el futuro[30]. Precisamente por eso Tanabe pensará que Heidegger toma el camino de *ōsō* (ir

---

27. Ibid., 128.
28. Ibid., 161.
29. Ibid., 162.
30. HEIDEGGER 2003A, 346.

hacia el absoluto) y se olvida del regreso al mundo (*gensō*)[31]. En cambio, para Tanabe, dado que lo absoluto no es opuesto a la existencia, sino que la acción de la mediación absoluta establece la relación recíproca entre lo absoluto y lo relativo, la nada absoluta media constantemente el presente. La mediación está en íntima relación con la acción y la práctica de la nada:

> Así la nada trascendente, que no es ni pasado ni futuro, sino que los trasciende a ambos, media al presente transformando al ser de la facticidad del presente en una mediación de la nada y de ahí en un relativo fundado en lo absoluto. Esto es lo que entiendo por inmanencia de la trascendencia[32].

En lugar de la resolución, como el momento que transforma arrojamiento en poder-ser propio, Tanabe piensa a la mediación como «la acción y práctica de la nada», es decir, como acción y práctica de la metanoesis.

### Del poder ser al eterno presente

Solo al encontrarse con la metanoesis como acción y práctica de la nada, en la que lo relativo se transforma en mediador de lo libre que es la nada absoluta podemos darnos cuenta que la nada absoluta es el fundamento de la libertad humana[33]. Someterse al absoluto, servir de su mediador, es la manera en que lo trascendente deviene inmanente y lo inmanente trascendente. Es evidente el lugar que el budismo de la Tierra Pura tuvo en Tanabe. Sin embargo, no debemos olvidar el aprecio que tuvo al zen con todas las críticas que pudo hacerle, como fueron la de pertenecer a la puerta de los sabios, o carecer de compromiso ético. Así cuando ilustra, ejemplifica, y da forma entendible a sus lectores de cómo lo inmanente se vuelve trascendente y lo trascendente inmanente desde la mediación de la nada absoluta, piensa en la libertad como el espíritu de desapego del budismo zen al hablar del «no tener nada» (*muichimotsu*) o del «rostro original del yo»[34]. Solo en el desapego o en el no tener nada, lo absoluto convierte al presente en un

---

31. Dice Tanabe: «su idea de trascendencia a través de los estados extáticos de la temporalidad (Éxtasis) no va más allá de la mera posibilidad del yo que se trasciende a sí mismo en dirección de un absoluto opuesto a él» (Tanabe 2014, 162).
32. Ibid., 163.
33. Ibid.
34. Cfr. Ibid.

verdadero estado de ék-stasis, el cual al producir una dislocación, una salida de sí, el yo es atravesado dando lugar a la eternidad del presente, o lo que se llamará el eterno presente en la metanoética. Podemos decir que el eterno presente es presente que ha sido atravesado por lo absoluto y se ha dado a luz desde lo absoluto.

Ahora bien, en el eterno presente se manifiesta una «espontaneidad más alta», podemos decir que se manifiesta una más alta que aquella que la filosofía occidental llegó a concebir como la acción libre considerada como actuar conforme a los propios planes. La espontaneidad más alta es el *jinen-hōnin*, «naturalidad» o acción-sin acción. Se trata de una actividad sin un yo actuante donde la acción es acción de lo absoluto. Desde la metanoética emerge una facticidad de cuño diferente a la facticidad heideggeriana. Tanabe le llama facticidad trascendente. Si la facticidad en Heidegger significa estar en el mundo de manera tal que el Dasein se encuentra ligado a los entes que comparecen dentro de su propio mundo como en «habérselas con algo, producir, cultivar y cuidar, usar, abandonar y dejar perderse, emprender, llevar a término»[35]; en Tanabe, esa facticidad es transformada en la acción mediadora de la nada absoluta que no es la acción del yo. En la facticidad trascendente «los planes y quehaceres del yo están mediados, subsumidos y negados»[36]. En cambio Heidegger «mantiene al yo como el sujeto de la autoconciencia»[37].

### La fuerza conversora de la nada

Llegados a este punto, Tanabe ha saltado de la ética a la religión. La acción es el resultado de la fe en la cual el yo se abandona completamente a sí mismo. Siendo la fe «autoconciencia de la aniquilación del yo»[38], y la acción, acción de la nada absoluta. En el planteamiento de la nada de *Ser y tiempo* como en el que aparece en *¿Qué es metafísica?* no se advierte la fuerza conversora de la nada, no se advierte a ese «principio trascendente que con-

---

35. Heidegger 2003a, 82 & 12.
36. Tanabe 2014, 164.
37. Ibid.
38. Ibid.

vierte al yo aniquilándolo»[39]. Y aunque Heidegger logre plantear en *¿Qué es metafísica?* que la nada es al mismo tiempo ser, y que esa es la cercanía con el pensamiento de Tanabe, carece del carácter conversor de la nada como principio de muerte y resurrección quedando atascado «en la clara noche de la angustia». Como piensa Tanabe, el sujeto que no es aniquilado en la crítica o crisis de las antinomias sigue «preservado y sostenido»[40].

En Tanabe la nada es trascendente y, en la medida que se relaciona con el yo e iluminación de uno mismo, es también inmanente, pero cuando no se puede pensar que la nada sea algo que se relaciona con lo relativo, y que lo media continuamente, entonces pasa como sucede con Heidegger: su nada es un principio de dirigirse a lo absoluto, un camino de *ōsō*, o más bien un eterno camino a *ōsō*, de ir-hacia, un apuntar eternamente a una posibilidad, permaneciendo la muerte un postulado, en un nivel meramente hermenéutico. Para Tanabe: «Solo demostrando la transformación absoluta de un fallecer en la muerte y regresar en la resurrección, puede la nada absoluta devenir completamente *für sich*[41]». Y aunque Heidegger hable de «enfrentar la muerte resueltamente», no es atravesar y trascender la muerte misma y atestiguar la resurrección, tal y como nos propone la metanoética. El problema de Heidegger es que al disolver lo absoluto, que es lo libre mismo, desbaratamos la posibilidad de la transformación, destruimos el trabajo de ese proceso. «La libertad necesita el fundamento de la nada trascendente para que el yo pueda atravesarse a sí mismo sin destruir su espontaneidad en el proceso»[42]. Finalmente, Tanabe resume su crítica a Heidegger de la siguiente manera:

> [...] la dialéctica que subyace a la teoría del tiempo de Heidegger ha sido desarrollada insuficientemente debido a su postura hermenéutica; de acuerdo con esto, la trascendencia de la nada absoluta que provee una base para la unidad extática del tiempo no puede devenir la acción-fe-iluminación de la eternidad. La conversión del pasado en el futuro, y la interpenetración de los dos que tiene lugar en el presente, permanece como un postulado que es asumido inmediatamente por el yo hermenéutico sin que el yo sea consciente de este

---

39. Ibid., 167.
40. Ibid.
41. Ibid., 168.
42. Ibid., 170.

como una manifestación de la nada eterna y trascendente. De acuerdo con esto, la ética, basada en el poder del yo, permanece ligada a la estrecha postura de la existencia humana y no abre una nueva visión de lo eterno[43].

### Las fuentes del tiempo

Para Tanabe, la superación de la disrupción es la no extinción de la disrupción. Es decir, el que la disrupción del yo no desaparezca permite un nuevo y continuo comienzo. Tanabe llama a ello circularidad. Dado que la disrupción realiza esa mediación entre lo absoluto y relativo, pasado y futuro, en el presente, en cualquier lugar que nos encontremos aquí y ahora, «permite comprometernos con la acción auténtica», esto es, realizar en y por la mediación de la nada la confrontación con lo relativo. Y es que semejante compromiso con la acción auténtica es indetenible, la mediación de la nada es un acontecer en el presente absoluto que se renueva incesantemente, donde lo establecido al desvanecerse gracias a la mediación absoluta de la nada da paso a una acción futura. Así, la nada, al girar sobre su propio eje en el presente eterno, posibilita «el despliegue y transformación del tiempo»[44]. Esta es la nada absoluta de Tanabe, creadora de otra temporalidad. Como trascendente es inobtenible y, como inobtenible, permite que lo establecido del pasado también se encuentre en la acción de la renovación constante como algo que todavía no se ha obtenido. A esto Tanabe llama historia. El tiempo está mediado por la práctica, por la acción-testimonio de renovación:

> Esta es la nada en la que se cree y es atestiguada en el autodespertar de la acción. Es algo que podemos buscar, pero no obtener, pero también algo que se obtiene incluso si no lo buscamos. Sin embargo, como nada, lo absoluto es el principio de esta mediación absoluta; paradójicamente, nos trasciende aun

---

43. Ibid., 175.

44. Dice Tanabe: Pues el ser que es atestiguado en la acción como la manifestación de la nada rápidamente se desvanece en el pasado como un hecho establecido, el cual necesita entonces ser mediado nuevamente para renovarse a sí mismo como ser, e implica ya, y de manera predestinada, la posibilidad de la acción futura basada en la mediación de la nada. La circularidad del futuro es mediada por el pasado, a la vez que el pasado es mediado por el futuro. En una palabra, la nada que es el principio de esta mediación gira sobre su eje que es el presente eterno, y manifestándose a sí misma incesantemente, posibilita permite comprometernos con la acción auténtica» (Ibid., 181).

cuando permanece por siempre inmanente en nosotros. Nuestra percepción de su inasequibilidad atestigua que ha sido obtenida. Al mismo tiempo, el pasado establecido como algo ya obtenido, requiere la acción de renovación constante como algo que todavía no se ha obtenido. El eterno autodespertar de tal desarrollo circular, basado en la nada absoluta, es la historia. Y lo absoluto, de lo cual nos hacemos conscientes a través de la práctica, esto es, a través de la absoluta disrupción de la crítica absoluta, se cree y se atestigua solamente en esta historia[45].

Tras la lectura de Heidegger de Tanabe que inició con el problema de la contingencia, el filósofo puede decir que la contingencia, gracias a la práctica de la metanoética, pierde su fijeza al abrirse a la renovación constante del comienzo. La nada absoluta inmanente-*qua*-trascendente en el presente puede ser pensada como el principio de esa renovación. Por eso, pensará Tanabe, la metanoética es «[...] un historicismo radical en el cual la continua repetición de *zange* provee principios básicos para el desarrollo circular de la historia»[46].

### La interpretación de Tanabe de las tres mentes siguiendo las señas de Shinran y Soga Ryōjin

La interpretación que realizó Tanabe del pensamiento de Heidegger con respecto a las relaciones entre pasado y futuro, así como el lugar determinante del presente eterno que encontró tras su lectura de Heidegger, lo hicieron acuñar una temporalidad metanoética. Pues bien, esa temporalidad metanoética toma suelo de la obra de Shinran titulada *Kyōgyōshinshō* (*Doctrina de la práctica, fe e iluminación*), particularmente de las interpretaciones del fundador del budismo Shin de las tres mentes. Dice Tanabe de Shinran: «[...] su idea de los tres estados de transformación religiosa y su interpretación de las «Tres Mentes» (*sanshin* 三心) es única en la historia de la filosofía de la religión en cuanto explicación de la estructura de la salvación»[47]. Fue Takeuchi Yoshinori, estudiante de Tanabe, quien escribió *La filosofía del Kyōgyōshinshō*, quien le acercó a Shinran y a su obra

---

45. Ibid.
46. Ibid., 65.
47. Ibid,. 66.

fundadora del budismo verdadero de la Tierra Pura (budismo *Shin*). Sin embargo, fue Soga Ryōjin quien lo acercó a la dimensión temporal de las tres mentes. Así declara Tanabe: «quiero hacer notar que la idea según la cual las tres mentes contienen una estructura temporal, fue propuesta primero por Soga Ryōjin, con cuya interpretación sobresaliente estoy en deuda»[48]. Después de leer el conjunto de textos agrupados en la sección *The Core of Shinshō* presentados en el libro *Soga Ryojin A reader* de Van Bragt, es preciso reconocer que Soga es el gozne hermenéutico indispensable entre Tanabe y Shinran[49].

### El sentido metanoético de la lectura de Soga de las tres mentes

Para entender la elucidación de Soga Ryōjin de las tres mentes, la cual permeó sobremanera *Filosofía como metanoética*, primero tenemos que recordar dos contextos de gran relevancia en el budismo de la Tierra Pura donde aparecen las tres mentes. Uno de ellos se encuentra en uno de los *Sutras de la Tierra Pura*, en el *Sutra de la Meditación*. En dicho sutra Buda Sakyamuni, tras enseñar a Vahidehi las diferentes clases de visualización de la Tierra Pura, de los budas y los bodisattvas, señala como condición indispensable para el nacimiento en la Tierra Pura tres clases de mente: la mente sincera, la mente profunda y la mente de aspiración al nacimiento por la trasferencia de los propios méritos. El pasaje donde se señala la presencia de las tres mentes es consignado en *Filosofía como metanoética* como sigue:

> Si hay seres sintientes que desean nacer en la Tierra Pura, pueden satisfacer sus deseos a través de establecer las tres mentes. ¿Cuáles son estas tres? La primera es la mente sincera; la segunda, la mente profunda; y la tercera, la mente de aspiración al nacimiento por la transferencia de méritos. Con estas tres mentes, pueden, con seguridad, nacer en la Tierra Pura[50].

El segundo contexto se encuentra en uno de los 48 votos pronunciados por Dharmākara, devenido Amida Buda para el establecimiento de su Tie-

---

48. Ibid., 328.
49. Cf. Soga 2017.
50. Tanabe 2014, 131.

rra, esto es, en el voto decimoctavo, el cual aparece del siguiente modo en *Filosofía como metanoética*:

> Si después de haber obtenido la budeidad, los seres de las diez direcciones con una mente sincera, una fe serena y el deseo de nacer en mi país, no renaciese, aun cuando hayan recitado diez veces (el *nenbutsu*), que yo no obtenga la Iluminación perfecta —con excepción de aquellos que han cometido los cinco pecados mortales y violado el *dharma* correcto[51].

Soga Ryōjin, al pensar la dinámica de la fe que encierra el voto decimoctavo, encuentra que la fe es al mismo tiempo el otro lado del voto original de Amida Buda de renacer en su Tierra dirigido a los seres sintientes como lo sugirió Shinran[52]. Para Soga, se trata de volver consciente este movimiento de la fe como el movimiento de las tres mentes. Dice Soga:

> Las tres mentes es el proceso de auto-examen del Primer Voto a través del cual el Tathāgata hace que el *shinjin* surja en nosotros; consecuentemente, este es el proceso de autoconciencia a través del cual nosotros nos volvemos a la mente del voto del Tathāgata[53].

La fe no es fe en el otro poder, como la fe en algo creído, en algo que finalmente es tomado como un objeto. Más bien, la fe es concedida por Amida. Shinran comprendió esto radicalmente antes que nadie. La fe es un regalo de la mente sincera de Amida surgida de su Gran Compasión y acaece en nosotros como conciencia plena de la nulidad de nuestros méritos y esfuerzos, como lo ha esclarecido Soga. «Recibimos por primera vez la revelación de habernos considerado durante mucho tiempo *merecedores* de recibir al otro poder [...]. Esto es un cambio de sentido al cual llamamos conversión»[54]. Solo al negar la transformación por el propio poder «uno puede empezar a confiar en el regalo del otro poder»[55]. Dado que Soga pensará la conversión como el giro de mente desde el punto de vista en el cual uno se considera merecedor del voto de Amida al punto de vista de volverse consciente del regalo proveniente de Amida, Tanabe piensa que la interpretación de Soga

---

51. Ibid., 301.
52. SOGA 2017, 506.
53. Ibid., 394..
54. Ibid., 535.
55. Ibid.

es metanoética en esencia, lo cual presta un gran soporte a su propia interpretación.

Habrá otras cercanías con la interpretación de Soga por parte de Tanabe, como es la de considerar la interpretación de Zendō o Shandao una interpretación sostenida en el propio poder. Y definitivamente es así, según Soga para Zendō la transformación de la transferencia del propio poder a la transferencia del otro poder, requiere abandonar absolutamente todo para permitir la trasferencia del otro poder, pero esto sigue permaneciendo en el ámbito del propio poder. Insistimos: para Soga fue Shinran quien se dio verdaderamente cuenta de que es el otro poder quien concede transferir los méritos al interior de la mente sincera y a ese momento el autor del *Kyōgyōshinshō* lo llamó «la fe de la trasferencia del otro poder» o «transferencia de la mente sincera»[56]. Antes *se creía* en el otro poder, así lo hizo Zendō, incluso Hōnen, pero ellos no pensaron en la trasferencia del otro poder como cumplimento del voto original.

Tanabe piensa que Soga dio una estructura temporal a las tres mentes. Y es que, efectivamente, ese instante de receptividad del regalo de Amida produce un gran despertar que da lugar de una vez por todas a la verdadera fe del abandono en el presente de la vida diaria[57]. Con ello lo que encuentra Soga es ese punto donde acontece la inmanencia en la trascendencia y la trascendencia en la inmanencia, las cuales en *Ser y tiempo* de Heideger quedaron completamente desdibujadas y que es lo que fuertemente critica Tanabe. A pesar de la gran ayuda que Soga presta a la consecución de una filosofía como metanoética, Tanabe tiene una seria reserva a la lectura de Soga: para este gran intérprete de Shinran, «el deseo de nacer en mi tierra» es algo a través de lo cual el Tathāgata hace un llamado a los seres sintientes a su Tierra. Y este llamado «es el verdadero despertar de la conciencia de nuestra receptividad religiosa»[58]. Para Soga «el deseo de nacer en la Tierra es el corazón de la fe confiada»[59]. Es en este punto donde Tanabe tiene la necesidad de otra interpretación de las tres mentes. Para Tanabe, el corazón de las

---

56. Ibid., 536.
57. Ibid., 537.
58. Ibid.
59. Ibid., 538.

tres mentes es la mente profunda y la mente profunda es metanoesis, como lo veremos en lo siguiente.

### La recuperación de Shinran en su lectura de las tres mentes

Shinran encuentra en el pensamiento de Zendō sobre las tres mentes que mente sincera (*Shijōshin*) es aquella que cree en la sinceridad y pureza de los propios pensamientos, actos y palabras en tanto que ellos fueron actuados por Amida con una verdadera y real mente. Veamos lo que dice Zendō sobre la mente sincera:

> Si tú actúas el bien en los tres modos de acción (palabras, actos y pensamientos) continuamente, considera como absolutamente necesario que el Buda actuó con verdadera y real mente. Esto es debido a que una persona considera la verdad y lo real como indispensable, ya sea que se encuentre afuera o dentro, en la luz o en la oscuridad, a eso es a lo que se refiere con «mente sincera»[60].

Asimismo, en Zendō fe profunda o mente profunda (*shinjin*) es una doble mente. Por un lado, la creencia profunda de ser un ser plagado de ciegas pasiones cautivo en el mar del nacimiento y la muerte que deambula en la transmigración desde un tiempo sin principio: «sin condición alguna que pueda conducir a la emancipación»[61]. Y, por otro lado, es la creencia profunda en el voto compasivo de Amida Buddha y los 48 votos establecidos por Amida para salvar a los seres sintientes. Por último, tenemos la mente de aspiración al nacimiento a la que decididamente el Tathāgata conduce a los seres sintientes enseñando en el *Sutra de la Contemplación* las conductas meritorias y las clases de bien, e impulsando a la resolución inamovible de nacimiento en la Tierra Pura por la transferencia de méritos en el futuro.

---

60. «...if you perform good in the three modes of action, unfailingly take as essential what the Buddha performed with true and real mind. It is because a person takes the true and real as essential, whether he be within or without, whether of brightness or darkness, that the term «sincere mind» is applied.» (SHINRAN 1997, 85).

61. Ibid.

## La oposición entre la lectura moral de Zendō y la lectura metanoética de las tres mentes de Shinran

En esta presentación de las tres mentes de Zendo desde Shinran, vemos que él interpreta estas tres mentes que aparecen en el *Sutra de la Visualización* desde el punto de vista de la aspiración al nacimiento mediante el *nenbutsu* del propio-poder. Y aunque Zendō tiene de manera *implícita* el *zange* o metanoesis, él no fue capaz de escapar del «idealismo de la obligación moral»[62]. Shinran, que se encuentra ya en el camino de *zange*, en cambio, es incapaz de mantenerse en las demandas de la obligación moral y, por el contrario, más bien es lanzado al corazón del mal y del pecado, hasta la propia autonegación, hasta abandonarse a sí mismo. Zendō, que no sigue el camino de la metanoesis, se mantiene dentro de los límites del ideal moral y, por lo mismo, aparece en su pensamiento una contradicción entre el *nenbutsu* y el autoesfuerzo que necesariamente acompaña a la idea de obligación. El giro que da Shinran a esta interpretación de Zendō es un giro metanoético, esto es, desde la perspectiva de la fe en el Otro Poder. Lo esencial para Tanabe, siguiendo a Shinran, es que «la función transformadora del Otro Poder» debe ser esencial para la interpretación de las tres mentes, en lo cual Soga vio una perspectiva iluminadora.

Por su parte, Tanabe se da cuenta que el acontecimiento de las tres mentes queda completamente desdibujado si se hace una lectura moral de las mismas y no una lectura desde la práctica del abandono y el arrepentimiento como tarea mediadora de la nada absoluta. Por esta razón, de acuerdo con Tanabe, la interpretación de Zendo de las tres mentes basada en el *Sutra de la Contemplación* no es congruente ni en cuanto a su descripción ni en cuanto a su relación. Ahí se produce una antinomia entre actos meritorios (mente sincera) y el inconcebible voto de Amida (que se encuentra en la mente profunda), por lo que es necesario llevar los contradictorios a una unidad dialéctica por la mediación de la nada absoluta. Para Tanabe esta confrontación entre mente sincera y mente profunda debe apuntar al «camino dialéctico de la metanoesis»[63]. Shinran ya abre este camino cuando advierte la contradicción profunda contenida en la mente de los seres sintientes y desarrolló

---

62. Tanabe 2014, 334.
63. Ibid., 330.

esa contradicción en una dialéctica. Para Shinran, el hombre desde su propio poder no puede ser salvado porque él es poseedor de una ignorancia infinita que lo arrastra desde tiempos inmemoriales en el mar del nacimiento y muerte, la consecuencia de ello es que el ser humano es impotente para salvarse a sí mismo, así la tentativa moral está destinada al fracaso. El ser humano está hecho de tal manera que él no puede salvarse a sí mismo, pues está preso de una ignorancia infinita. Pero entonces, ¿cómo es posible la salvación? El yo ha de perderse absolutamente a sí mismo por la acción transformadora del otro poder. Shinran, al sacar las tres mentes del *Sutra de la meditación* y al releerlas desde el *Sutra mayor*, las puede interpretar desde la transformación absoluta del otro-poder.

### El yo como mediador del otro-poder: un punto de vista esencial para resolver las antinomias entre las tres mentes

Para Tanabe el ser relativo solo como mediador de la nada absoluta puede ser transformado en algo que no es ni yo ni otro y ser conducido a una «naturalidad» donde «el yo se pierde a sí mismo»[64]. El yo deviene así acción del Otro-poder y su acción es transformación del yo. Las tres mentes son el reconocimiento de esa fuente transformadora del pasado que es la nada absoluta, sí y solo si el yo se convierte una y otra vez en mediador de la nada absoluta, esto es, si se transforma continuamente en «ser vacío». Solo de esta manera las tres mentes de Zendō, que presentan una estructura ideal, pueden ser leídas desde la metanoética. Como vemos, una de las virtudes de la interpretación de Tanabe es hacer de un esqueleto moral, una estructura dinámica del tiempo desde la transformación radical del *Existenz*.

Para Tanabe, a pesar de presentarse contradicciones en la interpretación de Zendō de las tres mentes, es posible llevar esas contradicciones a una transformación dialéctica. La primera contradicción que observa Tanabe es la que se encuentra entre la mente sincera y la mente profunda. Por un lado, para Zendō la mente sincera pide una pureza de corazón donde el bien que hacemos externamente esté en armonía con el interior. Y al mismo tiempo, en la mente profunda se experimenta una gran confianza en la

---

64. Ibid., 336.

mente de Amida que va junto con el despertar de nuestra profunda ignorancia y pecaminosidad como personas que desde un pasado sin fin nadan en el mar samsárico. Para Tanabe estos dos aspectos no pueden permanecer en un dualismo entre el *es* de nuestra pecado original y el *deber*. Si así fuera no se podría hablar de las tres mentes-*qua*-una mente. Entonces, ¿cómo se reconcilian estos contradictorios? Solo por vía de la metanoesis, donde la autonegación es transformada en resurrección, la cual está mediada por el poder de la Gran Compasión del Absoluto. Así, el ideal moral es abandonado, el poder del yo para salvarse también es abandonado, y justo en el abandono de la arrogancia moral, acontece una resurrección como acción-de-la-no acción del Otro Poder de Amida, que es la mente profunda. De modo que es la confesión de la ignorancia y del pecado sin fin, de la inhabilidad y de la experiencia de la finitud, la que media a la mente sincera. Por lo que la metanoesis que opera en la mente profunda se encuentra mediando a la mente sincera[65]. Así, lo que presenta Zendō como mente sincera no toma en cuenta la profunda transformación que ya ha operado la mente profunda para que a través del voto original acontezca la acción de la no acción, que es la mente sincera verdadera y en la cual los actos meritorios mediados por el propio poder han desaparecido.

Tanabe, asistido por Shinran, encuentra que la mente sincera no se logra a través del propio-poder, sino a través del reconocimiento metanoético de nuestra propia inhabilidad. De manera que es la mente profunda la que logra la unidad con la mente sincera. Aquí hay una transformación del pasado (representado por el mar kármico del nacimiento y muerte) en el presente gracias a la metanoesis continua, por lo que si la mente sincera se orienta al

---

65. «¿Cómo es posible reconciliar estos contradictorios? Solo mediante la confesión metanoética de nuestra incapacidad para alcanzar los ideales de la obligación moral y la aceptación humilde del hecho de nuestra finitud existencial. A través del obrar maravilloso del poder de la transformación absoluta que media el autoabandono de la metanoesis, nuestra mera autonegación se convierte en una negación de la negación —es decir, en una autoafirmació— y la muerte es convertida en resurrección. La esencia de la obligación moral es transferida a la "acción de la no-acción" del Otro-poder absoluto, y a través de esta experiencia, la metanoesis media la mente profunda que confiesa su propia ignorancia y pecaminosidad a la honestidad de la mente sincera» (ibid., 340–1).

pasado no puede ser pura. La mente sincera a la que da lugar la metanoesis es verdadera mente sincera como acción de la no acción[66].

Con respecto a la contradicción entre la mente profunda y la mente de aspiración al nacimiento por la transferencia de méritos, Tanabe considera que si la transferencia de méritos refiere a la resolución de nacer por la transferencia de nuestras buenas acciones y la de todos los seres sintientes hacia el nacimiento en la Tierra Pura, esto entra en contradicción con la «mente profunda del Dharma» (*hō no jinshin*), es decir, con la mente que unida al poder del voto de Amida «ya no siente necesidad de realizar ningún bien suplementario»[67]. ¿Cómo es posible superar esta contradicción de creer profundamente que el nacimiento depende absolutamente en el poder del voto de Amida de salvar a todos los seres sintientes y pensar que el nacimiento es obra del propio poder y de sus buenas acciones? No hay manera de salvar esa antinomia a menos que se considere que la mente de aspiración es una dimensión también mediada por la fe profunda, deviniendo dicha aspiración en una esperanza sin esperanza, en un buscar sin buscar, revelándose así el único sentido de futuro de las tres mentes. Así, en la interpretación que inaugura Tanabe de las tres mentes la transferencia de méritos es transformada en una esperanza sin esperanza o en un buscar sin buscar, lo cual reinterpreta completamente lo que se entendía por aspiración al nacimiento gracias a la mediación de la negación que descansa en el Voto original[68].

Ahora veamos la contradicción entre la mente sincera y la mente de aspiración al nacimiento. Esta contradicción radica en que si se posee la mente sincera de creer en la pureza de las acciones pasadas como piensa Zendō, entonces ¿porqué aspirar al nacimiento? Aspirar al nacimiento es más bien señal de la falla de la mente sincera que según Zendō es confianza en la sin-

---

66. «El reconocimiento de la metanoética de la incapacidad para lograr la mente sincera a través del propio-poder debido a la ignorancia y al pecado, al mismo tiempo, media un proceso a través del cual lo que fue alguna vez imposible por la ignorancia y el pecado, deviene ahora posible a través de la gratitud sumisa de la transferencia del Otro-poder. En este maravilloso poder, la mente sincera y la mente profunda son llevadas una unidad dialéctica fundada en la metanoesis» (ibid., 341).

67. Ibid., 342.

68. «Solo una esperanza de renacimiento que está mediada por la fe profunda y sostenida por la fe profunda puede gozar de estabilidad y resolución de una «esperanza sin esperanza» o de un «buscar sin buscar» cuya negación profunda yace en el voto original» (ibid., 342).

ceridad de nuestros actos y pensamientos del pasado. Además, la continuidad del pasado es incompatible con la transformación creadora de futuro. Como vemos, Tanabe está pensando las relaciones entre pasado y futuro tal y como lo hizo Heidegger en *Ser y Tiempo*. Para tratar de llevar esa contradicción a su unidad dialéctica, Tanabe nos propone que la mediación entre la mente sincera y la mente de aspiración acontece través de su mutua transformación en el presente a través de la metanoesis. Es a través de la mediación transformante de la metanoesis en el presente que el antagonismo entre pasado y el futuro puede reconciliarse. Gracias a la metanoesis el pasado pierde su apariencia de fijeza y acepta su continua renovación de sentido, de manera que propulsa el presente hacia el futuro. El futuro, piensa Tanabe, no puede realizar ninguna renovación de sentido sin la tradición del pasado, pero acepta la determinación del pasado solo como mediación negativa, de manera que el pasado solamente puede renovarse desde sus profundos fundamentos o fuentes y devenir creatividad desde la actividad transformante de la nada absoluta como metanoesis, es decir, desde su negación. Gracias a la metanoesis el pasado es continuamente renovado. Así acontece una síntesis creativa gracias a la nada absoluta que no es ni pasado ni futuro, pues el futuro como renovación de sentido se remonta a las fuentes del pasado como nada absoluta, reconciliándose pasado y futuro mutuamente en la unidad del presente[69]. Solo de manera no mediada la mente sincera y la mente de aspiración son opuestas, en cambio, la mente profunda que según Tanabe tiene lugar como metanoesis permite la unidad de ambas en su mutua negación y transformación. Gracias a la metanoesis que sirve de

---

69. «Solo a través de la mediación mutuamente transformadora de ambas en el presente puede este antagonismo reconciliarse. Es decir, en esta mutua mediación, el pasado cesa de aferrarse a su identidad, a pesar de su continuidad, y experimenta una conversión en la metanoesis de modo tal que puede aceptar la continua renovación de su significado como mediador que propulsa el presente hacia el futuro. Mientras tanto, el futuro necesita también darse cuenta de que no puede producir ningún tipo de contenido creativo sin la tradición del pasado. Debe de aceptar las determinaciones del pasado como mediación negativa, obediencia a la cual puede renovar al pasado desde el interior de sus propias fuentes más profundas y posibilitar una creatividad a través de la actividad transformadora de la nada absoluta. De este modo, una nueva síntesis creativa puede ser realizada, la cual no es ni pasado ni futuro, sino que revitaliza a ambos a través de la negación, estableciendo una unidad trascendente en el presente como la transformación absoluta a través de la cual tanto el pasado como el futuro son mutuamente reconciliados en un todo armonioso» (Ibid., 344).

pivote entre las tres mentes, encontramos «la unidad dialéctica negativa de las tres mentes»[70].

### Metanoesis, renovación y comienzo

A través de un largo camino hemos tratado de demostrar porqué para Tanabe «el concepto de las tres mentes profundiza más que los intentos de la filosofía occidental[71]» en el gran problema del tiempo. Gracias a la metanoesis el pasado es transformado en una «naturalidad» de la «acción de la no-acción», que es la mente sincera, y a su vez, el futuro como mente de aspiración al nacimiento por la transferencia de méritos es transformado en el nacimiento en la no-transferencia de méritos, en un buscar sin buscar. Tanabe no transforma pasado en futuro, ni arrojamiento en proyecto, hace algo que va más acá, transforma la contingencia en un presente eterno, que servirá de gozne entre pasado y futuro, creando una circularidad continua, gracias a la metanoesis. Desde esta lectura de las tres mentes «el pasado y el futuro se transforman y penetran mutuamente en el ahora eterno»[72].

> La acción de la metanoesis en el ahora eterno permite la continuidad del pasado y el renacimiento en el futuro a través de la negación de la mente profunda realizada como metanoesis[73].

Solo en tanto el pasado y el futuro es mediado negativamente por la metanoesis, es posible la resurrección y, en esa medida, son posibles la continuidad y la renovación en el ahora eterno. Tanabe pensaría que Heidegger en su planteamiento de *Ser y tiempo* no ha alcanzado la radicalidad de la nada absoluta. Al encontrarse concentrado en hacer posible al sí mismo propio, pierde la radicalidad del verdadero sí mismo que solo vive en su morir en el ahora eterno. Soga, por su parte, no logró desarrollar y ser consecuente con su descubrimiento de la conversión y hace de la aspiración al nacimiento prueba de la fe en Amida. Para Tanabe es la metanoesis el trasfondo para la unidad dialéctica y dinámica entre pasado y futuro, siendo la metanoesis el corazón de las tres mentes y del ahora eterno. En medio de esos encuentros

---

70. Ibid.
71. Ibid., 329.
72. Ibid., 344.
73. Ibid.

Tanabe logró pensar la metanoesis como lugar del comienzo: como principio de renovación de la vida humana y de las sociedades. De este modo abre la posibilidad de dar un giro del pasado entendido como estar nadando en el mar del nacimiento y muerte debido a nuestras pasiones ciegas desde un pasado sin fin, a un tiempo donde desde el ahora eterno uno es traído a la naturalidad y donde los errores del pasado de obra, palabra y pensamiento son transformados desde la fuente renovadora siempre bullente del tiempo que es la nada absoluta.

La temporalidad metanoética es insistente, porque es continua metánoia, continuo abandono, continuo des-endurecimiento y des-pejamiento y en ese mismo movimiento, continua renovación y creación. El yo como ser vacío se transforma en eje temporal de transformación. Y ese gozne que permite la relación entre pasado y futuro, en su unidad y diferencia, es también el que permite la relación entre *ōsō* y *gensō*, absoluto y relativo, que se traduce en una sociedad metanoética, o sociedad religiosa, cuyo principio es salvarse a sí mismo, salvando a los demás. Aquí encontramos el lazo que une a Tanabe con el Heidegger de *Beiträge zur Philosophie*, para quien la nada da lugar a las más profundas y amplias oscilaciones.

### Una hipotética réplica de Heidegger a Tanabe

Años antes de que Tanabe escribiera *Filosofía como metanoética*, Heidegger en *Aportes a la filosofía*, obra escrita entre 1936 y 1938, realiza su propia autorevisión de *Ser y tiempo*. En dicha obra, Heidegger considera que *Ser y tiempo* difícilmente podía acercarse al sentido del ser partiendo del hombre o del nosotros y pensando la decisión en términos de elección y resolución, quedando, por lo mismo, dicha obra encallada en lo «moral antropológico»[74]. Así en el contexto de La fundación [*Die Gründung*], ensamble de *Aportes a la Filosofía*, Heidegger hace de la nada el auténtico ámbito de proyección en el que el ocultamiento es aclarante ocultamiento [*lichtende Verbergung*][75]. En el esenciarse del ser, desde la nada, el ser «se abre como lo

---

74. Heidegger 2004b, 84 & 43.
75. En La Fundación leemos: «dejar esenciarse el fundamento como fundante» o «el fundamento funda» (ibid., 250 & 188).

que se oculta»[76], por eso indica, hace señas, instaurando el juego entre clamor del Ser y pertenencia al Ser, vacío y donación. El espacio-tiempo, otro de los nombres para este juego entre ocultamiento y desocultamiento, es lo previo a la matematización que supone el espacio *y* el tiempo. Es otra cosa al del transcurrir de un tiempo tras otro, y es también otra cosa a la eternización, a lo que es constante y presente. Es surgir en el instante y lo que se puede sustraer en el instante. El espacio-tiempo se origina de la verdad del ser y de su esenciarse. El espacio-tiempo es cercanía y lejanía, impulso y titubeo. Esta es la experiencia originaria del espacio-tiempo. Desde las categorías no se llega al acceso originario al esenciarse de la verdad del ser, pues el rehuso (*Verweigerung*) del Ser inaugura la disposición afectiva de la retención (*Verhaltenheit*), la cual soporta el rehusarse del ser y se sostiene en lo aún no decidido de una seña (*Wink*), en el sentido de que aquello que se acerca no sabemos si realmente lo hace o si se aleja. Todo este vacilante rehuso de la seña, que se muestra ocultándose, es anterior insisto al espacio *y* al tiempo que transcurre. Para pensar esta esencia ocultante-desocultante del espacio-tiempo, es necesaria «la remoción de la esencia humana al ser ahí», al claro de la verdad. Y ahí el estremecerse de la oscilación del ser, el desentumecimiento de la verdad del ser, aprisionada durante siglos en la *adequatio*, es ahora sí el fundamento del yo y nosotros, pues el espacio-tiempo es superación de toda subjetividad: es abismo. Así para el Heidegger de *Aportes a la filosofía* el vacilante rehuso que aguarda y espera, extasía lo venidero y abre un sido en la historia del ser marcado por la verdad del ente que constituye el ingreso al presente como abandono del ser en el ente. Por lo que el espacio-tiempo es la ruptura de la historia de occidente y su continua entificación, propiciado por lo noedor (*Nichtung*).

> El ser [Seyn]: el evento, en el contraimpulso, noedor y así *contencioso*. El origen de la contienda —ser o no ser.
> La verdad: fundamento como abismo. Fundamento: no de donde, sino en donde como lo perteneciente. Abismo: como espacio-tiempo de la contienda; la contienda como contienda de tierra y mundo, ¡porque referencia de la verdad del ente[77]!

76. Ibid.
77. Ibid., 279 &279.

Tal vez por esta vía sea posible también pensar que la metanoesis comparada al espacio-tiempo (Der Zeit-Raum) de Heidegger tenga aún un sentido demasiado «antropológico-moral», a menos que ella misma sea el acontecimiento del otro poder, que abre a las más profundas oscilaciones: pasado-futuro, *ōsō-gensō*, vida-muerte en el instante.

### Nota sobre los modos del tiempo en la escuela de Kioto: para una crítica a la temporalidad metanoética

La posición de Nishitani y Ueda es bastante alejada a la de Tanabe con respecto al gran tema del tiempo. En el caso de Ueda, la nada absoluta que rompe al yo apegado a sí mismo, al encuentro con la naturaleza nos devuelve a la posibilidad de ser ahí en el presente como en «Mira los lirios del campo» o «¿escuchas cómo susurra el río?»[78]. A esta posibilidad de retrotraernos al presente, en este caso a la presencia del río o la presencia de los lirios, Ueda le llama la fuerza presencial de la naturaleza[79]. Sin lugar a dudas se trata de un acontecimiento como «inicio decisivo de la vida verdadera»[80]. En el caso de Nishitani, esto que está más acá de las palabras y de los pensamientos, nos retrotrae a un tiempo originario, tiempo pleno, que es cada vez comienzo: «Cada día maravilloso día», dice Nishitani repitiendo las palabras de Unmon[81]. Estos modos de lenguaje son testimonios de «dejar caer cuerpo mente[82]» (Dōgen-Nishitani) o testimonios de haber roto «la cerrazón del yo[83]» (Ueda) y son el acaecer de otra temporalidad al unísono con la fuerza presencial de la naturaleza. En Tanabe es la metanoesis continua la que nos conduce también a una naturalidad de otro cuño, y nos lleva a una acción sin acción y a una esperanza sin esperanza en el presente, donde pasado y futuro son plenamente transfigurados. Sin embargo

---

78. Ueda 2004, 130.
79. Ibid.
80. Ibid.
81. Nishitani 2004, 244.
82. Ibid., 247.
83. Ueda 2004, 131.

en Tanabe encontramos un olvido de la naturaleza en términos de «¿oyes cómo susurra el riachuelo de ahí abajo?»[84].

Asimismo podemos decir que también desde Ueda y Nishitani es posible el giro del tiempo samsárico a un tiempo donde uno es traído gracias a la fuerza presencial de la naturaleza al ahora eterno. Tenemos en Nishitani y Ueda un tiempo dehomocentrico marcado por el acontecer del florecer y del fluir del río, siendo tanto Ueda como Nishitani apropiados por la fuerza presencial de la naturaleza. Frente a la fuerza presencial de la naturaleza que inaugura el ahora eterno, la temporalidad metanoética aparece demasiado subjetiva y homocéntrica, prueba de ello es el gran olvido de la naturaleza que caracteriza a *Filosofía como metanoética*. ¿Podemos prescindir de la naturaleza para pensar el problema del tiempo? Para Nishitani y Ueda definitivamente no. Sin embargo si no fuera por el proyecto metanoético de Tanabe, nos perderíamos de la fuerza conversora de la nada que sin tener nada por objeto nos conduce a las fuentes del tiempo.

* Este texto fue realizado dentro del marco del proyecto de investigación del ministerio FFI2015-65662-P «El pensamiento topológico en Japón. Un estudio de la concepción de la naturaleza, el espacio y el lugar en la filosofía, la religión y la estética japonesas» coordinado por Raquel Bouso (Universitat Pompeu Fabra). Y, fue escrito en una estancia sabática en el Nanzan Institute of Religion and Culture gracias al apoyo de la DGAPA de la Universidad Nacional Autónoma de México.

## Referencias

Heidegger, Martin
    2003a  *Ser y tiempo*. Trad., Jorge Eduardo Rivera C. Barcelona, Editorial Trotta.
    2003b  *Aportes a la filosofía. Acerca del evento*. Trad. Dina V. Picotti, Buenos Aires, Editorial Almagesto-Editorial Biblos.

Nishitani Keiji
    1999  *La religión y la nada*. Trad., Raquel Bouso García. Madrid, Siruela.

Shinran
    1997  *The Collected Works of Shinran Volumes I and II*. Translated by Dennis Hirota, Hisao Inagaki, Michio Tokunaga and Ryushin Uryuzu. Shin Buddhism Translation Series. Kioto, Jodo Shinshu Hongwanji-Ha.

84. Ibid., 130.

Soga Ryōjin
 2017 Jan Van Bragt, *A Soga Ryōjin Reader*. Edited by Wamae Muriuki, Nagoya, Chisokudō Publications.

Takeuchi Yoshinori
 2004 «The Philosophy of Nishida.» In Frederick Franck, ed., *The Buddha Eye: An Anthology of the Kyoto School and its Contemporaries*. Bloomingon, Indiana: World Wisdom, 183–208.

Tanabe, Hajime
 2014 *Filosofía como metanoética*. Trad., Rebeca Maldonado con Andrés Marquina, Sasha Jair Espinosa y Cristina Pérez Díaz. Barcelona, Herder.

Ueda Shizuteru
 2004 *Zen y filosofía*. Trad., Raquel Bouso García and Illana Giner Comín. Barcelona, Herder.

Marc Peeters
*Université Libre de Bruxelles*

Kuki Shūzō

Contingence et temps

> Reposant la question de la structure logique de la modalité chez Kuki, cette étude vise à mettre en évidence les multiples dimensions du temps humain. Une telle méditation s'accompagne d'une réflexion sur le « vécu » de la vie concrète dont Kuki fournit une élucidation que l'on pourrait qualifier de métaphysique. Cette métaphysique de la vie est à rapprocher de la pensée de l'Instant tel que Kierkegaard le pense, de la temporalisation heideggerienne et de la durée chez Bergson. Mais le philosophe le plus important convoqué par Kuki reste Nietzsche dont la pensée fulgurante de l'éternel retour du même nourrit la catégorie de la contingence de l'existence. Sauf que précisément, la contingence ne peut pas être une catégorie. La philosophie nietzschéenne traverse et nourrit l'œuvre de Kuki. La présente étude a pour ambition de laisser se confronter la pensée du retour et le temps de la durée. C'est dire qu'il est question ici de réflexion métaphysique sur cette dimension fondamentale de la conscience qu'est la forme du sens interne. Utiliser cette notion c'est *eo ipso* faire référence à Kant. Quels sont les rapports de ces multiples temporalités avec le temps éternel des dieux et du destin, telle est la question que soulève l'*opus magnum* de Kuki. Nous montrons les articulations d'abord logico-métaphysiques, ensuite existentiales de la structure de l'existant. C'est le raffinement esthétique de l'aristocrate qu'était Kuki qui a nourri notre essai de penser et de comprendre la structure de l'Iki.
>
> KEYWORDS: Contingence—modalité—existence— temps— logique

Dans cette étude, je vais vous entretenir de philosophie : d'une voie métaphysique parmi d'autres comme dit Heidegger[1]; des concepts fondamentaux d'une architectonique possible réfléchissante sans système – une finalité sans fin ; de la contingence constitutive de la pensée *philosophique;* et du temps de cette contingence[2]. C'est dire que le *Problème de la contingence, opus magnum* de Kuki pourrait bien être une tentative de réponse à la question qui n'aura eu de cesse de le tarauder : qu'est-ce que la philosophie ?[3] Kant demandait, à la fin de l'*Architectonique de la raison pure,* troisième chapitre de la *Méthodologie transcendantale* (relevant donc de la catégorie de la relation) : Qu'est-ce que la philosophie ? – nul ne le sait ; où est-elle ? – nulle part ; qui la détient ? – personne![4] Voyons donc comment s'articulent ces questions chez Kuki. Nous avons travaillé le *Problème de la contingence*; *La structure de l'Iki* et la belle thèse de Takako Saito, *La pensée du temps dans la pensée de Kuki,* 1998[5].

1. HEIDEGGER Martin, *Qu'est-ce que la philosophie? Questions I et II*, Paris, Gallimard, 351 : « Qu'est-ce que la philosophie ? De cette manière, nous conduirons notre entretien dans une réflexion bien assurée. L'entretien sera par là amené sur un chemin. Je dis : sur *un* chemin. Ainsi nous concédons que ce chemin n'est certainement pas le seul chemin ».
2. Je renvoie ici à mes deux ouvrages Marc PEETERS, *Discrépance et simulacre. Kant, Lesniewski et l'ontologie*, Amay, Lamiroy, 2013 ; *Kant et le problème logique de l'ontologie dans la « Critique de la raison pure »*, Nagoya, Chisokudo, 2016.
3. KUKI Shūzō, *Le problème de la contingence*, trad. &introd. par OMODAKA Hisayuki, Editions de l'Université de Tokyo, 1966 (cité : C & n° de page). Cf. la thèse de Takako SAITO, *La question du temps dans la pensée de Kuki*, 1998. Nous remercions chaleureusement Madame Saito pour avoir mis son texte doctoral à notre disposition.
4. KANT Immanuel, *Critique de la Raison pure* A838/B867 : « Jusque-là on ne peut apprendre aucune philosophie ; car où est-elle ? Qui la possède ? Et à quoi la reconnaître ? On ne peut qu'apprendre à philosopher... »
5. SAITO Takako, *La Question du temps dans la pensée de Kuki*, Université Paris 1 – Panthéon-Sorbonne, thèse de doctorat, 1998.

S'étant agi de la philosophie, et plus précisément de la philosophie de la contingence et du présent comme d'un « thaumazein » (Aristote) – un étonnement devant le monde et les dieux (qui se jouent du destin, C163), le visible et l'invisible, le moi et l'autre (C163); aussi bien de l' « admiration » (Descartes) – savoir, « l'expérimentation de ce qui est en nous » ou encore de la *reprise* kierkegaardienne[6], des situations-limites de Jaspers (C175), ou de la contingence originelle, l' « auto-analyse » qu'est la philosophie est une « expérimentation » intérieure ; en fin de compte, une introspection, selon une temporalisation du présent du doute. Descartes écrit en effet dans les *Passions de l'âme* :

> Lorsque la première *rencontre* de quelque objet nous *surprend*, et que nous le jugeons être de nouveau, ou fort différent de ce que nous connaissions auparavant ou bien de ce que nous supposions qu'il devait être, cela fait que nous *l'admirons* et en sommes étonnés. L'admiration […] n'a point de contraire, à cause que, si l'objet qui se présente n'a rien en soi qui nous *surprenne*, nous n'en sommes aucunement émus et nous le considérons sans passion[7].

Mais la philosophie est aussi *Stimmung* (*Stemning* en danois), disposition compréhensive fondamentale de la *reprise* (Kierkegaard) que Kuki ne cite pas. Telle l'angoisse – ou la contingence originelle de l'existence – l'interrogation de la vie de l'esprit, dans son ek-stase verticale et nouménale, se résout dans la temporalité de l'instant[8].

> Qu'en est-il de la relation entre la contingence originelle et la nécessité métaphysique ? demande Kuki. La première est un concept obtenu dans l'horizon hypothétique comme départ original de la série des causes. On arrive au concept de contingence originelle comme idée lorsqu'on remonte indéfiniment la série des causes de la nécessité d'expérience. La contingence originelle est le phénomène premier, le commencement de l'histoire. (C178)

Le phénomène originel est comme la reprise, une suspension téléologique rétrojective de l'historicité transcendantale, un laisser-apparaître de la discrépance originaire – le temps lui-même comme temporalisation du recueil

---

6. Cf. KIEKEGAARD Søren, *La reprise*, Paris, GF, éd. Viallaneix, 1990.
7. DESCARTES René, *Passions de l'âme*, §53, Paris, Garnier, 1993, vol. III : 999 (nous soulignons).
8. Cf. HEIDEGGER Martin, *Être et Temps*, Paris, Authentica, 1985 (trad. Martineau).

de la conscience en dissonance originaire avec la pensée de la pensée et la forme du sens interne: il semble que « la contingence originelle et la nécessité absolue métaphysique soient identiques » (c179). Ainsi le temps de la série des causes est-il linéaire (la série d'*en-bas*, c179: *l'amor fati*), tandis que le temps métaphysique du retour est cercle (la série d'*en-haut*). Il y a bien un transcendant nouménal chez Kuki. Dans ces conditions, il n'est pas indu d'affirmer que l'histoire est une fiction heuristique, qu'obère la reprise. Ceci ne signifie pas qu'il n'y a pas d'histoire, mais que l'historicité transcendantale est, en l'occurrence, un existential signifiant le trésor de l'histoire et de la langue dans sa dimension anticipatrice du futur, pour suivre le Thucydide de la *Guerre du Péloponnèse*. La « reprise », quant à elle, est un existential (un *ens philosophicum et abstractum*[9]) important: Kuki montre la différence entre le temps de la musique (la reprise musicale) et celui du poème. La reprise est en effet ressouvenir en avant, projection et rétrojection du temps dans l'objet idéel que sont la praxis et l'idée-schème architectonique de la philosophie. « Présent et instant » sont les temps qui sont nôtres. Ce qu'il importe de comprendre et d'élucider, c'est le rapport entre la modalité et le temps, ou plus précisément, l'ancrage dans la vie de l'esprit de la philosophie dans la forme symbolique de la contingence.

Possibilité-Impossibilité, Existence-Non-existence, Nécessité-Contingence sont les modalités des jugements selon Kant. La modalité a toujours un statut semi-régulateur, et se déploie dans le temps et sous des concepts sans fin, l'*Aus-sein* à partir du germe (un schème analogique symbolique) de toute philosophie instituée et reprise comme une détermination de l'historicité transcendantale. C'est par la rétrojection de l'idée que peut être pensée la discrépance essentielle de l'esprit (le *Gemüth*). En termes nietzschéens, la philosophie est toujours « inactuelle » et « intempestive ». Il convient de noter ici l'universalité de la pensée de Kuki, et ce, en pleine période nationaliste. Kuki est authentiquement un philosophe, qui a aussi étudié en Allemagne et en France, et qui connut tous les penseurs importants de son époque. Donc, la contingence, nous y revenons, n'est-elle pas dans un rapport d'extériorité par rapport à l'institution transcendantale et existentiale de la philosophie, qui ne cesse de chercher ce qu'elle est, en vain et également sans concept? Soulignons d'emblée une difficulté: dans son *Kant et*

---

9. Descartes René, *Règle xiv*, atx 442–3; Garnier, vol 1: 171–2.

*le problème de la Métaphysique*, Heidegger parle du Dasein en l'homme[10]. Peut-on y voir quelques linéaments de philosophie transcendantale, alors que Heidegger n'a cessé d'insister sur l'absence de résurgence transcendantale dans sa pensée ? Kuki ne semble pas être tombé dans ce 'piège'. On ne confondra pas 'existential' et 'transcendantal' qui sont des « êtres philosophiques abstraits ». Comme nous le comprenons – et même si Kuki ne fait pas cette distinction – je pense qu'il refuserait, comme Kant, une « faculté de juger réfléchissante » avec concept qui nous donnerait un accès direct à l'architectonique, comme chez Fichte. Si le présent est le temps de l'humain, l'instant est ce présent permanent – l'éternité au sens classique – littéralement incompréhensible et irreprésentable: le temps métaphysique du retour, non pas asymptotique de la durée, mais infini. Ainsi, le temps métaphysique cristallise-t-il dans l'Instant, une « réminiscence en avant »: catégorie singulière qui est celle de l'Individu métaphysique selon Kierkegaard et Heidegger. Or les êtres philosophiques abstraits que nous avons mentionnés (*entia philosophica et abstracta*, comme dit Descartes), ont un rapport singulier avec le temps.

Nous mettons en évidence deux couples de concepts, le mathématique et le dynamique, qui répondent aux prescrits du fil conducteur kantien en philosophie: le simulacre, la discrépance, la reprise et l'historicité transcendantale, soit *l'Unter-sein*, *l'In-sein*, le *Mit-sein* et *l'Aus-sein*.[11] De même que le simulacre abolit apparemment la discrépance; de même la reprise abolit-elle la temporalité de l'historicité transcendantale. Si le temps du passé est la nécessité, le temps du futur, le possible, la temporalisation modale de l'humain ou du *Dasein* en lui est la contingence. La mondification, (*l'Umwelt*) comme *horizon* phénoménologique de prédonation des *Dingen* (les Choses et non les objets), renvoie à l'être-jeté du souci, au long du temps de l'ennui (Langeweile – l'ennui). Kuki ne cite pas ce texte de Heidegger de 1928 (*Les concepts fondamentaux de la métaphysique*) consacré à la temporalité du *Dasein* dans une de ses dispositions compréhensives fondamentales, l'ennui[12]. Une telle disposition-compréhensive est saisissable depuis ses trois

---

10. Cf. HEIDEGGER Martin, *Kant et le problème de la métaphysique*, Paris, Gallimard, 1953.
11. Cf. Mes ouvrages déjà cités.
12. HEIDEGGER Martin, *Les problèmes fondamentaux de la métaphysique. Monde-Finitude-Solitude*, Paris, Gallimard, 1992.

manifestations, dont la première (l'ennui banal – sans doute le plus profond), la seconde et la troisième, l'impersonnel du « il s'ennuie en moi », signifie, comme dit Pascal, « que nous ne nous tenons jamais au temps présent » mais le laissons échapper pour des temps qui ne sont pas nôtres[13]. La première forme de l'ennui – à rapprocher du divertissement pascalien – s'exemplifie: Une gare. L'attente d'un train. La montre sur le quai indique qu'il reste une heure à l'attendre. L'homme qui attend compte les arbres qui bordent le quai, les pierres dévalées par terre. Il regarde la montre, décompte les minutes, le temps est long, il ne passe pas et – il s'ennuie. Le rapport au temps est essentiel dans cette disposition fondamentale. L'ennui révèle le temps, est un laisser-advenir de l'essence du *Dasein* (le *souci*). Ainsi, Kuki appréhende la contingence dans son rapport au temps comme l'auto-décomposition désintégrative de la conscience du temps et, plus fondamentalement, du temps de la conscience – pour le dire dans mon vocabulaire – ou une « auto-analyse » comme dit Alexis Philonenko. Pour reprendre la formule de Kuki dans *Le problème de la contingence*:

> Quant au rire devant la contingence d'une grande signification existentielle, c'est le rire clair de Zarathoustra, le surhomme, le rire qui moque la surprise de la mesquinerie humaine. En somme, la drôlerie de la contingence est un sentiment qui se produit par la réflexion de soi qui est surpris. (c163)

Surprise et réflexion sur soi: deux éléments constitutifs de la pensée philosophique. Je renvoie au texte de Descartes déjà cité. Avec de forts accents heideggeriens, la contingence se décline comme autant de manifestations métaphysiques du néant. Cette catégorie intrinsèque à la contingence ne doit pas être confondue avec le « rien abstrait » kantien – la non-chose (*Unding*) pour autant que l'on aura déployé le « rien » comme la *Table modale du rien* qui clôt l'*Analytique transcendantale*; à moins justement de considérer, comme le fait Heidegger dans son célèbre *Kantbuch* de 1929, le *nihil privativum* comme horizon horismatique des « non-choses » (l'espace et le temps) sous le concept réfléchissant de l'objet transcendantal=x comme matrice de l'expérience infinie. C'est dans la contingence catégorique – sous le concept – que la convertibilité des transcendantaux chez l'Aquinate est soumise à une suspension téléologique du concept, le « rien »

---

13. PASCAL Blaise, *Pensées*, Paris, Gallimard, Bibliothèque de la Pléiade, 1954, 1132.

étant abstrait du quelque chose (*aliquid*) à partir d'un autre *quelque chose* (l'*aliud quid*)[14]. Mais l'*anima* d'une certaine manière est toute chose. Si on abstrait quelque chose de quelque chose; il ne reste rien (*nihil*). Et pourtant, il s'agit bien d'une abstraction de raison raisonnée et non de raison raisonnante. Au sujet de cette convertibilité des transcendantaux dans le *De veritate*, question 1, article 1, entre l'*ens*, le *verum*, l'*aliquid*, l'*aliud quid*, et l'*unum*, Heidegger écrit dans *Sein und Zeit*:

> Au sein de la tâche d'une dérivation des «transcendantaux», c'est-à-dire des caractères d'être qui dépassent toute déterminité réale-générique possible d'un étant, tout «modus specialis entis», il convient également [...] de mettre en évidence le *verum* comme un *transcendens* de cette sorte. Ce qui advient en invoquant un étant qui, conformément à son mode d'être, a lui-même la propriété de «con-venir» avec tout étant quel qu'il soit. Cet étant insigne [...] c'est l'âme (*anima*). Le privilège du «Dasein» sur tout étant qui apparaît ici, même s'il reste ontologiquement non clarifié, n'est pas moins sans commune mesure avec une mauvaise subjectivisation du tout de l'étant. (SZ Martineau, 34)

C'est également ainsi que Bergson déploie, au-delà du concept, la durée créatrice de l'homme. Mais s'il est plus question de Husserl et de Heidegger chez Kuki, qui les connaissait personnellement, que de Kant, la philosophie de ce dernier est constamment présente même si c'est en filigrane dans le texte de Kuki. Et pour commencer, les trois types de contingence, dont Kuki, nous dit qu'ils sont à rapprocher de la classification des logiciens (on pourra se référer à Lotze), se trouvent chez le Kant de la *Première Critique* dans la *Table des jugements*. Il ne sera dès lors pas inutile de repenser cette *Table des jugements* déclinée sous l'*Unter-sein* d'un simulacre, comme dit Lambert, une subreption du temps et de l'espace dans la raison. Cette *Table* est à comprendre sous le concept, selon la catégorie de la relation, soit, le *Mit-sein* de l'*In-der-Welt-Sein* heideggerien que j'appelle l'historicité transcendantale; ce que j'appelle également un transcendantal: la *reprise*.

Par l'opération d'abstraction isolante ou réfléchissante de la sensibilité dans l'esprit (le *Gemüth*), la logique a affaire à la simple forme de l'entende-

---

14. Cf. THOMAS D'AQUIN, *Première question disputée sur la vérité. La Vérité (De Veritate)*, trad. C. Brouwer et M. Peeters, Paris, Vrin, 2002; HEIDEGGER Martin, *Sein und Zeit*, 34.

ment[15] (CRP §9, A70–6/B91–101) dans la pensée déterminante et réfléchissante. Il ne faut pas oublier que l'entendement ne peut faire l'abstraction de lui-même, comme la conscience d'ailleurs. La *Table des jugements* – penser, c'est juger – de l'*Analytique transcendantale* (la première des *Tables* de la *Critique*), « semble s'écarter sur quelques points, à la vérité non-essentiels, de la technique accoutumée des logiciens » (CRP A72). Il ne peut s'agir ici de donner une interprétation architectonique de cette *Table*. Cette interprétation métaphysique a été réalisée. Quels sont donc les points à mettre en évidence ? Avant même de commencer, il faut prendre bonne note que les jugements ont lieu dans le temps. Ainsi les jugements analytiques, d'un point de vue pragmatique, requièrent le temps, et donc ont « lieu », pour utiliser une métaphore de métaphore, dans le recueil synthétique, c'est-à-dire temporel, de la conscience. La *Table des jugements* est la première *Table* de l'*Analytique*. Elle doit donc être pensée sous la catégorie de la quantité. De ce point de vue (le simulacre – *Unter-sein*), la catégorie régulatrice des jugements est la relation (l'être-dans-l'exprérience). Le simulacre (*simulacrum*) est une subreption de l'espace et du temps dans la raison. Par exemple, dire que « p et -p » ne peuvent être vrais *en même temps*. On introduit donc le temps dans la formulation du principe de contradiction. Cette introduction du temps est le *\*simul*: *similitude, simultané* dans la raison. Ainsi, la décomposition des jugements est-elle déclinée sous le transcendantal de la *reprise*, l'activité philosophique elle-même. Donc se placer dans la catégorie de la relation, c'est faire référence à l'activité même de philosopher, la *praxis* du philosopher. C'est dire également que le choix par Kuki de la catégorie de la contingence totalement immanente à la praxis de la philosophie, puisque nous n'en avons pas de définition, s'impose : il n'y a pas de métatexte, de métasystème de la raison. L'architectonique n'est pas le calque de la raison. S'agissant dès lors des rapports de la pensée dans des jugements, ces derniers sont ceux (a) du prédicat au sujet – jugement catégorique ; (b) du fondement à la conséquence – jugement hypothétique ; (c) de la connaissance divisée et de tous les membres de la division entre eux – jugement disjonctif. Donc :

(1) Relation réciproque entre deux concepts ;

(2) Rapport de deux jugements ;

---

15. KANT Immanuel, *Critique de la raison pure*, que nous citons CRP plus n° de page (A/B pour première et seconde édition).

(3) Rapport de plusieurs jugements entre eux. Voyons les quelques remarques de Kant et de Kuki sur ces jugements disjonctifs (métaphysiques): ils contiennent un rapport entre propositions, (CRP A71–2/B97–8) rapport non consécutif, mais d'opposition logique, en tant que les *sphères* exclusives des différents jugements constituent ensemble «la *sphère* de la connaissance proprement dite». Et Kant ajoute: «Il y a donc dans un jugement disjonctif une certaine communauté des connaissances qui s'excluent réciproquement les unes les autres, mais par-là déterminent cependant en son tout la vraie connaissance, puisque prises ensemble elles constituent tout le contenu d'une unique connaissance donnée» (CRP A74/B99). La disjonction renvoie à l'absolu métaphysique. «L'absolu, comme absolu est un, (absolument, c'est-à-dire à tous égards comme le montrent les jugements infinis; C176). «Cette nécessité de l'absolu, on peut l'appeler nécessité métaphysique» (C176). Kuki, se référant à Lotze, fait des remarques semblables à celles de Kant sur la *Table des Jugements*. Il convient de noter la récurrence du terme de «sphère» dans ce passage de la *Critique*. Il s'agit de la sphère – l'extension – de la connaissance; mais ici, Kuki vise la totalité ontologique des infinis. Dans son analyse des jugements, Kuki constate que «dans la contingence, l'existence est en face du néant» (C3).

(4) Il s'agit aussi bien de «déborder l'existence»; d'«aller au transcendant en dépassant la forme», soit de «transcender la forme dans la métaphysique». La métaphysique traite de l' «être véritable» si et seulement si elle met en rapport cet «être véritable avec le non-être, c'est-à-dire le néant» (C3). Il semble qu'ici, et à la différence de Kant, mais en accord avec Hegel, le paradigme parménidien ne soit pas de mise: l'être est et le non-être n'est pas. Il y a une positivité du néant – telle celle que nous trouvons dans des théorèmes vrais sur la contradiction, le vide, rien, l'indicible et l'invisible. Telle est la spécificité de la science métaphysique, qu'une lecture architectonique laisse apparaître dans la *Première Critique* de Kant. La contingence est la question métaphysique ultime, puisqu'elle renvoie à la contingence originaire qui est, comme je l'ai déjà dit, l'originaire de la philosophie. La nécessité – ce dont le contraire est impossible – est une ipséité, une identité, qui repose sur le principe d'identité logique «A est A». Je reviendrai dans un instant sur cette identité. De même qu'il y a trois nécessités, il y

a trois contingences. Contingence logique, contingence de l'expérience et contingence métaphysique (c7).

Aussi bien Kuki – puisque les modalités sont de l'ordre de la logique – parlera-t-il de contingence catégorique, hypothétique et disjonctive. Nous voudrions ici faire une remarque. Que la première contingence relève de l'ipséité ou de l'identité ne va pas de soi. La logique développementale contemporaine repose sur la fracture des objets dans des espaces méréologiques empiétants les uns sur les autres en composant des espaces ouverts. Tel est le déploiement de l'epsilon logique éternel dans des thèses-théorèmes ontologiques. Il y a à l'heure actuelle une méditation sur le temps logique au-delà des modèles standard. Il s'agit aussi bien de penser la temporalité des morceaux d'objets qui sont équiformes mais différents dans l'espace et le temps. Bien entendu, il ne peut s'agir d'une restriction vis-à-vis de Kuki, mais il est intéressant de noter que la métaphysique contemporaine – pas plus que la logique développementale – ne repose sur le principe d'identité forte. Le néant habite les logiques paraconsistantes (basées sur la logique de Hegel) comme les logiques développementales, bien qu'il n'y ait aucune classe vide dans ces logiques. Il est question de cristallisation de l'éternité dans des ontologies partielles. Notons que l'intégration de l'infinité des ontologies partielles possibles nous donne un infini qualitatif en puissance. On pourrait dire aussi que l'infini ontologique au sens de Kuki, est qualitatif, donc synthétique. Mais il y a là une autre difficulté puisque le schème de la quantité correspond à la création du temps et celui de la qualité, au remplissement du temps. Or, ces deux schèmes sont ceux qui relèvent de la logique : ce sont les schèmes des catégories de la quantité et de la qualité, soit les catégories mathématiques. Certes Kant lui-même ramène-t-il la synthèse à la contingence et la nécessité à l'analyticité (c13). Mais le problème est ici différent. Le modèle logique de Kuki est strictement classique (Lotze) mais on pourrait aussi bien le rapporter à Frege ou Russell qui posait *eo ipso* la classe vide en même temps que la classe universelle pour éviter le monisme ontologique. La question philosophique que pose Kuki est celle du temps métaphysique qui est aussi l'instant, et qui est commun avec l'éternité. Ce problème est d'autant plus intéressant que l'epsilon méréologique, donc extralogique, est le laisser-advenir d'un temps qualitatif, contrairement au modèle quantitatif de la logique classique.

Voyons donc quelle est la temporalité de la contingence. Notons que c'est la discrépance (*l'In-sein* qualitatif) entre la synthèse temporelle de la conscience et la forme du sens interne (le temps) qui est le « lieu » du « laisser-advenir » du temps et, comme peut-être l'imagination est la source de toutes les facultés, en ce compris l'entendement et la raison, le laisser-advenir du schème de tous les phénomènes possibles. Conformément à la leçon heideggerienne sur le temps (*Sein und Zeit*), le possible est l'ek-stase du futur. L'être-jeté, déjeté dans la déchéance (qui n'est pas morale) du monde ambiant, tout d'abord et le plus souvent, est un être-en-avant-de-soi.(C155). La nécessité répond à l'ek-stase du passé. Kuki écrit: De même que la possibilité est toujours le temps d'une anticipation du futur, de même la nécessité doit toujours garder un regard en arrière sur le passé. La temporalité de la contingence est le présent, schème exprimé par le mot « maintenant ». Kuki ajoute encore, avec beaucoup de profondeur (C157): « Quant à la contingence au sens le plus significatif, depuis une possibilité future réduite à l'extrême, soit depuis le néant de l'impossibilité sans avenir, cachée dans un coin d'inexistence présente, elle jaillit comme contingence » (C157). La contingence métaphysique est en même temps – dans un simulacre – possibilité et néant de l'impossibilité sans avenir. La contingence est donc tissée d'impossible, donc de néant. La néantisation de l'absolu, pour parler comme Hegel abondamment cité par Kuki, signifie que [rien] synthétise, par impossible, l'étant. Ce qui n'est possible que si, comme je l'ai dit, le paradigme parménidien n'est pas de mise. C'est la raison pour laquelle il est possible de penser le néant. Ce qui soulève le problème suivant: peut-on penser le néant dans un schéma parménidien? En fait, oui, si nous le pensons comme abstrait, conformément à la leçon de Kant dans la *Table* modale du rien. Ce qui, on l'imagine bien, n'est pas un hasard. Le possible, le contingent et le nécessaire relèvent de la modalité (*l'Aus-sein*).

Kuki procède ensuite à une analyse de la temporalité de *Sein und Zeit*. Aussi, me semble-t-il, et telle que je l'ai comprise, la leçon heideggerienne du temps ne signifie-t-elle pas que le passé est toujours devant soi et non derrière soi, de même que le futur est toujours derrière soi? C'est la culpabilité de n'avoir pu accomplir sa possibilité la plus fondamentale, l'être-pour-la-mort, qui anime les existentiaux, la disposition (*Befindlichkeit*), la compréhension (*Verstehen*) et le discours (*Rede*). L'expérience des « *modalités obliques* » (C158), passé et futur, se néantise:

> Si on voit directement l'état des choses par une intuition substantielle et originelle, la contingence n'est ni expérience comme une négation de la nécessité, ni perçue dans son rapport avec la possibilité. (c158–9)

Toutefois, c'est là une « théorie ». Le présent est le temps originaire, comme chez Heidegger ou Kierkegaard comme je l'ai déjà indiqué. La surprise métaphysique est « destin » (c169). « En somme, le concept de destin au sens fort, comportant une conscience de soi enthousiaste, s'immergeant dans la contingence, ne peut être, à cause de cela, que ce qui fait vivre fondamentalement le moi lui-même. Et ne nous étonnons pas que la contingence en tant que destin ait été comprise comme le présent éternel du temps métaphysique récurrent » (c176). Kuki affirme donc que le temps de la contingence est éternel, au sens du présent permanent, du temps du retour comme destin. Les accents nietzschéens sont ici patents. Ou encore, Kuki écrit: « Alors, cette contingence comme destin, dans sa liaison hétérogène avec la nécessité, manifeste une structure de 'contingent-nécessaire', prend une puissance transcendante, et domine de sa rigueur toute l'existence humaine » (c168). Nous sommes très proches du dit de Hölderlin: « deviens celui que tu es, du moment que tu ne saches pas qui tu es ». Qu'en est-il alors du monde saisi dans la philosophie de la contingence: « L'éternelle palpitation du présent (c159) » est aussi bien « une bizarre rencontre », une « bizarrerie du destin » (c161), de *l'amor fati* de la temporalité du retour, « excitation de surprise » devant l'être-jeté « sous les yeux tel quel et non résolu » (c161).Ce sentiment de surprise est précisément le *thaumazein*, l'admiration cartésienne, la reprise ou la contingence originaire:

> En vérité, c'est de la surprise devant la contingence que naît la philosophie, dit Kuki. Et on peut voir le sentiment de l'être comme évoluant de la surprise de la contingence à la tranquillité de la nécessité, en passant par l'inquiétude de la possibilité. (c162)

La contingence est non conceptualisée, sans corrélations, sans règle, sans arrangement, sans intérêt, sans préoccupation. « La contingence n'a pas de but » (c187). Elle est « sans fond », « sans raison ». « Dans la contingence, il y a une profonde pénétration de l'être par le néant » (c187). « Elle n'a qu'une exigence faible et ténue dans le *hic* et *nunc*, et toute contingence recèle en elle-même dans son principe une destinée d'effondrement et de mort » (c187). Mais quelle est cette surprise originaire de la philosophie de l'existence philosophique? « Quand la réalité s'affronte au néant vient frôler le réel, nous ne pouvons retenir notre surprise en nous écriant, si je l'ai compris: 'pourquoi?' » (c187).

On le voit, la pensée de Kuki est un existentialisme qui est proche de Heidegger (même si ce dernier n'est précisément pas un existentialiste ou *a fortiori* un moraliste). Il est vrai que la méditation sur le temps de la contingence a une connotation esthétique que l'on ne trouverait pas dans la philosophie française de cette époque. Ce que nous voulons dire, c'est que l'esthétique de Kuki relève plus du rapport fondamental à l'œuvre d'art au sens de Heidegger. Si nous rapportons ces quelques considérations sur Kuki a notre propre travail – avec la modestie qui s'impose – nous dirons que la *praxis* philosophique du philosophe japonais répond à notre conception de la *reprise* proche de celle de Kierkegaard. Cette *praxis* contient un rapport particulier au temps dans le sens où celui-ci est apparemment aboli dans ce rien qu'est la discrépance de la raison à elle-même. Le défi que nous lance Kuki n'est alors rien d'autre que penser l'émergence contingente de ce rien qui constitue notre conscience comme recueil de représentations imaginaires où s'enracine la totalité de l'esprit. La relation fondamentale entre contingence et temps n'est pas épuisée, loin s'en faut. À notre avis, une méditation sur le néant et le rien serait une piste intéressante dans le concert des études consacrées à notre philosophe. Les rapports entre logique et métaphysique sont le fil conducteur implicite dans l'œuvre de Kuki. La question reste celle de la possibilité d'une ontologie formelle qui n'obère pas la pensée de l'existence en tant que sa contingence est irréductible – même à la mort.

Quentin Hiernaux
*Université Libre de Bruxelles*

# Le statut du végétal dans *Fūdo* de Watsuji

Après avoir introduit les concepts de base de *Fūdo*, je propose une interprétation du texte problématisée autour du statut de la végétation. Il s'agira de montrer pourquoi et comment la place que tient la végétation joue un rôle médiateur fondamental en tant que principe de première importance, y compris et surtout ici pour la vie humaine décrite par Watsuji. Ce faisant, l'objectif est double. D'une part, montrer, à la suite d'Augustin Berque, la cohérence de la visée *mésologique* initiale de l'auteur en donnant un fondement théorique à ses exemples végétaux. D'autre part, se recentrer sur le rôle mésologique de la végétation permet de relativiser la place du climat et donc du déterminisme environnemental souvent surévalués dans beaucoup de traductions et commentaires de *Fūdo*.

KEYWORDS: Watsuji Tetsurō—*Fūdo*—Augustin Berque—milieu—philosophie de la nature—végétal—biologie—mésologie—plantes—environnement—écologie—climat

Dans son ouvrage *Fūdo*, écrit en 1935, Watsuji Tetsurō (1889-1960) lie pour la première fois explicitement l'ontologie et la géographie en réunissant l'organicité sociale et l'environnement terrestre dans une visée philosophique. D'après la traduction française d'Augustin Berque que je suis ici, *fūdo* 風土 peut se traduire par « étude de l'entrelien humain ». C'est-à-dire que la question des milieux est pour Watsuji ce qui fonde et tisse concrètement les sociétés humaines sur la terre. Berque traduit donc plus simplement *Fūdo*[1] par milieu et *fūdosei* 風土性 par le néologisme médiance qui rend « le moment structurel de l'existence humaine ». La médiance consiste donc à :

> Exprimer son existence par le milieu lui-même. Donc, non pas en soi, comme le sujet cartésien, mais dans son lien sensible avec les choses. (BERQUE 2014, 42)

Selon Berque, la mésologie (l'étude des milieux) est donc ce qui couvre le fossé entre écologie et sociologie (à l'instar de la géographie) (BERQUE 2014, 21). L'environnement n'est en effet pas synonyme de milieu, ce dernier est plus riche puisqu'il englobe aussi la réalité sociale. Berque le définit comme « la relation éco-techno-symbolique d'une société à son environnement » et l'ensemble des milieux humains forme ce qu'il appelle l'écoumène dans leur relation à l'étendue terrestre (ibid. note 19).

L'angle d'approche problématique dans le commentaire que je propose de *Fūdo* consistera à conserver la visée première de Watsuji en essayant de montrer en quoi des motifs universalisants de la mésologie traversent le

---

[1]. Le concept de *Fūdo* est complexe, sa réception dans d'autres cultures et sa traduction dans d'autres langues l'est tout autant. Mon ralliement à la traduction et à l'interprétation de Berque ne doit pas occulter les discussions qui existent à ce sujet. Le concept recoupe à la fois une dimension environnementale et sociale et a souvent été traduit par « environnement » voire « climat ».

livre. En tant que chercheur en philosophie de la biologie, mes observations sous-tendent aussi la pertinence de la mésologie pour la biologie (avec l'écologie et l'éthologie comme horizon). Plus précisément, *il s'agira de montrer pourquoi et comment la place de la végétation joue un rôle médiateur fondamental en tant que principe mésologique de première importance*, y compris, et surtout ici, pour la vie humaine décrite par Watsuji. Ce rôle passe le plus souvent inaperçu, malgré son aspect fondamental, ce qui explique qu'en dépit de sa forte présence dans les descriptions de Watsuji, ce dernier ne thématise pas explicitement son importance. Du point de vue méthodologique, mes arguments se basent essentiellement sur la cohérence interne du livre de Watsuji et sur l'interprétation qu'en a donné Berque[2].

Si l'importance ontologique du végétal est bien établie dans la littérature biologique, ses conséquences pour la philosophie et notre rapport humain au milieu restent largement à établir. Le végétal est en effet fondamental dans l'économie de la vie sur Terre, que ce soit sur le plan proprement biologique (autotrophie, chaîne alimentaire, production et maintien de l'atmosphère respirable), sur le plan écologique, ou même géologique et climatique (RAVEN et al. 2014, BOURNÉRIAS et BOCK 2006, SUTY 2015, SULTAN 2015). Les plantes sont les producteurs primaires de l'énergie dont tous les autres vivants dépendent, elles sont à la base de la structuration de la quasi-totalité des écosystèmes, ont façonné la structure de la Terre par leur action sur les sols et sur l'atmosphère et continuent à le faire aujourd'hui. Les plantes représentent aussi l'immense majorité de la biomasse de la planète: entre 99 et 99,5% (MANCUSO et VIOLA 2015, 40): elles sont donc qualitativement et quantitativement primordiales et essentielles pour toute forme de vie et donc aussi pour la vie humaine et son rapport au milieu. Leur rôle est essentiel pour la vie, tant du point de vue historique que médial. Je souhaite donc expliciter ici le rôle fondamental de la végétation pour la théorie des milieux, ce que Watsuji n'a pas fait et qui reste limité chez Berque. Chez Watsuji, les exemples végétaux sont pourtant omniprésents pour illustrer le propos sans

---

2. Les lecteurs de la langue japonaise pourraient, par ailleurs, trouver des éléments en rapport avec la problématique dans certaines reprises des idées de Watsuji par SUZUKI (1975; 1978). Je n'ai pas pu consulter personnellement ces ouvrages recommandés par l'un de mes relecteurs car je n'ai pas connaissance du japonais. Cependant, BERQUE (1986, 122) range Suzuki dans la catégorie des déterministes qui posent un lien causal et direct entre la végétation et le mode de pensée.

que leur caractère essentiel soit souligné ni même remarqué pour la théorie des milieux, tandis que chez Berque, c'est le rôle du paysage qui est, à juste titre, le plus souvent souligné[3]. Les différents paysages, envisagés comme milieux de vie possibles, dépendent pourtant intrinsèquement de la végétation et de sa dynamique. La végétation permet de dynamiser le concept plutôt statique de paysage pour en faire un véritable milieu. Les pensées de Watsuji et Berque ont toutefois le grand mérite de laisser une place à la vie végétale, contrairement à l'immense majorité des philosophes qui la néglige totalement. En outre, je voudrais montrer et défendre ici l'idée que se recentrer sur le rôle mésologique de la végétation permet de mieux relativiser la place du climat, et donc du déterminisme environnemental, surévalués dans certaines interprétations et traductions de *Fūdo*.

## Introduction aux idées de *Fūdo*

Il est possible de saisir la pensée de Watsuji dans son opposition avec une certaine tradition philosophique occidentale en la contrastant avec la pensée de Heidegger. Watsuji a probablement été influencé par Heidegger (sans doute par son séjour en Allemagne et sa lecture critique d'Être et temps), sa critique principale à son égard serait que l'existence n'est pas seulement structurée par le temps, mais aussi par l'espace (c'est la médiance) :

> Si l'on saisit d'abord le caractère duel de l'existence humaine en tant qu'essence de l'humain, il deviendra tout de suite clair que l'on doit en découvrir la spatialité simultanément et corrélativement à la temporalité. (Watsuji 2011, 50)

L'existence est chargée d'une histoire, mais aussi d'un milieu, le milieu incarne l'histoire ; en dehors de cela l'être n'est qu'une abstraction. L'histoire est une histoire médiale et le milieu un milieu historique. Les isoler revient à en faire des objets abstraits. Le milieu de Watsuji est originaire, antérieur à une telle abstraction (Watsuji 2011, 51).

Selon l'interprétation de Berque, la médiance regroupe les deux moments (humains), celui du corps social (sociologie) et celui du corps animal (écolo-

---

[3]. Mentionnons, néanmoins, le chapitre III dans *Le Sauvage et l'artifice* que Berque (1986) consacre à la végétation japonaise.

gie). En cela, Watsuji critiquerait aussi le *Dasein* heideggerien qui se résume en fait au corps animal pour-la-mort avec lequel tout s'arrête au moment du décès. Or, chez Watsuji, le corps social persisterait au-delà de la mort, par ses traces et les souvenirs qu'il laisse. C'est par exemple ce qui permet l'Histoire.

Dans la même veine, Watsuji reproche à l'anthropologie et à la sociologie d'aborder l'humain soit comme individuel, soit comme société, en ratant son essence duelle qu'il pose comme plus fondamentale. Chercher l'existence humaine au fond de la conscience individuelle est une erreur (typique de la modernité occidentale), ce n'en est qu'un aspect.

Selon Berque (BERQUE in WATSUJI 2011, 28–9), la perspective watsujienne est décisive pour fonder l'éthique de l'environnement, sinon comment fonder en valeurs humaines un environnement réduit à un objet, un espace détaché de l'histoire humaine ? L'environnement n'est justement pas un objet. En effet, pour Watsuji il y a un (entre)lien de l'humanité au territoire qui se manifeste en une *subjectité*[4] qui rend capable d'accorder de la valeur à l'environnement (comme moment structurel de l'humanité et vice versa).

Remarquons que, dans l'esprit de Watsuji, l'étude des milieux, contrairement à ce que beaucoup ont cru, n'est pas un déterminisme environnemental, c'est-à-dire une relation de cause à effet du climat sur la culture. Berque mentionne d'ailleurs qu'à ce niveau, les traductions objectivantes de *Fūdo* en « climat » n'ont pas facilité les interprétations (BERQUE in WATSUJI 2011, 13–17). Or, le but explicite de Watsuji est de rendre compte du rapport réciproque de l'humain à l'environnement. C'est-à-dire de fonder une étude des milieux, une mésologie dans le vocabulaire de Berque. Mais qu'est-ce que cette posture implique exactement ? En quoi est-elle différente du simple déterminisme environnemental pour Watsuji ?

> Le genre humain se médiatise lui-même, l'esprit d'un peuple comme son caractère son médiaux, et c'est cette réalité qui lui est donnée. En tout temps, l'humain n'apparaît que sous une forme médiale particulière. Le problème ici est donc d'élucider la relation entre l'humain et son milieu. La méthode pour ce faire peut approximativement se diviser en deux parties. La première

---

4. La subjectité n'étant pas un soi hypostasié en une subjectivité autonome et opposée à ses objets (à la Descartes) mais justement ce qui manifeste qu'il y a un soi à travers sa relation au milieu (à la Nishida) (BERQUE 2014, 31-6).

consiste à séparer l'humain et le milieu, à les considérer indépendamment, et ensuite à découvrir des relations de cause à effet entre les deux. La seconde méthode s'attache à la vie humaine médiale dans sa forme concrète. Elle ne s'occupe pas de ces abstractions que sont le milieu séparé de l'humain, l'humain séparé du milieu: elle examine le milieu en tant que moment structurel de la vie humaine. Dans la première méthode, le milieu est extrait de l'existence humaine et devient simplement un phénomène naturel objectif. On pense donc que cet objet exerce, sur le corps physiologique également réduit à un objet, une influence physique, physiologique, psychologique, et que l'homme médial apparaît en ce qu'il a, de ce fait, une particularité concrète. Sans en avoir clairement conscience, Herder n'a cessé de pointer les insuffisances de cette méthode, pour s'engager dans la seconde. (Watsuji 2011, 289)

La première méthode est évidemment celle du déterminisme environnemental qui envisage précisément le milieu comme environnement, c'est-à-dire comme un objet donné en relation extérieure et causale avec l'humain, lui-même objectivé et déterminé (par l'anthropologie, par exemple). Cette approche est aussi généralement celle des sciences modernes et celle dont a hérité l'écologie classique. Elle se distingue donc d'une mésologie attentive à l'expérience de l'organisme, humain ou animal, comme rapport avec son environnement qui devient dès lors un véritable milieu. L'intégration de cette perspective, bien que restée longtemps étrangère à la biologie pour ensuite se révéler avec les travaux de l'éthologue Jakob von Uexküll (1956), connaît aujourd'hui un renouveau avec le développement des études sur la construction de niche, l'écologie développementale des organismes et l'épigénétique. Disciplines s'inscrivant elles-mêmes dans une certaine crise de la synthèse néodarwinienne, dominante pendant tout le xx$^e$ siècle. Or, la synthèse néodarwinienne dans sa version classique la plus orthodoxe est un avatar du déterminisme. Elle établit un lien causal strict, interne et univoque, entre les gènes et le développement de l'organisme qui les porte en récusant toute influence directe de l'environnement, à l'instar de la vision cartésienne du sujet interne et isolé du monde des objets.

Pour Watsuji, c'est en éprouvant le milieu dans notre relation avec lui que nous pouvons le comprendre (le froid par exemple). Les données de l'environnement sont toujours saisies de manière relationnelle. L'air froid n'est pas réductible à une impression du moi. Cela ne signifie pas pour autant qu'il existe indépendamment du sujet. Ce qui est premier est bien la relation « avoir froid » qui permet dans un second temps de distinguer l'air froid objectivé de la sensation de froid subjectivée. Selon Watsuji, c'est se méprendre que de distinguer le sujet de l'objet, et par conséquent de distinguer un 'nous' d'un 'air froid', qui s'établiraient chacun indépendamment (Watsuji 2011, 39–41). De plus, le froid ne peut être compris qu'en relation avec la tiédeur, la pluie, le vent et tous les autres phénomènes climatiques. Et le climat lui-même n'est pas quelque chose que l'on expérimente isolément, mais en rapport avec le sol, le relief, la saison, etc. En outre, avoir froid n'est pas juste une impression du sujet, c'est quelque chose qui nous engage socialement, qui nous pousse à nous rapprocher du feu, à acheter du bois ou à en couper, à tisser des vêtements, donc à planter du lin, etc. On se rend déjà compte que le climat en soi est loin de constituer l'alpha et l'oméga du milieu.

Pourtant, Watsuji manque parfois de cohérence par rapport aux intentions qu'il annonce. Ainsi, si le but poursuivi au début de l'œuvre est bien de dégager les principes ontologiques d'une mésologie (une étude du milieu), le recours aux illustrations dans la suite de l'ouvrage glisse parfois vers le déterminisme environnemental qui est précisément dénoncé par l'auteur. Berque relate aussi l'une des faiblesses de *Fūdo* : la tendance à généraliser abusivement le point de vue subjectif de l'auteur japonais à l'ensemble d'une population étrangère (à laquelle il n'appartient pas) pour en tirer des conclusions erronées (Berque in Watsuji 2011, 24–5). En outre, la place importante accordée à l'étude du Japon dans les exemples a pu induire de nombreux commentateurs à penser que Watsuji inscrivait *Fūdo* dans la lignée des nipponologies traditionnelles (c'est-à-dire des textes vantant la spécificité du Japon). Berque souligne d'ailleurs que la postface de Inoue Mitsusada à l'édition de 1979 va dans ce sens en dépit de l'intention plus universalisante de Watsuji (ibid., 14).

### La place des végétaux dans *Fūdo*

Ce qui compte pour Watsuji, c'est bien l'étude de la relation de l'humain à l'environnement : sa subjectité (par opposition à l'idée de subjectivité autopoïétique cartésienne) et pas l'étude des deux envisagés comme entités séparées. Pour rappel, dans *Fūdo*, l'humain ne peut être compris authentiquement qu'à partir de sa dualité intrinsèque. Revenons un moment sur le reproche de Watsuji à Heidegger. Selon le philosophe japonais, ce dernier n'aurait pas été capable de donner tout son sens à la spatialité:

> Une temporalité à quoi ne répond pas la spatialité n'est pas encore une vraie temporalité. Si Heidegger s'en est tenu là, c'est parce que son Dasein n'est en fin de compte qu'un individu. Il n'appréhende l'existence humaine qu'en tant que celle d'un homme individuel. Vu la dualité de l'existence humaine, qui est à la fois individuelle et sociale, ce n'est là qu'un aspect abstrait. (Watsuji 2011, 36)

Ceci permet d'ouvrir une brève parenthèse biologique qui indique la portée des thèses watsujiennes. En effet, s'il est vrai que l'humain doit être spatialisé et ne peut être qu'abstraitement individualisé, on peut élargir la portée de la critique japonaise, car c'est aussi vrai des organismes en général comme l'ont montré l'écologie et l'éthologie. La dualité des organismes n'est pas forcément sociale, mais ils ne peuvent pas pour autant être envisagés comme de purs individus indépendamment de leur milieu. Au niveau spatial, l'écologie nous a appris qu'il y avait une dualité biologique entre les individus et leurs rapports à l'environnement. Ceci est particulièrement vrai pour les végétaux. C'est, par exemple, ce que montre aujourd'hui l'étude de la construction de niche (étude de l'influence de l'organisme sur son environnement) ou l'écologie du développement (*eco-devo*: étude de l'influence de l'environnement sur le développement de l'organisme). Dans cette perspective, c'est le rapport qui est premier pour saisir la vie (Sultan 2015). Comme l'a montré von Uexküll (1956) dans le monde biologique, ce rapport est celui de l'organisme à son environnement et c'est ce rapport qui constitue un milieu propre à chaque organisme. Par ailleurs, comme nous allons le voir, si la végétation constitue une des dimensions les plus fondamentales des milieux écologiques, son rôle est aussi capital pour la mésologie humaine. En outre, lorsque Watsuji critique Heidegger en déclarant: « Il n'y a pas plus de milieu séparé de l'histoire qu'il n'y a d'histoire séparée du milieu » (Watsuji 2011, 48), cette assertion est aussi vraie pour la biologie au-delà de l'humanité. La théorie de l'évolution nous a appris que l'histoire des espèces, la phylogénie, est intrinsèquement liée à leur milieu, aux contraintes environnementales orientant la sélection naturelle, et l'on sait aujourd'hui que leur milieu est aussi le résultat de leur histoire (par la construction de niches). Or, à la source de ces processus (tant du point de vue historique qu'effectif), ce sont bien les végétaux qui sont les champions du façonnage des milieux (atmosphère, autotrophie, cycle de l'eau et du carbone, érosion des sols, rhizosphère, rétention de l'humidité, base de la chaîne trophique, symbioses, etc.). L'humain, comme tous les autres animaux, en dépend aussi pour ses besoins biologiques les plus élémentaires; pas étonnant que les milieux humains se soient dès lors organisés pratiquement et symboliquement en fonction des végétaux dans la plupart des cultures. Cette influence est particulièrement visible dans la culture japonaise:

> La constante présence du végétal, dans la vie quotidienne et l'esthétique traditionnelle du Japon, a toujours frappé le visiteur occidental. Même de nos jours, en dépit de la profusion des matières nouvelles, l'usage du végétal reste beaucoup plus répandu que dans un pays comme la France. (BERQUE 1986, 100)

Je pense que c'est d'ailleurs la raison pour laquelle les plantes et l'agriculture occupent une si grande place dans *Fūdo*. C'est cette ligne d'interprétation qui va être poursuivie dans la suite de cet article.

Une lecture classique ou rapide de *Fūdo* pourrait laisser croire que les types de climats résument à eux seuls les types de milieux humains. Or, selon mon hypothèse de travail, chez Watsuji, ce sont davantage les végétaux qui constituent la médiation la plus directe entre l'homme et son environnement dont le climat est plutôt d'abord une condition et une manifestation brute. Je propose de le montrer à travers différents passages clefs qui égrainent le texte de Watsuji. Bien entendu, il ne s'agit pas de substituer à la dimension univoque du climat de certaines interprétations du texte une dimension végétale qui serait tout aussi univoque. Mon objectif consiste à démontrer que, dans l'économie générale du rapport au milieu, les plantes jouent un rôle charnière décisif et direct que ce soit au niveau biologique ou culturel (mais elles ne sont évidemment pas les seules à jouer un rôle).

Dès le deuxième chapitre, les impressions des milieux et des saisons décrites par Watsuji à l'égard de l'Asie du Sud-Est sont essentiellement liées aux végétaux: que ce soient les types généraux de végétation, des arbres ou des plantes particulières ou bien même des fruits. Il traite de cette région et de sa « monotonie qui déborde de force » en ces termes:

> Nous pouvons l'exprimer par une figure concrète. Le Jardin botanique de Penang, à la différence de celui de Singapour, est situé dans une vallée entre

des collines. Les arbres aux larges feuilles qui y poussent leurs frondaisons m'ont fait exactement la même impression de puissance envahissante que, pendant à peine deux ou trois semaines, donnent les shii [ndt Ou Shiinoki: Pasania cuspidata, arbre (fagacées) au feuillage toujours vert, représentatif de la forêt à feuilles luisantes qui à l'état naturel couvrait les plaines du Japon (sauf au nord) avant l'agriculture] et les chênes lorsqu'ils recouvrent nos montagnes au plus fort de la canicule. Ici, c'est toute l'année que cela dure. Mais quand on quitte le jardin, et que, passé la vaste forêt de palmiers, l'on commence à s'élever au flanc de la colline par le funiculaire, ce sont les épillets blancs d'une herbe qui évoque les susuki [ndt: Herbe des pampas (Miscanthus sinensis), emblème de l'automne au Japon] et de petites fleurs violettes qui ressemblent à celles de l'automne, et de ça de là des hévéas, avec leurs tendres feuilles nouvelles et leurs feuilles rougies. Au sommet, où il fait plus frais, se dressent des arbres qui ressemblent à des cyprès et des magnolias, et qui par l'allure de leur branchage et leurs troncs patinés, donnent l'impression que l'on est dans un jardin au Japon. Ceux-là non plus, de toute l'année ne doivent pas changer de forme, mais en comparaison avec la touffeur de la forêt estivale, c'est le printemps et c'est l'automne. Ainsi, même sans le passage des saisons ce milieu recèle toutes sortes de variations. (Watsuji 2011, 67–8)

Ce qui ressort de ce passage, c'est l'omniprésence du monde végétal pour structurer l'expérience humaine de la temporalité du milieu. La relation de l'homme a son milieu est donc en très grande partie, sinon essentiellement, liée à la structuration physique, écologique, mais aussi symbolique et émotionnelle du monde végétal. Comme le dit Watsuji, plus que la chaleur ou le calendrier, ce qui fait l'été (ou une autre saison) est un ensemble d'impressions du milieu. Je peux ainsi affiner mon hypothèse en suggérant que ce sont autant les plantes qui font passer le temps, que le temps qui fait pousser les plantes.

Dans la deuxième section sur le désert, Watsuji explique que lorsque la géographie s'est emparée du terme « désert », les gens ont cru qu'il s'agissait d'une « nature indépendante de l'homme. Il s'agissait là d'une immense étendue de terrain stérile engendrée par le manque de précipitations » (Watsuji 2011, 86). Ceci est évidemment une objectivation de l'environnement qui passe à côté du véritable sens du milieu que lui attribue Watsuji: « Personnellement, je traite du désert en tant que 'mode d'être de l'humanité' » (Watsuji 2011, 87). Mais qu'est-ce que cela signifie au juste?

> Il s'agit d'un endroit sans habitants, sans la moindre vie, rude et sauvage, repoussant à l'extrême. Ce milieu, les gens l'ont saisi non pas dans sa forme, mais dans son manque de vie. Ce n'est pas seulement une mer de sable, ce sont des chaînes de montagnes dressant des pics aux rocs décharnés, de vastes lits de rivières éventuellement sans eau et pleins de cailloux. Les gens qui se trouvaient au milieu de ces montagnes et de ces rivières y ont perçu un monde inhabité par les animaux comme par les plantes. De même qu'une 'maison inhabitée' est sans vie, vacante, ensauvagée, de même ces milieux sont du desert. Cependant, quand un milieu est ainsi appelé desert, ce n'est déjà plus simplement de la nature extérieure. Ce qui est desert, c'est la relation unitaire de l'homme et du monde. (WATSUJI 2011, 85)

La caractéristique principale du milieu désertique est donc l'absence de vie induite par la sécheresse, c'est-à-dire l'absence de rapport au milieu caractéristique de la vie tant végétale, qu'animale ou humaine. Ce n'est donc pas la forme physique, le sable, ni même tant l'absence ou la rareté d'eau (car il peut y avoir des rivières traversant le désert) qui caractérisent le désert, c'est l'absence de médiation avec la vie humaine. Or, selon moi, la possibilité de ces médiations dépend avant toute chose de la présence des végétaux qui structurent les conditions biologiques de la vie animale et humaine (par leur médiation primaire et primordiale avec l'environnement inorganique). Au niveau culturel, ce manque de végétation se traduit par l'impossibilité de se sédentariser, et donc l'impossibilité de vivre dans un milieu où les plantes permettent l'agriculture. Or, comme le souligne Watsuji, l'agriculture est une dimension fondamentale de la structuration des milieux humains (sinon la plus fondamentale). Mais la structuration des milieux par le végétal déborde l'organisation socioagricole, on en a déjà eu un aperçu avec la structuration temporelle des saisons dans l'extrait précédent, ce qui suit insiste davantage sur la structuration symbolique du végétal.

Le rôle symbolique attribué au végétal chez Watsuji ne se réduit pas à des métaphores éculées. Suivant Bachelard, qui parle de « l'unité profonde et vivante de certaines images végétales » (BACHELARD 1943, 262), il est préférable de supposer qu'il trouve son sens dans les raisons réelles et dynamiques qui ont présidé à l'élaboration de ces symboles:

> La vie imaginaire vécue en sympathie avec le végétal réclamerait tout un livre. Les thèmes généraux curieusement dialectiques en seraient la prairie et la forêt, l'herbe et l'arbre, la touffe et le buisson, la verdure et l'épine, la liane et

le cep, les fleurs et les fruits – puis l'être même: la racine, la tige et les feuilles – puis le devenir marqué par les saisons fleuries ou dépouillées – enfin les puissances: le blé et l'olive, la rose et le chêne – la vigne. […] La rêverie végétale est la plus lente, la plus reposée, la plus reposante. Qu'on nous rende le jardin et le pré, la berge et la forêt, et nous revivons nos premiers bonheurs. Le végétal tient fidèlement les souvenirs des rêveries heureuses. À chaque printemps il les fait renaître. Et en échange, il semble que notre rêverie lui donne une plus grande croissance, de plus belles fleurs, des fleurs humaines. (Bachelard 1943, 261–2)

Outre le rapport au devenir et aux saisons évoqués précédemment, on retrouve aussi chez Watsuji l'importance du caractère végétal pour la description du rapport au milieu montagneux qu'entretiennent spécifiquement les Japonais. Pour eux, la montagne est dite bleutée, en référence à la couleur bleu-vert dont la couvrent les forêts. C'est ce qui fait de Watsuji en tant que japonais, un « humain bleu-montain » comme le traduit Berque. C'est-à-dire quelqu'un qui ne peut voir dans les montagnes rocheuses noires et pointues de la ville d'Aden en Arabie autre chose qu'une altérité sinistre au milieu montagneux qui lui est familier (Watsuji 2011, 88–9).

> Être non-bleu-montain, pour le dire abstraitement, c'est être dépourvu de la moindre végétation. Les montagnes enveloppées de végétation, c'est de la vie végétale qu'elles sont enveloppées; c'est par conséquent la vie végétale que révèlent leurs couleurs et leur aspect. Là, c'est d'abord avec cette vie que le vent et la pluie conversent, ils ne touchent pas directement le non-vivant du roc et de la terre. Au contraire, les montagnes sans végétation ne montrent pas la moindre vie. Le vent et la pluie n'ont qu'une influence physique sur la surface des rochers. Cela, ce sont donc des 'ossements' de montagnes, c'est de la montagne morte. Le contour de la montagne, la manière de pointer qu'ont les rochers, leur couleur noirâtre, tout cela exprime la mort, ne fait pas sentir la force de la vie. (Watsuji 2011, 89)

Pour Watsuji (en tant que Japonais), de telles montagnes squelettiques sont hideuses, ce n'est pas une caractéristique physique de leur nature, mais un rapport existentiel de l'humanité qu'il y voit (ou n'y voit pas). Il parle d'ailleurs de « sécheresse médiale » à l'égard de ces sombres montagnes d'Aden. L'humain japonais est dit bleu-montain parce que la montagne japonaise est humaine comme le sont les « fleurs humaines » de Bachelard. Ce passage confirme que ce qui conditionne notre rapport au désert en tant que milieu, c'est la sécheresse, mais bien seulement en tant que c'est d'elle que proviennent l'absence de vie et d'habitants. En effet, la sécheresse en soi n'est pas compréhensible comme cause du milieu (elle en est seulement une condition), comme Watsuji y insiste, c'est dans son rapport à l'absence de vie qu'elle doit se comprendre, et cette absence de vie, comme sa présence, est avant tout déterminée par l'absence ou la présence de végétation en tant que ce qui structure le plus massivement et essentiellement nos milieux[5].

On retrouve également l'importance de la médiation du végétal dans le chapitre suivant sur la prairie, ce qui conforte à nouveau mon hypothèse de travail. Watsuji voit dans la prairie l'essence de l'Europe en tant qu'alliance du sec et de l'humide. Il ajoute que la couleur de l'herbe qui passe du vert au jaune en été témoigne de l'essence des pays d'Europe méditerranéenne (WATSUJI 2011, 120). L'humidité tempérée couplée à la sécheresse du sud empêcherait les mauvaises herbes de pousser massivement comme c'est le cas dans les pays humides et chauds de la mousson. Watsuji en conclut qu'en Europe, il n'y a pas de mauvaises herbes parce qu'elles ne conditionnent pas le rapport à l'agriculture de façon déterminante.

> Ainsi la sécheresse estivale et l'humidité hivernale excluent les mauvaises herbes, faisant un pré de tout le territoire. Cela ne laisse pas de conditionner la nature du travail agricole. (WATSUJI 2011, 119).

Ce rapport agricole à la végétation occupe une place capitale pour décrire les différents peuples. L'auteur en profite pour contraster l'Europe avec le Japon où le travail agricole consisterait en soi à lutter contre les mauvaises herbes, alors qu'en Europe il n'y aurait rien à faire contre elles une fois le terrain défriché... La terre y est « docile », elle se « subordonne aux humains » ce qui les rend paresseux... On peut évidemment contester les conclusions ethnologiques de Watsuji, mais le rapport au végétal demeure, à juste titre, central dans sa conception des milieux.

Watsuji prend à nouveau un exemple végétal pour illustrer une autre influence typique du milieu: le vent. Ainsi, c'est par la forme très régulière de

---

5. Cependant, c'est surtout sur le caractère social de la sécheresse que Watsuji glose ensuite, rapport de combat entre l'homme et la nature dont il tire une sorte de vision anthropologique surannée et péremptoire de la façon dont le désert a organisé les civilisations égyptiennes, juives, islamiques et indirectement européennes. Nous n'abordons pas ces aspects du livre qui sortent du cadre de la problématique.

la croissance des arbres méditerranéens, dont les branches poussent pareillement dans toutes les directions, que l'on peut saisir la faiblesse continue du vent. Cela donne aux Japonais une impression d'artificialité contraire à ce que le vent soutenu fait subir aux arbres du pays du soleil levant dont les formes sont naturellement tourmentées (en biologie, cette influence du vent sur la croissance des arbres est appelée l'anémomorphose). Si bien que les Européens ont lié le naturel (la régularité des arbres) au rationnel, ce qui n'est pas le cas au Japon (Watsuji 2011, 122–3). Ce nouvel exemple qui peut sembler de prime abord climatique, puisque centré sur le vent, n'est à nouveau compréhensible qu'à travers ses manifestations sur la végétation. Le climat seul n'est pas constitutif des milieux[6].

Le milieu caractéristique de l'Asie en général et du Japon en particulier est la mousson. Toutefois, le Japon se caractérise aussi par l'influence d'une zone froide en plus de la zone tropicale qui se manifeste à nouveau par le végétal:

> Cette dualité se remarque d'abord dans la végétation. Les plantes tropicales, qui demandent beaucoup de soleil et d'humidité, sont ici florissantes. En plein été, le paysage diffère peu de celui d'un pays tropical. Témoin le riz. En revanche, prospèrent aussi les plantes de la zone froide, qui demandent un air froid et peu d'humidité. Témoin le blé. De la sorte, la terre est couverte en hiver par le blé et les herbes de l'hiver, en été par le riz et les herbes de l'été. Quant aux arbres qui ne peuvent pas se succéder comme cela, ils ont eux-mêmes cette double nature. On cite souvent comme propres au Japon, ces paysages de bambous – plantes tropicales – recouverts de neige; mais d'être habitués à la neige, ces bambous eux-mêmes ont évolué en bambous du Japon, élastiques et capables de se courber sous la charge neigeuse. Ces caractères, que dans l'abstrait l'on peut considérer du point de vue du milieu seul,

---

6. Watsuji met aussi en rapport (un peu trop) direct les jours sombres de l'Europe du nord avec le repliement subjectif, l'acuité envers l'intériorité et donc le développement de la raison moderne. Toutefois remarquons que Berque tempère ces conclusions en les mettant en balance avec celles d'Hippocrate, ce qui lui fait dire que ce n'est pas la nature qui parle, mais bien la subjectivité de l'homme qui se sert de la nature (ce qui met par là même du plomb dans l'aile au déterminisme environnemental). Watsuji n'est pas pour autant un déterministe environnemental, en théorie du moins, car la mésologie ne défend pas un rapport de causalité entre l'environnement et la culture mais bien plutôt l'idée que le milieu influence la façon dont l'homme exprime sa condition. Certains aspects d'un milieu donné font prendre conscience davantage de certaines choses que l'homme va ensuite cultiver plus avantageusement.

sont concrètement pour les gens, le moment de leur vie historique. Le riz, comme les divers légumes de zone tropicale, et le blé, comme divers légumes de zone froide, sont produits par les gens eux-mêmes; par conséquent, c'est dans la vie des gens eux-mêmes que la pluie, la neige et l'ensoleillement qui leur sont nécessaires les arrosent ou les ensoleillent. Lorsqu'un typhon disperse les fleurs du riz, c'est la vie humaine qu'il menace. (WATSUJI 2011, 192)

Ce sont donc bien les plantes qui créent une médiation entre « l'environnement objectif » et « l'individu subjectif ». Ceci corrobore mon hypothèse de travail selon laquelle c'est le végétal qui constitue la première incarnation du milieu dans le sens où c'est avec le végétal que s'instaure un véritable milieu, c'est-à-dire une manière d'être au monde pour l'humain, une subjectité. Ici il s'agit surtout du rapport agricole comme rapport vital de l'humain à son environnement. Si de prime abord, Watsuji semble s'en tenir surtout à l'influence du climat en tant que tel on se rend compte qu'à travers tous ses exemples il oscille sans cesse vers l'idée que ce sont bien les végétaux qui instaurent un type de milieu humain (dont le climat est davantage une condition de possibilité). Le passage qui suit illustre cette ambivalence:

> Pareille singularité des climats, plus qu'on ne s'en rend compte soi-même, s'entretisse aux profondeurs de notre expérience. Même les plantes en témoignent à l'évidence. La jeune verdure que nous voyons au Japon croît et change de couleurs si vite qu'on a à peine le temps d'apprécier les teintes fraîches des premières pousses du printemps que l'on n'en pouvait plus d'attendre. On s'est à peine rendu compte que les feuilles de saule ont perdu leur duvet que déjà, si vite qu'on pourrait croire avec précipitation, elles sont toutes vertes et touffues. En Europe en revanche, les jeunes pousses donnent exactement l'impression qu'on observe les aiguilles d'une horloge. Elles croissent, certes, et en un mois elles changent bien quelque peu, mais elles ne montrent dans ce changement rien qui nous émeuve. Il en va de même pour les feuillages d'automne. Dès le mois d'août, les feuilles jaunissent et font un bruit sec. Aucun charme pourtant ne se dégage de cette verdure noircie, qui se dresse toujours mélancolique. Puis insensiblement, elle pâlit petit à petit, et se change en un jaune faiblard. Jusqu'au moment où, fin octobre, toutes les feuilles caduques ont jauni, pas une seule fois elles ne nous accrochent le regard. On ne voit jamais cette vive métamorphose qui, avec les premières gelées, lorsque la température tombe la nuit brusquement, colore les feuilles du jour au lendemain. L'on peut sans doute transposer aux formes de notre sensibilité ces liens entre le climat et la végétation. (WATSUJI 2011, 271–2)

Ce passage, au-delà de son ethnocentrisme réducteur à l'égard de la sensibilité européenne, confirme que c'est justement le végétal et ses changements qui constituent l'expérience médiatrice principale entre le climat, situé plutôt du côté d'un pôle « objectif », et notre expérience « subjective » de la vie, qu'elle soit biologique ou sociale. Si Watsuji le met en évidence pour la culture japonaise, les manifestations du végétal et ses changements affectent tout autant les Européens, même si c'est peut-être d'une autre manière[7]. En effet, le climat seul est une abstraction qui se manifeste en premier lieu et avec le plus d'importance sur le monde végétal qui est lui-même l'élément primordial et essentiel du milieu humain en raison de l'agriculture (et même plus généralement et fondamentalement en raison de l'alimentation). L'agriculture est la base de la sédentarisation et du mode de socialisation dans lesquelles nos sociétés humaines s'inscrivent. On se souviendra que c'est d'ailleurs par son absence que Watsuji caractérise le milieu désertique.

> Au Proche-Orient, que ce soit en Arabie, en Égypte etc., les terres y sont extrêmement sèches. Sauf cas particulier, ce sont partout des déserts, des étendues sauvages dépourvues de végétation, pareilles à des squelettes.
> (WATSUJI 2011, 268)

Cependant, tout en défendant le caractère original du végétal pour de nombreux milieux, sinon la plupart, il convient de remarquer qu'il est peut-être « mésocentré » de l'absolutiser, malgré son importance, comme l'essence de tout milieu, y compris le désert. Une caractérisation négative du désert semble en effet ethnocentrée: l'absence de végétation ne serait pas nécessairement perçue comme un manque essentiel de leur milieu par les autochtones. À l'inverse, si l'on veut pousser la thèse de l'universalité du végétal comme créateur de tout milieu, il est possible d'envisager que la rareté des végétaux dans le désert soit justement ce qui guide ses peuples à la recherche d'eau et de pâturage pour le bétail dont ils dépendent puisqu'ils ne peuvent

---

[7]. Berque écrit à ce sujet dans une note relative à ce passage: « On notera encore une fois, que pour apprécier les subtilités d'un milieu quelconque, il faut être soi-même de ce milieu-là. Cela dit, la sensibilité avec laquelle la culture japonaise a détaillé les variations de son propre milieu est effectivement hors du commun, comme en témoignent par exemples les milliers de termes des 歳時記, ces recueils des 'mots de saison' (季語) qui sont aussi nécessaires aux haïkus que la structure sujet-verbe-complément l'est à une phrase en français » (BERQUE in WATSUJI 2011, 272).

pratiquer l'agriculture. Il ne s'agit alors plus que d'une absence toute relative du végétal qui confère un sens de l'importance, et donc un rôle d'autant plus déterminant, à la rare végétation du désert. Cette importance se décline simplement sur un autre mode que celui de l'agriculture, mais la végétation resterait un besoin vital au cœur du rapport de l'humain avec son milieu. Cette question reste partiellement ouverte.

Enfin, il me reste à écrire quelques mots sur le quatrième chapitre qui porte sur le caractère médial de l'art. Remarquons que l'exemple principal (qui n'est cependant pas le seul) que Watsuji choisit et développe le plus pour illustrer l'influence du milieu sur l'art est celui du jardin. Ce n'est pas un hasard étant donné l'importance des réflexions japonaises sur l'esthétique des jardins. Le discours sur l'esthétique des jardins japonais s'interprète le plus souvent comme une intégration de la nature en tant que paysage. Toutefois, parallèlement à cette interprétation tout à fait fondée, on peut aussi comprendre que chez Watsuji, l'art des jardins est l'art qui est au plus proche de la médiation entre la nature et l'homme qui y vit. Pourquoi ? Si l'on suit mon hypothèse de travail, le milieu influence l'homme et ses productions (sans que l'on soit déterministe à cet égard) et le milieu est avant tout d'essence végétale, il est alors cohérent que *Fūdo* privilégie l'art des jardins comme exemple paradigmatique de la jonction entre ce milieu et l'art comme production la plus intrinsèque aux humains. L'art des jardins serait en quelque sorte un aboutissement de la médiation, culturellement magnifiée, que la végétation instaure initialement à travers l'agriculture. Une version déterministe « fréquente » et un peu simpliste existe à cet égard. Par exemple celle de Karaki, consiste à voir l'origine de l'attention (japonaise) au végétal dans les soins intensifs exigés par la riziculture (Berque 1986, 103). BERQUE (1986, 101–7) témoigne aussi plus largement du lien fort qui existe entre le végétal et l'esthétique japonaise, que ce soit directement avec l'art floral ou indirectement dans la peinture, la littérature, l'architecture (TAKAHASHI 1978, 2: 105–30; KARAKI 1976, 1:164). Les nombreux exemples végétaux utilisés par Watsuji pour rendre compte de sa sensibilité culturelle constituent autant d'éléments anticipant implicitement une sensibilité végétale de l'art[8]. Sur le fond, Watsuji contraste le

---

8. Thierry MARIN (2012) défend explicitement une thèse assez similaire de l'influence du végétal sur l'art en Occident.

jardin à l'européenne comme une volonté de rationalisation de la nature par une tentative de domination géométrisante artificielle avec le jardin japonais qui est une composition à partir de la nature plutôt que contre la nature. L'art des jardins est ainsi l'archétype qui permet à Watsuji de généraliser ses idées aux autres arts:

> De ces différences dans l'art des jardins, nous pourrons facilement passer à la spécificité des autres arts. (Watsuji 2011, 261)

Ce qu'il va d'ailleurs faire en abordant la sculpture, la peinture, la littérature ou la musique. Néanmoins, cette visée esthétique sort de ma problématique.

## Conclusion

Ce que l'on retiendra de l'analyse des extraits commentés de Watsuji, c'est que pour être tout à fait cohérent avec son optique mésologique, il aurait dû dépasser le stade du climat comme axe théorique explicite. La théorisation d'une mésologie ne peut en effet se satisfaire d'un critère trop univoque comme le climat pour rendre compte des milieux humains. Ce sont bien plutôt des ensembles complexes de facteurs qui en sont à l'origine; on pourrait dire des complexes « écologiques ». En ce sens, nous rejoignons l'interprétation d'Augustin Berque sur cette question, mais en y adjoignant des arguments plus spécifiques sur la nature du végétal. En effet, une pensée « écologique » s'enracine nécessairement dans la vie végétale. Je pense avoir démontré ici que les exemples de Watsuji vont d'ailleurs eux-mêmes dans ce sens puisqu'en convoquant sans cesse le végétal dans la diversité et la complexité de ses formes et de ses usages, il suggère de fait que le climat ne doit pas être envisagé comme une cause ni même un élément plus déterminant de la création des milieux humains. En se recentrant sur la végétation on se rend compte que le climat est davantage une condition de possibilité de la végétation, et donc des milieux et par conséquent de la vie humaine, avec laquelle il forme un complexe expérientiel: un milieu humain. Car *in fine*, il semble bien que ce soit le végétal qui constitue le nexus ontologique privilégié pour structurer le plus directement notre expérience de notre milieu qu'elle soit vitale, biologique, perceptive, mais aussi sociale et symbolique.

## Indications bibliographiques

BACHELARD, Gaston
    1943    *L'air et les songes*. Paris, José Corti.

BERQUE, Augustin
    1995    *Les raisons du paysage. De la Chine antique aux environnements de synthèse*. Paris Hazan.
    2014    *Poétique de la terre. Histoire naturelle et histoire humaine, essai de mésologie*. Paris, Belin.
    1986    *Le sauvage et l'artifice: les japonais devant la nature*. Paris, Gallimard.

BOURNÉRIAS, Marcel et Christian BOCK
    2006    *Le génie des végétaux. Des conquérants fragiles*. Paris, Belin.

KARAKI Junzō 唐木順三
    1976    『日本人の心の歴史』 [A history of the Japanese mind]. Tokyo, Chikuma Shobō, 2 vols.

MANCUSO, Stefano et Alessandra VIOLA
    2015    *Brilliant Green: The Surprising History and Science of Plant Intelligence*. Translated by Joan Benham. Washington, Island Press.

MARIN, Thierry
    2012    *Le principe de floraison, manières végétales de faire des mondes*. Paris, Max Milo.

RAVEN, Peter, Ray EVERT et Susan EICHORN
    2012    *Biologie végétale*. 3e éd., trad. fr., J. Bouharmont. Bruxelles, De Boeck.

SULTAN, Sonia E.
    2015    *Organism and Environment: Ecological Development, Niche Construction, and Adaptation*. Oxford: Oxford University Press.

SUZUKI Hideo 鈴木秀夫
    1975    『風土の構造』 [The structure of *Fūdo*]. Tōkyō, Daimeidō.
    1978    『森林の思考・砂漠の思考』 [Thinking in forests, thinking in deserts]. Tōkyō, Nihon Hōsō Shuppan Kyōkai.

SUTY, Lydie
    2015    *Les végétaux, les relations avec leur environnement*. Versailles, Quae.

TAKAHASHI Kazuo 高橋和夫
    1978    『日本文学と気象』 [Japanese literature and climate]. Tokyo, Chūōkōronsha, 2 vol.

UEXKÜLL, Jakob von
    1956    *Milieu animal et milieu humain*. Trad. fr., C. Martin-Freville. Paris, Rivages, 2010.

WATSUJI Tetsurō
    2011    *Fudô. Le milieu humain*. Trad. fr., A. Berque. Paris, CNRS éditions.

Leon Krings
*Universität Hildesheim*

# Leibliches Üben als Teil einer philosophischen Lebenskunst
## Die Verkörperung von *Kata* in den japanischen Wegkünsten

> In this paper, I try to show how Japanese practices of self-cultivation found in the so-called "ways" (道 *dō, michi*) can be interpreted as embodied forms of "caring for oneself" (*epimeleia heautou*) and, therefore, as part of a philosophical *Lebenskunst* or art of living. To this end, I refer to phenomenological accounts of the body as well as to a unique notion of practice found in the writings of Dōgen Kigen, a thirteenth-century Japanese Zen master. Central to this essay is a concern with embodying *kata* or pre-defined patterns of movement and posture used in nearly all practices of self-cultivation in Japan. To approach this question, I look at the etymological roots of the term *kata* and its use in the writings of Zeami, the foremost representative of classical Noh theater, both as author and as actor. This is followed by an analysis of certain aspects of the embodiment of *kata* and the way it is described in Japanese literature.
> 
> KEYWORDS: Verkörperung—embodiment—leibliches Spüren—Lebenskunst—Kata—Übungswege—Wegkünste—Dōgen—Nishida Kitarō

> Jede Seele erkennt das Unendliche, erkennt alles, freilich in undeutlicher Weise, so wie ich etwa, wenn ich am Meeresufer spazieren gehe und das gewaltige Rauschen des Meeres höre, dabei auch die besonderen Geräusche einer jeden Woge höre, aus denen das Gesamtgeräusch sich zusammensetzt, ohne sie jedoch voneinander unterscheiden zu können. Unsere undeutlichen Perzeptionen sind eben das Ergebnis der Eindrücke, die das gesamte Universum auf uns ausübt.[1]

All unsere Lebensvollzüge sind mit unserem Körper und unserer leiblichen Wahrnehmung verbunden und jede Haltung oder Bewegung, die wir mit unserem Körper einnehmen oder ausführen, hat eine bestimmte Form, die unser Dasein – gemeinsam mit anderen Faktoren – im jeweiligen Augenblick bestimmt. Als leibliche Wesen sind wir in unserem Denken und Handeln in jedem Moment unseres Lebens auch dadurch bestimmt, wie wir uns als Körper und zugleich mittels diesem zu uns selbst und zu unserer Umwelt verhalten: ob wir uns in einer hastigen oder gemächlichen, verspielten oder disziplinierten, mit anderen in Kontakt tretenden oder von anderen abgrenzenden Weise bewegen, ob wir eine aufrechte oder gekrümmte, angespannte oder entspannte, offene oder verschlossene, liegende, sitzende oder stehende Haltung einnehmen. Dies mag uns nicht immer oder gar nur in den seltensten Fällen bewusst sein, prägt jedoch die Art und Weise, wie wir uns zu uns selbst und zur Welt verhalten, als ein uns zumeist kaum gewahr werdender Hintergrund unserer selbst, ein beständiges Rauschen dunkler Regungen, aus dem heraus unser bewusstes Dasein erwächst. Diese nur undeutlich wahrgenommenen Strukturen unseres spürbaren Leibes

---

1. Leibniz 1982, 19.

sowie die zur Selbstverständlichkeit gewachsenen Haltungen und Bewegungen unseres Körpers können jedoch auch bewusst gestaltet und kultiviert werden, und eine Beschäftigung mit den Möglichkeiten einer derartigen Selbstkultivierung erfordert eine Aufarbeitung der körperlichen Übungssysteme, die uns aus verschiedenen Kulturen überliefert sind, denn in diesen können wir auch heute noch lebendige Praktiken und Artikulationsformen der Erforschung des Körpers entdecken.

Meine mir eigentümlichen Bewegungen und Haltungen sind sowohl höchst individuell als auch gesellschaftlich geprägt, sie scheinen aus meinem Inneren hervorzuquellen und zugleich von außen an mich herangetragen zu werden. Eine Unterscheidung zwischen natürlich Gegebenem und kulturell Erlerntem ist in Bezug auf meine körperlichen Gewohnheiten nur schwer zu treffen, da sich beide Ebenen ununterbrochen zu verkreuzen und zu durchdringen scheinen. Unsere Bewegungen und Haltungen sind nicht nur expressiv, sondern performativ, indem sie Bedeutung nicht bloß zum Ausdruck bringen, sondern in ihrem Vollzug erst hervorbringen. Wir erzeugen in jedem Augenblick unseres Lebens – eben dadurch, dass wir leben – Sinn, ob wir dies beabsichtigen oder nicht. Dieser Sinn entfaltet sich in einer Unzahl von Bedeutungsdimensionen zugleich: individuell, sozial, technisch, künstlerisch, materiell, geistig, geschlechtlich, erotisch, ästhetisch, ethisch usw. Es scheint uns kaum möglich, die Wucherungen des Sinns, an deren Auswüchsen wir teilhaben, jemals reflexiv einzuholen, da auch unsere Reflexion selbst im Akt ihrer Ausführung wiederum ein Mehr an Sinn schafft, das sie sich nicht zum Inhalt gemacht hatte.[2]

Diese Sinn- und Formgebung, die im Vollzug unseres körperlichen Daseins unentwegt neue Gestalten des Sinns und körperliche Relationen erzeugt, sollte dem philosophischen Leben nicht fremd sein, sondern gerade dort bewusst ergriffen und bedacht werden. Wenn Philosophie sich nicht in beruflich betriebener Theoriebildung erschöpft, sondern als eine Weise der Lebensführung begriffen wird, die alle Facetten unseres Daseins betrifft, sollte sie die Bedeutung der körperlichen Formgebung reflektieren und ihre Möglichkeiten praktisch ausloten. Dies erfordert sowohl eine theoretische

---

2. Allerdings kann eine körperlich gebundene, performative Sinnkonstitution zugleich auch eine reflektierende sein, in welchem Fall die Reflexion nicht erst „im Nachhinein" stattzufinden braucht und an der performativen Sinnkonstitution selbst teilhaben kann.

Auseinandersetzung mit der systematischen Relevanz des Körpers und seiner Formkräfte für das, was wir „Geist", „Erkenntnis", „Selbst", „Gemeinschaft" etc. nennen, als auch eine – möglicherweise erst neu zu entdeckende – Übungspraxis, die diese Formkräfte *in concreto* ernst nimmt und in die menschliche Lebensform als einen Teil derselben integriert.

Ich denke, dass sich für beide Aspekte – den theoretischen wie den die Übung betreffenden, asketologischen – Ansatzpunkte in den ostasiatischen Denk- und Übungstraditionen finden, die mögliche Formen einer umfassenden philosophischen Lebenskunst zumindest andeuten können, selbst wenn sich eine schlichte Übernahme vorliegender Denk- und Übungsmuster als unangemessen erweisen sollte. Die Formen der Selbstkultivierung und der Selbstsorge, die sich in den asiatischen Übungstraditionen entwickelt haben, sind in bestimmten wesentlichen Zügen mit den Praktiken der antiken Askese (im ursprünglichen, weiten Sinn von „Übung") vergleichbar, da auch einige der buddhistischen, daoistischen und konfuzianischen Praktiken sich als „Techniken des Selbst"[3] verstehen lassen, die auf Formen der Ausbildung oder auch des Abbaus eines „Selbst" (自己)[4] des Praktizierenden abzielen und dessen Lebensvollzug sowie den Horizont seines In-der-Welt-Seins als Ganzes betreffen. Ich möchte in diesem Aufsatz hierzu japanische Körperpraktiken heranziehen und mich dabei vor allem auf den Zen-Buddhismus beziehen, da dieser sich für die Entwicklung verschiedener japanischer Übungsformen als besonders relevant erwiesen hat. Anschließend möchte ich die in den sogenannten „Übungswegen" bzw. „Wegkünsten" (道) noch heute praktizierte „Kata-Übung" und ihre mögliche Relevanz für eine gegenwärtige philosophische Lebenskunst thematisieren.

In Bezug auf ein mögliches Verständnis der Übungswege als Formen einer Praxis, die für eine philosophische Lebensform von Bedeutung sind, sollte angemerkt werden, dass es nicht darum gehen kann, die Praktiken der Übungswege sowie ihre lebensweltliche und theoretische Fundierung einfach kritiklos zu übernehmen. Schon die historische Tatsache, dass der

---

3. Siehe FOUCAULT 2009, 507f. Peter Sloterdijk spricht auch von „Anthropotechniken". Siehe SLOTERDIJK 2009.

4. Bei Verweisen auf asiatische Begriffe werde ich in diesem Aufsatz nur die jeweilige japanische Terminologie angeben, auch wenn natürlich beachtet werden muss, dass diese sich in vielen Fällen auf die chinesische und indische Begrifflichkeit zurückbezieht.

Zen-Buddhismus ebenso wie die Wegkünste zur Untermauerung einer nationalistischen Hypostasierung eines vermeintlichen „Wesens" des japanischen Volkes missbraucht wurden,⁵ macht deutlich, dass die Gefahr einer ideologischen Überformung dieser Praktiken besteht, obgleich sie ihrem Selbstverständnis nach umfassende „Lebenswege" darstellen, die ästhetische ebenso wie ethische Aspekte umfassen. Das heißt, leibliche Übungspraktiken müssen von einem kritischen Diskurs über ihre gesellschaftlichen, politischen und ethischen Implikationen sowie ihre institutionellen Rahmenbedingungen begleitet und vor Missbrauch bewahrt werden. Die hier beschriebenen Übungspraktiken können daher immer nur als mögliche Ansatzpunkte und nicht schon als endgültige Antworten auf die Frage nach einer körperlichen Übungspraxis im Rahmen einer philosophischen – und das heißt für mich hier vor allem forschenden und zugleich selbstkritischen – Lebensführung gelten.

### Die Übung des Selbst im Zen-Buddhismus

Als erste Annäherung an die leiblichen Übungspraktiken im japanischen Kontext möchte ich zunächst exemplarisch einen zen-buddhistischen Denker heranziehen, der ein für die japanischen Wegkünste einflussreiches Verständnis von Übung entwickelt hat. Es handelt sich um Dōgen Kigen (1200–1253), den Begründer der japanischen Sōtō-Schule des

---

5. Siehe BENESCH 2014. Aber auch umgekehrt gilt, dass die in den körperlichen Übungsformen anzutreffenden disziplinierenden Subjektivierungspraktiken, die das Individuum einem Kollektiv integrieren, nicht per se ethisch verwerflich sind und auch keine Besonderheit „traditionalistischer" asiatischer Gesellschaften im Gegensatz zu vermeintlich „individualistischen" westlichen Gesellschaften darstellen, sondern ebenso zu einer positiven Vermittlung zwischen Individuum und Gemeinschaft führen und in einen globalen Kontext gestellt werden können, wie Denis Gainty in seiner Behandlung des Ende des 19. Jahrhunderts entstandenen japanischen Kampfkunstverbandes *Dainippon Butokukai* feststellt:
> Instead of serving as an Orientalist oddity, the example of the Butokukai—like those of English rugby players, American footballers, Jewish weightlifters, Swedish calisthenicists, Chinese boxers, and Hindu, Persian, and Ottoman Turkish wrestlers—can help us to ask how the immediacy of the body in the co-construction of nation and self was itself a central feature of *global* modernity. (GAINTY 2013, 144)

Zum Verhältnis von Disziplinierung und Befreiung im Zusammenhang des Übens siehe MENKE 2003, 283–308.

Zen-Buddhismus. In seinem Hauptwerk *Shōbōgenzō* findet sich folgende Passage zum Erlernen des „Buddha-Weges" (仏道):

> Den Buddha-Weg erlernen heißt, sich selbst erlernen. Sich selbst erlernen heißt, sich selbst vergessen. Sich selbst vergessen heißt, durch die zehntausend *dharma* von selbst erwiesen werden. Durch die zehntausend *dharma* von selbst erwiesen werden heißt, Leib und Herz meiner selbst sowie Leib und Herz des Anderen abfallen zu lassen. Die Spur des Erwachens kann verschwinden, die verschwundene Spur des Erwachens [*soll man*] lang, lang hervortreten lassen.[6]

Wie bereits unmittelbar ersichtlich wird, spielt das Selbstverhältnis des Übenden in der zen-buddhistischen Praxis eine zentrale Rolle. Dabei ist es für die buddhistische Tradition charakteristisch, dass das eigentliche Selbstverhältnis mit negativen Ausdrücken beschrieben wird. In der Praxis des Zen soll sich „übend erweisen" (修証する), dass das eigene „Selbst" im Wesentlichen ein „Nicht-Selbst" (無我) ist. Der Ausdruck „Nicht-Selbst" verweist auf das Fehlen eines substanziellen, überzeitlichen Kerns des persönlichen Selbst und damit auf dessen radikale Abhängigkeit von ihm fremden, aber gleichursprünglichen Daseinsfaktoren. Die prinzipielle „Leerheit" (空) und Substanzlosigkeit aller Phänomene (法) und der sie erfahrenden Subjekte ist somit eng verknüpft mit ihrem Entstehen in wechselseitiger Abhängigkeit (縁起), noch radikaler formuliert mit der wechselseitigen Durchdringung der gestalthaft erscheinenden Phänomene und der ihnen zugrunde liegenden, gestaltlosen Leerheit (理事無碍), sowie der wechselseitigen Durchdringung der einzelnen Phänomene und Subjekte untereinander (事事無碍).[7]

Das in die Achtsamkeit gehobene und sich dabei kontinuierlich verändernde Verhältnis des Übenden zu sich selbst und zu den Phänomenen ist dabei ein eminent leibliches, da die gesteigerte Aufmerksamkeit während der Übungspraxis dazu führt, dass jedes noch so kleine Detail der körperlichen Haltung und der sinnlichen Wahrnehmung eine ungeahnte Bedeutsamkeit

---

6. Dōgen 2006, 38f. Die im Original vorhandenen japanischen Termini in Klammern werden bei Zitaten aus Gründen der Leserlichkeit ausgelassen.

7. Der Gedanke einer wechselseitigen Durchdringung von Prinzip und Sachverhalt/Phänomenen (理事無碍) sowie von Phänomen und Phänomen (事事無碍) geht auf das Avataṃsaka-sūtra und die chinesische Huayan-Schule des Buddhismus zurück. Siehe hierzu Fazangs Abhandlung zum „Goldenen Löwen" in Elberfeld et al. 2000.

entfalten kann. Bei der paradigmatischen Übungspraxis der Sitzmeditation (座禅) etwa kann jede Modifikation des Körpers – in der Weise des Atmens, der Blickrichtung, der Streckung der Wirbelsäule und des Kopfes, der Lage der Hände usw. – eine so umgreifende Modulation der leiblichen Wahrnehmungssphäre bedeuten, dass sich das Verhältnis des Übenden zu sich selbst sowie zur Welt von Grund auf verändert.[8]

Aufgrund der innigen Verschränkung von Selbst und Welt im Üben kann Dōgen davon sprechen, dass sich das Vergessen des Selbst als ein „Erwiesen-Werden" durch die „zehntausend *dharma*" (= sämtliche Phänomene der Welt) ereignet: „Sich selbst tragend die zehntausend *dharma* übend erweisen, das ist Irren; die zehntausend *dharma* kommen her und erweisen übend mich selbst, das ist Erwachen."[9] Das heißt, die Übung ist nicht einfach eine individuelle Anstrengung meinerseits, sondern sie ereignet sich als Erweisungsgeschehen, das mich ebenso wie die mir begegnenden Phänomene umfasst. Daher muss ich meine persönliche, individuelle Übung aus Dōgens Sicht in das Feld einer universellen – sich jedoch stets in den konkreten Phänomenen vollziehenden – übenden Selbst-Erweisung der Welt als Ganzes einbetten und mich selbst von den mir begegnenden Phänomenen her verstehen, da die Weise, wie sie mir begegnen, mir zeigt, was ich bin.[10]

Ein weiteres Charakteristikum des Übungsverständnisses bei Dōgen ist der Gedanke einer „Einheit von Übung und Erweis" (修証一如), d. h. einer wesensmäßigen Identität der ununterbrochenen Übungspraxis mit ihrem Erweis in Form eines In-Erscheinung-Tretens bzw. Offenbar-Werdens (現成)[11] des jeweiligen Augenblicks in seiner Fülle. „Erweis" bzw. „Bewäh-

---

8. Dies gilt insbesondere für die von Dōgen empfohlene Praxis des „Einfach-nur-Sitzens" (只管打坐), bei der das konkrete Sitzen selbst – und nicht etwa die Meditation über ein paradoxes Handeln oder Sprechen der alten Meister (公案) – der Inhalt der Übung ist.

9. Dōgen 2006, 38.

10. Selbst und Welt stellen bei Dōgen somit keine Gegensätze dar, sondern erlauben ein wechselseitiges Ineinander-Übergehen. Sein Denken ließe sich daher etwa mit Merleau-Pontys Chiasmus von Leib und Fleisch oder mit Nishida Kitarōs wechselseitiger Bestimmung der „handelnden Anschauung" (行為的直観) des individuellen Selbst und der „Selbstgestaltung der Welt" (世界の自己形成) in Verbindung bringen. Siehe Merleau-Ponty 1986. Zum Begriff der „handelnden Anschauung" bei Nishida siehe Elberfeld 2011, 313–44. Siehe auch Nishida 2016, 217–46.

11. Der japanische Ausdruck *genjō* (*su*), der sowohl als Nomen als auch als Verb verwendet werden kann, stellt einen Schlüsselbegriff in Dōgens Denken dar und wird sehr unterschied-

rung" (証) und „Offenbar-Werden" können dabei als eine Form von prozessual sich entfaltendem Erleuchtungsgeschehen verstanden werden, sodass man auch von einer Einheit von Übung und „Erleuchtung" (悟り) sprechen kann. „Erleuchtung" realisiert sich als ein wechselseitiges Offenbar-Machen der Phänomene und des Selbst, das heißt, sie ereignet sich in der Weise eines Sich-Zeigens der „objektiven" Wirklichkeit, das zugleich erst durch mein „subjektives" Erleben dieses Sich-Zeigens und mein Einüben in es realisiert wird. Erleuchtung ist demnach kein Zustand, der auf einer bestimmten Stufe des Übens erreicht wird, sodass sich das Üben anschließend erübrigen würde, sondern die Übung selbst ist es, die das Offenbar-Werden von Welt konkretisiert und verkörpert, d. h. im Üben als leiblichem Präsenzgeschehen zum Ausdruck bringt. Der Praktizierende erweist übend die Welt und wird dabei zugleich übend von der Welt erwiesen, die Verkörperung der Welt durch den Übenden ist zugleich eine Selbstverkörperung der Welt bzw. eine Verkörperung des Selbst durch die Welt.

Die Übung zielt somit nicht auf eine außerhalb ihrer selbst liegende, theoretische Einsicht ab, sondern ist in ihrem Vollzug selbst das leibliche In-Erscheinung-Treten der Wirklichkeit im Prozess ihrer Verkörperung durch die Ko-Präsenz von Übendem und Welt.[12] Übung ist demnach etwas Unabschließbares, ein „Üben-Halten" (行持) bzw. „anhaltendes Üben", das letztlich nicht mehr von den Handlungen des Alltags getrennt werden kann. Jede alltägliche Bewegung oder Haltung wird zu einem übend verkörperten Erweis der Wirklichkeit in ihrer gegenwärtigen Fülle: „Die Bedeutung von Tee[trinken] und Reis[essen] ist seit langem überliefert, [es] ist das Offenbar-Werden (現成) dieses Jetzt (而今)."[13] Trinken, Essen, Schlafen und Sprechen sind daher ebenso Möglichkeiten eines übenden Erweises der Wirklichkeit wie die formelle Sitzmeditation. In jedem Fall ist es entscheidend, dass die jeweilige Tätigkeit mit einer möglichst aus-

---

lich übersetzt. Ōhashi und Elberfeld übersetzen ihn mit „volles/vollkommenes Erscheinen", Heinemann mit „Verwirklichung", Waddell und Abe mit „manifestation", Steineck mit „offen zutage treten".

12. Zum Verständnis der Zen-Meditation als eines Verkörperungsrituals siehe Leighton 2008, 167–84.

13. Aus dem Kapitel 家常 (Kajō) des Shōbōgenzō, zitiert nach Heinemann 1979, 153. Heinemanns Übersetzung von genjō als „Verwirklichung" wurde hier durch „Offenbar-Werden" ersetzt.

schließlichen Sammlung der Aufmerksamkeit auf das gegenwärtige Jetzt und die in ihm erscheinende Fülle des sinnlich Gegebenen ausgeführt wird, ohne die so gesteigerte Aufmerksamkeit auf das intentional-gegenständliche Bewusstsein eines bestimmten Phänomens zu verengen. Die Sammlung der Aufmerksamkeit ist kein rein „innerliches" Geschehen im Bewusstsein des Übenden, sondern eine Form von leiblicher Präsenz, die sich als eine wechselseitige Verkörperung von Selbst und Welt realisiert, an welcher der oder die Übende ebenso wie alle anderen Wesen und „Dinge" (物) teilhat.[14]

### Die Kata-Übung in den japanischen Wegkünsten

Es ist an dieser Stelle nicht möglich, ausschöpfend auf die verschiedenen Formen des Übens im japanischen Zen-Buddhismus einzugehen. Dōgens Ausführungen, die hier nur angerissen werden konnten, stellen sicher einen Höhepunkt in der sprachlichen Beschreibung des Übungsgeschehens dar. Der Zen-Buddhismus übte in den folgenden Jahrhunderten nach Dōgen zusammen mit Daoismus, Konfuzianismus und Shintōismus einen entscheidenden Einfluss auf die Entwicklung einer Vielzahl von Künsten und Übungspraktiken aus, die häufig unter der allgemeinen Bezeichnung „Wegkünste" bzw. „Übungswege" (道) zusammengefasst werden.[15] Der

---

14. Im Hintergrund dieser Auffassung steht die schon das Denken im alten China leitende Voraussetzung, dass „Wirklichkeit in ihrer Vermittlung durch die Anschauung nicht als ‚Sein', sondern als ‚Wirksamkeit' verstanden" wird (OBERT 2007, 26). An dieser „Wirksamkeit" des Wirklichen haben nicht nur bewusste Akteure, sondern auch andere fühlende Wesen sowie unbelebte Dinge teil, da sie als konkrete Verkörperungen der Wirklichkeit gewissermaßen den Erfahrungsraum „krümmen" und gestalten. Dieses aus dem antiken China stammende Wirklichkeitsverständnis zeigt sich noch bei dem modernen japanischen Philosophen Nishida Kitarō, der etwa davon spricht, dass „die Dinge kommen und mich erleuchten", oder dass „wir denken, indem wir zu den Dingen werden und handeln, indem wir zu den Dingen werden." Siehe NISHIDA 1978–1980, Bd. 10, 157 f.

15. Hierzu zählen die „Wege der Kunst" (芸道), d. h. der „Teeweg" (茶道), der „Weg der Kalligraphie" (書道), der „Wegs des Blumensteckens" (花道, auch 生け花) und der „Weg des Duftes" (香道), sowie die „Wege des Kampfes" (武道), d. h. Karate-dō, Jūdō, Aikidō usw. Auch das Nō-Theater und andere Aufführungskünste (芸能) können zu den Wegkünsten gezählt werden. Die älteste Bezeichnung einer ästhetischen Praxis als „Weg" liegt in Japan wohl bei der Waka-Dichtung vor, die schon sehr früh als „Weg der Dichtung" (歌道) dem „buddhistischen Weg" (仏道) korreliert wurde. Siehe MINAMOTO 1989, 58. Auch in anderen Bereichen findet

japanische Kultur- und Literaturwissenschaftler Katō Shūichi geht sogar so weit zu behaupten, der Zen-Buddhismus habe die japanischen Künste nicht beeinflusst, sondern sei selbst zur Kunst geworden.[16] Die geschichtliche Entwicklung des Buddhismus und der Übungswege ist natürlich zu komplex, um sie in dieser Weise zusammenzufassen. Aus den Traktaten der verschiedenen Wegkünste ist jedenfalls ersichtlich, dass der Zen-Buddhismus einen entscheidenden Faktor in deren Entwicklung darstellt.[17]

Vom Übungsverständnis des Zen-Buddhismus übernehmen die klassischen Wegkünste wesentliche Elemente, die noch bis heute weitestgehend erhalten geblieben sind: Sie verstehen sich als eine Praxis der Selbstwerdung des Übenden, die sich zugleich als eine Negation des Selbst vollzieht. Das in intensiver Übung erlebte Selbst ist ein Nicht-Selbst, das sich im Idealfall von einem rein egozentrischen Standpunkt distanziert. Das Selbst wird erlernt, indem es vergessen wird, und findet sich auf diese Weise in die übende Selbststoffenbarung der Welt ein, worin es paradoxerweise zugleich die Entfaltung seiner vollen Konkretion und Individualität findet. Leib und Geist des Übenden können dabei zwar zum Zweck der Analyse provisorisch unterschieden werden, in der Übung selbst bilden sie allerdings einen untrennbaren Zusammenhang auf dem „Weg des Übens mit Leib und Geist" (身心学道).[18] Die zu erreichende „Einheit von Leib und Geist" (身心一如)[19] stellt jedoch keinen naturgegebenen Zustand dar, sondern tritt erst in der Übung performativ in Erscheinung. Daher beschäftigt sich die ostasiatische Tradition meist nicht vornehmlich damit, welches Verhältnis zwischen Körper und Geist *besteht*, sondern wie es sich übend *transformieren* lässt.

Eine Eigenart der japanischen Übungspraxis besteht darin, dass sich die

---

die Weg-Metapher Verwendung, etwa bei den Brettspielen Go und Shōgi, die auch als „Weg des Spielsteins" (棋道) bezeichnet werden.

16. Katō Shūichis „thesis is that during the long years of its seclusion Japan became so internalized that the artistic impulse, aesthetics, quite took the place accorded to religion in other countries […]: ,The art of Muromachi Japan was not influenced by Zen.' Rather, ,Zen became the art'" (RICHIE 2007, 68).

17. Siehe etwa Zeami Motokiyos *Neun Ränge* (九位) in ZEAMI 1986, 145–9, sowie die verschiedenen Traktate zur Schwertkunst in WILSON 2014.

18. Siehe das gleichnamige Kapitel in Dōgens *Shōbōgenzō*. DŌGEN 1970, 74–80. Im vorliegenden Aufsatz wird das japanische Wort *shin* (心, auch: *kokoro*), das wörtlich „Herz" bedeutet, mit „Geist" übersetzt.

19. Ebd. 23.

geistige Übung stets als körperliche Praxis vollzieht. Dies steht im Gegensatz zu der im antiken Griechenland zu beobachtenden Tendenz, körperliche Übungen entweder als bloßes Mittel zum Zweck der geistigen Vervollkommnung zu betrachten oder den Leib sogar als ein Übel zu verwerfen, mit der Begründung, er sei untrennbar mit den Leidenschaften verbunden und stehe daher der klaren Selbsterkenntnis der Seele im Weg. Dies zeigt sich etwa in der von Platon formulierten Ansicht, es ginge darum, sich vom Körper wie von einem Kerker zu befreien.[20] Die große Bedeutung, die der leiblichen Übung in den japanischen Übungswegen beigemessen wird, zeigt sich hingegen etwa in Dōgens genauen Anweisungen zur körperlichen Haltung in der Sitzmeditation[21], sowie in der Betonung der körperlichen Technik, wie sie in den Worten Zeamis (1363–1443), des Begründers des klassischen Nō-Theaters, zum Ausdruck kommt: „Willst du die Blüte wissen, mache dich zunächst mit dem Samen vertraut. Die Blüte ist der Geist, der Samen ist die [körperliche] Technik."[22]

Was hier als „Technik" wiedergegeben wurde, ist das japanische Wort *waza*, das mit unterschiedlichen Schriftzeichen geschrieben werden kann, die jeweils eine andere Konnotation aufweisen. Die Bedeutung des Ausdrucks *waza* changiert dabei – ähnlich wie beim griechischen Begriff der τέχνη – zwischen einem handwerklichen Können und einer ästhetischen Kunstfertigkeit. In jedem Fall verweist er auf ein mit dem Körper verbundenes, praktisches *knowing how* im Gegensatz zu einem theoretischen, propositional verfassten *knowing that*. Das im Zitat verwendete Schriftzeichen für *waza* (態) trägt die Bedeutung einer herausragenden Kunstfertigkeit, die ein Leben lang aufs Neue eingeübt werden muss. Eine solche körperlich angeeignete Technik steht in enger Verbindung zu dem, was in den Wegkünsten allgemein als Kata (型 oder 形) bekannt ist.[23]

---

20. Siehe Sokrates Rede in Platon *Phaid.* 82e f.
21. In der Schrift *Fukanzazengi*. Siehe DŌGEN 1970, 74–80.
22. 花を知らんと思はば、先づ、種を知るべし。花は心、種は態なるべし。Aus Zeamis Schrift *Fūshikaden*. Siehe ZEAMI 1974, 37. Übersetzung des Autors.
23. Das Schriftzeichen 態, das im Zitat mit der Lesung *waza* versehen wurde, kann im klassischen Japanisch ebenso wie das Schriftzeichen 形 als *nari* gelesen werden und bedeutet dann soviel wie „Form, Gestalt; Körperhaltung; äußere Erscheinung". Das Schriftzeichen 形 wiederum wird zur Wiedergabe von *kata* verwendet, woraus schon ein Zusammenhang zwischen *waza* und *kata* ersichtlich wird.

„Kata" bedeutet im Japanischen zunächst „Form, Gestalt, Muster", spezieller auch (im Fall von 型) „Gussform", im Sinne einer Vorlage, die zur Herstellung von Kopien verwendet werden kann. In den Übungswegen sind Kata körperliche Haltungs- und Bewegungsmuster, die von paradigmatischen Situationen (Meditation, Schwertkampf) oder auch alltäglichen Verrichtungen (Teetrinken, Schreiben) abstrahiert und auf ihre wesentlichen Elemente reduziert wurden, um sie sich in intensiver Übung anzueignen und von Meister zu Schüler zu tradieren. So können sowohl die Haltung des Körpers in der Sitzmeditation als auch Techniken und Bewegungsabläufe aus den Kampf- und Aufführungskünsten als „Kata" bezeichnet werden. Minamoto Ryōen (geb. 1920) bestimmt die Bedeutung des Ausdrucks folgendermaßen:

> Das Wort „Kata" (型) [...] hat die Bedeutung einer „Form der Form" (形の形). Kata finden sich in Japan vor allem in den ästhetischen und kriegerischen Künsten im Zusammenhang bestimmter körperlicher Bewegungen, sind aber nicht auf diese Künste beschränkt, sondern können ganz allgemein definiert werden als charakteristische Muster, die aus den bewussten und unbewussten Bewegungen des Menschen ausgewählt und anschließend im Prozess einer Akkumulation der hingebungsvollen Bemühung, sie immer weiter zu verfeinern und ihre Realisierung dauerhaft zu etablieren, sprunghaft angeeignet wurden. Mit anderen Worten: Sie sind „Formen, die dadurch vollendet werden, dass sie eine wahrnehmbare Gestalt besitzen und diese zugleich übersteigen." Als etwas, das die äußere Gestalt übersteigt, ist die *Kata* der Idee ähnlich. Während die Idee jedoch etwas rein Transzendentes ist, das die wahrnehmbare Gestalt [einfach nur] übersteigt, kann sich die Kata nicht anders als in wahrnehmbaren Formen zeigen.[24]

Ähnlich wie bei einer begrifflich erfassten „Idee" stellt die Kata das allgemeine „Wesen" einer Sache bzw. einer Bewegung dar. Im Gegensatz zu ersterer erhält die stoffliche, materiell-körperliche Manifestation der Kata ihre Bedeutung aber nicht erst aus einer Teilhabe an dieser, sondern die sinnlich wahrnehmbare Verkörperung der Kata selbst ist das genuine Medium, in der sich diese als das zeigt, was sie ist. Die Kata, das „Wesen" bzw. der „geistige Gehalt" einer leiblichen Bewegung oder Haltung, hat keine ihrer räumlichen und zeitlichen Erscheinung vorausliegende und von

---

24. MINAMOTO 1992, 29. Übersetzung des Autors.

dieser unabhängige Existenz, sondern ist nur im Moment ihrer Verkörperung und Einübung – die zugleich ihre eigentliche Ausübung darstellt – verwirklicht.

Die Kata übersteigt ihre spezifischen Aktualisierungen zwar in dem Sinne, dass sie das Ideal einer bestmöglichen Übungsform darstellt und intersubjektiv von Körper zu Körper übermittelt werden kann, ist aber von der fundamentalen Zeitlichkeit der körperlichen Welt insofern weiterhin betroffen, als sie sich mit dem leiblich-geistigen Selbst- und Weltverhältnis der sie ein- und ausübenden Übungsgemeinschaft verändert. Die Kata ist daher gewissermaßen ein performatives Artefakt, das sich nicht objektiv fixieren, sondern nur am eigenen Leibe spüren und verkörpern lässt. Die von anderen Menschen in leiblicher Mimesis übernommene Kata transformiert den leiblich Übenden und der individuelle Körper des Übenden individualisiert die Kata.

Die eigentliche Wirksamkeit der Kata entfaltet sich erst in einer auf ständiger Wiederholung aufbauenden *Habitualisierung*, bei der das performative Muster mitsamt seinen synästhetischen Gehalten und den in ihm eingelagerten Weisen des leiblichen Selbst- und Weltbestverhältnisses in den allgemeinen Lebensvollzug des übenden Individuums und seiner Gemeinschaft übergeht. Die jeweils habitualisierte leibliche Gesamtgestalt der individuellen und kollektiven Existenz bildet dann die geformte Ausgangsbasis für weitere iterative Transformationen und Folgehabitualisierungen, in einem auch auf das alltägliche Handeln übergreifenden Prozess der körperlichen Selbstgestaltung des Übenden und seiner Gemeinschaft in Form von Bewegungsmustern und Gesten.

Der grundlegende Ansatz der Kata-Übung besteht dabei darin, die sich im jeweiligen Augenblick vollziehende Konstitution des leiblichen Bewusstseins dadurch zu transformieren, dass dem Körper eine spezifische Form gegeben wird, die dem Übenden als Anhaltspunkt dient, sich spürend und zugleich handelnd in sich selbst und seinen Weltbezug zu vertiefen, um schließlich eine neue Form des verkörperten In-der-Welt-Seins daraus hervorgehen zu lassen.

ZUM SCHLUSS: DAS VERHÄLTNIS VON KÖRPER UND LEIB IN
DER KATA-ÜBUNG UND DIE PHILOSOPHISCHE LEBENSKUNST

Die Kata-Übung stellt sowohl eine Formgebung des objektiv wahrnehmbaren *Körpers*, als auch eine spürbare Wandlung des in unmittelbarer Selbstwahrnehmung (Propriozeption) gegebenen *Leibes* dar.[25] Die Bedeutung des leiblichen Spürens für den Übungsprozess besteht vor allem darin, dass es den genuinen Bezug des Übenden zu sich selbst als eines leiblichen Wesens herstellt. Es handelt sich um einen non-repräsentationalen, da in unmittelbarer Präsenz vollzogenen Bezug des Übenden zu sich selbst, der aufgrund der Einbettung desselben in seine Umwelt zugleich einen Selbstbezug des situativen Handlungsgeschehens als Ganzem darstellt. Da im Spüren kein deutlicher Unterschied zwischen Eigenem und Fremdem getroffen werden kann, vermittelt es in einem weder rein aktiv erzeugten noch rein passiv erlebten, sondern medial sich ereignenden Übungsprozess zwischen beiden Polen.[26]

Dieser spürend zu gestaltende und handelnd zu erspürende Selbstbezug der Kata-Übung macht die Übungswege zu Künsten im Medium der Propriozeption.[27] So wie sich Malerei primär im visuellen und Musik im auditiven Sinnesfeld entfalten und diese Künste die Möglichkeit bieten, das Offenbar-Werden bzw. In-Erscheinung-Treten der jeweiligen Sinnesfelder *in statu nascendi* zu zeigen, das heißt, den vorgegenständlichen Bedeutungshorizont der in ihnen erscheinenden gegenständlichen Phänomene in Form einer nur vage zu greifenden „Atmosphäre"[28] anzudeuten, so bietet die Kata-Übung der Wegkünste die Möglichkeit, den Konstitutionsprozess des leiblich spür-

---

25. Zur Leib-Körper-Unterscheidung siehe DEMMERLING 2011, 7–27. Zum leiblichen Spüren siehe SCHMITZ 1965. Es wird an dieser Stelle davon ausgegangen, das Leib und Körper keine ontologisch getrennten Kategorien darstellen, sondern sich auf verschiedene Bereiche sinnlicher Wahrnehmung beziehen, die gemeinsam mit anderen Sinnesmodalitäten ein gemeinsames Feld der Synästhesie bilden, in welchem die verschiedenen Sinnkonstitutionen der Einzelsinne wechselseitig aufeinander Bezug nehmen.

26. Die Bedeutung des leiblichen Spürens für die ostasiatischen Philosophie- und Übungstraditionen zeigt sich in dem reichhaltigen Wortfeld rund um den Begriff des „Ki" (氣 oder 気, chin. *Qi*), der sich auf eine eng mit dem Atmen verbundene, leiblich spürbare Form dynamischer Lebensenergie bezieht. Siehe ELBERFELD 2014, 303–12.

27. Für eine Behandlung der Kampfkunst als einer Kunstform im Medium der Propriozeption siehe SCHRENK 2014, 101–16.

28. Zur Bedeutung des Begriffs der „Atmosphäre" für die Ästhetik siehe BÖHME 2014.

baren Sinnesfeldes übend zu erforschen und ein praktisch erworbenes Wissen hierüber zu erlangen. Die Übungswege bieten diese Möglichkeit, indem sie Kunst nicht als *poiesis*, d. h. als Herstellung gegenständlicher Werke, vielleicht auch nicht nur als „Erfahrung"[29], sondern als Verkörperungsübung verständlich machen. Die Übung kennt keine klare Differenz zwischen Künstler und Publikum – das primäre Publikum des oder der Übenden ist er oder sie selbst; und eine mögliche Zuschauerin kann nur dann wirklich erfahren, was eine Kata bedeutet, wenn sie sie mit dem eigenen Körper übt und am eigenen Leib spürt.

Aufgrund des sich im Spüren konstituierenden Selbstbezugs ermöglicht die Kata-Übung eine reflektierte Auseinandersetzung des oder der Übenden mit der eigenen leiblichen Existenz in gegenwärtiger Selbstgegebenheit, und damit eine Form von Selbstsorge (*epimeleia heautou*), die einen Beitrag zur philosophischen Lebensführung leisten kann. Da sich das leibliche Spüren immer in einer Ambivalenz zwischen Selbst- und Fremdbezug bewegt, kann die innere (nicht bloß externe) Relation meiner selbst zur Welt und zu anderen Wesen in der Entfaltung leiblicher Resonanzen erforscht werden, worin sich auch ein innerer Zusammenhang von Ästhetik (Sinnlichkeit) und Ethik (Mitgefühl, Responsivität) im Üben ankündigt.

Da die Wegkünste sich neben dem Spüren auch am visuell beobachtbaren Körper vollziehen, ist zudem die Möglichkeit einer intersubjektiven Auseinandersetzung gegeben. Denn aus meinem Vollzug der Kata wird ersichtlich, ob dieser offensichtliche Mängel aufweist, etwa wenn ich Körperregionen anspanne, die keiner Anspannung bedürfen, oder wenn ich eine Bewegung nur mit dem Arm ausführe, ohne meinen Körper als Ganzes einzubeziehen, d.h. ohne eine Relation zwischen Arm, leiblichem Zentrum (腹 bzw. 丹田) und „Himmel und Erde" (天地) herzustellen. In der Übung durchdringen sich körperliche Handlung und leibliches Spüren wechselseitig, weshalb es erfahrenen Übenden möglich ist, bei der visuellen Beobachtung der körperlichen Bewegungen einer anderen Person zugleich zu *spüren*, ob das die Kata durchziehende leibliche Kräfteschema stimmig ist oder nicht. Auch bei Partnerübungen (etwa in den Kampfkünsten) wird dies ersichtlich, da ich und mein Partner uns sowohl wechselseitig als Körper visuell wahrneh-

---

29. DEWEY 1934. Mit Deweys Begriff der Erfahrung ließe sich jedoch durchaus an Formen des Übens anknüpfen.

men, als auch den von uns gemeinsam gebildeten leiblichen Zusammenhang intersubjektiv erspüren, d. h. uns sowohl körperlich voneinander absetzen als auch leiblich miteinander verschmelzen.[30]

Die (immer wieder aufs Neue zu vollziehende) Vollendung der Kata-Übung wird in den Übungswegen zumeist darin verortet, dass die Kata nicht mehr bewusst ausgeführt wird, sondern sich „von selbst" (自然) ereignet. Man spricht in diesem Fall auch davon, dass sich der Übende nicht mehr im Zustand des „seienden Geistes" (有心), sondern des „Nicht-Geistes" (無心) befindet.[31] Das heißt, es ist nun nicht mehr sein vermeintlich für sich bestehendes Selbst, das den Körper bewegt, sondern der Übungsvollzug ereignet sich aus sich selbst heraus, ohne erkennbares Handlungszentrum. Es gibt keinen Ort, an dem der Geist (im Sinne eines Handlungszentrums) verortet werden könnte, er wird zu einem *Erewhon*, einem „Nirgendwo", das zugleich überall ist. Das heißt jedoch nicht, dass der geistige Aspekt des Übungsgeschehens in einer abstrakten Transzendenz jenseits des körperlichen Vollzugs verschwindet, er geht vielmehr so umfassend in der körperlichen Präsenz des Übenden auf, dass er mit dem körperlich-leiblichen Vollzug selbst verschmilzt, zum verkörperten Horizont des situativen Übungsgeschehens an sich wird. In einem derartig radikal verkörperten Übungsvollzug erweist sich das Selbst als Nicht-Selbst, konkretisiert sich der Geist zum Körper, ermöglicht die körperliche Kopräsenz von Übendem und Welt das Offenbar-Werden ihres Entstehens in wechselseitiger Abhängigkeit, verschwimmen Bewegung und Beweger ineinander, verschmilzt das Subjekt mit seinem Handeln und Spüren, ist der Übende sein Leib, und doch bleiben die Differenzen erhalten, möglicherweise nur in sublimierter Weise. Diese performativ konstituierte wechselseitige Durchdrin-

---

30. Die innere Verfasstheit eines solchen Übungsvorgangs, die sich prinzipiell in jeder leiblich-körperlichen Erfahrung findet, lässt sich letztlich wahrscheinlich nur mithilfe einer paradoxen Struktur beschreiben. Mit dem japanischen Philosophen Nishida Kitarō könnte man von einer „diskontinuierlichen Kontinuität" (非連続の連続) zwischen Selbst und Anderem bzw. Selbst und Welt sprechen. Zur im Hintergrund dieses Begriffs stehenden Logik der „absolut widersprüchlichen Selbstidentität" (絶対矛盾の自己同一), die unter anderem auch von der buddhistischen Prajñāpāramitā-Literatur beeinflusst wurde, siehe NISHIDA 2014, 56–114.

31. Zum Begriff des *mushin* im Zusammenhang mit der Schwertkunst siehe die Schriften des Zen-Meisters Takuan Sōhō, die dieser an den Schwertmeister Yagyū Munenori adressiert hat. TAKUAN 1986.

gung der Gegensätze stellt zugleich eine Übergangsschwelle dar, an der die körperliche Nachahmung der vorgegebenen und als Einschränkung der eigenen Individualität erfahrenen Kata in den Hintergrund tritt und eine freie Variation derselben im Spiel der leiblichen Kräfte ihren Ausgang findet. Eine solche Erfahrung kann als höchst konkrete und individuelle, d. h. verkörperte Erfahrung von Freiheit verstanden werden, die allerdings nicht nur dem persönlichen Individuum zugerechnet werden kann, sondern sich zugleich „welthaft" ereignet.

Derartige Erfahrungen und die in den japanischen Übungswegen verwandte Terminologie müssen jedoch noch genauer phänomenologisch ausgewiesen und differenziert werden, bevor eine eingehendere Analyse ihrer Bedeutung für die menschliche Lebensform sowie für eine selbstkritische Gestaltung derselben erfolgen kann. Die phänomenologische Methode scheint mir hierfür insofern besonders sinnvoll, als dass das Üben der Kata stets an eine direkte und konkrete Erfahrung am eigenen Leibe geknüpft ist und die Phänomenologie eben darin besteht, derartige „Erste-Person-Erfahrungen" für die philosophische Reflexion fruchtbar zu machen. Bei der Aufarbeitung der Möglichkeiten des körperlichen Übens für eine reflektierte Lebenspraxis stehen wir noch immer am Anfang. Es erfordert m. E. eine genaue Auseinandersetzung mit den aus unterschiedlichen Kulturen überlieferten theoretischen Hintergründen sowie einen Einbezug der dort zu finden Praktiken des leiblichen Übens in die phänomenologische Methode, um dieses Forschungsfeld weiter zu erschließen.

## Literaturverzeichnis

Benesch, Oleg
 2014 *Inventing the Way of the Samurai: Nationalism, Internationalism, and Bushidō in Modern Japan.* Oxford (u.a.): Oxford Univ. Press.

Böhme, Gernot
 2014 *Atmosphäre. Essays zur neuen Ästhetik*, 2. Aufl. der 7., erw. und überarb. Aufl., Berlin: Suhrkamp.

Demmerling, Christoph
 2011 „Den Leib zur Sprache bringen: Überlegungen zur Leib-Körper-Unterscheidung", in: *Allgemeine Zeitschrift für Philosophie* 36/1: 7–27.

Dewey, John
 1934 *Art as experience*, London: Allen & Unwin.

Dōgen
- 1970 Terada Tōru 寺田 透, Mizuno Yaoko 水野弥穗子 (Hg.).『道元』[Dōgen], 日本思想大系, Bd. 12. Tōkyō: Iwanami Shoten.
- 2006 *Shōbōgenzō. Ausgewählte Schriften; anders philosophieren aus dem Zen*, übersetzt, erläutert und herausgegeben von Ryōsuke Ōhashi und Rolf Elberfeld. Tokyo/Stuttgart: Keio Univ. Press/Frommann-Holzboog.
- 2002 *The Heart of Dōgen's Shōbōgenzō*, transl. and annot. by Norman Waddell und Masao Abe, Albany, NY: SUNY Press.

Elberfeld, Rolf
- 2011 „Handelnde Anschauung (kōiteki chokkan): Nishida und die Praxis der Künste", in: *Allgemeine Zeitschrift für Philosophie* 36/3: 313–44.
- 2014 *Sprache und Sprachen. Eine philosophische Grundorientierung*, 3. Aufl., Freiburg: Alber.

Elberfeld et al.
- 2000 *Denkansätze zu einer buddhistischen Philosophie in China: Seng Zhao – Jizang – Fazang. Zwischen Übersetzung und Interpretation*, Köln: edition chōra.

Foucault, Michel
- 2009 *Hermeneutik des Subjekts. Vorlesungen am College de France (1981/82)*, übersetzt von Ulrike Bokelmann, Frankfurt a. M.: Suhrkamp.

Gainty, Denis
- 2013 *Martial Arts and the Body Politic in Meiji Japan*, London (u.a.): Routledge.

Heinemann, Robert Klaus (1979)
- 1979 *Der Weg des Übens im ostasiatischen Mahāyāna. Grundformen seiner Zeitrelation zum Übungsziel in der Entwicklung bis Dōgen*, Wiesbaden: Harrassowitz.

Leibniz, Gottfried W.
- 1982 *Vernunftprinzipien der Natur und Gnade/Monadologie*, übers. v. A. Buchenau, Hamburg: Felix Meiner.

Leighton, Taigen Dan
- 2008 „Zazen as an Enactment Ritual", in: Steven Heine und Dale S. Wright, *Zen Ritual: Studies of Zen Buddhist Theory in Practice*. Oxford (u.a.): Oxford Univ. Press, 167–84.

Menke, Christoph
- 2003 „Zweierlei Übung: Zum Verhältnis von sozialer Disziplinierung und ästhetischer Existenz", in: Honneth, Axel; Saar, Martin (Hg.): *Michel Foucault: Zwischenbilanz einer Rezeption. Frankfurter Foucault Konferenz 2001*, Frankfurt a. M.: Suhrkamp.

Merleau-Ponty, Maurice
- 1986 *Das Sichtbare und das Unsichtbare, gefolgt von Arbeitsnotizen*, hg. u. mit

einem Nachw. versehen v. Claude Lefort, übers. v. Regula Giuliani und Bernhard Waldenfels, München: Fink.

MINAMOTO Ryōen 源了圓編
1989 『型化』[Kata]. Tokyo: Sōbunsha.
1992 (Hg.) 『型と日本文化』[Kata und die japanische Kultur]. Tokyo: Sōbunsha.

NISHIDA Kitarō
1980 『西田幾多郎全集』[Nishita Kitarōs Gessamelte Werke], 3. Aufl. Tokyo: Iwanami, 1978–1980.
2014 „Selbstidentität und Kontinuität der Welt", übers. u. kommentiert v. Elmar Weinmayr, in: Ohashi Ryōsuke (Hg.): *Die Philosophie der Kyôto-Schule*, 3, erw. und mit einer Einf. vers. Aufl., Freiburg: Alber, 56–114.
2016 „Der geschichtliche Leib", übers. u. kommentiert von Leon Krings, in: *European Journal of Japanese Philosophy* 1: 217–46.

OBERT, Mathias
2007 *Welt als Bild. Die theoretische Grundlegung der chinesischen Berg-Wasser-Malerei zwischen dem 5. und dem 12. Jahrhundert*. Freiburg (u.a.): Alber.

RICHIE, Donald
2007 *A Tractate on Japanese Aesthetics*. Berkeley, CA: Stone Bridge Press.

SCHMITZ, Hermann
1965 *System der Philosophie 2.1: Der Leib*, Bonn: Bouvier.

SCHRENK, Markus
2014 „Is proprioceptive art possible?", in: Priest, Graham; Young, Damon (Hg.): *Philosophy and the Martial Arts: Engagement*. New York: Routledge, 101–16.

SLOTERDIJK, Peter
2009 *Du mußt dein Leben ändern. Über Anthropotechnik*. Frankfurt a. M.: Suhrkamp.

STEINECK, Christian et al.
2002 *Dôgen als Philosoph*. Wiesbaden: Harrassowitz.

TAKUAN Sōhō
1986 *The Unfettered Mind: Writings from a Zen Master to a Master Swordsman*, transl. by William Scott Wilson. Tokyo: Kodansha International.

WILSON, William Scott
2014 *The Swordsman's Handbook: Samurai Teachings on the Path of the Sword*. Boston (u.a.): Shambhala.

ZEAMI 世阿彌
1974 『世阿彌・禪竹』[Seami, Zenchiku], 日本思想大系, Bd. 24, Tōkyō: Iwanami Shoten.
1986 *Die geheime Überlieferung des Nō, Aufgezeichnet von Meister Seami, aus dem Japan*. übertr. und erl. von Oscar Benl, 2.Aufl., Frankfurt a. M.: Insel-Verlag.

Jordančo Sekulovski
*Temple University, Japan*

# Watsuji's Ethics from the Perspective of *Kata* as a Technology of the Self

This paper investigates the history of systems of thought different from those of the West. A closer look at Japan's long philosophical tradition draws attention to the presence of uniquely designed acculturation and training techniques designed as *kata* or *shikata* (型 or 仕形), shedding light on *kata* as a generic technique of self-perfection and self-transformation. By seeing *kata* as foundational to the Japanese mind and comparing it to Michel Foucault's research on technologies of the self, the groundwork is laid for a comparative analysis in terms of the principle of ἐπιμελεῖσθαι σαυτοῦ (taking care of oneself), an ethical and aesthetic paradigm dating back to European antiquity. Not only does this bring to light their similarities as techniques of individuation, it also reinforces the importance of Watsuji's relational understanding of human being.

KEYWORDS: *kata*—Watsuji Tetsurō—Michel Foucault—technologies of the self—*aidagara*—*rinrigaku*—interrelation—in-betweenness

The word *kata* is used in Japanese to refer to a set of uniquely designed acculturation and training techniques and practices known as *shikata* or *kata*. Contemporary research has neglected the importance of *kata*, whose various expressions developed over centuries, in favor of notions like *ambiguity* (曖昧さ), *dependency* (甘え), *the Japanese sense of beauty* (美学) and even *bushidō* (武士道, the way of the samurai). In so doing, a fundamental pillar of the Japanese pursuit of self-transformation and a potential key to a more comprehensive understanding of the Japanese mind has fallen by the wayside. Admittedly the idea of *kata* is as elusive to scholars at home as it has been to their counterparts in the West. This is not to say that we lack resources on the subject but only that the notion of *kata* itself docs not seem to have received the fuller attention it deserves.[1]

*Kata* or *shikata* refers to a particular way of doing things that puts the emphasis on the form and order of an actual process. Analyzing the etymology of the compound term *shikata*, we see that *shi* 仕 has the double sense of *support* and *serve*, while *kata* 型 or 形 commonly translates as *form* or *pattern*. Boyé De Mente has defined *kata* as a relationship between

> an inner order (the individual heart) and a natural order (the cosmos), and these two were linked together by form—by *kata*. It was *kata* that linked the individual and society.[2]

In his view, *kata* is to be seen as a sort of repetitive self-actualizing process or action, while at the same time it serves the formal function of unifying the

---

1. One notable scholar known for his extensive research on the topic of *kata* is Minamoto Ryōen. Unfortunately, none of his works have been translated into English and the only available reference to his comprehensive work on this subject remains the excerpt in HEISIG, KASULIS, MARALDO 2011, 930–5.
2. DEMENTE 2003, 15.

physical and the spiritual aspects of the human existence. It is not a question of embodying or harmonizing with any universal, metaphysical principles. *Kata* is not a vehicle for conveying hidden truths or uncovering the inner nature of things, rather it is simply a *model for shaping interrelational experience*. De Mente further argues the institutional and ritual characteristics of *kata* suggest a connection with morality in the sense that one's actions can be said to be "in *kata*" or "out of *kata*" (型にはまる・はまらない). To be "out of *kata*" is to oppose reason or the will of society, and in this sense, as we shall see, puts us in touch with the foundations of ethics in Japan.

## Watsuji's *Rinri* and *Aidagara* in Relation to *Kata*

Watsuji Tetsurō's major work *Rinrigaku* (*Ethics*)[3] offers an original and critical perspective on modern attempts to ground ethics solely on the actions and decisions of the conscious individual subject. Watsuji argues against western conceptions of human being that put the individual at the center of all modes of existence and then substitute it for the totality of all human existence . This view of the world, Watsuji claims, can be traced back to the assumption that the isolated ego is the proper starting point for modern philosophy.[4] When this approach is applied to the field of ethics and the existential problems that face us as human beings, it ends up with a flawed account of human agency for the simple reason that the solitary, isolated subject is merely an abstraction from a wider complex of interpersonal relationships. Consequently, this fixation on the isolated ego as a conceptual pivot distracts attention from what Watsuji sees as the true starting point for ethics: *concrete human existence* with an emphasis on human beings as contemplating subjects. This is why he insists that ethical problems cannot properly be framed without reliance on ideas such as social happiness or human welfare, therefore ethics cannot rely on individual consciousness

---

3. This paper is a result of multiple presentations aimed at expanding my earlier research by encompassing Watsuji's use of the notion of *rin* as an expression of *kata*. In my doctoral thesis (SEKULOVSKI 2013) I argue that François Laruelle's non-standard philosophy, as an all-encompassing posture and practice of Man, has similarities to the notion of *kata* and can therefore help generate new forms of what Laruelle calls *generic knowledge*.

4. WATSUJI, 1996, 11.

alone and needs to give way to a more relational and interdependent understanding of human being.

## Kata and the Grand "rin" of human beings

While Watsuji acknowledges that the notion of *rinri* (倫理 the Sino-Japanese term for ethics) is rooted in ancient Chinese thought, he makes it clear that he does not intend to argue for a revival or modern reconstruction of the Chinese classics in order to restore the significance of ethics as a Way. Rather, he attempts to situate ethics firmly and irrevocably within human relationships, and to center its attention on what goes on in the "in-between," on the actions and consequences that arise in interactions among individuals. Watsuji understands the glyph *rin* to carry the sense of *nakama* (なかま) or "fellowship," that is to say, a system of relationships among a given group of individuals that determines their mode of human existence. *Nakama* is thus intended not as an abstract logical principle but as a concrete point of reference to the interactions that bring people into contact with one another. At the same time, Watsuji continues, *rin* includes the dimension of *kimari* (決まり) agreement) or *kata* (form) as the basis of bringing order (秩序) to human relationships. In a word, *rin* is the *Way of human beings*.

Watsuji understands the second glyph, *ri*, to connote a general sense of *rationality*. It refers to the patterns of activity or relationship that can be seen to take place in the fellowship of *rin*:

> Therefore, *rinri*, that is, ethics, is the order or the pattern through which the communal existence of human beings is rendered possible. In other words, ethics consists of the laws of social existence.[5]

The significance of *rin*, as *nakama*, *kimari*, and therefore also *kata*, constitutes the order among human beings, in this manner, *rin*, *kata*, and, *aidagara* are correlated in such a manner that the latter empowers the *rin* (as a form) rendering it possible and empowering its continuity.

## What lies in-between?

On this basis, Watsuji postulates:

5. Watsuji 1996, 11.

The locus of ethical problems lies not in the consciousness of the isolated individual, but precisely in the in-betweenness of person and person. Because of this, ethics is the study of *ningen*.[6]

It is precisely the emphasis of this "in-betweenness" among individuals that allows Watsuji to rethink the concept of ethics and move away from the kind of individual-centered ethics that runs deep in the philosophical traditions of the West. There is no way to get at the heart of ethical problems solely in reliance on the experiences and contemplative efforts of individuals. Attention to the in-betweenness of person and person is crucial if we are to shift ethics away from regulative principles and the clarification of moral responsibilities towards our fellow human beings and towards the study of the human. The Japanese word Watsuji uses for "human" is composed of two characters: *nin* or *hito* (人), meaning person or human being, and *gen* or *aida* (間) meaning space or between. Watsuji insists that a human being is not simply an individual but a member of various social groupings, and as such should be defined fundamentally as a "we" rather than as an "I." Accordingly, "to be an I" means "to be a part of a correlative we," that is, a "we" composed of multiple "I"s. This in turn implies that for a human individual to "exist" means to "be among" one's fellow human beings. This essential correlatedness is what Watsuji calls *aidagara* or *betweenness*.

The term *aidagara* is composed of two glyphs: *aida* or *gen*, referred to in the previous paragraph, and *gara* (柄), which can mean nature or—more in keeping with Watsuji's usage—pattern. Putting the two together, then, *aidagara* translates literally as a "between pattern" or more simply, a relationship. The appearance of the same glyph 間 in both *ningen* and *aidagara* has nothing to do with the physical distance between individuals. If Watsuji's notion of "in-betweeness" were basically spatial, it might easily be dismissed as a kind of naïve realism. Avoiding that sense complicates our efforts to translate the word in the various contexts in which it is used. At times, *among* helps elucidate its intended meaning, as in the phrase *among one's fellow human beings*. In any case, the "space" that *gara* refers to is a *mid-place* in-between individuals, not a place that exists prior their interaction. This mid-place is defined, in turn, by an all-encompassing form or *rin* of human

---

6. Ibid., 10.

relationships that *are individuated among and within the interrelational pattern.* To capture this all-inclusive interrelationality in which individuals are wrapped up, we might better render the word *aidagara* "with-in" instead of the usual "in-between."

### Foucault's technologies of the self in late antiquity

Michel Foucault argued that the pursuit of ethical and aesthetical ideals in European antiquity stressed the importance of a unified practice and theory to empower a particular aesthetic of existence. The ancient principle of ἐπιμελεῖσθαι σεαυτόν or *taking care of oneself* stands behind the time-worn idea of caring not only for one's body but also and primarily for one's mind or soul. This ideal flourished at a time in European history when the view of the human being as an individual agent was taking shape and thus enabled the emergence of a specific set of what Foucault liked to call "technologies of self-creation."[7] These acculturation and training techniques allowed individuals to pursue, alone or with help of others, a course of disciplined practice for body, soul, thought, conduct, and overall state of being. The aim was a self-transformation that would usher in a state of happiness, purity, wisdom, perfection, or even immortality. As a result, the guiding principle of *taking care of oneself* was replaced with the principle γνῶθι σεαυτόν, *know thyself*.

This shift of direction in intellectual practice affected the subsequent orientation of European civilization, accentuating the place of reason and the role of the contemplating subject while at the same time sidelining technologies of the self nurtured under the earlier ideal of *taking care of oneself*. To this day, Foucault argues, western culture is guided by the principle of *knowing thyself*, effectively enshrining the individualist spirit as the very epitome of what it means to be human. Numerous ancient cultures, like the Greeks, fostered an interest at various times throughout their history in techniques and aesthetic practices aimed at enhancing existence, in modes of individuation and forms of self-discipline carried out through observation and experimentation whose only goal was to transform and better one-

---

7. For further details, see Foucault 1984.

self. In the case of Japan, the same *kata* that played a role in morality was also employed to facilitate and mediate one's pursuit of a certain aesthetics of existence. As was the case with the ancient Greeks, *kata* was also equated with beauty.

## *Kata* as a technology of the self

As disciplines for body, mind, and conduct aimed at achieving purity, wisdom, and perfection, *kata* and the ancient principle of *taking care of oneself* appear to be interchangeable. A consideration of the Tea Ceremony, one of the most emblematic of the traditional arts of Japan, bears this out. *Chadō* (茶道), the Way of Tea, is based on the use of *kata* and its principles reflect the will to master oneself through various disciplines of body, mind, and conduct. Precepts of *chadō* like harmony (和), respect (敬), purity (清) and tranquility (寂) show striking similarities to precepts articulated in European antiquity. The influence of Zen Buddhism on *chadō* and other traditional arts has carried over to Japanese modes of living and ways of thinking in general. In the same way, the use of *kata* came to serve as a *generic technique for the self-creation and self-transformation of individuals*, thus expanding its impact on Japanese society as a whole. The shift in paradigms that Foucault points out in Europe does not directly apply to Japan, where the old paradigm has survived down the centuries. Simply put, we may say that *kata* serves as a means of practical connection or fellowship, and that these specific forms or patterns circumscribe the topology of human interaction within which human relationships take place.

### *Kata as a dynamic principle*

Watsuji defines these kata of practical interaction as something that

> cannot itself exist apart from these connections. As specific forms in which human beings act, they exist only together with these practical connections. But when dynamic human existence is actualized repeatedly, in a definite manner, we can grasp this pattern that constantly makes its appearance in separation from the basis of this dynamic sort of existence.[8]

---

8. Watsuji 1996, 11.

The repetition of *kata* in a defined manner discloses the pattern of relationships within which human beings define themselves.

John Maraldo points out that Watsuji's conception of *ningen* represents a dynamic concept of the self in which identity is not fixed or determined but shaped interrelationally, in-between person and person, and thus subject to continual change. For Watsuji, to be human is also to be ethical, and one cannot be either unless one is both an individual and at the same time correlated to others. Watsuji, we recall, defined ethical conduct as the order or the pattern through which the communal existence of human beings is rendered possible; in other words, to be *ningen* means to navigate freely between the social and the individual. Maraldo goes on so say that *ningen*,

> although being subjective communal existence as the interconnection of acts, at the same time, is an individual that acts through these connections. This subjective and dynamic structure does not allow us to account for *ningen* as a 'thing' or 'substance.'[9]

To be *ningen* is to stand in a dynamic relationship—between the individual and the social, never just one or the other—and therefore cannot be conceived of in terms of a stable or complete structure or mode of being. Watsuji conceives *ningen* both as an individual and at the same time as a *subjective communal existence*, pointing at the non-dualist character of *ningen* seen as a totality of human beings established through the negation of individuality and expressed through the relational existence or pattern in-between person and person.

In this vein, Watsuji remarks of human existence that it

> infinitely aims at the realization of communal existence by virtue that human beings are *ningen*. Because of this, the pattern of practical connections already realized serves, at the same time, as a pattern yet to be achieved.[10]

This pattern of connections and its resultant ethic are regarded not as a goal to be reached but as something that needs to be *achieved infinitely*. It is, we may say, a *kata* that allows human existence to be realized as com-

---

9. Maraldo 2002, 185.
10. Watsuji 1996, 12.

munal existence. Its inclusive character provides for the emergence of the in-between or *aidagara* as an essential dimension of existence for *ningen*, a dimension in which the in-between is not an empty void but a form with an individuating function. The elusive character of this *kata* of interconnectedness accounts for its role as a pillar of the nondual, communal existence of *ningen* in-between the social and individual. As such, *kata* is not metaphysical in nature but relational. It presents as a model that give shape to *aida*, the with-in. For these reasons, I am persuaded that *kata* is the most fundamental constituent in the makeup of the Japanese mind in the sense that it defines the respective roles and forms that constitute the actual relational matrix of each individual *rin* in relation to the totality of *ningen*.

## Concluding remarks

The foregoing has tried to present a rationale for comparative research on the notion of *kata* in relation to Foucault's research on the technologies of the self in the ancient Greco-Roman world, and to suggest further examination of the role of *kata* as a fundamental pillar and technique for individual self-creation and self-transformation in Japan. My aim was to highlight possible commonalities between alternative systems of thought that appear at first to be closed in on themselves and inaccessible to one another. There is no doubt that common practices are a way to enhance mutual understanding. Further attention to the role played by *kata* in shaping the aesthetics of existence in Japan can make a contribution in the same direction.

## References

De Mente, Boyé Lafayette
  2003 *Kata: The Key to Understanding and Dealing with the Japanese*. Rutland, vt: Tuttle Publishing.
Foucault, Michel
  1984 *Histoire de la sexualité III. Le souci de soi*. Paris: Gallimard.
Heisig, James W., Thomas P. Kasulis, and John C. Maraldo
  2011 *Japanese Philosophy: A Sourcebook*. Honolulu: University of Hawai'i Press.

MARALDO, John
    2002    "*Watsuji Tetsuro's Ethics: Totalitarian or Communitarian?*" in Rolf Elberfeld and Günter Wohlfart, eds., *Komparative Ethik. Das gute Leben zwischen den Kulturen*. Köln: Edition Chora.

SEKULOVSKI, Jordančo
    2013    *Postures et pratiques de l'Homme. Libéralisme, philosophie non-standard et pensée japonaise*. Paris: L'Harmattan.

SOSHITSU Sen
    1994    *Vie du thé, esprit du thé*. Paris: Jean-Cyrille Godefroy.

WATSUJI Tetsurō
    1996    *Wastuji Tetsuro's Rinrigaku: Ethics in Japan*. Translated by Yamamoto Seisaku and Robert E. Carter. Albany, NY: SUNY Press.

Kuroda Akinobu
*Université de Strasbourg*

Lieu de médiation

Nishida, Tanabe, Simondon

Nous nous proposons dans cette intervention de structurer synchroniquement trois moments philosophiques d'origines différentes : l'intuition agissante chez Kitarō Nishida, la dialectique de la médiation absolue chez Hajime Tanabe et la philosophie de l'individuation chez Gilbert Simondon, dans un contexte de réflexion philosophique sur la nature de la vie humaine. Les trois moments semblent susceptibles de se croiser, se critiquer et se compléter dans un terrain *transductif* au sens où l'entend Simondon. C'est ce nouveau terrain que nous entendons défricher afin d'ouvrir une perspective où un individu humain se transforme en agent responsable d'un transhumanisme à travers le processus de l'individuation dynamique et *transindividuelle*, laquelle nous préparerait à l'émergence du posthumain dans un futur proche.

KEYWORDS: intuition agissante—logique de l'espèce—dialectique de la médiation absolue—individuation—transduction—information—antisubstantialisme—synchronisation structurée—habitude—relationalism

Ce texte se propose de présenter Nishida, Tanabe et Simondon comme trois moments philosophiques : moment critique représenté par Tanabe, moment réactif représenté par Nishida et moment médiateur représenté par Simondon ; ces trois moments, comme nous le verrons, se critiquent, mais surtout se complètent les uns les autres. Nous présentons ainsi ces trois philosophes directement dans un espace discursif en une langue commune. Nous souhaitons nous concentrer ainsi d'entrée de jeu sur une discussion philosophique sans passer par des démarches philologiques et chronologiques. Il ne s'agit donc pas d'une étude *comparative* qui se contente de recéler des points communs ou bien d'une affinité cachée derrière les apparences textuelles qui sont visiblement différentes les unes par rapport aux autres.

A travers cette démarche argumentative, nous allons constater, malgré une manière quelquefois schématisée et simplifiée, comment ces trois moments philosophiques peuvent-ils fonctionner ensemble afin d'ouvrir une nouvelle perspective sur la notion d'humain, voire celle de *transhumain*.

L'ordre selon lequel les trois philosophes seront convoqués en tant que moments philosophiques dans ce qui suit n'est donc pas l'ordre chronologique, mais un ordre *synchronique structuré*, c'est-à-dire un ordre discursif par lequel une discussion philosophique peut se déployer de manière cohérente à partir d'éléments constitutifs d'origines différentes.

Ainsi, tenterons-nous de rétablir le dialogue interrompu entre Nishida et Tanabe qui aurait pu être plus fructueux et productif s'ils avaient été plus patients l'un avec l'autre de leur vivant, en sollicitant Simondon, en tant que médiateur, pour faire une intervention en faveur de cette tentative de réconciliation.

Afin de ne pas nous perdre sur le chemin qui s'annonce pénible, nous repérons rapidement, à titre préparatif et provisoire, quelques points qui nous permettront de rapprocher nos trois philosophes sur un terrain d'entente, qui n'est pas dépourvu de tension productive.

Premier point commun facile à constater, c'est que leurs textes sont tous redoutables. Leurs textes demandent une lecture remplie de patience et d'attention de notre part afin de pouvoir accéder à leur pensée philosophique véritablement dynamique.

Le deuxième point commun qu'on peut constater, c'est qu'ils sont tous anti-substantialistes. Ils s'opposent à tous les types de substantialisme qui présupposent d'une manière ou d'une autre qu'il y a quelque chose d'immuable et toujours identique à soi-même au-delà de l'existence réelle évolutive[1].

Un troisième point, c'est que nos trois philosophes accordent une première importance au processus et aux relations dynamiques par rapport aux termes fixes entre lesquels ils se forment et se réalisent. Ces termes sont considérés chez les trois comme conséquences d'un processus ou de relations se formant, non pas comme entités établies antérieurement au processus ou aux relations.

### Moment critique
*Tanabe s'oppose à Nishida*

Commençons à partir d'un moment critique qui sert comme un point de départ ou déclencheur de discussion. D'abord nous allons présenter Tanabe.

En 1930, Tanabe publie une critique virulente sur la philosophie de Nishida reçue comme assez brutale auprès de ses disciples proches dont la plupart étaient également disciples proches de Nishida. L'article[2] dans

---

1. Chez Tanabe, on relève un problème quant à la conception de la substance lorsqu'il s'agit du statut de l'État dans sa logique de l'espèce. Le philosophe japonais était notablement enclin à l'absolutisation de l'État de l'humanité, ou État universel. Pourtant, les États réellement existants sont tous des États toujours relatifs aux conditions historiques et ne sont donc jamais susceptibles de se transformer en État universel. Il est d'ailleurs impensable qu'une espèce comme l'État existant se transforme en genre dans la mesure où la logique de l'espèce ne fait qu'un avec la dialectique de la médiation absolue suivant laquelle aucun terme, aucune entité, aucun niveau ne constituent une substance qui reste toujours identique à elle-même, indépendamment des autres.

2. Il s'agit d'un essai signé par Tanabe Hajime, intitulé 「西田先生の教えを仰ぐ」 [Je sollicite un enseignement auprès du Professeur Nishida], paru initialement dans la revue 『哲学研究』

lequel Tanabe déploie une argumentation contre Nishida, selon laquelle « l'éveil à soi du néant absolu » constitue une idée métaphysique insaisissable par le raisonnement et qui dépasse donc par essence toutes les déterminations conceptuelles ; où la notion anti-substantialiste de Nishida, englobante de tous les êtres dans le néant, serait une idée mystique telle que la procession plotinienne, de sorte qu'elle n'indiquerait qu'une expérience religieuse n'ayant rien en commun avec le principe d'une connaissance conceptuelle en général, ni avec l'établissement d'un système de connaissance philosophique, opposé par définition à d'autres systèmes conceptuels. En un mot, Tanabe a ainsi critiqué l'absolutisme nishidien.

En d'autres termes, le point crucial de la critique de Tanabe consiste à dire que chez Nishida il manque d'une manière fatale un élément médiateur entre le tout qu'est le néant absolu, insaisissable selon Tanabe, et l'individu qui ne peut qu'être englouti dans le néant absolu et pour lequel il n'y a aucune voie lui permettant de raisonner étape par étape avec un certain degré de certitude. Dans ces conditions, le particulier (ou le singulier) ne peut qu'être subsumé dans l'universel sans aucun intermédiaire, de sorte qu'il se perd totalement dans l'universel.

Face à cette critique notablement brutale, Nishida, quant à lui, tâche de s'en défendre dans un essai écrit vers la fin de 1930[3]. Tout en admettant que la notion de « néant absolu » contient une signification religieuse, Nishida s'efforce de faire comprendre qu'il s'agit d'un principe épistémologique fondamental consistant à fonder toutes les connaissances sur le *fait* de la détermination auto-éveillée du néant absolu[4], là où la *connaissance immanente de soi* s'éprouve le plus intimement et se révèle la plus globale. Mais cette réponse implicite de Nishida à la critique de Tanabe reste insuffisante dans la mesure où Nishida n'arrive pas à proposer un point médiateur à l'intérieur de sa philosophie.

Concernant le problème d'un point médiateur chez Nishida, en parti-

---

[Etudes philosophiques], N° 170, p. 429–68, repris dans TANABE 1964, 303–28.

3. 「私の絶対無の自覚的限定といふもの」[« Ce que j'appelle la détermination auto-éveillée du néant absolu »]. In 『無の自覚的限定』[Détermination auto-éveillée du néant] (1932), repris dans NKZ 5: 93–141.

4. « Ce que je nomme la détermination auto-éveillée du néant absolu […] possède une signification religieuse, en même temps qu'il constitue le fondement de l'établissement de la connaissance, au sens où le fait se détermine lui-même », NKZ 5: 127. Voir aussi *ibid.*, 107–8.

culière sa dernière tentative de concevoir l'espèce comme étant plastique, à laquelle nous reviendrons plus tard, lorsque nous nous penchons sur le deuxième moment de notre argumentation, le moment réactif.

*Qu'est-ce que «la logique de l'espèce»?*
Nous allons maintenant voir à quoi aboutit la critique de Tanabe sur Nishida, à savoir sa logique de l'espèce.

Dans les textes que Tanabe consacre à la présentation et développement de la logique de l'espèce, nous relevons trois traits représentatifs de cette logique.

*1. Une logique de l'intermédiaire.* C'est une logique dynamique en trois termes: individu – espèce – genre[5] qui se déterminent les uns les autres sans s'accorder une priorité d'ordre absolue. Si un problème se produit à un de ces trois niveaux il doit être médiatisé par les deux autres niveaux pour qu'il puisse être résolu. Pour la solution d'un problème qui se produit au niveau d'individu, d'espèce ou de genre, il est absolument nécessaire de passer par les deux autres niveaux.

*2. La dialectique de la médiation absolue*[6]. La logique de l'espèce et la dialectique de la médiation absolue sont les deux faces d'une même pièce.

La dialectique de la médiation absolue est une dialectique *négatrice* et non pas négative, dans laquelle tous les trois termes jouent le rôle de médiation. Dans cette logique, aucun élément n'est autodéterminé indépendamment des autres. La dialectique de la médiation absolue est conçue non seulement comme une logique suivant laquelle la réalité historico-sociale se dynamise, mais elle pourrait fournir aussi une méthode de pensée *transductive*[7]. La médiation absolue n'admet jamais un terme qui s'absolutise tout seul. En ce sens, la philosophie de Tanabe est un anti-absolutisme radical.

*3. La logique de la praxis pour une philosophie de l'être social.* La logique de l'espèce est aussi une logique de la praxis (en tant qu'action sociale) qui

---

5. Ces trois termes correspondent respectivement aux trois termes japonais: 個, 種, 類.
6. 絶対媒介の弁証法.
7. Sur ce point, nous reviendrons lorsque nous penchons sur le troisième moment philosophique de notre argumentation, moment médiateur, en faisant appel à la philosophie de Simondon.

se veut une théorie de base des individus afin que ceux-ci participent activement comme acteurs avec un objectif général de se donner l'humanité par l'intermédiaire de l'espèce à laquelle ils appartiennent sans absolutiser l'égocentrisme, ou bien devenir assujettit à la totalité.

*Le problème du substantialisation — une dérive fatale pour la logique de l'espèce.*

Lorsque la priorité ontologique est accordée au terme d'espèce par rapport aux deux autres termes constitutifs de « la logique de l'espèce » dont l'« individu » et le « genre », on se trouve forcément dans une aporie, pour autant que « la logique de l'espèce » et « la dialectique de la médiation absolue » soient indissociables l'une de l'autre chez Tanabe. Car, selon cette dernière, chacun des trois termes constitutifs de la logique de l'espèce doit passer nécessairement par les deux autres comme médiateurs indispensables, afin que tous les trois termes fonctionnent pleinement dans l'ensemble de cette logique, de sorte qu'il n'y aurait aucune priorité à accorder à l'un d'entre eux. En effet, Tanabe a dû être confronté à cette aporie, lorsqu'il considère l'État comme « l'être le plus concret »; à savoir une dernière instance à laquelle tous les individus devraient être, en fin de compte, assujettis. Cette aporie serait insurmontable dans la mesure où l'espèce occupe une place prépondérante et indéclinable au détriment des individus dans l'économie de la logique de l'espèce. Cette difficulté théorique majeure nous amènerait donc à remettre en cause la priorité discutable et la substantialisation injustifiée qui auraient été attribuées à l'espèce.

Pour autant que nous suivions rigoureusement la dialectique de la médiation absolue qui ne fait qu'un avec la logique de l'espèce chez Tanabe, les rapports dynamiques de l'individu à l'État auquel il appartient se définissent de la façon suivante.

L'État s'établit en tant qu'espèce, uniquement si l'individu s'établit comme étant autonome, indépendant et libre face à l'État auquel il appartient. Quant à l'individu, il n'est autonome, indépendant et libre que s'il exprime un intérêt étatique et fondateur et vise l'universel au-delà de l'État. Si l'État incarne un intérêt universel à travers des actions individuelles d'une manière ou d'une autre, cela ne présuppose pas qu'il soit susceptible de s'auto-identifier avec cet intérêt. C'est-à-dire que l'État ne justifie jamais son pouvoir, indépendamment des actions libres des individus.

MOMENT RÉACTIF

*Une pièce manquante dans l'économie de la philosophie de Nishida*

La notion d'espèce, indispensable pour la formation d'une philosophie de la vie à la fois sociale et collective, était une pièce manquante et théoriquement difficile à introduire dans l'économie de la philosophie nishidienne, qui consiste essentiellement en opposition entre l'individu et l'universel, et celle entre les individus. Dans les dernières années de sa vie, Nishida trouve une piste prometteuse qui aide à surmonter cette difficulté théorique épineuse dans la notion d'habitude chez Ravaisson, permettant ainsi de concevoir une logique de l'espèce en tant qu'élément constitutif, mais plastique et non substantiel, du monde de la réalité historique. Cette tentative, malheureusement interrompue par la rédaction de son dernier essai consacré au problème de la religion, reste définitivement inachevée à cause de son décès, néanmoins nous invite à la réflexion sur la conception d'une nouvelle philosophie de l'être social.

*Une critique nishidienne de la notion d'habitude bergsonienne*

Lorsqu'il présente une critique vigoureuse de l'interprétation bergsonienne de l'habitude ravaissonienne[8], Dominique Janicaud cite l'expression utilisée par Bergson afin de qualifier l'habitude en général en tant que : « le résidu fossilisé d'une activité spirituelle[9] », à propos de laquelle il considère que « cette expression peu ravaissonienne minimise la portée de *L'Habitude*[10] ». Se référant à cette même expression de Bergson ou au moins à une idée similaire que l'on peut trouver dans *Matière et mémoire* ou *L'évolution créatrice*, Nishida présente son idée sur l'habitude, qui s'oppose manifestement à celle de Bergson, de la façon suivante :

> Bergson a considéré l'habitude comme matérialisation de la vie. Pourtant, je pense, au contraire, que l'élan vital est un développement de l'habitude active. Bergson accorde la priorité au temporel auquel est assujetti le spatial. Pour ma part, je pense de façon contraire. Si l'on considère que la vie est constitutive, il nous sera impossible de penser autrement. La vie non consti-

---

8. JANICAUD 1997, 42 : « De toute évidence, Bergson n'a pas discerné le côté positif de l'habitude chez Ravaisson ».
9. BERGSON 2009, 267.
10. JANICAUD 1997, *op. cit.*, 43.

tutive ne serait pas objective, et elle ne serait pas la vie historique. Ce ne serait que ce qui est conçu au fond du soi subjectif. Certes, lorsqu'il s'agit de l'habitude, l'on considère normalement qu'elle est continuelle. Toutefois, cela tient au fait que l'on suppose le substantiel au fond de l'habitude. Quand on pense de cette manière, à partir d'où pourrait-on alors concevoir la formation de l'habitude ? L'habitude devra consister en l'auto-détermination du néant, inobjectivable en soi. Après avoir rédigé ce texte[11] sur l'habitude, j'ai eu par hasard l'occasion de lire *De l'habitude* de Ravaisson, ce qui m'a permis de savoir que Ravaisson avait déjà profondément réfléchi sur l'habitude. Bien que sa pensée n'ait pas atteint la réalité du monde historique, je ne peux que l'apprécier comme une belle pensée riche en remarques perspicaces sur l'habitude[12].

### *L'intérêt profond de Nishida pour* De l'habitude *de Ravaisson*

Ce qui est remarquable dans ce passage, c'est que Nishida avait conçu une pensée sur l'habitude très proche de celle de Ravaisson, avant même la lecture de la thèse de celui-ci. Certes, Nishida a auparavant étudié l'idée d'« habitude active » chez Maine de Biran, mais il a bien saisi dans *De l'habitude* l'enjeu philosophique cher à Ravaisson, notablement différent de celui de Biran et beaucoup plus important quant à la possibilité de développement théorique que ce dernier, à partir du concept d'habitude qu'il forge lui-même. Cet intérêt profond et l'affinité indéniable que Nishida désormais éprouve pour Ravaisson nous semblent bien expliquer le fait que Nishida présente une étude minutieuse sur *De l'habitude* neuf ans plus tard dans son essai intitulé « La Vie ».

Pourtant il est conscient des défauts théoriques de sa pensée de la vie au sujet des rapports des individus au monde de la réalité historique, composée de sociétés humaines évolutives. La solution à ce problème se trouve — efforts pour tenter d'établir une logique susceptible de procurer une médiation entre la théorie de la vie et celle de la société — dans les dernières pages de l'essai « La vie », entièrement consacrées à l'œuvre majeure de

---

11. Il s'agit du corps du texte de l'essai intitulé 「行為的直観の立場」 [La position de l'intuition agissante], auquel aurait été ajouté ce passage comme une note complémentaire lors de la publication de cet essai dans l'ouvrage intitulé 『哲学論文集第一』 [Recueil d'essais philosophique, le premier] en 1935.

12. NKZ 7: 157.

Ravaisson, *De l'habitude*. Nishida cherche dans cette œuvre une piste possible pour surmonter la difficulté théorique incontournable, révélée à travers le questionnement de l'espèce.

Il n'a pas complètement réussi à intégrer la notion d'espèce dans l'économie de la logique de la vie historique, où l'auto-identité contradictoire de l'un et du multiple est prédominante. Tout en admettant la nécessité d'introduire la notion d'espèce pour cadre intermédiaire dans la constitution du monde de la vie, il refuse catégoriquement de considérer l'espèce comme une substance toujours identique à soi, d'une part, et il s'efforce, d'autre part, d'établir l'effectivité de l'espèce au sein du monde de la vie historique et son irréductibilité aux individus et à la Vie. Il cherche à situer l'espèce entre les dimensions individuelle et universelle, de telle sorte que la créativité du monde auto-formant soit garantie. Il recherche ainsi quelque chose de pluridimensionnel se trouvant entre les deux vecteurs opposés, ceux de la différenciation et l'unification, vecteurs donnant une forme spécifique auto-formant à chaque individu. Nishida pense pouvoir le trouver dans la pensée ravaissonienne de l'habitude, conçue comme *disposition*, qui tient un rôle foncièrement intermédiaire au sein de la nature. En suivant tout à fait fidèlement l'ordre des argumentations de Ravaisson[13], il se propose de saisir dans la thèse ravaissonienne de l'habitude un moment concret qui lui permettra d'intégrer, selon l'ordre plastique de la nature, le concept d'espèce, dans la logique de la vie historique, comme une catégorie vitale, variable et intermédiaire qui rende possible effectivement l'auto-formation de la vie, cela en évitant consciemment la substantialisation définitive du concept d'espèce.

*La méthode ravaissonienne*

La méthode ravaissonienne est *descendante*, en ce sens que l'habitude nous permet de descendre en continu du plus haut degré de la nature, à savoir de la conscience proprement dite, jusqu'aux profondeurs de la nature à « la

---

13. La traduction japonaise de *De l'habitude* parut pour la première fois en 1938: 『習慣論』 *Shûkan-ron*, trad. par NODA Matao, Tôkyô, Iwanami Shoten. Apparemment, Nishida se réfère principalement à cette traduction scrupuleuse pour citer des textes assez fidèlement sans préciser pourtant la référence, cela en consultant le texte français; témoin la citation de quelques termes en français.

limite du mouvement de décroissance de l'habitude[14] », et cela sans perdre la lumière de la conscience[15].

C'est la même force qui, sans rien perdre, d'ailleurs, de son unité supérieure dans la personnalité, se multipliant sans se diviser, s'abaissant sans descendre, se résout elle-même, par plusieurs endroits, en ses tendances, ses actes, ses idées, se transforme dans le temps et se dissémine dans l'espace[16].

L'*habitude* en tant que méthode éminemment analogique nous permet de « reconstituer l'unité de l'ensemble du monde[17] ». Avec l'habitude reconnue comme une méthode universelle, nous *redescendons* la « spirale dont l'origine se trouve dans les profondeurs de la nature et dont l'aboutissement est dans la conscience[18] ». « C'est cette spirale que l'habitude redescend, et dont elle nous enseigne la génération et l'origine[19] ». Le *progrès* de l'habitude « conduit la conscience, par une dégradation non interrompue, de la volonté à l'instinct, et de l'unité accomplie de la personne à l'extrême diffusion de l'impersonnalité[20] ». L'habitude, parcourant le chemin inverse, nous fait comprendre qu'« il y a une infinité de degrés qui mesurent les développements d'une seule et même puissance[21] ».

Enfin, non seulement la forme la plus relevée de la vie dans l'humanité, l'activité motrice, renferme en abrégé toutes les formes inférieures qui se développent dans les fonctions subordonnées; mais la série de ces foncions n'est

---

14. RAVAISSON 1999, 139.
15. Voir aussi ibid., 137: « Non seulement, donc, les mouvements que l'habitude soustrait graduellement à la volonté ne sortent pas par cela même de la sphère de l'intelligence pour passer sous l'empire d'un mécanisme aveugle; mais ils ne sortent pas de la même activité intelligente où ils avaient pris naissance ».
16. Ibid., 137–8.
17. « Introduction » par Jacques BILLARD, RAVAISSON 1999, *op. cit.*, 43.
18. Ibid., 99. Voir aussi ibid., 158: « une spirale dont le principe réside dans la profondeur de la nature, et qui achève de s'épanouir dans la conscience ».
19. Ibid., 158.
20. Ibid., 147. Nous soulignons.
21. Ibid., 158. Voir JANICAUD 1997, *op. cit.*, 30: « L'unité de la loi de développement est d'autant mieux confirmée que son domaine d'application se révèle lui-même plus continu et que les différences qu'on y décèle n'exigent pas des sauts qualitatifs, mais peuvent se graduer suivant une unique mesure. Le principe leibnizien de continuité est sous-jacent à cette pensée fondamentale chez Ravaisson: il n'y a qu'une seule trame, la nature n'est que l'esprit enveloppé à l'état de puissance infinitésimale, les ruptures apparentes de la chaîne masquent les insensibles transitions. »

elle-même que le résumé du développement général de la vie dans le monde, de règne en règne, de genre en genre, d'espèce en espèce, jusqu'aux plus imparfaits rudiments et aux éléments les plus simples de l'existence[22].

## La méthode nishidienne

Par rapport à cette méthode *descendante* ravaissonienne, on peut qualifier la méthode nishidienne en tant qu'*ascendante*, ayant même sens que l'intuition agissante, Nishida situe son discours à l'origine de la conscience dans le monde de la vie historique — cela, dans le but de parcourir le développement de l'intuition agissante en tant que processus de l'auto-formation du monde, processus qui s'élève jusqu'à l'auto-éveil du monde éprouvé en tant que soi corporel. En posant l'intuition agissante à l'origine de la conscience, Nishida cherche les conditions de possibilité d'une conscience évolutive dans le monde auto-formant qu'est le monde de la vie historique : où et comment se saisit la conscience comme telle dans le monde ?

> En tant qu'habitude, notre conscience subsiste dans la mémoire du monde de la formation historique [...] en tant que disposition[23].

L'habitude, se manifeste comme une conscience de soi, et nous fait comprendre qu'il y a une capacité unique d'auto-formation en nous, qui n'est pas plus réductible à un mécanisme du monde matériel, qu'à l'activité pure de l'esprit incorporel ; cette capacité constitue la disposition qui peut se développer jusqu'à la créativité individuelle, créativité consistant à donner une nouvelle forme au monde en se donnant une forme singulière pouvant fonctionner comme un principe de configuration du milieu[24]. Il s'agit là du processus effectif de l'approfondissement de l'auto-éveil, processus qui se déroule à partir de l'intuition agissante nous ouvrant initialement au monde, jusqu'à l'auto-éveil au monde, éprouvé comme tel dans le soi corporel, point auto-expressif d'un monde auto-expressif ou point créateur d'un monde créateur.

22. Ravaisson 1999, *op. cit.*, 146.
23. NKZ 10 : 293.
24. Cette description de l'habitude s'applique parfaitement à la définition de l'information au sens où l'entend Simondon.

## L'espèce comme une habitude collective contractée

Les deux méthodes, ravaissonienne et nishidienne, ne s'excluent pas l'une l'autre, mais bien au contraire, elles sont complémentaires l'une pour l'autre. La logique de la vie historique fournit une fondation ontologique à la théorie générale de l'habitude, tandis que celle-ci, considérée comme « la seule méthode réelle[25] », nous permet d'éprouver intérieurement cette logique formative de la vie en vertu de l'aperception interne immédiate, portée par notre corps autoformant, qui agit par et dans le milieu où il vit.

Ici, nous entrevoyons la possibilité, malheureusement si peu développée par Nishida, de concevoir l'espèce comme une habitude collective contractée « entre le dernier fond de la nature et le plus haut point de la liberté réflexive[26] » dans « l'histoire de l'Habitude », qui « représente le retour de la Liberté à la Nature[27] ». Cependant, il n'est pas question ici d'une séparation catégorique de la nature et de la volonté, mais d'une inclusion ontologique de la mouvance de la volonté dans l'unité universelle de la Nature. Cette Nature comprend en elle ces trois *positions*: *vouloir être*, *devoir être*, *pouvoir être*, celles qui se transforment les unes en les autres dans « la continuité de la discontinuité », en vertu de l'habitude qui est par excellence une *disposition*.

Dans cette perspective, l'espèce peut se concevoir comme n'étant ni *naturelle* ni *abstraite*, mais *habituelle*: elle n'est pas déterminée comme un *être*, tout à fait indépendamment de notre volonté; elle n'est pas inventée tout à fait arbitrairement par la pensée spéculative; au contraire déterminée comme une habitude contractée par un groupe d'individus qui partagent une certaine *forme* de vie, créée, conservée et développée comme une histoire collective par eux-mêmes. L'histoire de l'Habitude nous amène à comprendre *de l'intérieur* le processus de formation de l'espèce à laquelle nous appartenons, et à situer celle-ci dans le cours de l'histoire évolutive allant de

---

25. Ravaisson 1999, *op. cit.*, 139.
26. Ibid., 158.
27. Ibid. Voir Janicaud 1997, *op. cit.*, 45: « La nature désigne alors la plénitude de la réalité, l'être, non plus en général, mais par excellence. Elle est à la fois non intellectuelle et non passive. Elle échappe à l'entendement, parce qu'il ne saisit, de manière discontinue, que les cadres de la réalité, donc seulement la nature en ses contours. Elle n'est pas passive, parce qu'elle n'est pas déterminée de l'extérieur par notre volonté. Nous découvrons ici le caractère le plus important de la nature: si elle échappe à notre volonté, c'est qu'elle est en elle-même spontanéité. »

ce qui est créé à ce qui crée. Autrement dit de la spontanéité naturelle impersonnelle à la conscience où s'épanouit la spontanéité singulière, auto-éveillée en l'individu. Nous pouvons ainsi parvenir à considérer d'une manière cohérente, tout en suivant la logique de la vie historique, la plasticité des espèces existantes, qui imposent à chaque individu une forme spécifique d'activité vitale, d'une part, et, d'autre part, la créativité des individus auto-éveillés, qui sont susceptibles de briser la forme qui leur est imposée pour donner au monde une nouvelle forme créatrice, en se donnant une nouvelle forme normative de vie en vertu de l'habitude[28].

Le concept d'espèce, ainsi reformulé à partir de la pensée de l'habitude ravaissonienne et son interprétation nishidienne, nous permettra d'envisager une logique de l'espèce élaborée par Tanabe avec sa dialectique de la médiation absolue, dans une perspective à la fois ouverte et bien déterminée pour la conception d'une nouvelle philosophie de l'être social.

Nous pourrons également nous pencher sur la question comment intégrer la logique de l'espèce de Tanabe afin de la faire fonctionner comme une logique de base pour la création d'une espèce nouvelle en tant que catégorie intermédiaire et plastique entre les individus et la société à laquelle ils appartiennent.

Nous avons ainsi trouvé une piste prometteuse par laquelle nous pourrions rétablir le dialogue interrompu entre Nishida et Tanabe.

## Moment médiateur

Enfin, nous sommes arrivés chez Simondon, philosophe français qui me semble susceptible de jouer un rôle de médiateur entre Nishida et Tanabe. Or, comme nous avons constaté, nous avons déjà trouvé un terrain d'entente entre Nishida et Tanabe qui permet une collaboration afin d'élaborer une logique de base pour la création d'une nouvelle espèce en tant que catégorie intermédiaire et plastique entre les individus et la société à laquelle ils appartiennent. Alors, avons-nous encore besoin de solliciter Simondon pour faire une intervention dans cette discussion pour réconcilier les deux philosophes japonais, cofondateurs de l'École de Kyôto ? À

---

28. C'est exactement dans ce sens-là que Simondon utilise le terme « information », c'est-à-dire au sens de donner une forme et se donner une forme.

dire vrai, Simondon a *déjà joué* ce rôle de l'intermédiaire entre Nishida et Tanabe, à visage caché, tout au long de l'argumentation que nous avons suivie jusqu'ici. Autrement dit, si nous avons réussi à réconcilier les deux philosophes japonais sur un terrain précis, c'est justement grâce à la philosophie de l'individuation de Simondon qui m'a fourni des dispositifs conceptuels me permettant de faire dialoguer à nouveau Nishida et Tanabe.

Par suite, nous allons présenter quelques éléments prépondérants de la philosophie de Simondon et quelques contributions possibles de la part de Nishida et Tanabe pour clarifier des problèmes qui demandent davantage de précisions chez Simondon.

Lisons d'abord quelques passages de l'introduction de l'œuvre majeure de Simondon, *L'individuation à la lumière des notions de forme et d'information*, afin de saisir son intention principale, sa méthodologie, et quelques concepts fondamentaux.

*Individuation*

> L'intention de cette étude est donc d'étudier les *formes, modes et degrés de l'individuation* pour replacer l'individu dans l'être, selon les trois niveaux physique, vital, psycho-social. Au lieu de supposer des substances pour rendre compte de l'individuation, nous prenons les différents régimes d'individuation pour fondement des domaines tels que matière, vie, esprit, société. La séparation, l'étagement, les relations de ces domaines apparaissent comme des aspects de l'individuation selon ses différentes modalités; aux notions de substance, de forme, de matière, se substituent les notions plus fondamentales d'information première, de résonance interne, de potentiel énergétique, d'ordre de grandeur[29].

L'individuation c'est l'ensemble du processus de devenir l'être à trois niveaux différents: physique, vital (ou biologique) et psycho-social. L'être humain est un être individué, c'est-à-dire un individu formé comme un moment évolutif de l'individuation. Se dotant de la dimension psycho-sociale, il n'est pas toujours identique à soi-même, mais il exprime un état métastable obtenu par la solution d'un problème posé au milieu dans lequel il vit. Il s'agit d'un 'état provisoire qui est susceptible à se restructurer en fonction d'un nouveau problème auquel il serait confronté et devrait donc résoudre.

---

29. Simondon 2005, 32.

La position philosophique de Simondon sur l'individuation pourrait se résumer en deux thèses suivantes: il n'y a pas d'individu élémentaire, d'individu premier et antérieur à toute genèse; le devenir n'est pas devenir de l'être individué, mais devenir d'individuation de l'être.

*Méthode*

> La méthode consiste à ne pas essayer de composer l'essence d'une réalité au moyen d'une relation *conceptuelle* entre deux termes extrêmes, et à considérer toute véritable relation comme ayant rang d'être. La relation est une modalité d'être; elle est simultanée par rapport aux termes dont elle assure l'existence. Une relation doit être saisie comme relation dans l'être, relation de l'être, manière d'être et non simple rapport entre deux termes [...][30].

Cette méthode simondonienne, qui accorde plus d'importance aux relations elles-mêmes qu'aux termes extrêmes encadrant celles-ci, nous permettra de mieux comprendre les individus individués que nous sommes à travers nos relations dynamiques et évolutives, en les considérant comme plastiques et déterminées toujours en fonction de différents niveaux et dimensions.

*Méthode, information*

> Nous entendons par transduction une opération, physique, biologique, mentale, sociale, par laquelle une activité se propage de proche en proche à l'intérieur d'un domaine, en fondant cette propagation sur une structuration du domaine opérée de place en place: chaque région de structure constituée sert à la région suivante de principe de constitution, si bien qu'une modification s'étend ainsi progressivement en même temps que cette opération structurante[31].

Selon Simondon, ni la déduction ni l'induction ne peuvent saisir l'individuation qui est le processus même de la réalité. Si la transduction consiste des processus où s'effectue la génération de l'acte de penser et de son objet à travers sa propre structuration, c'est seulement dans la transduction que le processus de l'individuation de la réalité pourrait se saisir de l'intérieur en temps réel comme sa propre affaire. Par cette notion de transduction, nous

30. Ibid.
31. Ibid.

pourrions mieux expliciter le mécanisme du développement de l'auto-éveil du monde ou de la détermination auto-éveillée du monde chez Nishida.

*Information*

> L'information suppose *un changement de phase d'un système* car elle suppose un premier état préindividuel qui s'individue selon l'organisation découverte; l'information est la formule de l'individuation, formule qui ne peut préexister à cette individuation; on pourrait dire que l'information est toujours au présent, actuelle, car elle est le sens selon lequel un système s'individue[32].

La notion d'information est très complexe chez Simondon. Mais ce qui est évident malgré cela, c'est que l'information au sens simondonien ne se réduit jamais aux renseignements sur quelque chose ou à l'action de les obtenir ou de les transmettre. Pour lui, l'information est l'*apparition* même d'une forme ou le processus de génération d'une forme dans ce monde. Autrement dit, l'information est une action de donner une forme ou de se donner une forme dans ce monde. Cette donation d'une forme se fait toujours avec celle d'autres formes. Aucune forme ne se forme jamais toute seule, mais elle se forme toujours en rapport avec d'autres formes qui se forment à leur manière. Ces rapports entre formes se génèrent en même temps que la génération de formes. Ces rapports font donc aussi partie de l'information en tant que processus de génération.

C'est dans cette théorie de l'information de Simondon que nous pourrions intégrer la pensée de l'auto-formation de la forme de Nishida afin d'appliquer celle-ci à différents systèmes de formes à différents niveaux plus concrets. Nous pourrions ainsi développer une logique de la forme dans différents domaines de façon transdisciplinaire.

*Résonance de thèses nishidiennes chez Simondon*

> L'individualité est un aspect de la génération, s'explique par la genèse d'un être et consiste en la perpétuation de cette genèse; l'individu est ce qui a été individué et continue à s'individuer; il est relation transductive d'une activité, à la fois résultat et agent, consistance et cohérence de cette activité par laquelle il a été constitué et par laquelle il constitue; il est la substance héré-

---

32. Ibid., 31.

ditaire, selon l'expression de Rabaud, car il transmet l'activité qu'il a reçue ; il est ce qui fait passer cette activité, à travers le temps, sous forme condensée, comme information[33].

En lisant ce passage, nous sommes tentés de résumer la thèse de Simondon en cette formule: « ce n'est pas l'individu qui précède l'individuation, c'est au contraire l'individuation qui précède l'individu. L'individuation est plus fondamentale que l'être individué ». Cette formule est parfaitement symétrique à celle de Nishida lorsqu'il parle de l'expérience pure: « ce n'est pas l'individu qui précède l'expérience, c'est au contraire l'expérience qui précède l'individu. L'expérience est plus fondamentale que la distinction individuelle[34] ».

Par ailleurs, en lisant le même passage, nous nous rappelons aussi cette formule de Nishida: « de ce qui est créé à ce qui crée[35] ».

## Un point de croisement entre Tanabe et Simondon

Lorsque Simondon écrit que « le véritable principe d'individuation est médiation[36] », il est évident qu'il ne s'agit pas de la médiation entre les termes qui auraient existé chacun séparément et indépendamment les uns des autres. L'individuation n'est autre que le surgissement d'une intermédiation elle-même qui se génère avec les termes qui la constituent. C'est dire que la théorie de l'individuation de Simondon est fondée sur une logique de médiation absolue. Autrement dit, le principe de la théorie anti-substantialiste de l'individuation n'est autre que le principe de la médiation absolue. C'est là que l'on trouve un point de croisement tout à fait intéressant entre Simondon et Tanabe à partir duquel l'on pourrait développer la logique de la médiation absolue de façon transductive afin d'éviter le piège posé par le substantialisme.

---

33. Ibid., 191.
34. NKZ 1: 6–7:「個人あって経験あるにあらず、経験あって個人あるのである、個人的区別より経験が根本的である」
35.「作くられたものから作るものへ」
36. SIMONDON 2005, 27.

*Au moyen de la logique de l'espèce*

> L'information exprime l'immanence de l'ensemble en chacun des sous-ensembles et l'existence de l'ensemble comme groupe de sous-ensembles, incorporant réellement la quiddité de chacun, ce qui est la réciproque de l'immanence de l'ensemble à chacun des sous-ensembles. S'il y a en effet une dépendance de chaque sous-ensemble par rapport à l'ensemble, il y a aussi une dépendance de l'ensemble par rapport aux sous-ensembles. Cette réciprocité entre deux niveaux désigne ce que l'on peut nommer résonance interne de l'ensemble, et définit l'ensemble comme réalité en cours d'individuation[37].

Suivant la thèse simondonienne, les catégories de genre, d'espèce et d'individu ne sont pas tout à fait adéquates pour saisir une réalité composée des ensembles et des sous-ensembles qui sont dynamiques et immanents les uns aux autres. Car ces catégories sont considérées chez le philosophe français comme étant fixes et qu'il n'y a aucun rapport dynamique entre elles. Pourtant, si ces trois termes sont ressaisis et redéfinis suivant la logique de la médiation absolue de Tanabe, ils pourront être traités comme éléments constitutifs de la réalité dynamique.

## Conclusion

Nous avons ainsi parcouru un chemin quelque peu sinueux à partir du moment critique représenté par Tanabe jusqu'au moment médiateur représenté par Simondon en passant par le moment réactif représenté par Nishida. Nous avons ainsi tenté de rétablir le dialogue interrompu entre deux philosophes japonais par l'intermédiaire d'un philosophe français.

La notion d'espèce était une pièce manquante dans l'économie de la philosophie du néant absolu chez Nishida. Chez Tanabe, elle était une des trois pièces primordiales dans la dialectique de la médiation absolue, Pourtant, elle a été considérée à tort comme une substance dans la logique de l'espèce lorsqu'il s'agit de l'État, car cette substantialisation de ce dernier n'est cohérente par rapport à la dialectique de la médiation absolue qui est indissociable à la logique de l'espèce.

La philosophie de la vie de Nishida a tenté de résoudre cette aporie en

---

[37]. Simondon 2005, 330.

introduisant la notion d'habitude ravaissonienne dans le monde de la réalité historique. L'espèce pourrait ainsi être saisie comme étant habituelle, non substantielle, donc comme une réalité historique, susceptible d'être modifiée, modulé, amplifiée, élargie ou éventuellement diminuée. Cette tentative philosophique potentiellement fructueuse a été malheureusement laissée inachevée chez le premier fondateur de l'Ecole de Kyoto. Elle n'a pas été reprise non plus par son successeur à la chaire de la philosophie première à l'Université impériale de Kyoto.

Chez Simondon, la notion d'espèce peut être saisie comme un moment du processus d'individuation. Elle n'est donc pas une substance, mais un état métastable, donc provisoire. Dans le processus d'individuation, en général, l'espèce se forme comme un état d'information au sens simondonien, c'est-à-dire comme expression de l'auto-formation de la forme au sens nishidien.

La notion d'espèce, ayant ainsi passé une épreuve philosophique en trois moments, critique, réactif et médiateur, a abouti au stade où elle est devenue ou redevenu dynamique et surtout transductive.

C'est un chemin qui reste à frayer encore plus loin afin de poursuivre le dialogue rétabli entre Nishida et Tanabe, mais aussi d'ouvrir un espace discursif où les deux philosophes japonais et le philosophe français pourraient se lancer et s'engager dans une discussion productive sur d'autres questionnements comme ceux qui sont relatifs à la technique ou plus précisément au corps technique, au corps historique, au sujet éthique et à la dimension sacrée du monde *etc.*

## Références bibliographiques

*Abréviations*

NKZ 『西田幾多郎全集』 [Œuvres complètes de Nishida Kitarō], Tokyo, Iwanami Shoten, 24 volumes, 2002–2009.

Bergson, Henri
    2009 *La pensée et le mouvant*. Paris, PUF, coll. « Quadrige Grands textes ».

Janicaud, Dominique
    1997 *Ravaisson et la métaphysique. Une généalogie du spiritualisme français*. Paris, Vrin, 2ᵉ éd.

Ravaisson, Félix
    1999 *De l'habitude. Métaphysique et morale*. Paris, PUF, « Quadrige ».

Simondon, Gilbert
　2005　*L'individuation à la lumière des notions de forme et d'information*, Grenoble, Jérôme Million.

Tanabe Hajime
　1964　『田邉元全集』[Œuvres complètes de Tanabe Hajime], vol. 4, Tokyo, Chikuma Shobō.

KATSUMORI MAKOTO
*Akita University, Japan*

# Reading Hiromatsu's Theory of the Fourfold Structure

Hiromatsu Wataru's philosophical thought revolves around an analysis of what he calls the "fourfold structure." According to Hiromatsu, all phenomena in the world are structured in such a fourfold manner that "a given presents itself as something to someone as Someone," and these four moments of the phenomenon are not independent elements, but exist only as terms of the functional relationship. This paper surveys and critically examines this theory of the fourfold structure, and shows, in particular, how this theory, while largely presented as synchronic structural analysis, contains some conceptual motifs going beyond the synchronic framework. Specifically, with a focus on the process in which there arises a meaning common to different phenomenal givens and to different knowers, my analysis suggests the way in which phenomena are dynamically structured and thereby displaced in meaning as well as in the knowers' role relationship.

KEYWORDS: Hiromatsu Wataru—phenomenon—meaning—intersubjectivity—fourfold structure—reification—synchronic structure—structuring movement—displacement—general signifier—general signified

Hiromatsu Wataru 廣松 渉 (1933–1994) describes the basic motif of his philosophy as a systematic critique of the "modern worldview" (近代的世界観), which he characterizes as ontologically "substantialist" and epistemologically bound by the "subject/object schema."[1] Inspired by the thought of Karl Marx and Marxism as well as by the philosophical implications of twentieth-century physical science,[2] he strives to replace the modern worldview with a new philosophical orientation marked by "the primacy of relation" and what he calls the intersubjective "fourfold structure" (四肢構造).[3]

In this article, I will survey and critically examine Hiromatsu's general philosophical theory of the fourfold structure.[4] As Hiromatsu notes, this theory is largely developed as a "synchronic" structural analysis of the phenomenal world.[5] A closer reading will show, however, that his texts contain some lines of thought that differ from, and stand in latent tension with, his overall synchronic approach. In the first section, I outline his theory of the fourfold structure in its primarily synchronic framework. I then set out to analyze this theory and show how his synchronic framework may be sur-

---

1. HWC 1: 13, 15: xvii.

2. Hiromatsu's systematic philosophy goes hand in hand with his novel interpretation of Marx's thought. In the present study, however, except for referring to part of his reading of Marx in the second section, I will not enter into this area of his scholarship. For a discussion of Hiromatsu's analysis of Marx's theory of the commodity, see KATSUMORI 2016B. For a study of his approach to modern physical science (specifically, Ernst Mach's thought and Einstein's relativity theory), see KATSUMORI 2016A.

3. HWC 15: xiii, xviii.

4. Major prior inquiries into Hiromatsu's theory of the fourfold structure include chapter 3 of KOBAYASHI 1987 and part 2 of KUMANO 2004. In the present study, however, I do not enter into these or other authors' readings of his philosophy.

5. HWC 1: 29.

passed by some of his dynamic conceptual motifs. More specifically, in the second section, I investigate the structuring of the known side of phenomena, and, in the third, the fourfold structuring of phenomena, with a focus on what may be called the dynamic displacement of meanings and cognitive roles.

### An overview of the theory of the fourfold structure[6]

Hiromatsu's overall philosophical project revolves around the theory of the fourfold structure, which he developed in his 1972 book *The Intersubjective Being-Structure of the World* 『世界の共同主観的存在構造』 and several subsequent works, most systematically in *Being and Meaning* 『存在と意味』, vol. 1 (1982) and vol. 2 (1993). This theory begins with a structural analysis of phenomena "as they unfold *cognitively*."[7] For Hiromatsu, the cognitive aspect of the world, or the world "in a provisional abstraction from such moments as practical significance or value significance," has no priority over the practical, but is rather just a "structural moment or perspectival cross section" of the latter.[8] Yet, in order to confront effectively the modern philosophical tradition, which has primarily been concerned with the cognitive dimension, he finds it convenient to *start* with this dimension.[9] His philosophy thus sets out to analyze the cognitive aspect of the phenomenal world—"the world as it appears to pre-reflective consciousness."[10] In the present study, I largely restrict myself to this part of his work engaging with the cognitive dimension.

Hiromatsu rejects the modern subject/object schema, which underlies the realist copy theory as well as various kinds of idealism, and—up to a point following Ernst Mach's phenomenalism—conceives phenomena as neither simply subjective nor purely objective, but prior to the very divi-

---

6. A large part of this section has been adapted from a section of KATSUMORI 2016A, 168–75.
7. HWC 15: xvii.
8. HWC 15: 5, vii.
9. The first and the second volumes of *Being and Meaning* are devoted to an analysis of the cognitive and the practical dimensions, respectively.
10. HWC 1: 30.

sion of subject and object. However, he breaks with Machian phenomenalism insofar as it fails to grasp the "meaningful moment" of phenomena.[11] Rather, in a manner reminiscent of phenomenology, he emphasizes that all phenomena "bear meaning," or, in other words, that they appear *as* something. As he explains it:

> The phenomenon always already appears in itself *as something* more than a mere "sensuous" (感性的) given. The sound that is just heard appears intuitively *as* a car horn; what is seen outside the window appears *as* a pine tree. When I see a thing that lies on the desk, I am aware of it directly *as* a "pencil."[12]

This applies not only to perceptions, but to all kinds of phenomena, including representations as well as linguistically mediated judgments.[13] All these phenomena appear as something more or something other than "the phenomenal given" (現相的所与).[14] Put differently, the phenomenon is such that, "in showing itself…, it always already shows something else."[15] Hiromatsu designates this something more or something else as "the meaningful cognized" (意味的所識)" or simply the "meaning."[16] Any phenomenon thus consists of these two factors, given and meaning, linked to each other in such a way that the former appears *as* the latter. If we denote the phenomenal given by p and the meaningful cognized by [p], the phenomenon is structured in the form of "p as [p]."[17]

---

11. HWC 3: 546. See Katsumori 2016a, 158.

12. HWC 1: 33.

13. In what follows in the text, while treating not only nonverbal perceptions and representations but also linguistic signs, I will not directly enter into Hiromatsu's thematic discussion of language, specifically his analysis of judgment (see HWC 1: 47ff., 15: 281ff.).

14. HWC 15: 39.

15. HWC 1: 34.

16. HWC 15: 39, 1: 35. In his early works, Hiromatsu used the term 意味的所知 (the meaningful known) instead of 意味的所識, thus giving rise to a double meaning of 所知: as against the knower (能知) and as against the given (所与). To remove this ambiguity, he introduced in *Being and Meaning*, vol. 1, the neologism 所識 (the cognized), while reserving 所知 for what comprises both given and cognized (or meaning) (see HWC 15: xxvii). The words 所知 and 所識 are hardly distinguishable, however, in terms of the intrinsic meanings of the component characters.

17. This expression is based on a notation that Hiromatsu introduced in his graduation thesis (HWC 16) and later used in his analysis of Marx's theory of the commodity. More specifically, he employs the expression "a as [a]" for the relation between what Marx calls use-value and value

This twofold or dual character of the phenomenon, Hiromatsu continues, is "manifest most typically in the case of signs," such as a series of sounds or ink stains appearing as a meaningful word. Yet this twofoldness is not unique to what are commonly called signs, but, conversely, all phenomena are, in a sense, "of a signitive (symbolic) character."[18] It is precisely by virtue of this general character of phenomena that signs in the narrow sense can function as signs. From this point of view, borrowing terms of Ferdinand de Saussure's linguistics, Hiromatsu renames the phenomenal given the "signifier" and the meaningful cognized the "signified."[19]

While emphasizing the duality of phenomena, Hiromatsu in no way maintains a *dualism* of mutually independent terms. On the contrary, he seeks to de-substantialize the two moments of phenomena by what may, in a sense, be characterized as an extension of the Saussurean views of signs to all phenomena.[20] First, he argues that not only are all phenomena meaningful, but also any meaning (or signified) exists only to the extent that it is tied to, or, as it were, is "incarnated" in a phenomenal given (or signifier).[21] In other words, far from being self-contained, both the given and the meaning can be what they are only in their interrelation. Second, Hiromatsu points to the differential character of meaning: It is not that the meaning A is distinguished from non-A because of A's independent self-identity, but that "A is taken… as self-identical insofar as it is distinguished from non-A."[22] In this way, with regard both to the relation between given and meaning and to the relation between different meanings, he offers a radically "relationist" account, rejecting the reifying notion of meaning as self-contained.

Hiromatsu goes on to determine more closely the character of the meaningful cognized. Meaning is, he maintains, neither a "real object" referred

---

of commodities, which, in Hiromatsu's view, exemplify two factors of the phenomenon in the practical domain, corresponding respectively to given and meaning under discussion here (see HWC 12: 148).

18. HWC 1: 34.

19. HWC 15: 149.

20. On the other hand, Hiromatsu criticizes Saussure for presupposing the dichotomy of things and ideas, and conceiving signs as psychical entities (MARUYAMA and HIROMATSU 1993, 22ff.).

21. HWC 1: 36.

22. HWC 15: 26.

to, nor a "mental image" associated with the phenomenal given. For what are called real objects as well as mental images are themselves phenomena, already consisting of the two moments of given and meaning. Rather, meaning is, if considered as such, marked by its "ideal" character. Suppose a series of phenomena such as this pine, that cedar, and so on, equally appear as one and the same meaning "tree." Here, as we can see, unlike the pine or cedar located at a particular place, the meaning "tree" "exists anywhere"; in contrast to the individual trees, which grow, change, and finally die, the latter remains unchanged; and the meaning "tree" is "a universal that is not *any* of the individual phenomena, but can be any of them." In this way, while givens are "individual, local, and variable" and may thus be called "real," the meaning exhibits a "universal, trans-spatial, and invariable," in short, "ideal," character.[23] It should be noted, however, that this ideality of meaning holds only insofar as one attempts in thought to "isolate" the meaning from the whole phenomenon and to "treat it as if it were an independent term." In other words, as Hiromatsu admits, his characterization of meaning as ideal contains a kind of "reification,"[24] and this critical and self-critical insight marks his decisive break with Husserlian phenomenology. In an effort to avoid this reification, Hiromatsu reformulates meaning as "functional," in the sense of the mathematical function into which specific values—corresponding to phenomenal givens—are each time inserted.[25] He holds this analogy to be appropriate insofar as the function is not considered in separation from the specific values it takes.

This motif of criticizing reification further leads Hiromatsu into a certain relativization of the given/meaning distinction itself. He points to the possibility of the "manifold process" or "multi-layered structure" in which "the given-cognized formation at one level… stands in the position of a given in relation to a higher-level meaningful cognized."[26] Conversely speaking, the

---

23. HWC 15: 21; cf. 78f.

24. HWC 15: 17.

25. HWC 15: 22f., cf. 74f. It seems to me that, without compromising what Hiromatsu means here, meaning could well be likened to the mathematical *variable* rather than to the function. The analogy to the function is employed, however, in order to emphasize the relational character of meaning (private communication with Hiromatsu).

26. HWC 1: 45, 15: 7. The term "multi-layered structure" is cited from HIROMATSU 1988, which is not included in his *Collected Works*.

phenomenal given at any level can be a twofold formation at a lower level. In the series of such different levels, he continues, "there is no fixed, unique lowest-level given."[27] For, as soon as one is aware of the phenomenal given as such, this can no longer be a pure given, but is already known *as* something. This being the case, "sensuous elements" in Mach's philosophy as well as what positivists call "sense data" cannot be ultimate givens, but already assume the duality of given and meaning.

Thus far, while de-substantializing and relativizing the twofold structure of phenomena, Hiromatsu has restricted himself to their "known" side in a provisional abstraction from the subjective or "knowing" side. As he points out, however, a phenomenon is every time a phenomenon "*for* someone,"[28] and this someone—the "knower" (能知)—is, also like "the known" (所知), twofold in character. When, for instance, a child sees a cow, saying, "that's a doggie," it is indeed to the child, and not to me, that the phenomenon appears as a "doggie." Nevertheless, Hiromatsu continues:

> …without in a sense taking the cow as a doggie, I could not even know that the child has "mistaken" it for a dog. I can recognize the child's mistake only insofar as I myself also in a sense take the cow as a doggie.[29]

Here we see the "self-dividing unity" of "oneself as oneself" and "oneself as (playing the role of) another." While this is most manifestly seen in linguistic communication, the duality of "someone as someone (else)" can be recognized generally in phenomenal consciousness. The latter someone, "initially a concrete individual," tends, through human intercourse, to be depersonalized into "the one" (ヒト),[30] so that the knower takes on the form of "someone as the one." Insofar as the known is attributed to this someone as the one, Hiromatsu designates the someone as the "knowing someone" (能知的誰某) and the one as the "cognizing Someone" (能識的或者), for-

27. HWC 15: 8.
28. HWC 1: 38/973. The second page number refers to the English translation (Hiromatsu 2011).
29. HWC 1: 39/974 (translation modified).
30. HWC 15: 133f. In Hiromatsu's account, what he means by "the one" more or less overlaps with Martin Heidegger's concept of "*das Man*" (HWC 1: 44/977). As the English translator Viren Murthy comments, however, the one is "free of some of the pejorative connotations" of *das Man* (Hiromatsu 2011, 973).

mulating the duality of the knower: P as [P].³¹ He characterizes the cognizing Someone in a manner similar to the meaningful cognized seen above: While the knowing someone may be called "individual, variable, and local," that is, "real," the cognizing Someone, if considered as such, exhibits a "universal, invariable, and trans-spatial," in short, "ideal" character.³² Thus structured in parallel with the known, the knower "exists as a cognizing Someone who is more than a knowing someone."³³

It might appear to the reader that Hiromatsu is simply calling the subject and the object by other names—knower and known, respectively—and dividing each of them into two factors. Yet, as he emphasizes, unlike the traditional notions of subject and object, knower and known are not "ontically separate," but are, as is illustrated by "the expansion and contraction of the bodily self," just the two non-fixed aspects of a "state of union."³⁴ This internal link between knower and known is further specified as follows. First, the phenomenal given and the knowing someone are necessarily connected in such a way that the former is "each time perspectively given" to the latter.³⁵ Second, and more importantly, the formation of a meaning is correlative with the process through which different knowers make themselves intersubjectively isomorphic to become a cognizing Someone. Not only the meanings of linguistic signs, but also the perceptual articulations of phenomena are already conditioned by the "intersubjective cultural setting"—as is illustrated by the fact that the dog's bark, which native Japanese speakers hear as *wanwan*, sounds like "bow-wow" to native English speakers.³⁶ In this way, "intersubjectivity" (間主観性 or 共同主観性) serves as the

31. HWC 15: 148. Just as in the case of 所知 and 所識, one can hardly distinguish between the intrinsic meanings of 能知的 (knowing) and 能識的 (cognizing)—Hiromatsu's neologisms—or between 誰某 (someone) and 或者 (Someone). The philosophically relevant distinctions rest entirely on his original usage of the terms.

32. HWC 15: 135.

33. HWC 15: 132.

34. HWC 15: 92, 98, 96. As examples of the expansion of the bodily self, Hiromatsu cites "the blind person's cane and the medical doctor's stethoscope" as well as the "observational instrument" in physics, which is given special importance in the context of quantum theory. On the other hand, he takes a "paralyzed arm or leg" as an example of the contraction of the bodily self (HWC 15: 91–3).

35. HWC 15: 185.

36. Hiromatsu 1988, 90f.

essential link between meaning and Someone.[37] Intersubjectivity lies in the fact that "while I and others have as givens different perspectival phenomena," we can share one and the same meaning.[38]

As is suggested by our consideration so far, the twofold structures of both knower and known are combined to form what Hiromatsu calls the fourfold structure (四肢構造) of the phenomenon: "a given presents itself as something to someone as Someone," or, in fully technical terms, "a phenomenal given is valid as a meaningful cognized to a knowing someone as a cognizing Someone" (p as [p] for P as [P]).[39] For instance, something outside the window appears as a pine tree to me as a "one" (general knower); and the sound "tree" bears the meaning of tree for someone as an English speaker. As Hiromatsu repeatedly stresses, the above four moments of the phenomenon are not self-contained elements that subsequently enter into relation to one another, but themselves "subsist only as terms of the [fourfold] functional relationship."[40] Furthermore, a fourfold-structured phenomenon itself is "not closed in on itself as a four-term relation," but exists only in relation to other phenomena, that is, to other fourfold formations.[41] Insofar as the phenomenon is thus relationally structured, Hiromatsu names it the *koto* (事)—a Japanese term that defies simple translation, but may roughly be rendered as "state of affairs" or *Sachverhalt*.[42] Hiromatsu counterposes this *koto* to the *mono* (物), namely, the thing (*Ding*, *res*) that is taken as substantial and self-contained.

In terms of this contrast between *koto* and *mono*, Hiromatsu defines the term "reification" (物象化), broadening Karl Marx's concept of reification (*Versachlichung*)—the reification of the social relation between humans—into a concept that covers the whole phenomenal world. By reification he means mistaking a *koto* for a *mono*, that is, a misconception of the fourfold

---

37. Hiromatsu uses the two Japanese terms 間主観性 and 共同主観性 as translations of "intersubjectivity" with their nuances somewhat different from each other, but without an explicit conceptual distinction between them. I will discuss issues concerning these terms toward the end of the third section.
38. HWC 15: 189.
39. HWC 15: 198.
40. HWC 1: 45.
41. HWC 13: 260.
42. HWC 15: 199.

structural relation such that one or more terms of the relation are taken as independent of other terms or of the whole relationship.[43] More strictly, in terms of the quasi-Hegelian we/it perspectival difference, reification is defined as the circumstance that "a *koto*, which is determined relationally from the point of view of scholarly reflection (*für uns*), appears as a *mono* to the immediate consciousness involved (*für es*)."[44] While the hypostatization of meaning represents the most typical mode of reification, Hiromatsu is no less critical of the Machian or other modes of reification of the phenomenal given, or of the reification of the known or the knower as a whole. A continual uncovering and overcoming of reification in this manner constitutes the leading motif of his philosophical enterprise.

It should be noted, however, that this idea of reification in its relation to the fourfold structure is formulated within the framework of static or synchronic structural analysis. Yet, as we will see below, Hiromatsu's philosophy does not entirely confine itself to, but at least partly goes beyond, the synchronic frame of analysis, and, moreover, his formulation of synchronic structure itself depends in part on motifs exceeding the synchronic dimension. This being the case, there may also arise circumstances in which the concept of reification as defined above synchronically can no longer be maintained as it is. In the next section, I will pursue such more or less latent lines of thought of Hiromatsu, with a focus on the way in which phenomena are dynamically structured and thereby displaced in meaning.

---

43. According to Hiromatsu, not only individualism or atomism, which "substantializes terms of a relation," but also holism, which "substantializes the totality of a relation," is a "reifying misconception" (HWC 16: 282). The primary target of his critique, however, is the individualist and elementalist type of reification, because this type is characteristic of the modern worldview (see HWC 10: 496).

44. HWC 13: 245. As Hiromatsu notes, the "we" in his—as well as Marx's—sense differs from the Hegelian we (*wir*) in that it does not stand in the position of absolute knowledge, but is relative to the specific stage of the dialogical-dialectical processes in which it is formed (HWC 4: 425; cf. 2: 357).

## Displacement and reification in the structuring of the known

In his 1979 book *Things, States of Affairs, Words* 『もの・こと・ことば』, when discussing the fourfold structure of linguistic phenomena, Hiromatsu adds the following note to the text:

> While in this work I have studied [linguistic phenomena] provisionally as they are *reified* in the mode of the *langue*, it is necessary to note in a more rigorous discussion that the linguistic formation is "produced" (reproduced) each time it is spoken and understood in hearing, and that this is also the case with "meaning." In reality, the identity and invariability of meaning hold, as it were, only on a meta-level, that is, only insofar as the intentional moment that each time occurs "productively" is identified reflectively from our point of view (*für uns*).[45]

Does reification here also mean the hypostatization of the meaning or any other term of the fourfold structure? It can hardly be so, because Hiromatsu's main text to which the above note refers is devoted entirely to a critique of reification in this sense. Rather, it seems that the term "reified" in the above quotation is concerned with the structure in which an identical meaning is maintained over a series of phenomena, that is, with the synchronic given/meaning structure itself. Correlatively, the critique of this reification is being made from a point of view that surpasses the synchronic framework.

The possibility of such a shift in the meaning of reification will be still more difficult to ignore if we look—here briefly—at Hiromatsu's analysis of the practical world. First, Hiromatsu characterizes as "reified" the circumstance that the rules and norms of action appear as rigid and self-identical "despite their plasticity."[46] Second, maintaining generally that human action is carried out "as something more than a mere bodily behavior," namely, as

---

45. HWC 1: 445 (first emphasis mine). Elsewhere, in discussing the practical dimension, Hiromatsu makes a parallel remark: The "norms and rules" of action are "produced and reproduced each time the subjects involved act in a specific manner" (HWC 16: 416).

46. HWC 16: 450. As regards historical laws, Hiromatsu maintains that "it is through a reification of the activity of individuals that historical-social lawfulness holds" (HWC 10: 175f.). In his analysis of the cognitive world, however, he characterizes as reifying, not so much law or lawfulness itself, but rather the notion that laws "govern" individual facts (HWC 15: 485). This seems to illustrate the fact that Hiromatsu's dynamic conceptions come to the fore more visibly in the practical than in the cognitive dimension.

an interhuman "role-playing," he points out that roles (役割) tend to be "reified" into fixed "Roles" (役柄) such as statuses and positions.[47] In this "institutional reification of the connection of role actions," he continues, individual actors become "impersonal and anonymous."[48] These points seem to raise questions for the cognitive dimension as well, insofar as we are to avoid inconsistency between the cognitive and the practical: If a self-identical meaning and, correlatively, a depersonalized "one" or cognizing Someone are established, is not this circumstance already reified? If this is so, is not the fourfold structure itself, as understood in the synchronic framework, already a product of reification?

Before directly examining these questions, I wish to qualify the parallels that I earlier drew between Hiromatsu's and Saussure's relationist views. First, Hiromatsu's concept of the signifier is not, as the Saussurean signifier (*signifiant*), a formal factor within the already structured *langue*, but the "material moment" each time phenomenally given.[49] This conception of the signifier makes it possible to inquire into processes prior to the establishment of a *langue*-like structure. As a concrete inquiry along this line, Hiromatsu enters into the process in which perceptual phenomena are progressively articulated. In his account, this process consists of the following series of stages: (a) Something is congealed from the "nothing-ground" (無－地) to become a "figure"; (b) the figure and the ground are differentiated so that the former appears as self-identical; and (c) two such figures become distinct from each other in the mode of "this and that."[50] While, in the first stage (a), there is already a potential duality in which something appears as a figure, it is not until stage (b) that this figure is grasped as a meaning through the mediation of the reflexive relation to the ground.[51] Conversely speaking, Hiromatsu's theory includes within its scope the cir-

---

47. HWC 1: 113, 16: 99, 5: 139. In his later work, Hiromatsu introduced a distinction between 役割 and 役柄, both of which are commonly translated as "role." While by 役割 he means "role" in general, he reserves 役柄 for the role that is already fixed as status or position. In this study, I render 役割 and 役柄 as "role" and "Role," respectively.

48. HWC 5: 220, 228.
49. HWC 15: 168.
50. HWC 15: 151ff.
51. HWC 1: 347f.

cumstance that "something other than the given" is *not* yet established as the self-identical meaningful cognized.

These points suggest that Hiromatsu's philosophy, while primarily a synchronic structural analysis, diverges from Saussure's position (at least in his *Course in General Linguistics*)[52] and structuralism, and opens itself to the dimension of "structural change"—in a broad sense of the term covering "the formation, maintenance, and transformation of structure."[53] Notwithstanding Hiromatsu's remark that "my developmental arguments are largely an auxiliary means for a theory of being-structure,"[54] the developmental, or better, the dynamic dimension seems to be an indispensable moment of his thought. This dynamic dimension is concerned not so much with the merely diachronic transition of already structured systems, but rather with the very process through which phenomena are structured.[55] It is no doubt in terms of this structuring movement—in the sense including both de- and re-structuring—that we can adequately understand what Hiromatsu calls reification "in the mode of the *langue*" or "institutional reification." In what follows, I will accordingly explore this dimension of structuring with a provisional restriction to the known side of phenomena.

Some important clues for understanding Hiromatsu's dynamic conceptions may be found in some apparently minor details of his texts. First, there seems to be an ambiguity when he characterizes meaning as either "something more" or "something other" than the phenomenal given. Yet, well aware of this apparent ambiguity, Hiromatsu seeks to remove it by noting that, strictly speaking, a meaning can be said to be "something more" not relatively to the phenomenal given itself, but only to another, lower-level meaning in a multi-layered structure. In relation to the phenomenal given on the same level, he continues, the meaning may only be called something

---

52. Here I leave on one side the question of whether and to what extent Saussure's *Course in General Linguistics*, posthumously compiled and published, represents his original thought. For a thematic study of this and related questions about Saussure's thought, see MARUYAMA 1981.

53. HWC 14: 199.

54. HWC 15: 36.

55. Hiromatsu remarks, for example, that the fourfold structure "consists solely in the *process* relationship" (HWC 1: 43f., my emphasis) among the moments of phenomena, notably between meaning and cognizing Someone in their correlative formation.

*else*. In this sense, it is not more-or-lessness, but "otherness" that is basic to the relation between given and meaning.⁵⁶

Second, however, there remains another ambiguity, not mentioned as such by Hiromatsu himself, in his formulation of the duality of phenomena. On the one hand, as we have seen, Hiromatsu claims that a phenomenon appears as something "more than a mere 'sensuous' given," or more precisely, something other than the phenomenal given. This type of formulation readily leads to the synchronic structure in which the phenomenon comprises the two moments of given and meaning. On the other hand, he also maintains that the phenomenon is such that, "in showing itself…, it always already shows something else."⁵⁷ This mode of expression implies that p appears as *something other than p itself*, or, in other words, that the phenomenon contains in itself a movement of becoming other than itself or a displacement of itself. It is no doubt this latter formulation that is relevant to the dynamic dimension, which is rendered invisible in the first formulation.

To make a third point, I wish to start by specifying what Hiromatsu means by the phrase "in itself" (即自的 *an sich*) as in the statement that "a phenomenon… appears in itself as something more than a mere 'sensuous' given." By this qualification "in itself," he means that the knower is not always actually—but in many cases only potentially—conscious of the twofoldness of phenomena. According to Hiromatsu, "in the *immediate* consciousness of the subject involved," the phenomenon is commonly a full unity of given and meaning. In *reflective* consciousness, however, it is readily "bifurcated" into the two moments.⁵⁸ This indicates that, despite his preliminary characterization of the phenomenal world as "the world as it appears to pre-reflective consciousness,"⁵⁹ one cannot maintain the twofold structure without including reflection on phenomena in the phenomenal world itself.

56. HWC 1: 349.
57. Hiromatsu also says that consciousness "does not receive the given as such, but is aware of it as something other or something more than the given" (HWC 1: 34).
58. HWC 1: 348.
59. Hiromatsu acknowledges the "fictional" character of such a pre-reflective world, noting that it is "nothing more than our basic prejudgment" relative to our historical and social conditions (HWC 1: 31, 15: 32).

What is more important, however, is Hiromatsu's argument directly following the above: As soon as one is thus aware of the phenomenal given in distinction to the meaning, this given is no longer a given as such, but is itself dualized into a given and a meaning.

> For instance, when one is aware of a "comma" [in a written text] and then tries to make explicit "the given" of which one has just been aware *as a comma*, one is now aware of that moment as, say, a *black spot*. That is, one is aware of the given anew in a twofold structure, *as* a cognized "black spot," which differs from the initially cognized "comma."[60]

This passage from Hiromatsu's *Things, States of Affairs, Words* is meant to prove the non-presence of the phenomenal given "purified" from meaning, which is an important point of his synchronic analysis as seen earlier. In my view, however, what is more relevant here lies in the course of the argument itself: Reflective consciousness not only makes explicit the twofoldness of the phenomenon (p as [p]), but also produces a new twofold formation (p′ as [p′]), that is, dualizes the phenomenon differently than earlier.[61] Reflection on a phenomenon, itself involved in the phenomenal world, cannot simply be to view the phenomenon just as it is, but necessarily redetermines it in meaning. That is to say, a phenomenon, as soon as it is reflected upon, undergoes a displacement in meaning.

While this point has been made about reflection on the phenomenal given, the same point will basically apply to reflection on the meaning or the given/meaning as a whole. A series of such reflections leads to what Hiromatsu calls the "manifold process," mentioned earlier, which may be expressed as "p as [p] as [[p]]…." Here the as-connection "…as [[p]]," for example, may provisionally be called an addition to the preceding as-connection "p as [p]." Yet, despite the architectonic image easily evoked by Hiromatsu's expressions such as "multilayered structure" or "piling-up,"[62] the

---

60. HWC 1: 348. In this quotation, I have translated 所知 as the cognized, not as the known, because by 所知 Hiromatsu here means what he would call 所識 in his later work.

61. In *Being and Meaning*, Hiromatsu makes a similar point using the example of Rubin's figure. In his account, one may at first say that the black-and-white figure is seen either as a vase or as two facing profiles (HWC 15: 5). As soon as this black-and-white figure is perceived as such, however, it becomes "yet another meaningful cognized beside the two profiles and vase" (HWC 15: 7).

62. HWC 1: 349.

addition of a new dual connection, which is a reflection on the preceding dual formation, cannot leave the latter purely intact. Insofar as any reflection on phenomena is itself involved in the connection of phenomena, and the meaning of any phenomenon is determined in relation to other phenomena, it follows that the manifold process is also a process of displacement in meaning.

So far we have traced some of Hiromatsu's lines of thought that tend to surpass his synchronic framework, which suggest that phenomena, including reflections on phenomena, contain in themselves a movement of displacement or self-displacement in meaning.[63] Taking now one step further than his own accounts, let us examine whether and, if so, how such a displacement occurs in the process through which there arises a meaning common to different phenomenal givens. While meaning is a constitutive moment of a single phenomenon, its existence rather lies in the possibility[64] that it is reproduced as one and the same meaning over a (potentially indefinite) number of phenomena. This identical meaning, in Hiromatsu's view, does not exist independently of the phenomena, nor can it be derived from them through "inductive abstraction." Rather it derives from a "direct equating" of the phenomena with each other in terms of meaning.[65] This equating may be illustrated by such cases as recognizing the person just seen as an old friend, or regarding this pine and that cedar as similar things. Although the identical meaning ("tree" in the latter example), once established, seems to precede individual phenomena, let us start from the situation in which it does *not* yet exist, and examine how it emerges through the equating of phenomena.

Hiromatsu thematizes this kind of equating not so much in his major epistemological-ontological works as in his writings on Marx's thought,

---

63. In his analysis of the practical world, Hiromatsu briefly speaks of "displacement" (ズレ) as it occurs in the imitation of actions (HWC 16: 444).

64. The word "possibility" is needed here to reflect Hiromatsu's view that meaning, while it must be reproducible, need not be actually reproduced over different phenomena (see HWC 4: 78). Incidentally, we can see a parallel between this idea and Jacques Derrida's notion of "iterability" (DERRIDA 1972A, 375/315).

65. HWC 15: 158. This applies to phenomena in the third stage of the process of articulation as seen earlier, that is, a pair of phenomena that become distinct from each other in the mode of "this and that."

specifically in his 1974 book *The Philosophy of Capital*『資本論の哲学』. In it he analyzes Marx's theory of the commodity with a focus on the equating (*Gleichsetzung*) of different commodities in their exchange. Although Marx's discussion of "the two factors of commodities" and "the duality of labor," which correspond to the Hiromatsuan dualities of phenomena in the known and the knowing sides, respectively, already prefigures the outline of the fourfold structure, Hiromatsu's reading centers on Marx's subsequent analysis of the value-form, an analysis of the very process through which such a structure is formed.[66] Given the structural parallelism in Hiromatsu's philosophy between the cognitive and the practical dimensions, the problematic of the equating of commodities in value may reasonably be carried over into the equating of phenomena in cognitive meaning.

Let us first consider two phenomena $p_1$ and $p_2$, say, this pine and that cedar, and suppose that $p_2$ is equated with $p_1$ in meaning. Although this equating does not, as with that of commodities, have a quantitative character, I express it likewise by the equation $p_1 = p_2$. Following Marx, by this equation I mean the unidirectional relation in which $p_1$ is worth $p_2$, and not the other way around. By analogy with Marx's terminology, we can say that $p_1$ is determined in meaning relatively to $p_2$ and thus stands in the "relative form of meaning," whereas $p_2$ serves as the measure or "meaning mirror" of this determination (similar to what Marx calls the "value mirror") and is thus in the "equivalent form."[67] In this equating, $p_1$ assumes duality ($p_1$ as $[p_1]$) through the mediation of its reflexive relation to $p_2$. While, like any other phenomenon, $p_1$ is, prior to the above specific equating, already a dual formation of given/meaning, it is newly dualized through this equating, taking on a meaning other than the previous one ("pine").[68] That is, the

---

66. See MEGA II-6: 80ff./138ff. It should be noted, however, that Hiromatsu considers the simple form of value to be already a "constitutive moment" of the total or expanded form of value (HWC 12: 399), and does not treat the transition from the former to the latter—and further to the general form of value—as a dynamic process of structuring. I have elsewhere critically examined this aspect of Hiromatsu's reading of Marx (KATSUMORI 2016B). My analysis here, starting from the equating of two phenomena, will treat the subsequent process as a literally dynamic development.

67. See Marx's argument in MEGA II-6: 81/139f., 85/144.

68. As we can see, this process constitutes part of a manifold process as discussed earlier. The previous meaning "pine" was also formed through equating of phenomena, and, in this sense, the series of equating processes has no unambiguous origin. It is also worth noting that when

meaning of $p_1$ is determined in terms of $p_2$, as something equal in meaning to $p_2$. This state of affairs, a dualization through equating, may be expressed as:

$$p_1 \text{ as } [p_1 (=p_2)].^{69} \tag{1}$$

Next, let us suppose that a third phenomenon $p_3$, say, that oak, appears and is also equated with $p_1$ ($p_1 = p_3$). Then $p_1$ is again, but differently, dualized, where both $p_2$ and $p_3$ serve as $p_1$'s equivalents:

$$p_1 \text{ as } [p_1 (=p_2, p_3)]. \tag{2}$$

The transition from (1) to (2) indicates that the equating of $p_2$, $p_3$, and in general, $p_n$, with $p_1$ each time newly dualizes $p_1$ and redetermines it in meaning. This applies not only to $p_1$, but *mutatis mutandis* also to $p_2$, $p_3$, and other phenomena. It thus follows that each newly added equation "= $p_n$" redetermines all the phenomena with which it is equated, thereby incessantly rearticulating the phenomenal world. In other words, the equating of different phenomena, constitutive of an identical meaning, cannot be a pure reproduction of the same meaning, but contains a movement that each time displaces the phenomena in meaning.[70]

To be sure, it has been pointed out by many that the repetitive reproduction of meaning brings about its displacement or fluctuation. What is important here, however, is that the displacement of meaning, or the displacement of phenomena in meaning, is not simply due to a change in the context external to the phenomena, but that, as analyzed above, it arises structurally and unavoidably from the very constitution of the same meaning.[71] It should be noted that this displacement of meaning is not gener-

---

$p_2$ is equated with $p_1$, $p_1$ may perceptually have disappeared and be reproduced in memory. In this case, $p_2$ is equated not directly with the "original" $p_1$, but with a reproductive remembrance thereof.

69. As mentioned in the first section, Hiromatsu holds that any identification of a meaning, say [p], is already mediated by its difference from other meanings, [q], [r], …. For the sake of simplicity, however, this reflexive determination is not explicitly dealt with here.

70. As we can see, this point is again reminiscent of Derrida's conception of "iterability." According to Derrida, while the possibility of repetition or iteration is constitutive of the ideal identity of meaning, this iteration "always alters… that which it seems to reproduce" (DERRIDA 1990, 82/40). In my view, however, Derrida does not fully explicate why or how this "alteration" occurs, and thus his arguments may be supplemented by an inquiry comparable to the analysis attempted here with respect to Hiromatsu's philosophy.

71. This is related to Hiromatsu's (rather unelaborated) point that "in the mechanism

ally noticed by the consciousness directly engaged in the acts of equating. It can first be recognized as such by a reflective consciousness that directs attention to such a transition as that from (1) to (2). Since, however, as we saw above, reflection on phenomena and their meanings generally displaces what is reflected upon, reflection on a displacement of meaning gives rise to yet another displacement. From this it follows that the displacement of meaning cannot be unambiguously determined. This is analogous to the circumstance in quantum theory, as it is analyzed by Niels Bohr, that the interaction between objects and measuring instruments "cannot be controlled," because any attempt to determine such an interaction in its turn introduces "new possibilities of interaction."[72] We can thus borrow Bohr's terminology to characterize the displacement of meaning as in principle "uncontrollable."

Under certain prevalent, if not ubiquitous, circumstances, however, this uncontrollable displacement seems on the surface to disappear. Suppose that, from the series of phenomena, one picks out a specific phenomenon $p^*$, and gives priority to the equations having $p^*$ on the right side, namely $p_1 = p^*$, $p_2 = p^*$, …, and thus to the as-connections having $p^*$ as the sole equivalent (or meaning mirror), "$p_1$ as $[p_1 (=p^*)]$," "$p_2$ as $[p_2 (=p^*)]$," and so on. In this case, $p^*$ comes to serve as a sign in the narrow sense (e.g. the word "tree") that exclusively represents all the other phenomena in question, thus structurally stabilizing the connection of phenomena.[73] Here $p^*$ may be designated as the general signifier, and the meaning common to all the phenomena as the general signified.[74] Denoting this general signified by $[p^*]$, we can express the structure thus stabilized as:

---

of reproductive maintenance of structures lies also the possibility of structural change" (MARUYAMA and HIROMATSU 1993, 204).

72. BOHR 1987, 2: 40f. According to Bohr, this uncontrollability of interaction leads to the relation of "complementarity" between "the space-time co-ordination and the claim of causality" (BOHR 1987, 1: 54f.). Further, he extends this view beyond physics to the cognitive process in general, pointing to the complementarity of "the analysis of a concept and its immediate application" (BOHR 1987, 1: 20). This enlarged conception of complementarity seems to be essentially linked to the thematic developed here in the text. For a philosophical-historical analysis of Bohr's complementarity, see KATSUMORI 2011.

73. In his analysis of the practical world, Hiromatsu speaks of the "structural stabilization" of the relation of cooperative actions between different persons (HWC 5: 248).

74. These terms—general signifier and signified—appear, under the reified condition in the sense to be defined below, as what Derrida calls "transcendental signifier" and "transcendental

$$p_1, p_2, \ldots \text{ as } [p^*]. \qquad (3)$$

Again with reference to Marx's analysis of the value-form, this structure is analogous to the general form of value or the money form, where p* corresponds to the "general equivalent" or money, and [p*] to the value of commodities as commensurated by the general equivalent.[75] Since, from the Hiromatsuan point of view, sign p* is in principle nothing more than one phenomenon among others, its introduction does not alter the basic fact that the equating of phenomena displaces them in meaning. Moreover, privileging the relations with p* as the equivalent is itself a further displacement of the connection of phenomena. Nevertheless, these displacements tend to be concealed as a result of the above structural stabilization. For, under formula (3), it seems as if the meanings of phenomena $p_1$, $p_2$, ... were determined in terms of p* alone, thus fixed once and for all, without being incessantly redetermined. This leads to the notion that the series of phenomena shares the purely self-identical and directly present meaning [p*]. Furthermore, once the structure (3) is set up for phenomena $p_1$, $p_2$, ..., $p_n$, a further equating of $p_{n+1}$ with these phenomena seems to be confined to the same structure despite the fact that this equating again displaces the phenomena in meaning.[76] For example, although calling something a tree (instead of a grass or anything else) each time redetermines "tree" in meaning, it seems as if the meaning of "tree" were fixed in advance. Thus the displacing movement of phenomena apparently gives way to the synchronic structure of given/meaning. In my view, it is precisely this kind of concealment of the dynamic dimension that Hiromatsu means by reification "in the mode of the *langue*" or "institutional reification." This reification no longer primarily refers to a substantializing misconception of what is in synchronic relationship. The concept of reification may rather be redefined as the *apparent reduction of displacing movement to a synchronic structure*.

From this perspective, let us reexamine Hiromatsu's analogy of meaning or the meaningful cognized with the mathematical function. Hiromatsu

signified," respectively (DERRIDA 1967, 33/20; 1972B, 120/86).

75. See MEGA II-6: 96–101/157–62.

76. As Hiromatsu notes, although the linguistically expressed meaning is "in an incessant process of formation and change," it tends to become apparently fixed and ready-made (HWC 15: 179).

indeed stresses that, in this analogy, what really exists is solely the function $f(x, y, z, ...)$ with specific values inserted into its variables $x, y, z, ...$, and not the function itself as it is independent of inserted values. Yet our consideration above indicates a further point he does not make explicit. That is, the equating of different phenomena corresponds to the substitution of specific values, not into an already existing function, but rather *for other specific values*.[77] It is a series of such substitutions that first generates a "function," while at the same time altering and displacing it. In contrast, the mathematical function, while not independent of the whole set of insertable values, is in general considered as remaining purely the same regardless of the specific values inserted each time, insofar as these values are within the range for which the function is defined in advance. To this extent, contrary to Hiromatsu's remarks, "functional identity" can by no means be contrasted with "rigid self-identity."[78] Put differently, the validity (*Gültigkeit*) of a function implies its indifference (*Gleichgültigkeit*) to specific values. In fact, in his analysis of the practical world, Hiromatsu himself introduces the concept of the function to characterize the circumstance that the personality of individuals becomes "irrelevant (*gleichgültig*)" to their relation of roles.[79] This enables us to see how meaning differs in character from the mathematical function as it is commonly understood. It is by virtue of this difference that the "structural form" of phenomena, a specific kind of meaning, is subject to change.[80] This being the case, the analogy of meaning to the mathematical function, insofar as the latter is understood in the above manner, proves to be already reifying—reifying in the sense redefined above. In other words, reification, as it is dynamically reconceived, refers precisely to the circumstance that different phenomena $p_1, p_2, ...$ seems to be *functionally subsumed* under a general signified [p*]. In fact, this reification seems to be most

77. This is related to Hiromatsu's point in his analysis of the cognitive world that learning rules as objective knowledge is preceded by "imitation" of actions (HWC 16: 442; cf. 430).

78. HWC 15: 26.

79. HWC 1: 118.

80. HWC 14: 220. Hiromatsu remarks that meaning, while remaining self-identical "within certain limits," "can be experienced as something else… if it changes beyond [these] limits" (HWC 1: 350). It should be noted, however, that these limits are not, as in the case of the mathematical function, determined in advance.

strongly prompted in physical-scientific knowledge, which seeks to determine phenomena by subsuming them under mathematical functions.

In the present section, I have striven to extend some of Hiromatsu's conceptual motifs to show how his theory of the fourfold structure tends to move beyond itself. Focusing particularly on the displacement of phenomena in meaning and the reifying mechanism of its concealment, my analysis has also suggested that the functional relation, which, in his account, essentially characterizes "phenomena as they really are,"[81] is itself reified in character. The scope of this section, however, has still been limited to the known side of phenomena. Given the structural link between knower and known, we must explicitly take into account the knowing side, and thus the intersubjective dimension, of phenomena. In the next section, I will accordingly examine the fourfold structuring of phenomena in the mutual understanding of knowers.

### Displacement and Reification in the Fourfold-Structuring of Phenomena

Hiromatsu more or less implicitly supposes circumstances in which a meaning common to various phenomena, or a general signified, is not established, nor a cognizing Someone correlative with such a meaning. In fact, with regard to the knowing side of phenomena—as we have seen in the example of noticing the child's "mistake" of calling a cow a doggie—he starts from the twofoldness of "someone as someone (else)" where not only the former someone, but also the latter is a "concrete individual."[82] Furthermore, as suggested by his remarks that the duality of knowing someone and cognizing Someone holds "except for the latent 'knowing subject' in the developmentally initial phase," and that some kinds of mental illness may be characterized as a "disintegration" of the cognizing Someone, Hiromatsu seems to hold that there *are* phases or cases in which the cognizing Someone

---

81. HWC 15: 18.
82. Here it is not essential, however, to take the individual as the starting point, considering that, in Hiromatsu's view, the personal individual is not a primary being, but derives from the division of pre-personal phenomena into self and other (HWC 15: 112).

is either not yet established or has already collapsed.[83] He does not, however, fully analyze the formation or dissolution of the cognizing Someone, that is, the structuring process of the knower, or the process of intersubjective fourfold *structuring*, as distinct from the synchronic structure. In this section, starting from, but going one step beyond, Hiromatsu's ideas, I will accordingly investigate the dimension of fourfold structuring and thereby amplify my previous discussion of displacement and reification.

In what follows, for the sake of simplicity, I provisionally limit myself to the relation between two knowers and focus on their mutual understanding through linguistic communication.[84] Suppose an English and a Japanese speaker, $P_1$ and $P_2$, both of whom initially have no knowledge of each other's language, utter words $p_1$ and $p_2$—say "tree" and *"ki"*—respectively, and let us consider the process through which they come to grasp these words as having the same meaning.[85] If, to begin with, $P_1$ thinks that $P_2$'s word *"ki"* means "tree," he equates in meaning his own word $p_1$ with the word he has just heard, $p_2$, or, to put it differently, grasps $p_2$ as equal in meaning to $p_1$ ($p_2 = p_1$). That is to say, $P_1$ dualizes $p_2$ into

$$p_2 \text{ as } [p_2 (= p_1)]. \tag{4}$$

In a conjugate manner, the Japanese speaker $P_2$ thinks that $P_1$'s word "tree" means *"ki,"* that is, equates $p_2$ with $p_1$ ($p_1 = p_2$) and thereby dualizes $p_1$ into

$$p_1 \text{ as } [p_1 (= p_2)]. \tag{5}$$

It is important to note that, for the same reason as given in the previous section, these dualizations of phenomena are re-dualizations such that each of the phenomena in question are already displaced in meaning. Even though $p_2$ was, for $P_1$, initially nothing more than a sound lacking a specific linguistic meaning, it was already a phenomenon laden with meaning in the Hiromatsuan broad sense of the term. This $p_2$ or *"ki"* is, through the equat-

---

83. HWC 15: 148, 2: 453.

84. Hiromatsu is critical of the approach that treats language games or speech acts as "the general model of social action" (HWC 16: 341), and I also do not intend to make the following example in the text a paradigm of the intersubjective structuring of phenomena.

85. If, in this example, a tree or *ki* is perceptually given as in the earlier case of "cow/dog," it may be necessary to enter into the relation between such perceptual phenomena and the linguistic signs "tree" and *"ki"* (which are themselves phenomena). To avoid intricacies, however, here we abstract from such reference to perceptual phenomena.

ing relation $p_2 = p_1$, redetermined in meaning as something equal to "tree." *Mutatis mutandis*, the same applies to $p_1$.

The relation $p_2 = p_1$ and its converse $p_1 = p_2$ are different equating relations, and therefore the as-connections (4) and (5), which involve these relations, also differ from each other. That is, in (4), $p_2$ is determined in meaning—with $p_1$ as equivalent (or meaning mirror)—from $P_1$'s standpoint, while (5) represents a reverse determination of meaning from $P_2$'s standpoint. Insofar as the two knowers' points of view cannot be arbitrarily interchanged, (4) and (5) constitute two distinct connections of phenomena that are formally symmetrical and yet mutually exclusive. This being the case, at the present stage, we do *not* yet have the structure in which $P_1$ and $P_2$ jointly, as cognizing Someone, grasp $p_1$ and $p_2$ as the same meaningful cognized or, in other words, as a general signified—general in the still limited sense of being common to the two knowers and to the two known phenomena.

The formation of this kind of structure, that is, the fourfold structural stabilization of the connection of phenomena, is commonly mediated by the introduction of a general signifier as a correlative of the general signified, and takes on various forms depending on the way the general signifier is introduced. Here I will consider the following three types of cases:

(a) Either $p_1$ or $p_2$ is privileged over the other and becomes the general signifier;
(b) A third phenomenon is introduced and privileged over $p_1$ and $p_2$, thereby serving as the general signifier;
(c) A relation of transformation between $p_1$ and $p_2$ is set up in a manner differently from (a) and (b), and the signifying side of this relation itself serves as the general signifier.

Let us start by examining case (a), which seems to conform the most to substantialist ontology.

(a) In the above example, this corresponds to the case in which one of the two knowers, say $P_1$, privileges his own language and imposes it on the other, $P_2$, who comes to submit to this one-sided move by $P_1$. In this case, $P_2$ accepts $P_1$'s point of view, and—if we apply Hiromatsu's term "role" (役割) to the cognitive dimension as well—takes his knowing role as her own, coming to think herself that her word *"ki"* means "tree." Here the equating relation $p_1 = p_2$, which was initially set up by $P_2$, becomes repressed or excluded. In other words, phenomenon $p_2$, which served as $p_1$'s equivalent as well, turns into a term merely determin*ed* in meaning, while the relation $p_2$ = $p_1$ are privileged over $p_1 = p_2$ and thus relation (4) over (5). Through this process, $p_1$, or the word "tree," becomes the general signifier that unilaterally represents $p_2$, and a meaning common to both phenomena, a general signified $[p_1]$, is established. In this way, the set of relations (4) and (5) reduce to the single relation

$$p_1, p_2 \text{ as } [p_1]. \tag{6}$$

Correlatively, both knowers come to play $P_1$'s knowing role as the Role (役柄) of a cognizing Someone, $[P_1]$—let us call it the cognizing Role—and thus the connection of phenomena is stabilized in a fourfold structure ($p_1$, $p_2$ as $[p_1]$ for $P_1$, $P_2$ as $[P_1]$). Speaking again by analogy with Marx's account of the value-form, we can see not only that—similarly to the case (3) in Section 2—$p_1$ corresponds to the general equivalent or money and $[p_1]$ to the value as commensurated by money, but also that $[P_1]$ corresponds to the subject of abstract human labor.

(b) We can also think of another case, however, the case in which two knowers make themselves equal in their relation of roles when coming to mutual understanding. Suppose that a third word p*, say, the Esperantist "arbro," is introduced. In this case, the two knowers take the point of view of a "virtual" knower using this p*, set up the equating relations $p_1$ = p* and $p_2$ = p* with p* serving as the equivalent, and thus dualize $p_1$ and $p_2$ into "$p_1$ as $[p_1$ (= p*)]" and "$p_2$ as $[p_1$ (= p*)]," respectively. Here, if these as-connections are privileged not only over the possible relations "p* as $[p^*$ (= $p_1$)]" and "p* as $[p^*$ (= $p_2$)]," but also over (4) and (5), the series of the connections of meaning will reduce to the relation

$$p_1, p_2 \text{ as } [p^*], \tag{7}$$

where the third term p* serves as the general signifier. In this way, the conflictual relationship between (4) and (5) is dissolved, and $p_1$ and $p_2$ become horizontally translatable (or transformable) into each other. Correlatively, the two knowers jointly play the third knowing role, the role of the utterer of p*, as the cognizing Role, and thereby attain a consensus ($p_1$, $p_2$ as $[p^*]$ for $P_1$, $P_2$ as $[P^*]$).

(c) Further, there may also be the case in which the two knowers do not introduce the third in such a "substantialist" manner as above and yet attain an equal mutual understanding. In the example of "tree" and "*ki*," this is the process through which a stable relation of translation between the two terms is formed without being mediated by a privileged linguistic sign. This kind of case is, however, treated by Hiromatsu specifically in his epistemological analysis of the theory of relativity in such works as *Outpost to a Koto-based Worldview* 『事的世界観への前哨』(1975) and *The Philosophy of Relativity Theory* 『相対性理論の哲学』(1981), and let us take this as an example here.[86] According to Hiromatsu, in Albert Einstein's relativity theory, observers start by recognizing that their results of space-time measurement are relative to their coordinate systems (for example, the contraction of bodies moving relatively to the system), and, through "intersubjective communication and mutual understanding," each come to grasp the "phenomenon-for-the-self" and the "phenomenon-for-the-other" synthetically in one and the same intersubjective meaning.[87] I designate the results of measurement obtained by observers $P_1$ and $P_2$ or their linguistic representations (for instance, the length of a rod being $l_1$ and $l_2$) as $p_1$ and $p_2$, respectively. Here, too, the starting point of $P_1$ and $P_2$'s mutual understanding is their setting up relations (4) and (5), respectively, but, as it turns out, the subsequent process will differ from cases (a) and (b).

The characteristic feature of this process will become clearer if it is compared with the case of pre-relativistic electrodynamics (as represented by Hendrik Antoon Lorentz' theory), which precisely corresponds to case (b). In pre-relativistic electrodynamics, the results of measurement in a particular coordinate system such as the absolutely resting system or ether system are privileged, and the connection of phenomena is structured in such a way that those privileged results of measurement serve as the general signifier $p^*$. By contrast, in relativity theory, which rejects the assumption of

---

86. I have elsewhere surveyed and critically examined Hiromatsu's analysis of relativity theory with a focus on the same issue of intersubjective cognitive structure as discussed here (Katsumori 2016A, esp. 163–8, 181–5).

87. HWC 3: 284, 288. To be sure, in the same way as in the case of cow/doggie, for a stricter discussion we would need to distinguish between observational phenomena and their linguistic representations and enter into the relation between them. Here, however, for the sake of convenience, I will—as Hiromatsu himself often does—provisionally abstract from this aspect of the state of affairs.

such a privileged system, neither $p_1$ nor $p_2$, nor any other particular result of measurement, can serve as the general signifier. Rather, the observers adopt the procedure of deriving a general signifier/signified from the very relation between phenomena $p_1$ and $p_2$ in conjunction with their own observational standpoints (corresponding to the states of motion of the systems). The two observers each start by setting themselves (imaginatively) in each other's standpoint, that is, playing the other's role as the knower, so that relation (4) holds also for $P_2$, and (5) for $P_1$.[88] Then they reflectively objectify their observational standpoints and the results of measurement, or, in other words, shift part of their knowing roles as observers to the known side. Thus, in place of the initial phenomena $p_1$ and $p_2$, the phenomena *for* the respective observing knowers, "$p_1$ for $P_1$" and "$p_2$ for $P_2$" (which I denote by $p_1'$ and $p_2'$, respectively), become the known sides of new phenomena. The knowing sides of these new phenomena are constituted by a single theoretical knower, no longer bound by particular observational standpoints. $P_1$ and $P_2$, both playing the role of this theoretical knower as cognizing Role [$\tilde{P}$], make the transformation relation between $p_1'$ and $p_2'$ itself a general signified [$\tilde{p}$]. They thus set up the relation

$$p_1', p_2' \text{ as } [\tilde{p}] \qquad (8)$$

as the form of their mutual understanding ($p_1'$, $p_2'$ as [$\tilde{p}$] for $P_1$, $P_2$ as [$\tilde{P}$]). This may be called a relationist structural stabilization of the connection of phenomena, where there is no self-contained term that exclusively represents the meanings of phenomena. This is not to say, however, that no general signifier appears. Rather, the transformation relation between $p_1'$ and $p_2'$ is a dual formation of signifier-signified (given-meaning), whose signifying side, namely, the mathematical equations of the coordinate transformation (the Lorentz transformation in the case of special relativity), serve as the general signifier [$\tilde{p}$]. That is, here again it is not the case that the general signified [$\tilde{p}$] is purely ideally shared, but that the general signifier-signified—which is a phenomenon standing beside $p_1$ and $p_2$—is introduced and given a pivotal role in the structural stabilization of phenomena.

In all the above three cases, we can see how the phenomena undergo not only displacements in meaning, but also displacements in the knowers' role

---

88. See HWC 3: 400.

relationship. To begin with, just as there occurred displacements of meaning in (4) and (5), where $p_1$ and $p_2$ were equated and each dualized, there occur similar displacements in case (b), when p* is equated and thereby $p_1$ and $p_2$ are newly dualized. Moreover, the privileging of a specific as-connection in cases (a) and (b) is itself a displacement in meaning. On the other hand, a knower's playing the standpoint of another knower constitutes a displacement in their role relationship. Specifically, when $P_2$ plays $P_1$'s standpoint in cases (a) and (c), $P_1$'s knowing role becomes a role that $P_2$ also plays as a knowing subject. Further, in case (c), when the two knowers reflectively objectify their own observational standpoints, there occurs not only, in the same way as in the previous section, a displacement in meaning due to reflection, but also a displacement in the knower-known relation in such a way that part of the knowing role shifts to the known side. Finally, in all these cases, the formation of a stable structure is the establishment of new connections of meanings as expressed by (6), (7), and (8), where (the known sides of) the phenomena are displaced in meaning in such a way as to be represented by a general signifier, and also the two knowers are displaced in their knowing role so that they jointly play a cognizing Role.

These displacements in meaning and knowing role seem to be inevitable insofar as we dynamically extend Hiromatsu's relationist conception of both the knowing and the known sides of phenomena. Furthermore, a stable structure, even though once set up, cannot be maintained without being incessantly applied to new phenomena, and such an application each time newly displaces the connection of phenomena. This incessant displacement is, to be sure, not unrelated to what Hiromatsu calls the "incessant correction" of meaning. As he puts it:

> …needless to say, this intersubjective unity and identity of the meaningful cognized do not strictly hold from a transcendent point of view, but is a belief held each time by the consciousness involved. This belief can be subject reflectively to incessant correction. (However, in such reflective correction, an intersubjectively identical and unitary meaningful cognized is posited each time, and the structure of the intersubjective identity and unity of the meaningful cognized does not break down, but "persists.")[89]

---

89. HWC 15: 195.

Yet the movement of displacement as discussed so far, while it may contain as particular cases the knower's reflectively guided corrections, is in principle uncontrollable (for the reason given in the previous section) so that, even when reflected upon, displacement each time exceeds that reflection. This being the case, Hiromatsu's remark above may be reversed as follows: The intersubjective identity of meaning is always accompanied and affected by incessant displacement in meaning. The displacement of phenomena is not simply caused by factors external to the structure of intersubjective identity, but is structurally involved in the very positing of intersubjective identity itself.

However, this displacement tends to be concealed by the stabilization of structure as expressed by (6), (7), or (8), and, as may be suggested from our findings in the previous section, this tendency advances if such stable structures are formed not only between two knowers or two known phenomena, but among indefinitely many phenomena. That is, under these circumstances, the connection of phenomena in meaning as well as the knowers' role relation seems to be fixed so that not only are the phenomena apparently subsumed under a general signified, but also the knowers are apparently subsumed under a general cognizing Role. In other words, it now seems as if individual knowers did not *substitute* for each other in their roles in a "self-ridding (脱自的) way,"[90] but rather were simply *inserted* into a cognizing Role that maintains its functional self-identity. Precisely this state of affairs may be called reification in the dimension of fourfold structuring. This reification appears paradoxically to be more unavoidable in case (c), where the general signifier and signified are formed relationally, than in cases (a) and (b), where $p_1$ and $p^*$, respectively, serve as a general signifier. For in relation (8) in case (c), although the general signifier is the signifying side of a phenomenon that in principle stands side by side with phenomena $p_1$ and $p_2$, it nevertheless appears as a transformation rule standing above the two phenomena, as if it transcended the connection of phenomena in general. In this way, the signifying side of the transformation relation becomes seemingly transparent, and this leans toward the notion that only the meaning of the transformation relation, namely the general signified, is intersubjectively shared. This notion becomes all the more irresistible in the case where the

---

90. HWC 1: 169.

transformation relation is a mathematical function such as the coordinate transformation in the above example, which is marked by the apparent fixity and unambiguity of the connection between the transformation equations and their meaning.[91] This suggests that modern physics, which Hiromatsu values positively for its tendency to overcome substantialism and the subject/object schema, may be subject to a critique of reification in the dynamic dimension.[92]

This renewed conception of reification may be further elucidated with reference to Hiromatsu's central concept of intersubjectivity. To translate the Western philosophical term "intersubjectivity" or *Intersubjektivität*, Hiromatsu uses the two Japanese words *kanshukansei* (間主観性) and *kyōdōshukansei* (共同主観性) with their nuances somewhat different from each other. That is, the term *kanshukansei* (or at times *kanshutaisei* 間主体性), which consists of *kan* (between) and *shukansei* (subjectivity), thus reproducing literally the original sense of "inter-," is mainly used where knowers are personally polarized in the mode of self and other. On the other hand, *kyōdōshukansei* (or *kyōdōshutaisei* 共同主体性), with *kyōdō* meaning "common" or "joint," is often used where knowers, having already attained "mutual recognition," exist together in the mode of "we," so that the term could in some cases better be rendered as "cosubjectivity."[93] Yet Hiromatsu also holds that *kanshukansei* simultaneously means *kyōdōshukansei*, and does not treat the two words as technically distinct terms. However, our consideration so far suggests that the difference between the two terms is relevant to the dynamic conception of reification as proposed above. Here I accordingly introduce the following tentative terminological distinction: I reserve the English term "intersubjectivity" for the cases where knowers are polarized as self and other, while using the term "cosubjectivity" for the cases where they exist jointly as "we." With this terminological setting, we can

---

91. As I have suggested elsewhere, this reifying mechanism seems to underlie the following conceptual difference between Einstein's two theories of relativity: The dimension of intersubjective structuring, which is still visible in special relativity, tends to be concealed in general relativity with the adoption of the tensor formalism, which incorporates in itself the intersubjective validity of knowledge among coordinate systems. See KATSUMORI 1992, 578, 590; 2016a, 183ff.

92. See KATSUMORI 2016a, 185f.

93. See HWC 15: 130.

now characterize the above reification as the circumstance that *the intersubjective movement of mutual substitution of knowing roles apparently reduces to the cosubjective structure of their subsumption under a Role*. Put differently, reification as reconceived here pertains to the circumstance that knowers, deprived of mutual otherness, seem to constitute a cosubjective "we," and that a purely identical meaning presents itself to this "we."

In some cases, this "we" may be scholarly cognizers, that is, (the ideal moment of) subjects of scholarly reflection. Since the previous section, we have seen how reflection on a phenomenon, itself involved in the connection of phenomena, brings about a displacement of the phenomenon in meaning, and this should apply to scholarly reflection as well. To be sure, Hiromatsu maintains that the scholarly "we" is not a self-contained joint subject, but just the cognitive moment whose Role individual knowers play in scholarly reflection.[94] However, this is not the whole state of affairs with which we are concerned here. Rather, each time scholarly reflection on phenomena is carried out, the phenomena are redetermined as thus reflected upon and are displaced in meaning in correlation with the knowing role of the reflection. Specifically, Hiromatsu's (or my) analysis of communication between knowers, in imaginatively playing the roles of the knowers, involves itself in the communicative process and thus brings about a displacement of meanings and roles. In the reifying perspective, however, precisely this state of affairs is concealed from the scholarly reflective knower. That is to say—as Hiromatsu's texts may at times give rise to this impression—the scholarly subject apparently "looks on in a purely detached manner" at fourfold-structured phenomena as they really are.[95]

In this paper, I have surveyed and analyzed Hiromatsu's theory of the fourfold structure and thereby sought to extend it fully to the dynamic dimension. This extension is not simply an enlargement of the domain, but a qualitative change that contains kinds of inversion. First of all, we have seen how the equating of phenomena and the knowers' mutual understanding, which make possible the identity of meanings and roles, paradoxically displace these meanings and roles. We have also seen how this movement of

94. See HWC 4: 425.
95. HWC 15: 32; cf. 1: 31.

displacement tends to reduce apparently to a synchronic structure, which I have characterized as reification in the dynamic dimension. It has thus turned out that dynamic inquiry is not limited to an "auxiliary means" of synchronic structural analysis, but may be developed as a deconstructive critique of a reification that tends to make the latter apparently self-contained.[96] This enables us to see how Hiromatsu's concept of reification and related basic concepts have themselves undergone a series of *displacements* in meaning. Here we cannot simply answer the alternative question of whether the present study constitutes a criticism of Hiromatsu's philosophy or a positive reinterpretation thereof. What has been shown is, rather, how his philosophy—through a movement that at once sustains and disrupts it—opens itself to the possibility of a radical reconfiguration.

* This paper is based on Chapter 1 of my Japanese-language book 『現代日本哲学への問い：「われわれ」とそのかなた』 [Questioning contemporary Japanese philosophy: The "we" and beyond] (Tokyo: Keisō Shobō, 2009), 1–43.

## References

*Abbreviations*

HWC    『廣松渉著作集』 [Collected works of Hiromatsu Wataru]. Tokyo: Iwanami Shoten, 1996–1997.

MEGA   *Karl Marx/Friedrich Engels Gesamtausgabe*. Berlin: Diez Verlag; Amsterdam: Akademie Verlag.

*Other works*

Bohr, Niels
1987   *The Philosophical Writings of Niels Bohr*, 4 vols. Woodbridge, Conn.: Ox Bow Press, 1987–1998.

Derrida, Jacques
1967   *De la grammatologie* (Paris: Les Éditions de Minuit). English translation by

---

96. Hiromatsu himself at times characterizes his critique of reification as "deconstruction" (Maruyama and Hiromatsu 1993, 82). It is also noteworthy that, at a symposium held on the occasion of Derrida's visit to Japan in 1983, Hiromatsu outlined his philosophical views with reference to Derrida's thought, noting that the "unity of identity and difference" in the as-connection of given and meaning "corresponds precisely to Derridean *différance*" (Hiromatsu 1983, 10). Given the lack of his thematic account of Derrida's work, however, the relation between the thought of the two philosophers is yet to be examined.

Gayatri Chakravorty Spivak, *Of Grammatology* (Baltimore: Johns Hopkins University Press, 1976).

1972a *Marges de la philosophie* (Paris : Les Éditions de Minuit). English translation by Alan Bass, *Margins of Philosophy* (Chicago: The University of Chicago Press, 1982).

1972b *Positions* (Paris: Les Éditions de Minuit). English translation by Alan Bass, *Positions* (Chicago: The University of Chicago Press, 1987).

1990 *Limited Inc.* (Paris: Éditions Galilée). English translation by Samuel Weber and Jeffrey Mehlman, *Limited Inc* (Evanston, Ill.: Northwestern University Press, 1988).

Hiromatsu Wataru 廣松 渉

1983 "Autour de 'la différance." Translated by Adachi Kazuhiro, unpublished manuscript.

1988 『新哲学入門』[A new introduction to philosophy] (Tokyo: Iwanami Shoten).

2011 "The Subjective Duality of Phenomena," translated by Viren Murthy, in James W. Heisig, Thomas P. Kasulis, and John C. Maraldo, eds., *Japanese Philosophy: A Sourcebook* (Honolulu: University of Hawaii Press), pp. 973–8.

Katsumori Makoto 勝守 真

1992 "The Theories of Relativity and Einstein's Philosophical Turn," in *Studies in History and Philosophy of Science*, Vol. 23, 557–92.

2009 『現代日本哲学への問い:「われわれ」とそのかなた』[Questioning contemporary Japanese philosophy: The "we" and beyond] (Tokyo: Keisō Shobō).

2011 *Niels Bohr's Complementarity: Its Structure, History, and Intersections with Hermeneutics and Deconstruction*, Vol. 286 of *Boston Studies in the Philosophy of Science* (Dordrecht: Springer).

2016a "Hiromatsu on Mach's Philosophy and Relativity Theory," *European Journal of Japanese Philosophy* 1: 149–88.

2016b "Hiromatsu on Marx's Theory of the Commodity," *Frontiers of Japanese Philosophy* 8: 170–92.

Kobayashi Toshiaki 小林敏明

1987 『〈ことなり〉の現象学』[The phenomenology of *"différance"*] (Tokyo: Kōbundō).

Kumano Sumihiko 熊野純彦

2004 『戦後思想の一断面:哲学者廣松渉の軌跡』[A cross section of postwar thought: Traces of the philosopher Hiromatsu Wataru] (Tokyo: Nakanishiya Shuppan)

Maruyama Keizaburō 丸山圭三郎

1981 『ソシュールの思想』[Saussure's thought] (Tokyo: Iwanami Shoten).

MARUYAMA Keizaburō and HIROMATSU Wataru
　1993　『記号的世界と物象化』[The signitive world and reification] (Tokyo: Jōkyō Shuppan)

MARX, Karl
　1976　*Capital: A Critique of Political Economy*. Translated by Ben Fowkes (Harmondsworth: Penguin Books).

Roman Paşca
*Kanda University of International Studies, Japan*

# Parabola păsărilor
Andō Shōeki 安藤昌益

ORIGINAL TITLE: 「諸鳥会合シテ法世ヲ論ズ」『安藤昌益全集6巻』 [Opera completă a lui Andō Shōeki, vol. 6], Tōkyō: Nōsangyoson Bunka Kyōkai, 1997, 34–87)

KEYWORDS: Japonia—perioada Edo—filosofie—Andō Shōeki—parabola păsărilor

## Prezentare

Andō Shōeki 安藤昌益 (1703-1762) este, probabil, una dintre figurile cele mai misterioase din istoria intelectuală a Japoniei. Există extrem de puține informații certe despre viața lui: se știe, de exemplu, că și-a început activitatea ca filosof după vîrsta de 40 de ani, cînd se mutase deja la Hachinohe, un fief mic din nordul Japoniei; primii ani din viața lui reprezintă însă, în mare parte, o enigmă. Spre deosebire de mulți dintre intelectualii contemporani lui, Shōeki nu a aderat la nici unul dintre curentele majore de gîndire care predominau în epocă (neo-confucianism, budism, nativism etc.) ci, dimpotrivă, le-a criticat pe toate încercînd să propună în schimb un sistem filosofic propriu. A avut foarte puțini discipoli, iar după moartea lui scrierile sale au rămas practic necunoscute vreme de două secole pînă cînd au fost redescoperite din întîmplare în perioada Meiji (1868–1912), în a doua jumătate a secolului al XIX-lea.

Scrierea cea mai importantă a lui Shōeki, *Shizen shin'eidō* 『自然真営道』 („Adevărata cale de funcționare a naturii"), prezintă o viziune asupra universului în care există două lumi distincte: "lumea naturii" (自然の世) și lumea "legii private"[1] (私法世). Lumea naturii reprezintă un tărîm ideal, primordial, în care toate formele și manifestările de energie și viață există într-o stare nealterată și necoruptă, în vreme ce lumea legii private reprezintă societatea umană, marcată de introducerea de legi artificiale și, astfel, compromisă

---

1. Multe dintre noțiunile care apar în *Shizen shin'eidō*—„lege" 法, „cale" 道, „natură" 自然 etc.—fac parte din vocabularul budist, taoist sau confucianist, însă Shōeki se distanțează de sensul original susținînd că este incorect și propunînd în loc propria interpretare. Aceasta reprezintă una dintre modalitățile prin care, pe o parte, critică toate „doctrinele" și, pe de altă parte, atrage atenția asupra limitelor limbajului.

prin devierea de la adevărata cale a naturii. Scrierea este un text extrem de complex în care abundă idei, concepte și noțiuni care pot servi drept suport pentru o serie întreagă de interpretări foarte variate. Astfel, Shōeki poate fi considerat, de exemplu, un promotor al fiziocrației, sau un „filosof agrar(ian)", în special datorită conceptului de „cultivare directă" (直耕); în același timp, este și un critic social foarte vocal, nemulțumit de starea de fapt din Japonia perioadei Edo (1603–1868)—mai ales de sistemul de clase și de decăderea fermierilor—pe care o critică propunînd în schimb o viziune asupra lumii în care orice ierarhie socială este practic imposibilă; nu în ultimul rînd, este un filosof naturalist care descrie o imagine holistică a naturii ca tărîm autosuficient și complet, guvernat în exclusivitate de forțe și principii naturale. Shōeki este, însă, dincolo de toate aceste calificări, un filosof pur și simplu care propune un *Weltanschauung* nou și extrem de original.

Fragmentul tradus aici, „Parabola păsărilor", face parte dintr-o secțiune intitulată *Hōsei monogatari* 法世物語 („Povești din lumea legii private"), inclusă ca o anexă în textul *Shizen shin'eidō*. În afară de cea a păsărilor, există trei alte parabole: a jivinelor, a tîrîtoarelor și a peștilor, care se adună într-un soi de congres general al viețuitoarelor pentru a dezbate diferențele dintre lumile lor respective și lumea legii private (societatea umană). Concluzia este, în fiecare dintre aceste parabole, că lumea legii private nu este decît o imitație ieftină și meschină a lumii animalelor, un tărîm al corupției și al lăcomiei, care e limpede că s-a îndepărtat de la Adevărata cale a naturii.

Yasunaga (1992) susține că întreaga secțiune *Hōsei monogatari* reprezintă de fapt o anomalie stilistică în ansamblul scrierilor lui Shōeki și că filosoful nu ar fi plănuit să o includă inițial în *Shizen shin'eidō*. Într-adevăr, ca stil de scriere, secțiunea este diferită de restul textului—deși începe cu un scurt pasaj în proză inspirat de textele clasice chineze, trece aproape imediat la un amestec de ideograme și de silabar *kana*; în plus, tonul dezbaterii păsărilor este neprotocolar, presărat cu expresii colocviale și, pe alocuri, chiar licențioase.

Însă indiferent care au fost intențiile lui Shōeki, parabolele reprezintă un gen experimental hibrid (poate) unic în istoria filosofiei japoneze, în care autorul se dovedește a fi și un maestru al satirei, recurgînd la numeroase jocuri de cuvinte și de ideograme pentru a critica nu numai situația socială impusă de shogunatul Tokugawa, ci și doctrina budistă, confucianismul, taoismul, strategii militari din China antică, Shintoismul sau medicina tradițională. Iar satira aceasta constituie o introducere excelentă pentru filosofia lui Shōeki și ne oferă o perspectivă generoasă asupra *Weltanschauung*-ului pe care îl propune. După cum observă Tucker (2013), genul parabolei nu este ceva nou în istoria intelectuală a Asiei de Est, fiind folosit pe larg îndeosebi de taoiști precum Zhuang Zhou. Ce este interesant însă este faptul că Shōeki folosește acest mecanism al discursului tocmai pentru a critica (și) taoismul și pe Zhuang Zhou însuși, lucru inedit în peisajul intelectual al Japoniei din perioada Tokugawa.

Dincolo de valențele literare ale textului, „Parabola păsărilor" poate fi considerată un soi de pilulă concentrată care conține *in nuce* esența filosofiei lui Shōeki. Pe lîngă apariția în text a numeroase concepte-cheie precum *tenka* (転下), *tenchi* (転定), *kasshin* (活真), *chokkō* (直耕) sau cele trei tipuri de energii, parabola expune limpede și fără echivoc imaginea celor două lumi aflate în opoziție, cea a Naturii și cea a legii private, creionînd în același timp un portret dublu al ființei umane înainte și *după* devierea de la Adevărata cale a naturii.

Pentru realizarea traducerii—prima de acest fel în limba română—am folosit ediția operelor complete ale lui Andō Shōeki publicată între 1995 și 1998 în îngrijirea lui Terao Gorō, în care parabolele apar în volumul 6. De asemenea, pentru clarificarea unor termeni și concepte din original și pentru redactarea notelor am consultat o serie de lucrări și articole care discută filosofia lui Shōeki, în special Terao (1997), Joly (1996), și Inaba (2004); lista completă a acestora se găsește în bibliografia de la final.

# Andō Shōeki

# Parabola păsărilor

*Traducere și note Roman Pașca*

(諸鳥会合シテ法世²ヲ論ズ)

Cînd feluritele păsări s-au adunat să discute, primul care a vorbit a fost porumbelul:

> Iată care este părerea mea, bine cîntărită: pe cer și pe mare³, dar și pe pămîntul care se află între ele (大地) trăiesc o sumedenie de viețuitoare. Dintre acestea, oamenii sînt dominați de energia descendentă și conțin înlăuntrul lor energia laterală și pe cea ascendentă⁴—tocmai de aceea sînt oameni. Pe deasupra, de vreme ce oamenii sînt străbătuți de fluxul descendent de materie primară (活真) fără nici o opreliște, singura lor îndeletnicire pe lume⁵ trebuie să fie doar cultivarea directă⁶, fără nici o abatere către vreo altă ocupație. Prin

---

2. 法世 reprezintă de fapt o contracție a termenului 私法ノ世 („lumea legii private"), care se referă la o societate controlată printr-un sistem de legi bazate pe interese și dorințe personale. Termenul *hōsei* este folosit, deci, pentru a desemna sistemul și modelul teoretic dezvoltate în conformitate cu interesul propriu al clasei conducătoare. În lucrările lui Shōeki apare în opoziție cu 自然ノ世 („lumea Naturii"), care desemnează conceptul de „societate fără clase". Prin urmare, *hōsei* poate fi tradus și ca „societate divizată în clase".

3. *Tenchi*, care în mod normal este redat prin ideogramele 天地, este scris ca 転定 de către Andō Shōeki. Sensul său primar este de univers („cer și pămînt"), dar uneori—precum aici, în prima replică a porumbelului din *Parabola păsărilor*—este folosit pentru a indica cerurile și oceanele (și corespondența dintre ele). 央土 („pămîntul din centru") se referă la ceea ce se află între ceruri și oceane, și anume pămîntul.

4. Potrivit lui Shōeki, există trei tipuri de energii care circulă în natură: *tsūki* 通気 (energia descendentă), 横気 (energia laterală) și *gyakki* 逆気 (energia ascendentă). *Tsūki* circulă în jos dinspre cer spre pămînt și dă naștere ființelor umane, *ōki* circulă în lateral și dă naștere celor patru tipuri de viețuitoare (păsări, jivine, tîrîtoare și pești), iar *gyakki* circulă în sus dinspre pămînt spre cer și dă naștere plantelor (ierburi, arbori și cereale).

5. 転下 este versiunea lui Shōeki pentru 天下 („ceea ce se află sub cer"), termenul utilizat în China antică—și apoi adoptat și în Japonia—pentru a face referință la lume / univers în general. Ca și în cazul 天地, Shōeki înlocuiește ideograma 天 („cer") cu 転— cu aceeași citire *ten*, dar cu un sens diferit: „a se mișca", „a se roti", „a se învîrti" etc. Pentru Shōeki, utilizarea lui 転 este singura modalitate de a reda caracterul dinamic al lumii în întregul ei, precum și al structurii sale interne.

6. „Cultivarea directă" (直耕) este un concept creat de Shōeki pentru a se referi la

urmare, între oameni nu există diviziuni între superiori și inferiori, nobili și mireni sau săraci și bogați; oamenii nu mănîncă oameni și nici nu sînt mîncați de alți oameni, nu iau și nu dau unul de la celălalt și fiecare dintre ei își găsește soțul sau soața potrivită. Aceasta este adevărata situație⁷ a societății umane (人ノ世).

Însă noi, cele patru tipuri de animale⁸, sîntem dominate de energia laterală și conținem înlăuntru energia descendentă și cea ascendentă. Dacă energia laterală este în faza progresivă⁹, ne naștem ca păsări. În cazul nostru, așadar, energia descendentă este domolită și sîntem dominate de faza progresivă a energiei laterale. Iar vulturul, la care energia laterală este cea mai avansată, este conducătorul nostru (王). Cocorul este nobilul de la curte (公卿), marele dregător (大夫); șoimul este suzeranul feudal (諸候); cioara este meșteșugarul (工) în rîndul păsărilor; cotofana este negustorul (商); acvila este stăpînul nostru (主), iar păsările cele mici sînt toate slujitorii (奴僕) lor. Așadar, vulturul prăduiește și mănîncă gîște și șoimi, iar șoimul prinde și mănîncă ciori, vrăbii și toate celelalte soiuri de păsări. Cocorul prinde și mănîncă fazani, iar cioara prinde și mănîncă vrăbii și porumbei. Astfel e orînduirea, ca cel mare să îl mănînce pe cel mic (大ハ小ヲ食フ). Iar asta se întîmplă pentru că noi păsările sîntem născute din faza progresivă a energiei laterale și, prin urmare, materia primară e direcționată în lateral. Prin urmare, orînduirea aceasta ca cel mare să îl mănînce pe cel mic este îndeletnicirea noastră obișnuită, aceasta este cultivarea directă pentru noi, păsările. Și sîntem astfel pentru că materia primară a cerului¹⁰ circulă prin noi în lateral.

---

totalitatea activităților productive, de la aratul pămîntului pînă la recoltare. Într-un sens extins, *chokkō* e folosit și pentru a desemna orice activitate creatoare, de la energiile ontologice ale naturii pînă la toate îndeletnicirile și activitățile care susțin existența tuturor formelor de viață, de la ființe umane pînă la plante.

7. 通神 este un alt termen creat de Shōeki, care folosește ideograma 神 („zeu", „divinitate") interschimbabil cu 心 („suflet", „inimă", „minte") sau 真 („adevăr", „realitate") deoarece toate trei pot fi citite *shin*. În *Parabole*, *tsūshin* este adesea folosit cu sensul de „adevărata stare de lucruri", „situația reală".

8. 四類 (literal, „cele patru tipuri") este termenul utilizat de Shōkei pentru a desemna cele patru tipuri de viețuitoare: păsările (鳥), jivinele (獣), tîrîtoarele (虫) și peștii (魚).

9. 横進偏気 se referă la faza progresivă (de avansare ) a energiei laterale care domină animalele. Această fază dă naștere păsărilor, și este adesea menționată în contrast cu faza regresivă (de retragere) *ōtaihenki* (横退偏気), care dă naștere jivinelor.

10. *Tenshin* 転真 este încă unul dintre termenii în care Shōeki înlocuiește ideograma 天 cu 転. *Tenshin* este în principiu similar cu *kasshin* (sau *ikitemakoto*) 活真, însă e folosit de multe ori cu o intensiune mai vastă: *tenshin* nu reprezintă materia primară care există în oceane și pe pămînt, nici cea care se găsește în ființele umane sau în alte

Noi, toate cele patru tipuri de animale, avem această soartă: cel mare îl mănîncă pe cel mic, mîncăm și sîntem mîncate unele de celelalte. Oamenii, însă, nu ar trebui să prindă și să mănînce animale. Această practică a fost începută de sfinții din vechime[11] și reprezintă o fărădelege. De la bun început, sfinții au nesocotit Calea cerului[12]. Tu, prietenă cioară, ce părere ai despre acestea?

Cioara a răspuns:

Este întocmai cum ai grăit tu. Oamenii se nasc din materia primară a cerului care circulă prin ei de sus în jos și, în concordanță cu acea materie primară, trebuie să trăiască prin cultivarea directă a grînelor. Cu toate astea, cînd au apărut sfinții din vechime și Buddha[13], aceștia au refuzat să cultive pămîntul (不耕) și au nesocotit astfel calea cultivării directe impusă de materia primară a cerului: au furat și s-au înfruptat cu lăcomie din bucate pe care nu le cultivau. Apoi, au născocit propriile lor legi (私法) și astfel, odată cu apariția conducătorilor (王), a nobililor (公卿), a dregătorilor (大夫), a suzeranilor (諸侯), a războinicilor (士), a meșteșugarilor (工) și a negustorilor (商), a luat naștere lumea legii private (法世). Conducătorul a impus legea, iar mai departe fiecare a impus propria lege după poziție și rang; la fel au făcut și cei fără poziție și rang, iar dacă cineva nesocotea legea, acela era osîndit la moarte. Astfel, pentru că și cei superiori și cei inferiori deopotrivă sînt constrînși de legi, lumea lor se cheamă lumea legii private. Prin aceste legi, conducătorul îi pune pe nobili și pe dregători să trudească pentru el și apoi

---

viețuitoare, ci materia primordială care circulă între și prin ceruri. Astfel, *tenshin* este înțeles adesea ca o versiune mai abstractă a puterilor creatoare ale *kasshin*.

11. *Seijin* 聖人 indică „sfinții" din China antică, și anume: cei trei suverani auguști (Fu Xi 伏羲, Shennong 神農 și Împăratul Galben 黄帝) și cei cinci împărați (Shaohao 少昊, Zhuanxu 顓頊, Ku 黄帝, Yao 堯 și Shun 舜) de dinainte de dinastia Xia 夏朝, cei trei suverani (Yu 禹, fondatorul dinastiei Xia; Tang 湯王, fondatorul dinastiei Shang 商朝; Wen 文王, fondatorul dinastiei Zhou 周朝), suveranul Wu 武王 (primul din dinastia Zhou), ducele de Zhou 周公 (fratele regelui Wu) și Confucius 孔子. În anumite pasaje, Shōeki se referă la ei ca fiind cei „unsprezece sfinți", lăsînd deoparte trei dintre împărați (Shaohao, Zhuanxu și Ku).

12. 転道 este modul în care Shōeki alege să scrie 天道, „Calea Cerului", termen folosit de obicei în contrast cu 人道, „Calea Omului". În scrierile lui Shōeki, *tendō* desemnează legile care reglementează mișcările ritmice ale materiei primare *kasshin*.

13. 聖・釈 este termenul folosit de Shōeki pentru a face referire, sintetic, atît la „sfinții" din China antică (聖人), cît și la Buddha (釈迦). Într-o interpretare mai largă, termenul desemnează orice conducător sau lider, precum și principiile ideologice pe care acesta le susține.

mănîncă roadele strădaniei lor; nobilii și dregătorii mănîncă roadele strădaniei suzeranilor; suzeranii mănîncă roadele strădaniei războinicilor din suită; războinicii mănîncă roadele strădaniei meșteșugarilor și negustorilor—astfel, stăpînii se înfruptă mereu din munca servitorilor lor. La fel fac și călugării budiști, medicii, preoții de la altare și pustnicii din munți. Lucrurile acestea sînt aidoma orînduielii noastre ca cel mare să îl mănînce pe cel mic, așa că lumea oamenilor este întru totul asemenea lumii noastre. Lumea oamenilor nu e cu nimic mai bună sau mai presus decît a noastră. Tu ce părere ai, prietene uliu?

Uliul a răspuns astfel:

Și măcar de-ar fi numai faptul că lumea lor nu e cu nimic mai bună decît a noastră! Printre oameni sînt unii care au furat și și-au însușit cîmpurile care ar fi trebuit să fie ale tuturor celor din lume (転下), spunînd „Asta e țara mea! Ăsta e teritoriul meu! Ăsta e fieful meu!". Au atacat și au furat calea cultivării directe și s-au îmbuibat peste măsură. Pe deasupra, oamenii trăiesc într-o lume în care cel mare îl mănîncă pe cel mic—lumea legii umane (人ノ法世) este mult mai lacomă (重欲) și mai ignorantă (妄迷) decît a noastră.

Auzind acestea, vrabia a înaintat și a grăit astfel:

Domnul Uliu are întru totul dreptate: oamenii sînt foarte lacomi și ignoranți. Unde mai pui că printre ei există unii care fac meseria de păsărar, care ne prind cu momeală (鳥餅) și ne dau apoi de mîncare la șoimi, ba chiar ne mănîncă ei înșiși, prăjite (焼雀)! Noi, păsările, n-ar trebui însă să fim mîncare pentru oameni, oamenii ar trebui să mănînce grîne și legume. Astfel, pe lîngă faptul că nu cultivă ei înșiși grîne și le fură pe ale altora, oamenii ne mai și omoară și ne înfulecă drept delicatese. Iar asta este o mare fărădelege (大罪)!

În timp ce vorbea, i-au țîșnit lacrimi din ochi.

Auzind văicăreala vrabiei, rața, care participa și ea la taifas, a început să vorbească pe un ton tînguitor:

Într-adevăr, după cum spune și vrabia, oamenii sînt extrem de lacomi. Noi, rațele, ne naștem ca păsări de apă și ne hrănim prinzînd feluritele soiuri de pește (雑鯜) pe care ni le oferă materia primară a cerului (転真). Oamenii nu ar avea nici un motiv să ne urască, și cu toate astea ne prind cu momeală și ne omoară, iar apoi ne mănîncă susținînd că sîntem o gustare mai hrănitoare chiar decît ginseng. Asta este fără îndoială o mare fărădelege și arată că oamenii din lumea legii private sînt mult mai afundați în neleguiure decît noi, cele patru tipuri de animale. După moarte, cu siguranță însă că vor renaște în rîndul nostru și vor avea aceeași soartă ca noi, iar atunci va fi rîndul lor să fie omorîți de către oamenii din lumea legii private.

Fazanul, care era și el de față, a început atunci să vorbească și el tușind nervos:

> Noi, fazanii, ne naștem din vitalitatea focurilor de iarbă și tufișuri de pe coastele munților, ne hrănim cu iarbă și cu fructele din tufărișuri și trăim în conformitate cu soarta pe care ne-a hărăzit-o cerul. Nu i-am deranjat niciodată pe oameni și nu le-am dat niciodată vreun motiv să ne urască. Cu toate astea, oamenii din lumea legii private, cunoscînd prea bine faptul că din naștere—din pricina vitalității extraordinare a focurilor—rămînem foarte repede fără suflu și că din cauza asta nu putem zbura mult și la înălțime, ne urmăresc și, cînd sîntem cu suflarea tăiată, ne prind și ne omoară. Ne mănîncă apoi strigînd: „Fazanul de iarnă e delicios!" Energia descendentă a materiei primare a cerului i-a creat pe oameni și le-a dat hrana necesară, iar energia laterală ne-a creat pe noi și ne-a dat hrana potrivită. Deși calea (道) fiecăruia este limpede, de ce oare or fi fiind atît de ignoranți și lacomi și sfinții, și Buddha, și Shōtoku Taishi[14] și toți ceilalți din lumea legii private? Tu cunoști pricina, prietenă becață?

Becața a răspuns:

> După părerea mea, oamenii din lumea legii private au îngropat adînc înlăuntrul lor energia descendentă care ar trebui să îi domine; astfel, energia laterală a țîșnit în sus și a ajuns să-i domine, făcîndu-i să fie aidoma nouă. Prin urmare, cei puternici și iscusiți, cum e vulturul printre păsări, s-au făcut conducători prin forță ca să-și satisfacă o poftă egoistă. Au nesocotit calea cerului, au furat și s-au înfruptat din mîncarea tuturor celor de dedesubtul lor, creînd astfel societatea divizată în clase în care jaful și exploatarea (盗乱) nu încetează niciodată. Conducătorul nostru, vulturul, ne prinde și ne mănîncă pe toți cei care sîntem sub el, dar asta este soarta ce ne-a fost hărăzită de cer, iar noi, cei care sîntem mîncați, nu avem de ce să-l urîm. Însă conducătorul

---

14. Shōtoku Taishi 聖徳太子 (574–622), regent și politician important din perioada Asuka, este desemnat aici prin termenul 厩, care reprezintă o contracție de la Umayado no Ōji 厩戸皇子, unul dintre numele sale alternative. Shōeki îl critică în numeroase pasaje pe Shōtoku Taishi pentru introducerea și promovarea atît a confucianismului cît și a budismului, considerîndu-l răspunzător pentru haosul și confuzia care domnesc în Japonia.

din lumea legii private nu are permisiunea cerului și mănîncă roadele strădaniei tuturor celor de sub el—deși e om, e un hoț mai rău decît orice pasăre. Și chiar dacă e conducător, nu avem de ce să-l invidiem. Pînă la urmă, va ajunge să fie dominat de energia laterală și va avea aceeași soartă cu noi. Din asta, îmi dau seama că lumea noastră, a păsărilor, e mult superioară lumii legii private a oamenilor.

Tocmai atunci a venit în zbor și bîtlanul. Păsările au strigat toate într-un glas:

A sosit dregătorul de rangul al cincilea, cu gîtul și picioarele-i lungi, cu veșmintele lui nobile și coroana lui de pene răsucite!

I-au făcut loc să se așeze.

Bîtlanul s-a așezat și a început să vorbească:

Am auzit că stăpînul nostru șoimul e în trecere și m-am temut că mi-e viața în primejdie dacă mă întîlnesc cu el, așa că am stat ascuns. De-asta am întîrziat. Dar ia spuneți-mi, care e pricina acestei adunări a păsărilor?

Atunci, bufnița—învelită în veșmintele ei groase și moi—a ieșit în față cu un foșnet și a început să vorbească:

Eu, care sînt cunoscută drept matricidă[15], mă tem să apar dinaintea ciorii, care dă dovadă de pietate filială, așa că am să-mi fac paravan.

Și-a desfăcut aripile larg dinaintea ciocului și, cu ochii deschiși larg ca de pisică, s-a întors spre bîtlan și a continuat cu o voce aspră:

Nu pot să accept scuza pentru întîrziere a prietenului bîtlan. Mi se pare pur și simplu că face paradă de rangul lui. Această adunare a păsărilor este una la care dezbatem[16] una dintre cele mai importante chestiuni din vremurile trecute și prezente. Discutăm dacă există sau nu vreo diferență între lumea păsărilor și lumea legii private a oamenilor. Înainte de apariția sfinților din vechime și a lui Buddha, lumea oamenilor era o societate în care oamenii trăiau în conformitate cu calea cerului și se ocupau cu toții de cultivarea

---

15. Despre 嚢—bufnița—se spune că este matricidă deoarece una dintre teoriile privind etimologia cuvîntului susține că ar deriva din fraza 母食ラフ în japoneză clasică, frază al cărei sens literal este "a mînca mama". Sugestia este aici că bufnița este o pasăre lipsită complet de pietate filială.

16. 評詮 (cu versiunea prescurtată 評) este folosit de Shōeki cu sensul de „discuție", „dezbatere", dar are și nuanța de „evaluare".

directă—nici nu se compara cu lumea noastră, a păsărilor. După apariția sfinților și a lui Buddha, însă, oamenii au creat propriile lor legi (私法), au nesocotit cultivarea directă impusă de calea cerului și astfel au creat o lume a jafului și exploatării, o lume a îndoielii (惑心) care este întocmai cu lumea noastră. Iar faptul că lumea oamenilor a ajuns să fie la fel cu a noastră nu face decît să ne facă nouă cinste (面目). Iar tu, bîtlane, îți întinzi măreț gîtul și îți ridici coroana de pene ca și cum ai vrea să-ți arăți rangul și prinzi și mănînci creaturi mai mici decît tine. Purtarea ta e aidoma cu cea a oamenilor din lumea legii private.

Bîtlanul a răspuns:

Văd că aceasta este într-adevăr o dezbatere foarte importantă. Am înțeles lucrul ăsta acum.

Atunci, cîteva dintre păsările mai mici—prepelița, ciocîrlia, sfrînciocul, pitulicea, scatiul, ortolanul și cucul—s-au apropiat dinspre margini și au glăsuit în cor:

Noi sîntem cele mai sărace și mai umile din lumea păsărilor, cele care locuiesc în cătunele cele friguroase. Credem că adunarea aceasta este cea mai importantă din vremurile trecute și prezente și tocmai de aceea participăm și noi. Cioara, care este o pasăre de oraș și care își face cuibul în apropierea caselor oamenilor, este și ea aici, dar cocoșul de ce oare n-o fi prezent? Oare cioara și uliul nu și-au dat seama că lipsește? Dacă nu va apărea la această întîlnire, avem de gînd să-i informăm pe șoim, conducătorul nostru, și pe erete, generalul nostru.

Cioara și uliul au fost de acord, așa că au trimis un emisar să-l cheme pe cocoș, care a venit pînă la urmă.

Noi, orătăniile de curte, ne naștem din vitalitatea focului din casele oamenilor, trăim prin curțile lor și ne hrănim cu rămășițele de la mesele lor. Nici n-am știut că se ține această mare adunare a păsărilor. Am venit de îndată ce m-a chemat emisarul ciorii.

Prepelița a intervenit:

Atunci te întreb pe dumneata de ce ai creastă și pinteni ascuțiți și de ce cînți ca să anunți ora?

Cocoșul a răspuns:

Faptul că am creastă arată că eu cunosc riturile, faptul că chem găina cînd găsesc mîncare e dovadă de omenie, am pinteni pentru a apăra datoria morală, faptul că știu cînd e ceasul zorilor e dovadă de înțelepciune, iar faptul că nu greșesc niciodată ora arată loialitate. Faptul că mă lupt cu orice alt cocoș pe care îl întîlnesc arată că am curaj. Prin urmare, eu sînt omul ales și luptătorul curajos din lumea păsărilor. Omul ales din societatea oamenilor nu e decît o născocire egoistă și meschină. Eu, însă, sînt un om ales adevărat pentru că așa m-am născut în lumea păsărilor[17].

Prepelița a continuat:

Nu se poate să nu existe și în lumea păsărilor un om ales. Iar cele cinci virtuți[18] ale omului ales din lumea noastră sînt mai presus decît falsele virtuți ale omului pentru că sînt înnăscute. Să ne plecăm cu toții dinaintea cocoșului!

Păsările toate au făcut o plecăciune.

La adunarea aceea se afla și lebăda de vară, dar pînă atunci nu rostise nici un cuvînt. Ciocîrlia s-a întors către ea și a început să ciripească:

Prietenă lebădă de vară, de ce stai aici fără să spui nimic?

Lebăda de vară a răspuns:

Din pricina greșelilor mele, am făcut o boală venerică și mi s-a urcat către cap; de-asta am fața roșie, ciocul strîmb și vocea răgușită. Mi-e rușine și de-asta nu vorbesc.

Ciocîrlia a continuat:

---

17. 礼 („cunoașterea riturilor"), 仁 („benevolența"), 義 („datoria morală"), 智 („înțelepciunea"), 信 („loialitatea"), și 勇 („curajul") sînt toate virtuți postulate de către Confucius. Apar la 君子 („Omul Ales") și la 勇士 („războinicul curajos") ca trăsături morale imanente. În plus, există și o veche legendă chinezească potrivit căreia cocoșul este înzestrat cu cinci trăsături: 文 („cultură, civilizație")—motivul pentru care are creastă; 武 („capacitate de luptă")—motivul pentru care are pinteni; 勇 („curaj")—motivul pentru care se luptă cu alți cocoși; 仁 („benevolența")—motivul pentru care cheamă găina cînd găsește mîncare; și 信 („loialitate")—motivul pentru anunță întotdeauna ora cu exactitate. Shōeki modifică această legendă pentru a pune accentul, simbolic, pe Omul Ales și pe războinic. Este interesat de menționat că Shōeki, citînd toate aceste virtuți, face referire la modelul confucianist tocmai pentru a critica valorile pe care acesta le promova în Japonia perioadei Tokugawa.

18. 五常 sînt cele cinci (五) virtuți enunțate de Confucius, pe care Omul Ales trebuie să le respecte tot timpul (常). (cf. nota 17)

> Am crezut că numai oamenii din lumea legii private beau în neștire și fac boli venerice, de le putrezește trupul și le cade nasul, iar apoi ajung să aibă glasul gîjîit ca lebăda. Dar, de vreme ce și în lumea noastră există păsări care suferă de boli lumești ca tine, asta înseamnă că societatea umană și lumea noastră sînt la fel.

Atunci a sosit în zbor cocorul. Celelate păsări s-au dat deoparte ca să-i facă loc.

Cocorul a vorbit:

> Gîtul meu și ciocul meu cel lung reprezintă veșmintele mele de curte (狩衣), iar picioarele care-mi atîrnă în urmă în zbor reprezintă mantia mea de ceremonii (幞). Prin urmare, eu sînt nobilul și marele dregător din lumea păsărilor.

Toate păsările și-au plecat atunci capetele, umile.

Cocorul a continuat:

> Eu sînt cancelarul (太政大臣), cel mai important dintre miniștri. Prin urmare, zbor întotdeauna în înaltul cerului și nu cobor decît foarte rar în lumea de jos. Îi prind și îi mănînc pe cei mai mici și inferiori mie, întocmai cum dregătorii din lumea oamenilor înfulecă roadele muncii celor de sub ei. Luați aminte cu toatele: să nu cumva să credeți că nobilii și regenții din lumea păsărilor sînt cu ceva mai prejos decît cei din societatea oamenilor! Eu, de pildă, sînt la fel cu nobilii și dregătorii din lumea legii private. Faptul că nu există diferențe între societatea umană și lumea păsărilor este din pricina sfinților din vechime și a lui Buddha. Cele două lumi sînt exact la fel.

Rațele mandarine erau și ele prezente la taifas, însă bărbătușul și femeiușca erau pierduți în mîngîieri ațîțătoare, fără rușine de privirile celorlalte păsări. Aflată alături, lebăda a remarcat cu voce tare:

> E adevărat că eu m-am ales cu vocea asta hîrîită din pricina propriilor mele pofte trupești (色恋沙汰), dar n-am fost chiar în halul ăsta, ca voi! Vă văd toate păsările, ar trebui să vă înfrînați!

Atunci, una dintre rațele mandarine a replicat:

> Să știi că nu ai de ce să ne dojenești. În societatea oamenilor, un singur rege sau un singur nobil are mai multe ibovnice și se dedă la desfătări în miezul zilei fără vreo jenă de privirea cuiva. De vreme ce tocmai cei care sînt în fruntea societății umane se comportă astfel, dacă n-am exista noi în lumea păsă-

rilor, atunci ar fi mult prea diferită de lumea oamenilor și asta ar fi un mare păcat.

Lebăda a continuat:

Trebuie deci să îngăduim asta, de vreme ce lumea oamenilor imită lumea păsărilor în privința asta.

În răstimpul acesta, cele două rațe mandarine s-au pomenit despărțite de numeroasele păsări prezente la adunare, care s-au băgat între ele; copleșită de tristețe la gîndul că nu se vor mai putea întîlni niciodată, rața a murit cu inima frîntă. Cînd a găsit leșul iubitei, rățoiul și-a desfăcut aripile ca să-l acopere și apoi a murit și el.

Văzînd acestea, celelalte păsări s-au tînguit într-un glas:

Cît de profundă a fost dragostea lor!

Atunci, a vorbit rața mare:

Rătăcirea aceasta din dragoste nu se întîlnește numai la rațele mandarine. Buddha din societatea oamenilor susține că „legătura dintre soți durează și în viața următoare" (夫婦ハ二世ノ契リ). Tocmai de aceea, cînd un bărbat și o femeie din lumea legii private se îndrăgostesc, dar există opreliști care îi împiedică să se căsătorească, se sinucid împreună (心中) în speranța că vor fi împreună în viața următoare. Asta se întîmplă în societatea umană unde există legea budistă, iar lumea păsărilor nu e deloc diferită.

Gîsca sălbatică venise și ea din peregrinările ei ca să participe la întîlnirea păsărilor. Coțofana s-a întors spre ea și a întrebat-o:

Tu ai zburat peste toate țările și toate insulele din lume—ai văzut pe-acolo ceva interesant?

Gîsca a răspuns:

Noi zburăm într-adevăr peste toate țările și toate insulele de pe lume, dar faptul că nu avem un cuib statornic nu e alegerea noastră. Sîntem mînate[19] de

---

19. Termenul folosit aici este 感シ, care apare scris cu ideograma pentru verbul „a simți" (*kanjiru*), căruia Shōeki îi atașază, în diferite contexte, citirile *fureru* („a atinge", „a afecta", „a influența"), *hataraku* („a munci", „a produce un efect") sau *ugoku* („a se mișca", „a pune în mișcare"). Shōeki utilizează acest verb pentru a indica influența pe care o au energiile cerului și pămîntului. Citirile alternative sporesc dinamismul con-

energiile noastre înnăscute (生得ノ気行) și de energiile cerului și pămîntului (転定ノ気行). De aceea, iarna zburăm spre sud, vara spre nord, iar primăvara și toamna spre est sau spre vest—astfel, ne supunem energiilor cerului și pămîntului. Prin urmare, dacă în lumea păsărilor există cineva care vrea să afle despre țările din lumea largă, să ne întrebe pe noi orice.

În lumea legii private, oamenii își construiesc corăbii, pe care le folosesc ca să traverseze în alte țări, unde pornesc războaie. Unele țări cuceresc, altele sînt cucerite, dar e limpede că oamenii călătoresc în alte țări numai din lăcomie. Asta se întîmplă așadar în societatea umană, care e mînată de jaf, exploatare și avariție oarbă (妄欲). Noi călătorim din țară în țară ca să ne hrănim cu mîncăruri diferite din fiecare. Prin urmare, în lumea noastră a păsărilor facem același lucru cu oamenii care traversează în alte țări în corăbiile lor. Lumea oamenilor e la fel cu lumea păsărilor.

Rîndunica se afla și ea într-un colț al adunării. Sfrînciocul a întrebat-o:

Și tu, prietenă rîndunică, ai venit de departe. Ne poți spune dacă și viața ta seamănă cu cea din lumea oamenilor?

Rîndunica a răspuns:

Noi rîndunicile sîntem păsări mici și nu avem o țară sau o casă a noastră. Rătăcim din țară în țară și trăim în odăi de împrumut, sub vreo prispă sau sub vreo streașină, fără să avem vreodată o casă proprie. Cum doar insectele minuscule cu aripi ne sînt inferioare, le prindem și le mîncăm. Nu cunoaștem gustul vreunei delicatese și ne ducem traiul în sărăcie. În societatea umană, regii și nobilii se află în vîrf și duc o viață de huzur, cu bunătăți alese și veșminte minunate. Sub ei sînt o sumedenie de oameni într-o sărăcie lucie, care se adăpostesc de ploaie pe sub poduri și își găsesc sălaș în vreo cocioabă ici sau pe sub o streașină colo, se hrănesc cu te miri ce și au hainele zdrențuite. Aceștia din urmă sînt aidoma nouă, rîndunicile din lumea păsărilor. Lucrurile astea se întîmplă pentru că sfinții din vechime și Buddha au inventat propriile lor legi și au creat astfel societatea umană.

Stufărica se afla și ea într-un colț. Vrabia s-a întors spre ea și a întrebat-o:

Tu, prietenă stufărică, ești cunoscută drept o pasăre cu limba ascuțită și spiritul ager. De ce nu spui nimic?

Stufărica a răspuns:

---

ceptului.

Da, sînt vorbăreață și isteață: eu cînt despre cer, cînt despre pămînt, cînt despre treburile oamenilor, cînt despre toate cele—nu există nici un lucru despre care să nu ciripesc. Sfinții, înțelepții și cărturarii[20] din lumea oamenilor predică despre fenomenele și principiile cerului și pămîntului, omului și tuturor lucrurilor—astfel, născocesc tot soiul de teorii pe care le numesc „învățături" și pe care le scot la vînzare. Așa se înfruptă ei cu lăcomie și nesocotesc calea cerului. Buddha, toți *bodhisattva*, fiecare *arhat*[21] și călugări din toate sectele (諸宗ノ僧) propovăduiesc tot soiul de lucruri, dar ei sînt cu toții pierduți în iluzie și încearcă să ducă și restul lumii în iluzie. Învățăturile lui Confucius (儒), ale lui Buddha (仏), ale lui Laozi (老), ale lui Zhuangzi (荘), ale doctorilor din vechime (医) și ale lui Shōtoku Taishi (厩) nu propovăduiesc altceva decît egoismul (己利), jaful și exploatarea (盗乱), îndoiala (心惑) și lăcomia (妄行) care alcătuiesc lumea legii private; învățăturile lor însă nu se deosebesc cu nimic de ciripelile mele nătînge.

Înainte să apară sfinții și Buddha, lumea oamenilor respecta calea cerului și materia primară, iar toată lumea practica cultivarea directă—lumea noastră a păsărilor era umilă și smerită. Însă după apariția sfinților și a lui Buddha, societatea umană a nesocotit calea materiei primare (活真道) și a creat propriile legi artificiale, devenind astfel aidoma lumii păsărilor. Prin urmare, lumea păsărilor s-a extins cu alte creaturi asemănătoare, iar lucrul acesta nu poate decît să ne bucure.

Atunci, toate păsările au lăudat-o într-un glas:

Într-adevăr, ce pricepută și isteață e prietena stufărică!

20. 聖・賢・学者 sînt „sfinții", înțelepții și cărturarii din China antică care, în viziunea lui Shōeki, sînt responsabili pentru decăderea lumii legii private. Aici, Shōeki face referire la numele menționate de Nakae Tōju 中江藤樹, filosof neo-confucianist din secolul al XVII-lea. La Tōju, lista sfinților îl include pe Confucius 孔子, iar cea a înțelepților pe Mencius 孟子 (unul dintre cei mai reputați comentatori confucianiști) și pe Ō Yōmei 王陽明 (fondator al școlii Yōmei în China). Includerea lui Ō Yōmei pe lista înțelepților e firească avînd în vedere faptul că Tōju însuși este fondatorul școlii Ō Yōmei din Japonia—din școală fac parte și samuraiul reformator Kumazawa Banzan 熊沢蕃山 și Yoshida Shōin 吉田松陰, ai cărui discipoli aveau să devină lideri ai Restaurației Meiji din 1868. „Cărturarii" sînt discipoli și învățăcei ai sfinților și înțelepților. Și aici, Shōeki face referire la gînditorii confucianiști și la discipolii lor (și la Confucius însuși, de altfel) numai cu scopul de a critica din nou viziunea lor asupra lumii și faptul că au provocat distrugerea echilibrului Naturii.

21. *Bodhisattva* (în japoneză 菩薩) este termenul care îi desemnează pe cei care, motivați de compasiune, ajung la dorința spontană de a atinge starea de Buddha. *Arhat* (în japoneză 羅漢) reprezintă stadiul anterior celui de *bodhisattva*.

Lebăda era și ea de față la adunare. Rîndunica s-a întors spre ea și a întrebat-o:

Tu ești maiestuoasă și neprihănită, dar de ce nu spui nimic?

Lebăda a răspuns:

Eu sînt mare la trup și grea, și îmi e greu să-mi iau zborul și să revin pe pămînt. Sufletul îmi e însă neprihănit și lipsit de pofte, pe măsura penelor mele albe, fără de pată. Tocmai de aceea eu nu vorbesc fără rost. În lumea oamenilor există unii, precum Bodhidharma (磨)[22] și discipolii săi (僧) care, ignoranți, sînt obsedați de „purificarea" sufletului (清偏心・妄惑) și născocesc tot felul de metode pentru a-și atinge scopul. Ei sînt la fel ca mine, lebăda din lumea păsărilor.

Păsările au lăudat-o într-un glas:

Lebăda e călugărul nostru zen, starostele care a ajuns la iluminarea cea mare și profundă datorită obsesiei sale pentru puritate!

Cormoranul era și el de față, pitit în spate. Lebăda s-a întors spre el și l-a întrebat:

Cormorane, tu de ce nu ieși în față să-ți spui părerile?

Cormoranul a răspuns:

Tu ești pasăre de apă, ca și mine, dar deși trupul ți-e greu plutești foarte bine. Eu mă cufund adînc în apă și prind pești pe care îi mănînc întregi. Nici tu, nici eu nu putem trăi fără apă. În lumea oamenilor, Laozi este cel care laudă virtuțile apei, iar Zhuangzi este cel care se afundă în învățătura apei, fără a-i explica adevărata natură. Prin urmare, eu, care înghit peștii pe nemestecate, sînt asemeni celor din societatea umană care înghit doctrina vidului și a marii căi[23].

Lebăda și-a arătat aprobarea față de spusele lui.

Toate păsările mici au început atunci s-o caute neliniștite pe silvia de

22. Bodhidharma este un cunoscut patriarh budist, considerat a fi fondatorul sectei *Chan* din China (*Zen* 禅 în japoneză).

23. 虚無 („nimic") și 大道 („marea cale") sînt termenii pe care îi utilizează Shōeki pentru a se referi la învățăturile Taoismului și la Laozi și Zhuangzi. *Kyomu* este folosit depreciativ pentru a sugera că doctrina Tao este vidă și inutilă.

mlaștină.

Silvia de mlaștină are o voce încîntătoare, dar e oare printre noi? Sau n-a sosit încă?

Pe cînd discutau astfel, silvia a început să vorbească:

Eu sînt o pasăre mică și m-am născut din energia începutului primăverii. Am fost la taifas de la bun început, însă m-am străduit să nu fiu necuviincioasă și m-am sfiit să vorbesc de față cu atîtea păsări mari și impunătoare. Noi, silviile de mlaștină, ne naștem dominate de faza progresivă a energiei inițiale a elementului lemn[24], produsă de materia primară. Sîntem mesageri ai cerului, iar rolul nostru este foarte important pentru că anunțăm prin primul nostru ciripit (初音) venirea primăverii și momentul cînd trebuie să înceapă cultivarea directă. Tocmai de aceea, toate creaturile de pe lume încep cultivarea după ce aud primul nostru ciripit. Astfel, cu glasurile noastre minunate vestim poruncile naturii.

Noi ne facem cuiburile în locuri primejdioase și sîntem cu mare băgare de seamă să nu cădem pradă păsărilor mai mari. De aceea, unul dintre sfinții din vechime, invidios pe virtuțile noastre, a spus: „Silvia cea galbenă care ciripește întruna și-a făcut cuib la marginea unei creste. Dacă omul nu-și cunoaște locul cuvenit, asta înseamnă că este inferior păsării". Cel care a spus asta s-a născut ca ființă umană, dar s-a abătut de la calea cultivării directe, a nesocotit calea cerului și s-a înfruptat cu lăcomie din truda altora—și tot el e invidios pe noi! A căzut astfel în rîndul celor patru tipuri de animale. Voi, păsări, ascultați toate la ce vă spun: în lumea păsărilor, eu sînt superioară acelui sfînt din vechime. Mai mult chiar, îi sînt învățătoare.

Păsările toate au rămas mute de uimire.

Silvia de mlaștină a continuat:

Nu numai sfinții din vechime au auzit ciripitul meu. Buddha însuși, ascultînd cîntecul meu „*Hō, hoke chō*"[25], a strîns laolaltă roadele înțelepciunii acumu-

24. 初進木気行 înseamnă, literal, „faza progresivă a energiei inițiale a elementului lemn". Pentru Shōeki, aceasta este o energie extrem de pozitivă, iar uneori folosește termenul pentru a indica primăvara timpurie, anotimpul renașterii și al începutului creșterii. Alături de foc, metal și apă, lemnul este unul dintre cele patru elemente fundamentale (Shōeki discută pămîntul separat de această serie de elemente, atribuindu-i o fecunditate materială aparte și justificînd astfel tratarea lui drept încarnația materiei primare *kasshin* din care se nasc toate lucrurile și ființele).

25. *Hō, hoke chō* (法法華徴), onomatopeea folosită de silvia de mlaștină, reprezintă de

late într-o viață și a alcătuit Sutra Lotusului (法華経), care conține învățăturile adevărate ale Marelui Vehicul (実大乗). Eu m-am născut dominată de faza progresivă a energiei laterale, iar sufletul lui Buddha avea aceeași fază progresivă a aceleiași energii, și tocmai de aceea a fost inspirat de primul meu ciripit să întocmească Sutra Lotusului și să întemeieze lumea legii private. După ce-a murit, a renăscut din energia laterală și a devenit unul dintre noi.

Bucurați-vă, deci, păsări! Sfinții și Buddha au căzut în lumea păsărilor și au deveni aidoma nouă! Prin urmare, lumea noastră e cu mult superioară societății umane!

Păsările au rostit într-un glas:

Dacă lucrurile stau așa, înseamnă că lumea noastră e paradisul[26] pentru că aici se află și sfinții și Buddha!

Pasărea *ran*[27] se afla și ea acolo, cocoțată la înălțime. Glasul ei era melodios ca al unui cîntăreț.

Păsările au întrebat-o:

Tu vii din țările din sud[28]—ce har ai?

*Ran* a răspuns:

Eu m-am născut într-un ținut fierbinte și de aceea elementul foc e foarte puternic în mine. Din naștere, vocea mi-e aspră și tremurătoare. În ținuturile

---

fapt un joc de cuvinte care face trimitere la Sutra Lotusului (法華経). Pentru a reda ciripitul păsării, Shōeki folosește ideogramele din numele sutrei (法華), cărora le adaugă 徴, care poate avea și sensul de „semn" sau „anunțare". Astfel, sugerează că ar exista o legătură între ciripitul silviei și sutră, prima anunțind-o pe cea din urmă.

26. 極楽 înseamnă, literal, „fericirea supremă". Tradus adesea ca „paradis", este termenul folosit în japoneză pentru a reda *sukhāvatī* din sanscrită, care desemnează Tărîmul Pur de la apus al lui Buddha Amithāba (*Amida*).

27. 鸞 este o pasăre mitologică din China antică. Se credea despre ea că are un penaj multicolor și frumos, asemănător cu al unui păun, și că își poate schimba după plac tonalitatea vocii. Unii cărturari o considerau a fi o sub-specie a phoenixului. Cîteva texte de perioadă Edo menționează că *ran* este o pasăre reală și relatează o legendă potrivit căreia phoenixul se transformă de fapt în *ran* la bătrînețe. *Ran* era de asemenea considerată o pasăre cu virtuți morale superioare care nu-și făcea apariția decît în vremuri de pace și liniște.

28. 蛮国 este o prescurtare pentru 南蛮国, „ținuturile barbarilor din sud". Termenul a fost folosit inițial de către chinezi pentru a se referi la toate teritoriile aflate mai la sud de Marea Chinei de Sud, în special Indonezia. Despre aceste teritorii se credea că adăpostesc numeroase păsări mitologice, printre care și phoenixul sau *ran*.

din lumea legii private, în Japonia a existat un om care mi-a lăudat glasul foarte mult, ba chiar l-a imitat ca să facă incantații budiste. Și-a luat numele de Shinran (真鸞) și a fondat adevărata Sectă a Pămîntului Pur[29]. Prin urmare, lumea noastră, a păsărilor, oferă un model pentru cele mai profunde credințe din lumea oamenilor.

Păsările au strigat atunci într-un glas:

Asta înseamnă că numele tău adevărat este Buddha Amida!

Pițigoiul era așezat într-un colț întunecat al adunării.
Presura de munte l-a întrebat:

Pițigoiule, tu de ce nu participi la taifas?

Pițigoiul a răspuns:

La început, am fost o pasăre de munte, dar acum m-am mutat pe un deal mic din apropierea capitalei (本ハ大山ノ鳥ナリ。今ハ都近キ丘野辺). Caut întruna nuci și, cînd găsesc cîte una, zbor spre cer cu ea în cioc—îi dau drumul, mă reped în jos, mă așez pe o stîncă și aștept să cadă. Zgomotul pe care îl face nuca izbită de stîncă seamănă cu sunetul unui gong dintr-un templu budist (鍾鐇). Zgomotul pe care îl scoate ciocul meu lovind cojile seamănă cu bătăile unui clopot (打鐘). Arzînd de nerăbdare să înhaț și să înfulec ofranda sinceră (心施) pe care nuca o face din omenie (仁), lovesc pătimaș cu ciocul în coji cîntînd întruna „Mai mult, mai mult!" (南哺茂南哺茂) pînă reușesc să mănînc miezul. Pițigoiul cel mare era neîncrezător față de mine, așa că pînă la urmă am făcut un legămînt scris (起請): „Ba pot să înfulec tot mai mult și mai mult. Dacă nu e așa, fie să nu mai mănînc nuci și să pier." Atunci, și pițigoiul mare s-a apucat să ciocănească alături de mine cojile și să mănînce miezul cel bun[30].

29. 一向宗 înseamnă, literal, "religia unidirecțională". Reprezintă o apelație alternativă pentru Adevărata Sectă a Pămîntului Pur, făcînd aluzie la faptul că adepții sectei se concentrau asupra unui singur lucru: venerarea lui Buddha.

30. 本ハ大山ノ鳥ナリ。今ハ都近キ丘野辺 din replica pițigoiului reprezintă o aluzie la destinul lui Hōnen 法然, reformatorul religios din a doua jumătate a secolului al XII-lea care a fondat prima ramură independentă (japoneză) a Budismului Pămîntului Pur, numită 浄土宗. Inițial, acesta a făcut parte din secta Tendai 天台 la un templu pe muntele Hiei 比叡, dar mai tîrziu s-a mutat la Ōtani, la periferia capitalei Kyōto, și a început să propovăduiască ideea că *nenbutsu* 念仏 (incantarea constantă a numelui lui Buddha Amida) este singura condiție necesară pentru a pătrunde pe Pămîntul Pur al lui Buddha Amida. Se spune despre el că este cel care a consacrat fraza *Namu Amida Butsu*

În lumea oamenilor a existat un călugăr budist care era foarte invidios pe mine. La început, a stat într-o mănăstire pe un munte înalt, dar apoi a coborît în apropierea capitalei și a început să propovăduiască învățăturile sectei Pămîntului Pur. Îngîna mereu cuvintele fără nici un sens „Amida, Amida" și a scris și el un legămînt. Bătea întruna din clopot, propovăduia încoace și-ncolo și se înfrupta lacom din roadele muncii altora. Astfel, a devenit unul dintre noi. Lumea legii private e ticsită de energie laterală.

*Chin* (鳩), pasărea cea otrăvitoare, stătea pe unul dintre locurile de jos. Cioara s-a întors sprea ea și a întrebat-o:

*Chin*, tu ce har ai?

*Chin* a răspuns:

Eu sînt o pasăre foarte otrăvitoare, care mănîncă pești fără solzi și șerpi, așa că m-am sfiit să vorbesc în fața acestei adunări. De-asta n-am spus nimic pînă acum. Și în lumea legii private există oameni mieroși, dar plini de viclenie (佞人) care împart otravă încoace și-ncolo, imitîndu-mă. Sînt doctorii, care pretind că vindecă dar nu cunosc efectele leacurilor; tratamentele lor sînt prescrise orbește, căci meseria lor adevărată e cea de ucigaș. Iar lucrul acesta l-au învățat de la mine. Sînt mulți de teapa mea în societatea umană.

Toate păsările s-au arătat de acord cu acestea.

---

南無阿弥陀仏 („Slavă lui Buddha Amida, al Luminii Infinite") în Japonia. Shōeki duce paralela între pițigoi și Hōnen mai departe menționînd legămîntul (起請 în japoneză)—acesta este o aluzie la una dintre cele mai importante scrieri ale lui Hōnen, 一枚起請文 („Documentul-legămînt de o pagină"), pe care l-a scris cu două zile înainte de moartea sa din 1212, în loc de testament. Cum documentul lui Hōnen conține esența doctrinei și a practicilor pe care le promovase, e evident că în acest fragment Shōeki ia în derîdere secta Pămîntului Pur și pe fondatorul acesteia—așa se explică, de altfel, conținutul legămîntului pițigoiului. Ironia continuă însă și la un nivel mai subtil: făcînd aluzie la Hōnen, Shōeki se referă în același timp și la fraza *Namu Amida Butsu* și la faptul că trebuia să fie repetată la nesfîrșit pentru a avea acces la Pămîntul Pur. Astfel, cînd Shōeki descrie cîntecul pițigoiului mîncînd nuci ca fiind 南哺茂南哺茂 („Mai mult, mai mult!"), el persiflează de fapt invocația budistă (chiar și la nivel grafic, prin folosirea ideogramei 南). Mai mult, acest fragment în care pițigoiul și Hōnen sînt puși în opoziție conține și o referință depreciativă la adresa confucianismului: astfel, miezul comestibil al nucii este numit 仁, care reprezintă de fapt virtutea morală a benevolenței postulate de Confucius. Imaginea pițigoiului care înfulecă lacom miez de nucă devine o reprezentare extrem de plastică a ideii că confucianismul este complet irelevant în lumea ideală a Naturii pe care Shōeki o descrie în textele lui.

*Kiba* (耆婆), pasărea cu două capete, stătea cocoțată pe sus.
Pasărea *ran* s-a întors spre ea și a întrebat-o:

Tu ce părere ai?

*Kiba* a răspuns:

> Eu sînt o pasăre din legendele budiste, cu un singur trup și două capete. De aceea, sînt mai elocventă decît oricare altă pasăre—glasul meu are forța glasurilor a șase păsări laolaltă. În lumea legii private există unii călugări care pretind că stăpînesc învățăturile celor șase secte[31], dar doctrinele acestea sînt confuze și părtinitoare pentru că sînt influențate de energia laterală. Ele au fost create din invidie față de mine, care am două capete, cînt cu măiestrie despre toate lucrurile din lume și înfulec cu lăcomie roadele trudei altora. Călugării care se dedică ritualurilor budiste și ating iluminarea sînt dominați de percepții false și de energia laterală, ca și noi, așa că pînă la urmă cad în lumea păsărilor și ajung la fel cu noi. Tocmai de aceea, lumea noastră a păsărilor înflorește datorită acțiunilor din lumea oamenilor.

Toate păsările s-au arătat încîntate de vorbele ei.
Papagalul era și el așezat într-o margine.
Pasărea *Chin* s-a întors spre el și l-a întrebat:

Tu te-ai născut ca pasăre, dar de ce imiți vorbele oamenilor?

Papagalul a răspuns:

> Eu am o inimă mare și plină de vitalitatea focului. Elementul foc dinăuntrul meu intră în rezonanță cu spusele oamenilor și de aceea pot să le imit. În lumea legii private există oameni asemeni mie: niște călugări din Japonia au mers în China (漢土) și au început să imite vorbele călugărilor chinezi, iar apoi s-au întors și au transmis învățăturile sectelor Tendai 天台 și Shingon 真言, ambele dominate de percepții false și de energia laterală. Mai întîi, au fost ei înșiși amăgiți, iar apoi au amăgit la rîndul lor oamenii. Și au făcut lucrul acesta imitîndu-mă pe mine. Eu m-am născut dominat de energia laterală. Călugării din lumea legii private, amăgiți de legea budistă, au ajuns să fie și ei influențați de energia laterală și, căutîndu-și semenii, au căzut în lumea păsă-

---

31. Shōeki se referă la cele șase școli din Nara cunoscute colectiv sub numele de *rokushū* (六宗): Ritsu (律), Kusha (俱舎), Jōjitsu (成実), Hossō (法相), Sanron (三論) și Kegon (華厳). Acestea erau secte budiste cu o componentă academică puternică, introduse în Japonia din Coreea la sfîrșitul sec. VI—începutul sec. VII.

rilor și au devenit aidoma mie. Prin urmare, toți cei din societatea umană ne pizmuiesc și doresc să fie la fel cu noi.

Pasărea Paradisului se afla și ea la taifas, către apus.
Păsările celelalte i-au spus:

> Dă-te la o parte din calea vîntului. Tu înghiți doar aer, nu mănînci niciodată nimic și nici nu defechezi, doar tragi întruna pîrțuri. Ne deranjezi pe toate cîtă vreme rămîi sus în văzduh.

Pasărea Paradisului a răspuns:

> Mi-am dat și eu seama de asta și de-asta zbor de obicei împotriva vîntului. Adineauri, vîntul a început să bată dinspre răsărit, așa că m-am mutat înspre apus. Eu mănînc doar aer și trag întruna pîrțuri—nu am pic de hrană în stomac și nici un gînd în creier; nu știu ce înseamnă minte sau conștiință de sine, iar pentru mine nici o pasăre nu face nici măcar cît un pîrț. Dintre toate păsările din lumea noastră, eu sînt supremă, sînt singura care a ajuns la iluminare. Un călugăr din lumea legii private, invidios pe mine, a spus că „Nu se poate ajunge la iluminare prin nici o altă sectă. Doar prin Sutra Lotusului se poate atinge starea de Buddha"[32] și a fondat secta Nichiren 日蓮, care critică toate celelalte secte. A făcut asta imitîndu-mă pe mine. Tot budismul din societatea umană e de fapt influențat de surplusul de energie laterală (余横) care provine din lumea noastră.

Porumbelul sălbatic era și el așezat undeva jos.

---

32. În original: 成鳥ハ、諸鳥ハ無得鳥、風鳥ハ最第一. Această replică a Păsării Paradisului conține și un joc de cuvinte interesant care este foarte relevant pentru modul în care Shōeki alege să-și construiască discursul: astfel, vorbind despre iluminarea Păsării Paradisului, Shōeki inventează—exclusiv pentru acest episod—cuvîntul *jōchō* 成鳥 („a deveni pasăre"), care reprezintă de fapt o aluzie la sintagma *jōbutsu* 成仏 („a deveni Buddha"), folosită în general cu sensul de „a atinge starea de Buddha", „a ajunge la iluminare". Cu alte cuvinte, *jōchō* ar putea fi tradus drept „a atinge starea de Pasăre". În plus, fraza este și o referință transparentă la pasajul care apare mai jos: 諸宗ハ無得道、成仏ハ限法華 („starea de Buddha nu va fi atinsă de [nimeni din] nici o altă sectă; iluminarea poate fi obținută numai prin Sutra Lotusului"). Pasajul conține esența doctrinei și practicilor sectei Nichiren 日蓮, care a fost fondată în a doua jumătate a secolului al XIII-lea de călugărul Nichiren. Nichiren considera că celelalte secte au deviat de la ortodoxia Mahāyāna și predica devoțiunea față de Sutra Lotusului (numită *Myōhō renge kyō* 妙法蓮華経 în japoneză) ca fiind singura modalitate de a ajunge la iluminare, precum și incantarea repetată a frazei „Slavă Sutrei Lotusului" (*Namu myōhō renge kyō* 南無妙法蓮華経) ca practică esențială a sectei.

Porumbelul de casă s-a întors spre el și l-a întrebat:

Noi doi sîntem același soi. Tu de ce nu spui nimic?

Porumbelul sălbatic a răspuns:

Eu m-am născut din faza regresivă a energiei focului și, cînd vine anotimpul potrivit, mă apropii de satele oamenilor și strig cu glasul mei tulbure: „Ieșiți! Ieșiți!" (*dede kōke dede kōke* 出来出来)—sînt un emisar al materiei primare care le dă de știre oamenilor care respectă cultivarea directă (直耕ノ転人) că a venit vremea să planteze. Rolul meu este foarte important pentru că merg peste tot, din provincie în provincie, mă așez pe o creangă ici și uguiesc ca să dau de știre sau popesc pe o creangă dincolo ca să fac anunțul. Un călugăr din lumea legii private, imitîndu-mă, a creat secta Ji[33]; s-a apucat să-i lingușească pe cei puternici și să se înfrupte din roadele trudei altora. I s-a îngăduit să folosească în călătorii caii de poștă (伝馬) și se plimbă dintr-un tîrg în altul vînzînd tăblițe pe care stă scris „Șase sute de mii de credincioși pe pămîntul pur al lui Buddha Amida" (六十万人往生), dar nu se sfiește să înfulece ofrandele. S-a lăsat amăgit și tulburat de energia laterală și a ajuns asemeni nouă. Astfel, budismul din lumea noastră s-a răspîndit și în societatea oamenilor.

A apărut atunci și codobatura, întîrziată.
Păsările toate au dojenit-o într-un glas:

Codobaturo, tu ești una dintre păsările mici, de ce ai venit abia acum?

Vrabia a început să vorbească:

Te lauzi de multă vreme că tu i-ai învățat pe zeii Izanagi și Izanami tainele sexului—pesemne că ai întîrziat la taifasul nostru tocmai din pricina trufiei. Dar să nu uiți că odinioară te numeai vrabie de albie, și că erai una dintre noi. Ia nu-ți mai da aere!

---

33. 時宗 („Secta Timpului") este o ramură a sectei budiste a Pămîntului Pur. Numele este derivat din principala practică pe care o promova, și anume de recitare a *nenbutsu* tot timpul. A fost fondată în a doua jumătate a secolului al XIII-lea de un călugăr pe nume Ippen 一遍; în acest fragment, Shōeki face, desigur, referire la acest Ippen. 六十万人往生 („șase sute de mii de credincioși") reprezintă o aluzie la tăblițele pe care membrii sectei încercau să le vîndă, pe care era scris *Namu Amida Butsu, ketsujō ōjō rokujūmannin* 南無阿弥陀仏、決定往生六十万人 („Slavă lui Buddha Amida! Sînt hotărît să înmînez șase sute de mii de tăblițe [celor care vor merge în Pămîntul Pur]")—acesta era, de altfel, motto-ul lui Ippen, dar se pare că a reușit să distribuie doar în jur de două sute de mii de tăblițe.

Codobatura a răspuns:

> Mă învinuiești degeaba, nu sînt deloc cu nasul pe sus. De vreme ce eu sînt maestrul care i-a inițiat pe cei doi zei în taina importantă a sexului, zeii cei noi și fără de experiență vin în fiecare zi să învețe de la mine—am fost atît de ocupată încît pur și simplu am uitat de timp. Vă rog să mă iertați. Am ajuns să îi inițiez pe cei doi zei datorită obiceiului meu de a da mereu din cap și de a-mi flutura coada. Buddha și călugării din lumea legii private mă imită și dau și ei din cap și din coadă—la fel fac și sfinții, înțelepții și cărturarii. Cu toții mă imită și dau din capete și din cozi fără încetare, zi și noapte, dedicați practicării Căii sexului. Sînt aidoma unor armăsari ațîțați de pofte într-o luncă primăvara. Sînt dominați de energia laterală și au ajuns asemeni mie. În curînd, lumea noastră a păsărilor va vibra din pricina poftelor trupești.

Într-un glas, toate păsările au început să rîdă și să ciripească vesele:

> După cum spune codobatura, lumea păsărilor va fi în curînd un loc foarte animat!

Atunci, a sosit în zbor acvila, cîrîind cu glasul ei metalic (鉄棒音). Păsările celelalte au fost surprinse și s-au ghemuit înspăimîntate; acvila s-a oprit pe o creangă puțin deasupra lor și a început să vorbească:

> Ascultați-mă, voi păsări! Eu sînt pedestrașul din lumea păsărilor și am o suită numeroasă. Dacă vreuna dintre voi comite vreo nelegiuire, am să-i spun asta șoimului călător, însoțitorul cel mai de vază al suzeranului nostru (諸侯ノ家老). După cît de gravă e fapta, veți fi prinse, sfîrtecate și mîncate. Vă spun asta de la bun început.

A sosit atunci și șoimul călător, cu o suită numeroasă. S-au oprit pe un copac ceva mai înalt, iar șoimul a început să vorbească uitîndu-se în jos către acvilă:

> Le-ai făcut cunoscută proclamația mea?

Acvila a făcut o plecăciune și a răspuns:

> Da, le-am transmis-o întocmai.

Șoimul călător a vorbit:

> Luați aminte, păsări! Eu sînt însoțitorul principal al șoimului, care este suzeranul lumii noastre a păsărilor. Să mă țineți minte!

Toate păsările s-au înclinat.

Atunci au început să sosească păsărelele care erau înainte-mergătorii șoimului și, îndreptîndu-se spre șoimul călător, l-au anunțat:

Vine preaslăvitul șoim!

Auzind că vine șoimul, toate păsările s-au ghemuit înspăimîntate. Șoimul a venit în zbor și s-a oprit pe o creangă a unui copac înalt. L-a întrebat pe șoimul călător:

Șoimule călător, le-ai anunțat păsărilor proclamația mea?

Șoimul călător a răspuns:

Da, le-am transmis-o întocmai.

Șoimul a vorbit:

Eu sînt suzeranul (大名) din lumea păsărilor. Să mă țineți minte!

Și-a deschis ochii și le-a țintuit cu privirea. Cuprinse de spaimă la gîndul că ar putea fi prinse și sfîșiate pe loc, păsările s-au ghemuit și mai mult.

Precedat de fîlfîit mare de aripi, a sosit și eretele însoțit de o suită numeroasă—s-a oprit pe o piatră mare, cu fața spre adunare. Șoimul a făcut o plecăciune adîncă.

Eretele a început să vorbească șuierat:

Eu sînt generalul lumii păsărilor și țin toată această lume în ghearele mele. Am puterea să vă prind și să vă mănînc pe toate, de la tine, șoimule, pînă la păsările cele mai mici—și nu am să tolerez cîtuși de puțin delăsarea din partea voastră. Eu sînt generalul din lumea păsărilor! Să mă țineți minte!

A aruncat spre păsări o privire mînioasă, iar acestea s-au chircit și mai mult, moarte de spaimă.

A venit atunci în zbor vulturul, cu un foșnet de aripi înspăimîntător, însoțit de o sumedenie de alte păsări. Îngrozite de fîșîitul aripilor, păsările din adunare s-au ghemuit pînă s-au lipit de pămînt.

Vulturul s-a oprit pe vîrful unei stînci de partea cealaltă a adunării, a scos un țipăt puternic iar apoi a început să tune:

Eu sînt împăratul lumii păsărilor, lordul vultur suprem (上視又鷲王)—căci phoenixul e o pasăre din India. Voi toate, de la cocor, erete, șoim și șoim călător pînă la păsările cele mici, sînteți toate ale mele. Dacă vreuna dintre voi îmi nesocotește poruncile, am s-o prind imediat, am s-o sfîșii și am s-o înfulec. Voi păsări, să-mi ascultați poruncile!

Apoi a continuat:

Ierarhia mare—mic sau puternic—slab din lumea noastră a păsărilor e stabilită de materia primară a cerului. Lumea noastră apare cînd energia materiei primare circulă în lateral. Lumea legii private a fost creată cînd energia materiei primare circula vertical, de sus în jos, iar oamenii se îndeletniceau cu toții cu cultivarea directă. Pe vremea aceea, nu exista absolut nici o distincție (一切 ノ二別無ク) între superior și inferior, între mare și mic, între nobil și mirean. Au apărut însă sfinții din vechime și Buddha, care au creat propriile lor legi, iar societatea umană a luat drept model lumea noastră. Și-au creat împăratul lor imitîndu-mă pe mine, vulturul; și-au creat propriul general imitîndu-l pe erete; și-au creat nobilii imitîndu-l pe cocor; și-au creat suzeranii feudali imitîndu-l pe șoim; și-au creat însoțitorii, servitorii și toți funcționarii imitîndu-l pe șoimul călător; și-au creat pedestrașii imitînd acvila; au creat cele patru clase sociale (四民) imitînd puzderia de păsări mici; au creat ghicitorii (巫者) și pustnicii din munți (山伏) imitînd codobatura; au creat doctorii imitînd pasărea *Chin*; au creat preoții de la temple imitînd-o pe lebădă; i-au creat pe Laozi și Zhuangzi imitîndu-l pe cormoran; i-au creat pe cerșetori ( 乞食) și pe proscriși (非人) imitînd pitulicea și presura de munte. Astfel a fost creată societatea umană, imitînd mereu lumea păsărilor.

Între societatea oamenilor și lumea păsărilor există multe asemănări. În lumea păsărilor, firește, ierarhia hărăzită de cer e ca cel mare să îl mănînce pe cel mic. Însă dacă, de pildă, o acvilă e prinsă și crescută de oameni iar apoi i se dă din nou drumul în sălbăticie, nu mai poate face față păsărilor mici pe care le prindea și le mînca de obicei, ci mai degrabă zboară încoace și-ncolo ca să scape de ele și în cele din urmă moare de foame. La fel e și cu pedestrașii din lumea oamenilor: cînd rămîn fără soldă (扶持), ajung în rîndul cerșetorilor și al proscrișilor și se văd nevoiți să-i lingușească pe orășenii și pe fermierii pe care îi jefuiau înainte, și suferă mult. Dacă un șoim sau un șoim călător sînt prinși și crescuți de oameni iar apoi li se dă din nou drumul în sălbăticie, nu mai pot face față ciorilor, pe care le prindeau și le mîncau înainte, ci în cele din urmă ajung să fie sfîșiați și omorîți de ele. La fel stau lucrurile și cu însoțitorii, oficialii și suzeranii din societatea umană: cînd sînt învinși în bătălie, sînt nevoiți să-i lingușească pe fermierii și orășenii pe care îi jefuiau înainte. Dacă un erete e prins și crescut de oameni iar apoi i se dă drumul și se întoarce în munți, nu mai poate face față gîștelor sau lebedelor pe care le prindea și le mînca de obicei, ci zboară ici și colo ca să scape de ele și în cele din urmă ostenește, slăbește și moare. La fel e și cu generalii din societatea umană: cînd pierd o bătălie în timpul unei răscoale, cad în mizerie (落人ト成リ) și sînt nevoiți să-i lingușească pe fermieri și să cerșească de mîncare, iar în cele din urmă sînt descoperiți de dușmani și sînt uciși. Dacă un vultur e prins și crescut de oameni iar apoi i se dă drumul și se întoarce în munți, își pierde puterile, nu mai face față bîtlanilor și gîștelor și nu mai e în stare să îi prindă și să îi mănînce. În cele din urmă slăbește și moare. La fel e și cu împărații din lumea oamenilor: cînd pierd o bătălie în timpul unei răscoale, sînt nevoiți să se ascundă în cocioabele unor țărani, iar în cele din urmă sînt descoperiți de dușmani și uciși. Aceasta este o asemănare foarte mare între lumea păsărilor și societatea umană.

De vreme ce păsările se nasc dominate de energia laterală pentru că așa le hărăzește materia primară, greșeala nu e a lor. Oamenii se nasc dominați de energia descendentă și ar trebui ca fiecare dintre ei se îndeletnicească numai cu cultivarea directă, dar sînt influențați de o gîndire părtinitoare și de idei greșite și prin urmare cad în lumea păsărilor, iar asta este o greșeală atît de gravă încît nu poate fi exprimată în cuvinte sau cuprinsă cu gîndul[34]. Pe deasupra, toți oamenii de la Fu Xi (伏羲) pînă la Confucius au imitat stufărica cea gureșă care ciripește întruna fără rost și papagalul care repetă aiurea și așa au creat textele sfinte[35], poezia și proza (詩文). Învățăturile fraților Cheng Hao și Cheng Yi (程子) sînt imitații ale sfrîncîocului, iar cele ale lui Zhu Xi (朱子) imitații ale trilurilor ciocîrliei; învățăturile lui Sorai (徂徠) sînt o imitație a pitulicei, iar studiile despre poezie și proză din dinastiile Tang, Song și Ming imită ciripiturile prepeliței. Toate studiile literare nu sînt altceva decît imitații ale cîntecului păsărilor. Baladele vechi japoneze (小歌) sînt o imitație a gînguritului cucului, iar cînturile tradiționale și cele din teatrul Nō (謡ヒ・能) sînt o imitație a scatiului. Muzica rituală e o imitație a ortolanului, iar cîn-

34. 言語同断、心行絶無 este o altă expresie creată de Shōeki pentru a imita și a se referi la dictoanele budiste 言語道断 și 心行所滅. Primul înseamnă „vorbire întreruptă" și este folosit pentru a desemna procesele psihologice profunde a căror amploare nu poate fi exprimată în cuvinte, iar al doilea înseamnă, literal, „locul unde mișcările inimii dispar" și este folosit pentru a desemna stări mentale extrem de intense. Shōeki modifică frazele inițiale înlocuind al doilea termen din ambele cu 同断 („același", „la fel") și 絶無 („absolut deloc", „în nici un caz"), respectiv.

35. 聖学 înseamnă „învățătura sacră" și este un termen utilizat de obicei pentru a face referire la confucianism. Shōeki îl folosește pentru a trimite nu numai la Confucius și la scrierile sale, ci la toată literatura produsă de confucianiști și neo-confucianiști atît în China cît și în Japonia.

turile din teatrul de păpuși Jōruri sînt o imitație a strigătelor becaței. Oamenii cîntă la shamisen, koto și biwa[36] imitînd tînguirile pescărușului; imitînd rațele mandarine, își pierd mințile din pricina poftelor trupești și a băuturii. Fazanii, înspăimîntați de vultur și de erete, se ascund prin scorburi de copaci și ajung să se bată între ei pentru mîncare—imitîndu-i, oamenii se dedau jocurilor de noroc, iar jocurile duc în cele din urmă la incendii și jafuri. Toate activitățile din societatea umană sînt de fapt copiate după lumea păsărilor.

Cineva ar putea întreba: „Dar de ce ar imita oamenii păsările, mai ales în chestiuni de politică (政事)?" Iată răspunsul meu: oamenii nu sînt de fapt conștienți că imită lumea păsărilor. Păsările se nasc dominate de energia laterală, iar oamenii de cea descendentă—prin urmare, sînt diferiți din naștere. Oamenii se nasc însă influențați de ideea unilaterală de puritate[37] și, prin urmare, li se tulbură sufletul și li se mărginește mintea (偏心・偏知)—astfel, se blochează energia descendentă și așa ajung să creeze lumea legii private. Iar legea însăși este energie laterală. Legea nu poate fi creată cîtă vreme energia dominantă este cea descendentă, deoarece energia descendentă circulă foarte repede și în concordanță cu mișcările cerului—nu se mișcă niciodată în lateral. Cînd domină energia laterală, cea verticală este blocată și nu mai poate circula cum trebuie. Oamenii nu-și dau seama că sînt influențați de energia laterală și așa ajung să creeze legile. Prin urmare, în lumea legii private, totul este rezultatul energiei laterale. Tocmai de aceea, oamenii, deși nu sînt conștienți de asta, ajung să facă lucrurile întocmai ca în lumea păsărilor, care este dominată de energia laterală.

Păsările care sînt prinse de oameni și ținute în cuști vreme îndelungată nu-și pot urma ciclul vieții (形化) pentru că nu sînt în sălbăticie, unde s-au născut, așa că pînă la urmă mor. Iar păsările care sînt ținute multă vreme în captivitate nu mai pot supraviețui cînd sînt eliberate și trimise înapoi în sălbăticie, deoarece au fost influențate prea mult timp de energia descendentă a oamenilor și își pierd energia laterală de păsări. Nu se mai pot adapta la energia laterală din sălbăticie (山野) și mor. Pe de altă parte, una din șase sute de păsări este om, și chiar dacă celelalte păsări încearcă să o crească hrănind-o cu

---

36. *Shamisen* (三味線), *koto* (琴) și *biwa* (琵) sînt trei tipuri de instrumente japoneze tradiționale, toate cu coarde.

37. 清偏精 este încă o noțiune extrem de importantă pentru înțelegerea filosofiei lui Shōeki. Acesta critică ființele umane pentru că posedă *seihensei*—un spirit înclinat numai către puritate—deoarece, în viziunea lui, spiritul care domină toate ființele ar trebui să fie un amestec, o combinație subtilă și echilibrată de puritate (清) și impuritate (濁). Deși aceste două elemente sînt inseparabile, ființele umane resping constant impuritatea și devin astfel unilaterale, pierzînd armonia cu Natura.

grîne, va muri pentru că energia descendentă umană va fi înăbușită de energia laterală de pasăre.

Cînd stă ridicată, pasărea vede foarte departe în lateral pentru că are ochii de-o parte și de alta a capului, dar nu poate să vadă bine în sus și în jos—lucrurile stau așa pentru că e dominată de energia laterală. Sfinții și Buddha au privit lumea într-un mod artificial și cîmpul lor vizual era larg în lateral, dar era tulbure și murdar. Tocmai de aceea au creat propriile lor legi și au născocit tot soiul de învățături și practici: nu știau că, dacă vezi limpede și fără oprelisti de sus în jos, dacă sufletul și mintea îți sînt sincere, nu ai nevoie de nici o lege—și nu și-au dat seama de asta pentru că sufletul lor era dominat de energia laterală. Prin urmare, societatea umană a ajuns să semene foarte bine cu lumea păsărilor.

Atunci, păsările cele mici au vorbit toate într-un glas:

Deși societatea umană și lumea păsărilor sînt identice, există totuși o diferență, și anume că păsările nu pot să prindă oameni. În plus, păsările nu prind niciodată alte păsări și nu le țin în cușcă. Oamenii însă prind păsările mari, le țin captive în voliere (鳥部屋) și le dau să mănînce tot soiul de păsări mici; prind păsările mici, le țin în cuști și le pun să cînte ca să-și poată desfăta urechile. Astea sînt niște fapte care n-au nimic de-a face cu energia laterală a păsărilor!

Silvia a spus:

Da, sînt mulți oameni care le prind pe suratele mele!

Prepelița a adăugat:

De la o vreme încoace s-au înmulțit și cei care ne prind pe noi, a adăugat prepelița.

Presura a vorbit și ea:

Există pînă și oameni care prind nenumărate păsări, le țin în cuști și apoi le vînd și astfel își cîștigă traiul. Astfel de oameni, în sufletul cărora energia laterală se găsește cu asupra de măsură, sînt vicleni și meschini și comit fărădelegi grave—ei vor cădea repede în lumea noastră. Sînt oameni care n-au nici o fărîmă de discernămînt, care nu-și dau seama ce-ar însemna să fie ei înșiși închiși în cușcă, să le fie închiși nevestele și copiii și să fie scoși la vînzare! Nici măcar nu pot fi numiți oameni!

Păsările și-au spus atunci părerea finală:

Există printre noi vreo pasăre care să fi suferit de foamete (飢饉) sau din pricina vreunui an cu recoltă slabă (凶年)? Este vreuna care să fi ajuns la sapă de lemn pentru că n-a putut da înapoi un împrumut? Este vreo pasăre care să fi avut greutăți pentru că i s-au luat și dijma (年貢) și birul pe pământ (物成)? Vreuna care să ajungă să fure mîncarea unei alte păsări din pricina legii taxelor (税斂ノ法)? E vreo pasăre care să ia „contribuții" (用立金) și „împrumuturi" (貸上) de la altele? E vreuna care să facă paradă de bogăția și statutul ei? Există vreo pasăre care să cîștige într-o bătălie sau într-un război și să devină împăratul nostru, vulturul? Sau se poate ca împăratul nostru, vulturul, să devină un proscris dacă pierde un război? Să ne gîndim bine la toate lucrurile astea.

Atunci au ajuns toate la următoarea concluzie:

Asemenea suferințe și tulburări nu există decît în societatea umană. În lumea păsărilor nu se întîmplă astfel de lucruri—nici una dintre noi nu poate ajunge la sapă de lemn, să trebuiască să-și vîndă casa sau adăpostul. Prin urmare, lumea noastră, a păsărilor, e cu mult superioară lumii legii private. Lumea noastră e un tărîm paradisiac în care domnește pacea (極楽・太平ノ転下ナリ).

În lumea păsărilor nu există nici aur, nici argint; prin urmare, nu există nici lăcomie, nici tulburare, nici jafuri, nici războaie.

## BIBLIOGRAFIE

*Abreviere*

ASZ6 『安藤昌益全集6巻』[*Opera completă a lui Andō Shōeki, vol. 6*], Tōkyō: Nōsangyoson Bunka Kyōkai, 1997, pp: 34–87.

INABA Mamoru 稲葉 守
2004 『今にして安藤昌益』[*Andō Shōeki în prezent*]. Tōkyō: Fūtōsha.

JOLY, Jacques
1996 *Le naturel selon Andô Shôeki. Un type de discours sur la nature et la spontanéité par un maître-confucéen de l'époque Tokugawa: Andô Shôeki (1703–1762)*. Paris: Maisonneuve & Larose.

PAȘCA, Roman
2016 "*Homo Naturalis*: Andō Shōeki's Understanding of the Human Being", in T. Morisato, ed., *Frontiers of Japanese Philosophy 8: Critical Perspectives on Japanese Philosophy*. Nagoya: Nanzan Institute for Religion and Culture & Chisokudō Publications, 78–99.

Terao Gorō 寺尾 五郎
 1997 「諸鳥会合シテ法世ヲ論ズ 解説」["Comentarii la Parabola păsărilor"], in 『安藤昌益全集6巻』[*Opera completă a lui Andō Shōeki*, vol. 6]. Tōkyō: Nō-sangyoson Bunka Kyōkai.

Tucker, John A.
 2013 "Andō Shōeki's Agrarian Utopianism: An East Asian Philosophical Contextualization", in *Taiwan Journal of East Asian Studies* 10/1, 53–86.

Wada Kōsaku 和田耕作
 1989 『安藤昌益の思想』[*Gîndirea lui Andō Shōeki*]. Tōkyō: Kōyō Shobō.

Yasunaga Toshinobu 安永寿延
 1992 *Andō Shōeki: Social and Ecological Philosopher of Eighteenth-Century Japan.* New York: Weatherhill.

RALF MÜLLER
*Institut für Philosophie der Stiftung Universität Hildesheim*

# Über die Philosophie des Lebens

Nishida Kitarō 西田幾多郎

ORIGINAL TITLE:「生の哲學について」『西田幾多郎全集』旧版 [Alte Ausgabe: Gesammelte Werke Nishida Kitarōs]. Tokyo, Iwanami Shoten, 1978, 6: 428–51; 新版 [Neue Ausgabe]. Tokyo, Iwanami Shoten, 2009, 5: 335–53

KEYWORDS: Lebensphilosophie—Dilthey—Bergson—objektiver Geist—Person

# Einleitung

Der hier übersetzte Aufsatz wird am 1. Oktober 1932 in der 34. Ausgabe der Zeitschrift *Ideal* (理想) veröffentlicht. Nishida macht in seinen Tagebüchern keine genaueren Angaben zu seiner Entstehung, aber in einem Brief an Tosaka Jun (1900–1945) vom 4. Oktober desselben Jahres bezeichnet er den Aufsatz als Resümee der Abhandlung „Ich und Du"[1]. Es ist die neunte und letzte des dann im Dezember 1932 erscheinenden Buchs „Die sich selbst gewahrende Bestimmung des Nichts".

    Nishida schickt den Aufsatz zusammen mit dem Brief und bemerkt darin, dass sich Tosaka sicherlich an den theologischen Gedanken stoßen wird. Im Kern geht es Nishida um dem Begriff der „Person" 人格, der hier den Anlass bietet, sich von der Lebensphilosophie seiner Zeit abzugrenzen, explizit von Henri Bergson (1859–1941) und Wilhelm Dilthey (1883–1911). Nishida teilt das Anliegen dieser Autoren, „Leben" zum Thema der Philosophie zu erheben, ringt aber damit, wie es begrifflich gefasst werden kann, und zwar im Horizont des hegelschen Begriffs des objektiven Geistes, wie er von Dilthey zur Grundlage der Geisteswissenschaften gemacht wird. Ausgangspunkt ist dabei ein Lebensbegriff, den Nishida im Anschluss an einen zentralen Grundgedanken Johann Gottlieb Fichtes (1762–1814) einführt. Leben ist Selbstbewusstsein durch Setzung des Ich. Nishida schreibt: „Ohne ‚ich' gibt es kein ‚wahres Leben' […]. Das ‚wahre Leben' kann nicht noematisch, sondern muss noetisch erkannt werden"[2].

    Wie Nishida im Vorwort zur Aufsatzsammlung „Die sich selbst gewah-

---

1. 『西田幾多郎全集』[Gesammelte Werke Nishida Kitarōs], Tokyo, Iwanami Shoten, 2009, 21: 122.

2. *European Journal of Japanese Philosophy* 1 (2016): 165.

rende Bestimmung des Nichts" festhält, geht der Aufsatz zur Lebensphilosophie sachlich nicht über das in „Ich und Du" Gesagte hinaus[3]. Umso interessanter erscheint es daher, den Aufsatz als eine philosophiegeschichtliche Selbstverortung zu lesen. Die Abgrenzung zum Marxismus seiner Zeit ist bekannt, auch wenn sie in Teilen erst noch durch die von Nishida im Brief an Tosaka angedeutete Thematisierung des Praxisbegriffs ausgearbeitet wird. Ebenso kann der Bezug auf Bergson nicht überraschen, gilt er Nishida doch schon als Spiritus rector seiner *Studie über das Gute* (1911). Vielmehr muss Nishidas Verhältnis zu Dilthey an dieser Stelle genauer in den Blick genommen werden, da gerade Dilthey als Repräsentant einer Lebensphilosophie, die zugleich eine wissenschaftliche Begründung der Geisteswissenschaften leisten will, das Verhältnis von Begriff und Leben als Gegensatz von Mittelbarkeit und Unmittelbarkeit thematisiert und zu lösen versucht.

Zahlreiche Publikationen ab den 1920er Jahren zeigen, wie dieser Gegensatz von Begriff und Leben zum Kern einer philosophischen und sachlich bedeutsamen Debatte wird, zu der Nishida mit seinem Aufsatz 1932 Stellung bezieht. Nur einige Stimmen dieser Debatte aus den Jahren 1920, 1930 und 1931 seien genannt: Heinrich Rickert (1863–1936),[4] Ernst Cassirer (1874–1945)[5] und Georg Misch (1878–1965)[6]. Aus der heutigen Sicht zeigen diese Philosophen die Komplexität und Tiefe der Fragestellung, die auch im Anschluss an die Lebensphilosophie nicht notwendigerweise irrationalistisch beantwortet werden muss.[7]

Im Horizont der genannten Fragestellung erweist sich Nishidas Aufsatz nicht nur als hilfreich zur Orientierung in den Entwicklungslinien seines Denkens ab dem Ende der 1920er Jahre, sondern auch als ein spannen-

---

3. *Gesammelte Werke Nishida Kitarōs* 5: 8.

4. Heinrich Rickert: *Die Philosophie des Lebens. Darstellung und Kritik der philosophischen Modeströmungen unserer Zeit*, Mohr, Tübingen 1920.

5. Ernst Cassirer: „‚Geist' und ‚Leben' in der Philosophie der Gegenwart" (1930), in: ders. *Geist und Leben. Schriften zu den Lebensordnungen von Natur und Kunst, Geschichte und Sprache*, Leipzig, Reclam 1993, 32–61.

6. Georg Misch: *Lebensphilosophie und Phänomenologie. Eine Auseinandersetzung der Dilthey'schen Richtung mit Heidegger und Husserl*, Teubner, Leipzig/Berlin 1931.

7. Vor dem Hintergrund der Arbeit Georg Lukács' (1885–1971) (*Die Zerstörung der Vernunft. Der Weg des Irrationalismus von Schelling zu Hitler*, Berlin 1953; insbesondere das Kapitel: Die Lebensphilosophie im imperialistischen Deutschland, 351–473) wird die Lebensphilosophie lange Zeit als bloß irrationalistisch angesehen.

der Beitrag zur Auflösung des Gegensatzes von Begriff und Leben. Durch und ausgehend von diesem Beitrag, so die an anderer Stelle auszuführende These, lässt sich der kulturphilosophische Charakter der Philosophie Nishidas aufklären, insbesondere wenn man das bislang oftmals vernachlässigte Verhältnis zu Dilthey näher untersucht.

# Nishida Kitarō
# Über die Philosophie des Lebens
*übersetzt von Ralf Müller*

I

Es gibt nichts, das von alters her Philosophie genannt wird, das nicht in irgendeinem Sinn aus dem Verlangen[8] eines tiefgründigen Lebens 深い生命の要求に基づかざる entsteht. Wo gäbe es etwas, das als Philosophie zu bezeichnen wäre, ohne die ‚Frage'[9] 問題 des menschlichen Lebens'? In diesem Sinn hege ich eine große Sympathie gegenüber dem, was Philosophie des Lebens genannt wird. Aber wenn man sagt, lasst uns ‚Leben' zum Grundbegriff 根本概念 machen und [so] eine Philosophie konstruieren[10] 組織, muss [man] zunächst klären, was ‚Leben' ist, und die Beziehung von Leben und Logik muss ergründet werden. Wenn man etwas wie ‚Leben' nicht logisch erweisen kann, ist es natürlich auch nicht möglich, es begrifflich zu fassen. Es kommt hinzu, dass es wohl niemanden gibt, der mit dem Leben als unmittelbare Tatsache 直接の事実 nicht vertraut ist. Aber wenn die ‚Lebensphilosophie' als ein philosophisches System 哲学的体系, Wissenschaftlichkeit' 学問性 beansprucht, muss etwas wie die ‚logische Bedeutung 論理的意義 des Lebens' zutiefst erfasst werden. Wäre das ‚Leben' bloß etwas die Logik Übersteigendes, könnte man es nicht zum Grundbegriff der Philosophie machen. Es gibt heute vielerlei Weisen, in denen die Philosophie des Lebens gedacht wird, und im jeweiligen Standort hat sie ihre jeweilige Bedeutung, allein, es wird nicht über die tiefe immanente Beziehung zwischen Leben, das ihr [der Philosophie] Grundbegriff ist, und Logik nachgedacht. Darin liegt der grundsätzliche Schwachpunkt der ‚Lebensphilosophie', und [ich] denke, daraus entsteht auch die Kritik, die der Lebensphilosophie durch Leute zuteilwird, die eine Wissenschaftlichkeit der Philosophie fordern. Etwas wie das ‚logische Begreifen des Lebens' ist in der Weise der sogenannten Logik selbstredend nicht möglich, denn dort wird wohl etwas wie die

---

8. Alias: Bedürfnis, Anspruch.
9. Alias: Fragen.
10. Alias: organisieren, gliedern.

‚dialektische Logik' gedacht. Vielleicht sollte [man] die Philosophie Hegels nicht zur sogenannten ‚Lebensphilosophie' zählen, aber es ist wohl in diesem Sinn umgekehrt denkbar, dass [die Philosophie Hegels] die Bedeutung der wahren Philosophie des Lebens hat. Indessen kann man auch sagen, dass Hegel, der grundsätzlich am Standort des Idealismus stand, wohl die wahre Bedeutung der Dialektik nicht begreifen konnte und er zugleich das Leben nicht wahrhaftig in logischer Weise begreifen konnte.

Ich meine, dass das ‚wahre Leben' allein vom Selbstgewahren unseres persönlichen Selbst her gedacht wird. Ohne ‚ich' 我 gibt es kein ‚wahres Leben', ohne das ‚Persönliche' 人格的 gibt es kein ‚wahres Ich' 真の我. Das ‚wahre Leben' kann nicht noematisch, sondern muss noetisch erkannt werden[11] 知られる. Wir denken das ‚Leben' gewöhnlich basierend auf der ‚organischen Funktion von Lebewesen'. Aber teleologische Kausalität ist nicht unbedingt Leben, und letztlich führt man etwas wie ‚biologische Erscheinungen' naturwissenschaftlich in jedem Fall auf die mechanische Kausalität zurück, und etwas wie die ‚Zweckmäßigkeit' denkt man, kurz gesagt, nicht anders als das, was durch unser Subjekt[sein] 我々の主観 hinzugefügt wird. Ohne Bewusstsein gibt es kein ‚Leben'. Das, was als Leben gedacht wird, das man in keinem Sinn auf Natur reduzieren kann, ist nichts Anderes, als was man aufgrund der Tatsache unseres Bewusstseins fordert. Psychologen denken wohl, es gäbe ‚Bewusstseinsphänomene' ohne sich selbst gewahrendes Bewusstsein. Sie sagen wohl, ‚sich selbst gewahrendes Bewusstsein' sei im Gegenteil nur eine Art von Bewusstsein. Aber ohne ‚Bewusstseinseinheit' gibt es kein ‚Bewusstsein'. In der Einheit des Bewusstseins liegt das Vereinheitlichende nicht außerhalb des Vereinheitlichten, und das Ganze ist in den Teilen enthalten, und jedes Einzelne ist mit der Bedeutung des Ganzen versehen. Das ‚besondere Bewusstsein' 特殊の意識, das als sogenanntes sich selbst gewahrendes Bewusstsein gedacht wird, ist nicht das Selbst 自己, das unserem Bewusstsein eine Einheit gibt. In diesem Sinn muss unser Selbst etwas sein, dessen man sich in keiner Hinsicht bewusstwerden kann. Das ‚wahre Selbstgewahren' kann nicht anders gedacht werden denn als ein unendlicher Prozess, bei dem das Selbst im Selbst das Selbst sieht, und es bedeutet nichts Anderes, als dass das Ziel dieses unendlichen Prozesses im Ausgangspunkt enthalten ist. Was in diesem Sinn als Seiendes gedacht wird,

---

11. Alias: muss noetisch vertraut sein.

muss bedeuten, dass nicht das Teil vom Ganzen, sondern dass das Ganze vom Teil her gedacht wird. [Es] wird nicht in dem Sinn gedacht, dass das Einzelne 個物 als Selbstbestimmung des Allgemeinen gedacht wird, sondern es muss umgekehrt in dem Sinn gedacht werden, dass das Allgemeine dadurch gedacht wird, dass das Einzelne das Einzelne selber bestimmt; und es muss bedeuten, von einem Punkt zum anderen überzugehen, es muss als Kontinuität der Diskontinuität gedacht werden. Ohne ‚Einheit des Bewusstseins' gibt es keine ‚Bewusstseinsphänomene', und die ‚Bewusstseinseinheit' muss die oben [erörterte] Bedeutung besitzen. Denn ohne ‚Selbst' werden keine ‚Bewusstseinsphänomene' gedacht. Was als konkretes Bewusstsein gedacht wird, muss die Bedeutung haben, stets vom Grund des Selbst selber her das Selbst zu bestimmen, es muss die Bedeutung der Selbstbestimmung ohne Bestimmendes haben. Etwas wie das bloße Bewusstsein ohne Selbstgewahren ist nicht mehr als eine Seite des Bewusstseins, die durch die starke Verminderung der noetischen Bestimmung an der äußersten Grenze der noematischen Richtung gedacht wird.

Ohne ‚Selbst' gibt es kein ‚Bewusstsein', und wenn man annimmt, dass das ‚Selbst' etwas ist, wie oben [ausgeführt], müssen wir versuchen, auf einer noch tieferliegenden Ebene über unser ‚Selbst' nachzudenken. Was für eine Sache ist die wahrhaft sich selbst gewahrende Bestimmung? Gewöhnlich denken wir das ‚intellektuelle Selbstgewahren' als Selbstgewahren. Aber unser Selbst wird weder durch so etwas wie die sogenannte ‚innere Wahrnehmung' bewusst gemacht, noch ist es wiederum etwas wie das bloße Bewusstsein des Denkens. Unser Selbst muss frei sein, es muss wirken. Auch das, was als Selbstgewahren des Selbst der inneren Wahrnehmung gedacht wird, muss in Wirklichkeit auf [seiner] Kehrseite durch Handeln getragen werden. Ohne ‚Handeln' gibt es auch kein ‚Selbst'. Was als wahres Selbstgewahren gedacht wird, muss die Bedeutung der Selbstbestimmung des handelnden Selbst haben. Aufgrund der Tatsache der inneren Reflexion 内省的事実 wurde das ‚Selbst' herkömmlich als innere Kontinuität gedacht. Es ist nicht nötig zu sagen, dass ‚unser Selbst' nicht einfach etwas ist, das äußerlich gedacht wird, aber andererseits kann es auch nicht einfach als Bewusstseinsinneres gedacht werden. Am Grund unseres Selbst muss es etwas geben, das das Selbst selber übersteigt. Dort, wo das Innere das Äußere und das Äußere das Innere ist, wird die Tatsache des wahrhaft konkreten Bewusstseins gedacht. Nun, was ist das, was als unser handelndes Selbst gedacht wird, und auf welche Weise wird es wohl gedacht? Im Grund der Selbstbestimmung des handelnden Selbst muss es unbedingt etwas geben, das das Selbst übersteigt, muss es das Irrationale geben. Wenn das, was als unser wahres Selbst gedacht wird, nicht bloß etwas wie ‚Vernunft' ist, ist es auch nicht etwas wie das sogenannte ‚bewusste Selbst' als innere Kontinuität. Als handelndes Selbst müssen wir durch das Objektive, nein, durch das Irrationale fundiert sein. Aber würde im Wurzelgrund[12] 根底 des Selbst allein das Irrationale gedacht werden, gäbe es kein ‚Selbst'. Aus dem, was in welchem Sinn auch immer bloß als Natur gedacht wird, geht unser Selbstgewahren nicht hervor. Von diesem Standort her ist auch ‚unser Handeln', kurz gesagt, nichts als eine einfache Bewegung. Insofern das ‚Selbstgewahren' von uns wahrhaft gedacht wird, muss man [es so] denken, dass wir in unserem eigenen Grund überall den Anderen sehen. Was als unser Wissen oder Handeln gedacht wird, ist in diesem Selbstgewahren fundiert. Dort kann man sich etwas wie den ‚objektiven Geist' als Grund des Selbstgewahrens unseres handelnden Selbst denken. Und [ich] denke, dass unser Selbst dadurch, dass das Selbst selber darin eingeht, das Selbst selber entdeckt. Aber was muss der in diesem Sinn gedachte objektive Geist wohl sein? In welchem Sinn wird er wohl als objektives Sein gedacht? Das heißt, in welcher Seinsform[13] 存在形式 muss das Sein [des objektiven Geistes] gedacht werden? Und in welcher Beziehung steht [der objektive Geist] zu dem, was als unser individuelles Selbst gedacht wird? Wenn man ihn in dem Sinn, dass ‚wir in unserem Grund überall den Anderen sehen', als Vertiefung und Erweiterung des sogenannten inneren Selbst ansähe, wäre so eine Fundierung des objektiven Grundes des handelnden Selbst nicht möglich. Würde [der objektive Geist] demgegenüber gedacht werden als etwas wie das ‚große geistige Prinzip', als objektives Sein,[14] das unser individuelles Selbst übersteigt, könnten wir so die ‚Freiheit unseres individuellen Selbst' nicht erklären. Und ohne ‚Freiheit des individuellen Selbst' gibt es kein ‚Selbstgewahren des wahrhaft handelnden Selbst'. Genauso wenig ist es möglich, wie weit eine denkbare Selbstbestimmung eines einfachen Allgemeinen auch geht, das Einzelne zu erreichen.

Hier müssen wir zutiefst zu bedenken versuchen, in welchem Sinn das

12. Alias: Boden, Basis.
13. Alias: Existenzform.
14. Alias: Existenz.

zustande kommt, was als Leben unseres persönlichen Selbst gedacht wird. Was als Leben unseres persönlichen Selbst gedacht wird, wird wohl zunächst als in der Zeit Fließendes gedacht. Aber das, was wahrhaft als Leben unseres persönlichen Selbst zu bezeichnen ist, ist nicht so etwas wie die sogenannte ‚innere Kontinuität', sondern muss das sein, was in jedem Augenblick als unabhängig und frei gedacht wird. [Es] muss als etwas gedacht werden, das mit jedem Moment das Absolute berührt[15] 接する. Was als Leben des persönlichen Selbst gedacht wird, wird als diese Kontinuität der Diskontinuität gedacht. Daher ist, vom gegenwärtigen Ich 私 aus gesehen, das gestrige Ich ein Du 汝, und auch das Ich von Morgen muss ein Du sein, oder eher, wir müssen in jedem Moment so denken. Wenn in diesem Sinn die Einheit unserer ganzen Person gedacht wird, muss [sie] die Bedeutung von ‚gesellschaftlich' haben. Und das heißt, als Kontinuität der Diskontinuität wird [sie] gedacht als ein zeitlich Bestimmen des Selbst selber. Das, was als Leben unseres persönlichen Selbst gedacht wird, kann man so denken, dass [es] das Selbst selber gesellschaftlich und geschichtlich bestimmt. Daher denke ich als Grundprinzip der persönlichen Einheit etwas wie ‚agape'. Das, was das Ich dieses Augenblicks als Ich bestimmt, ist nicht etwas wie bloße Natur, sondern muss die Bedeutung des früheren Ich haben. Und das ist nicht wie ein bloßes ‚Ich', sondern muss gegenüber dem Ich dieses Augenblicks die Bedeutung des Du haben. Auch in dem Fall wiederum, dass das spätere Ich teleologisch so gedacht wird, dass es das jetzige Ich bestimmt, ist das nicht bloß wie die ‚entelechia', sondern muss in der Tat von der Bedeutung eines Du sein. Auch in dem Fall, dass demgegenüber das Ich so gedacht wird, dass es das zukünftige Ich bestimmt, bedeutet das nicht bloß, dass es ein späteres Ich bestimmt, sondern dass dem späteren Ich gegenüber das heutige Ich die Bedeutung des Du haben muss. In dem, was als Leben unseres persönlichen Selbst gedacht wird, muss gegenüber dem Ich der jeweiligen Augenblicke das Ich der anderen Augenblicke die Bedeutung des Du haben. Wir können sagen, dass ‚unsere persönliche Einheit' dadurch zustande kommt, dass wir im Selbst das Du sehen. Darauf muss die Idee der Selbstachtung 自敬 gegenüber unserem Selbst selber beruhen. Ohne ‚Selbstachtung' gibt es kein ‚Leben unseres persönlichen Selbst'.

Das Zustandekommen des ‚persönlichen Lebens unseres individuellen

---

15. Alias: an das Absolute angrenzent.

Selbst' muss wie oben [beschrieben] gedacht werden, aber das, was als unser persönliches Leben gedacht wird, kann nicht bloß als individuelles gedacht werden. Unser persönliches Leben muss etwas sein, das geboren wird und stirbt. Etwas, das bloß ungeboren und unsterblich ist, ist nichts Lebendiges. ‚Unser individuelles Leben' wird als ein Glied der Kette des Lebens 連鎖の一環 gedacht. Auch das, was als unser persönliches Selbst gedacht wird, muss in der Geschichte geboren werden und sterben. Und wenn im Wurzelgrund dieses Lebens etwas wie ‚die bloße Natur' gedacht wird oder wenn auch etwas wie die ‚bloße Vernunft' gedacht wird, nein, selbst wenn so etwas wie der ‚objektive Geist' gedacht wird, geht daraus kein ‚persönliches Leben des individuellen Selbst' hervor. Im persönlichen Leben des individuellen Selbst muss, wie oben gesagt, gegenüber jedem als Ich gedachten Augenblick ein anderer Augenblick als Du gedacht werden. Das heißt, in seinem Wurzelgrund muss etwas wie ‚Gesellschaft' gedacht werden, muss *agape* gedacht werden.

In gleicher Weise wird das ‚persönliche Leben unseres individuellen Selbst' dadurch gedacht, dass die Gemeinschaft Gottes 神的社会 gedacht wird, d.h. dass die *agape* des Absoluten am Wurzelgrund der Selbstbestimmung unseres individuellen Selbst gedacht wird, dadurch dass alles dem Ich Gegenüberstehende Du ist. Auch in dem, was als persönliches Leben des individuellen Selbst gedacht wird, sind wir in jedem Moment selbständig und frei und berühren in jedem Schritt das Absolute, aber zwischen Ich und Du ist es in jedem Sinn unmöglich, etwas wie die ‚noematische Kontinuität' zu erkennen. Und ich bin ich, indem ich dich erkenne, du bist du, indem du mich erkennst. Damit unser individuelles Selbst ein individuelles Selbst ist, muss es im Wurzelgrund seiner selbst das absolut Irrationale erkennen, muss es das absolut Andere sehen. Und wenn das als einfaches Anderes gedacht werden würde, gäbe es kein Selbst. Das heißt, es ist ein absolut Anderes und zugleich macht es das Ich zu einem Ich, es muss die Bedeutung des Du haben. Was als Du gedacht wird, muss die Bedeutung haben, dass es als das absolut Andere das Ich negiert und zugleich das Ich affirmiert. Ich und Du erblicken sich vermittels 通して der absoluten Negation. Die ‚absolute Negation zu passieren' 通する, bedeutet auf der einen Seite, sich unmittelbar zu erblicken. Dort entsteht, wie auch Gogarten sagt, die Geschichte durch die ‚zufällige Begegnung von Ich und Du', und zugleich bedeutet es, dass ‚wir uns in der Geschichte erblicken'. Wenn man von der Beziehung zwischen Ich und Du spricht, wird gewöhnlich eine abstrakte Beziehung zwischen [einem] bewussten Selbst und [einem anderen] bewussten Selbst gedacht. Deshalb erscheint es so, als ob die Beziehung zwischen Ich und Du von der Geschichte getrennt gedacht wird, aber die Ich-Du-Beziehung als konkreteste Beziehung des Einzelnen 個物的なるもの wird nicht ohne die geschichtliche Bestimmung gedacht. Das Einzelne wird allein als äußerste Grenze der Selbstbestimmung des Allgemeinen gedacht. Etwas wie ‚Kants Reich der Zwecke' ist die Welt der Vernunft, aber nicht die Gesellschaft handelnder Selbste und daher keine Gesellschaft lebendiger persönlicher Selbste.

Was ich *agape* nenne, bedeutet nicht etwas wie die sogenannte ‚Liebe' 愛, sondern bedeutet, ‚durch Sterben leben', es hat die Bedeutung des Opfers, und es wird in der Gegenrichtung zum *eros* gedacht. Wenn gedacht wird, dass das Selbst das Selbst ist dadurch, dass wir im Grund unserer Selbst den absoluten Anderen sehen, muss man denken, dass wir vom absoluten Anderen her bestimmt werden. Das, was in diesem Moment als dieses Ich gedacht wird, muss als von der unendlichen Vergangenheit her bestimmt gedacht werden. Alles Seiende ist in etwas, wir werden als aus einer unendlichen Umwelt her bestimmt gedacht. In diesem Sinn kann man von *agape* als dem Grundprinzip des absoluten Todes sprechen, und man kann sagen, dass [sie] nicht nur das Ich negiert, sondern auch das Du negiert. Das heißt, man kann denken, dass [sie] eine Bedeutung hat wie die Negationssebene des ewigen Jetzt, das man auch als das Bestimmen der räumlichen Welt denken kann dadurch, dass man in jeder Hinsicht die Zeit negiert. Aber das Ich ist nicht Ich dadurch, dass wir im Grund des Selbst selber bloß das absolute Andere sehen, und dadurch, dass man es so denkt, dass es durch das Andere bestimmt wird, sondern in dem Sinn, dass das Ich im absoluten Anderen das Ich sieht, ist das Ich das Ich. Der absolute Andere ist absolut der Andere und zugleich muss er das Ich zum Ich machen, d.h. es muss die Bedeutung des ‚Du' haben. Wie gegenüber dem Ich eines jeden Moments das Ich eines jeweils anderen Moments die Bedeutung des Du haben muss, bestimmen sich Ich und Du als Kontinuität des absolut Diskontinuierlichen. Wenn man die absolute Negation nicht passiert, ist das Du kein Du, sondern ein bloßes Ich, und so hört das Du auf, Du zu sein, und zugleich hört das Ich auf, Ich zu sein. Was als Bestimmung des absoluten Anderen gedacht wird, muss als Kontinuität der Diskontinuität als Bestimmung ohne Bestimmendes gedacht werden. Die Vermittlung des absoluten Anderen muss als Vermittlung des absoluten Nichts gedacht werden. Und unsere Gesellschaft, die als aus der Beziehung zwischen Ich und Du zustande kommend zu denken ist, hat gegenüber dem darin Seienden einerseits die Bedeutung, das Prinzips des Todes zu sein und zugleich muss es andererseits die Bedeutung haben, das Prinzip des Lebens zu sein, d.h., es muss die Bedeutung eines dialektischen Prinzips haben. Auch etwas wie der ‚objektive Geist', der als Wurzelgrund unseres persönlichen Lebens gedacht wird, muss in diesem Sinn etwas sein, das als Gesellschaft gedacht wird. In der äußersten Grenze, in der man denkt, dass wir im Grund des Selbst selber den Anderen sehen, wird durch die Bedeutung des dialektischen Selbstgewahrens, wo es heißt, dass dieser Andere das Selbst ist, die Selbstbestimmung des objektiven Geistes gedacht. So wie das Selbstgewahren unseres individuellen Selbst als Gesellschaftliches als Person gedacht wird, so wird es wohl auch eine Persönlichkeit besitzend gedacht. Nur muss beides in entgegengesetzten Richtungen der sich gewahrenden Bestimmung gedacht werden. Am Grund dessen, was als Gesellschaft gedacht wird, in der wir existieren und durch die wir bestimmt werden, wird eine ‚tiefe Irrationalität' gedacht. Man kann die Geschichte auch als Geschichte des Kampfes und der Sünde bezeichnen. Aber wenn am Grund der gesellschaftlichen Bestimmung in irgendeinem Sinn etwas wie die ‚Natur' gedacht wird, geht daraus kein persönliches Leben hervor. Auch was als Eigenliebe gedacht wird, die der Wurzelgrund des Kampfes und der Sünde ist, muss eine Seite der *agape* sein. Und wahrhaft das Selbst selber zu lieben, muss ein das Selbst selber Negieren sein. Eigenliebe als solche ist ein Widerspruch. Darin wird der ‚Kunstgriff der Vernunft' gedacht.

Wenn man denkt, wie oben ausgeführt, kann man nicht umhin, am Grund unseres persönlichen Lebens, als absolute, *agape*artige Einheit, etwas wie die ‚Gemeinschaft Gottes' zu denken. Und diese muss als Person[-sein] Gottes gedacht werden. Wie im persönlichen Leben des individuellen Selbst die ‚persönliche Einheit des Ich' dadurch zustande kommt, dass das Ich eines jeden Moments das Ich eines [je] anderen Moments als Du entdeckt, entsteht die ‚persönliche Einheit Gottes' dadurch, dass in jedem Punkt der geschichtlichen Entwicklung das gänzlich in der Geschichte existierende und durch die Geschichte bestimmte Ich alles andere als Du entdeckt. Dass das ‚Ich eines jeden Moments das Ich des [je] anderen Moments als Du sieht', bedeutet umgekehrt, dass das ‚Ich im Anderen das Ich selber sieht', und ‚unsere individuelle Person' wird gedacht durch das ‚im Selbst selber den absoluten Anderen Sehen'. Auf diese Weise muss das Person[sein] Gottes bedeuten, dass das als geschichtlich Einzigartiges bestimmte Ich den absolut Anderen als Du und ‚im absoluten Anderen Ich sieht'. Wie man in der christlichen Lehre sagt, muss die *agape* etwas Göttliches sein, durch die *agape* Gottes entsteht die *agape* der Menschen. Vom Standort des individuellen Selbst kann das, was man *agape* nennt, nicht gedacht werden. Und ohne *agape* gibt es nichts, das unser persönliches Selbst zu nennen wäre. Was als unsere persönliche Einheit gedacht wird, muss fundiert sein durch die Person Gottes. Das Selbstgewahren des individuellen Selbst ist vielleicht die *ratio cognoscendi*, aber nicht die *ratio essendi*. Als *agape*artige Bestimmung des Absoluten wird in ihm durch die persönliche Bestimmung Gottes, der gemeinschaftlich zu denken ist, ein Person[sein] bestimmt, das unbegrenzt gesellschaftlich ist. Es ist auch allgemein so, dass als Selbstbestimmung des ewigen Jetzt eine unbegrenzte Zeit gedacht wird. Und wenn man vom Standort unseres sich gewahrenden Selbst, das durch die Liebe dieses Absoluten bestimmt wird, im Grund seiner selbst den absoluten Anderen sieht, muss es eine uns bestimmende, unendliche gesellschaftliche Bestimmung geben. Wir müssen als bis ins Letzte gesellschaftlich und geschichtlich bestimmt gedacht werden. Und insofern das bedeutet, zugleich negiert und geboren zu werden, ist der objektive Geist als persönlich denkbar. Sein Inhalt ist auch als der einer Person denkbar. Und der Verlauf dieser gesellschaftlich-geschichtlichen Entwicklung ist durch und durch dialektisch zu denken. Was ich *agape* nenne, meint nicht die sogenannte ‚Menschenliebe', die sentimental ist. Denn dort, wo man die Negation des Absoluten wahrhaft umfasst, gibt es die *agape* der *agape*. Mit Tertullian kann man als einen Aspekt Gottes auch die Materialität anerkennen. Die Gemeinschaft Gottes bedeutet nicht das Reich der Engel im Himmel. Das heißt, im Grunde der Geschichte muss es etwas unser persönliches Leben Fundierendes geben. Nur, aus bloßer Irrationalität oder einfacher Materialität geht nichts hervor. Auch etwas wie die dialektische Bewegung wird von dort her nicht gedacht.

Ich denke unser persönliches Leben in der wie oben ausgeführten Art, und [ich denke,] dass die verschiedenen Weisen, Leben zu denken, von diesem Standort her gedacht werden müssen. Alles konkrete Seiende muss in diesem Sinn ein sich selbst Bestimmendes und in dem von mir genannten Sinn gesellschaftlich-geschichtlich sein. Auch Materie oder Natur bestimmen sich selbst zeitlich und daraus müsste alles hervorgehen. In Richtung der absoluten Negation der Selbstbestimmung des persönlichen Selbst, das im eigenen Grunde den absoluten Anderen sieht, werden Materie und Natur denkbar. Auch die teleologische Welt kann vom Standort des Selbstgewahrens des persönlichen Selbst durch die Vergegenständlichung seiner selbst gedacht werden. Es mag viele Einwände dagegen geben, etwas wie ‚agape' als dieses metaphysische Prinzip zu denken. Aber was ich *agape* nenne, bedeutet nichts anderes als ein gesellschaftliches Prinzip, das die dialektische, geschichtliche Bestimmung fundiert. Wie bereits öfter gesagt, wird das ‚Selbstgewahren des persönlichen Selbst' wahrhaft dadurch gedacht, dass man ‚im Selbst den absoluten Anderen und umgekehrt im absoluten Anderen das Selbst sieht'. Ohne mit dem absoluten Anderen identisch zu sein[16] 即する, wird kein ‚wahres Selbstgewahren' gedacht. Auch was als Element des persönlichen Selbstgewahrens als triebhaftes Bedürfnis gedacht wird, als auch was als vernunftmäßiges Sollen gedacht wird, es wird alles als ein Gesichtspunkt der *agape* gedacht. Und außerhalb der ‚Welt des persönlichen Selbst' ist es unmöglich, dass eine wahrhaft konkrete Welt der Wirklichkeit gedacht wird.

II

Ich habe jetzt nicht den Raum, von meinem Standort aus die verschiedenen Lebensphilosophien ausführlich zu diskutieren, aber ich denke, dass alles, was als Philosophie des Lebens gedacht wird, abgesehen von ihrem Metaphysischen und Erkenntnistheoretischen, durch die oben ausgeführte Bedeutung des Lebens fundiert werden muss. Das ‚persönliche Selbst' als Selbstgewahren des handelnden Selbst wird dadurch gedacht, dass ‚wir im Selbst den absoluten Anderen und umgekehrt im absoluten Anderen das Selbst sehen', und das, was als Leben des persönlichen Selbst gedacht wird, kommt zustande durch das Entdecken des absoluten Anderen als Du. Wenn man es so denkt, ist das, was als unser persönliches Leben gedacht wird, als *agape*artige Einheit nur als gesellschaftlich zu bezeichnen, und insofern gedacht wird, dass diese gesellschaftliche Einheit zustande kommt, wird von uns etwas gedacht wie die ‚Einheit des persönlichen Selbst', d.h. die ‚innere Kontinuität'. So ist das, was wahrhaft als Inhalt des Lebens zu bezeichnen

---

16. Alias: beruhen auf, übereinstimmen.

ist, als persönlicher Inhalt zu bezeichnen, und wenn man annimmt, dass der ‚persönliche Inhalt' als ideenartiger Inhalt イデヤ的内容 gedacht wird, können wir denken, dass man durch Handeln die Idee イデヤ sieht. Man kann wohl sagen, dass etwas wie die ‚reine Dauer' Bergsons einen Standort wie ‚die innere Kontinuität meines persönlichen Selbst' in jeder Richtung gründlich vorangetrieben hat. Wenn man sieht, dass dabei gedacht wird, dass [sie] innerhalb des Standorts des Selbstgewahrens des handelnden Selbst im Grund des Selbst das Selbst negiert und zugleich das Selbst gebiert und dass wir darin eingehen und zugleich dort heraus geboren werden, wird wohl etwas wie ‚unendliche innere Kontinuität des Lebens' gedacht. Etwas wie ‚die Schöpfung des inneren Lebens' kann man in dem Sinn denken, dass wir geboren werden, indem wir darin eingehen. Aber das, was als unser wahres Leben zu bezeichnen ist, wird nicht bloß in diesem Sinn gedacht. Was als wahres Leben gedacht wird, wird dort gedacht, wo man im absoluten Anderen das Selbst sieht, d.h. vom absoluten Tod aufersteht. Wie die ‚Zeit' nicht als bloße Kontinuität gedacht wird, sondern als die Kontinuität der Diskontinuität gedacht werden muss, muss auch das ‚wahre Leben' in diesem Sinn als Kontinuität gedacht werden. Auf der anderen Seite des Lebens muss es Räumlichkeit und Materialität geben. Das ‚Selbst' Bergsons ist bloßes, intuitives Selbst, aber kein handelndes Selbst. In Bergsons Selbst gibt es keinen ‚Tod' und das heißt, dass es zugleich kein wahrhaft lebendiges, wirkendes Selbst ist, es besitzt keine wahrhafte Objektivität. Unser wahres Selbst muss in der Geschichte geboren werden und in die Geschichte wirken.

Auch ‚Wissen' als Selbstbestimmung des handelnden Selbst muss als eine Art Handeln gedacht werden. ‚Handeln' bedeutet weder eine bloße äußerliche Bewegung noch ein bloßes innerliches Bewusstsein. Dadurch, dass man im Grund des Selbst selber den absoluten Anderen sieht und im Anderen das Selbst sieht, d.h. dadurch, dass man das Äußere im Innern sieht, wird die ‚Selbstbestimmung des handelnden Selbst' gedacht. Wenn man denkt, dass das, was als die Einheit unseres persönlichen Selbst gedacht wird, als *agape*artige Bestimmung die Bedeutung des Gesellschaftlichen hat, und in dem Sinn zustandekommt, dass durch die absolute *agape*artige Bestimmung in der Gesellschaft die Gesellschaft bestimmt wird, muss das, was als Inhalt der Selbstbestimmung des handelnden Selbst gedacht wird, die Bedeutung des Inhalts des Ausdrucks 表現 haben. Wenn das Selbst das Selbst ist, weil wir im Grund des Selbst selber den absoluten Anderen sehen und im absoluten Anderen das Selbst sehen, hat alles, was dem Selbst entgegensteht, die Bedeutung des Du und muss als das Selbst selber Ausdrückendes gedacht werden. Auch das, was als Inhalt der Selbstbestimmung unseres individuellen Selbst gedacht wird, kann man, insofern dies gesellschaftlich ist, als ausdruckshaft denken. Man kann auch denken, dass wir den Erlebnisinhalt des Selbst verstehen. Was als Inhalt unseres Erlebens gedacht wird, ist nichts Anderes als das, was man als Inhalt der Selbstbestimmung des von mir sogenannten handelnden Selbst denkt. Was als Inhalt der Selbstbestimmung des handelnden Selbst gedacht wird, wird als Inhalt des Lebens unseres persönlichen Selbst gedacht, und insofern durch die *agape*artige Bestimmung die ‚gesellschaftliche Einheit' gedacht wird, wird etwas wie die ‚innere Kontinuität des Erlebens' gedacht. Wenn man am Standort des handelnden Selbst steht und im Grund des Selbst den absoluten Anderen sieht, gibt es nichts, das von all dem, das dem Selbst entgegensteht, nicht Objekt des Verstehens ist. Verstehen bedeutet in diesem Sinn nichts anderes als die Selbstbestimmung meines handelnden Selbst. So kann man wohl von meinem Standort der Selbstbestimmung des handelnden Selbst etwas wie die Lebensphilosophie Diltheys denken. Wenn man am Standort des handelnden Selbst steht und überall im Grund des Selbst selber ein Du sieht, d.h. wenn man den absoluten Anderen als Du sieht, können wir im Selbst selber die Geschichte sehen. Dann man kann wohl auch sagen, dass etwas wie die ‚Struktur' oder ‚Beziehung' in dem Sinn gedacht wird, dass man in der Gesellschaft die Gesellschaft bestimmt, d.h. dass man in der persönlichen Einheit die persönliche Einheit bestimmt.

Aber ‚Wissen' ist nicht bloß Verstehen. Am Standort des handelnden Selbst ist das dem Ich als Du Gegenüberstehende nicht nur bloß ein Gegenstand des Verstehens, sondern muss auch bedeuten, dass [es] das Ich als Ich bestimmt. Im Selbstgewahren des individuellen Selbst muss [Wissen] bedeuten, dass das Ich dieses Moments das Ich eines anderen Moments als Du bestimmt und zugleich das Ich des anderen Moments das Ich dieses Moments als Du bestimmt. Das Selbstgewahren unseres individuellen Selbst kommt zustande als gesellschaftliche Bestimmung. Es muss bedeuten, im Selbst den Anderen zu sehen und zugleich im Anderen das Selbst zu sehen. Was als Inhalt des Erlebens unseres individuellen Selbst gedacht wird, muss einerseits als der Inhalt des Verstehens und zugleich andererseits als der Inhalt der Intuition gedacht werden, es muss im Ich unmittelbar evident

直証的 sein. Was bloß als Du gedacht wird, kann wohl bloß Gegenstand des Verstehens sein. Aber dem Ich gegenüber ist das Ich nicht nur Gegenstand des Verstehens, sondern muss auch als Gegenstand der Intuition gedacht werden. Was ich hier Intuition nenne, bedeutet, dass jeder Moment als absoluter das Andere bestimmt, es bedeutet, dass jeder Moment das ewige Jetzt berührt. Logisch bedeutet es, dass das Einzelne das Allgemeine bestimmt. Man kann dies wohl so denken, dass sich in der Gegenwart die Extreme von unendlicher Vergangenheit und Zukunft verbinden. Was als Selbstgewahren unseres individuellen Selbst gedacht wird, kommt zustande als Prozess der Intuition. Wenn man denkt, dass die Person durch die Person bestimmt wird und die Gesellschaft durch die Gesellschaft bestimmt wird, dann muss auch für unsere gesellschaftliche Bestimmung die Bedeutung der Intuition bedacht werden. Man kann auch denken, dass die Gesellschaft im Selbst das Selbst sieht. In der Selbstbestimmung unseres handelnden Selbst, die das Äußere zum Inneren macht, muss es diese Bedeutung geben. Insofern gedacht wird, dass wir in der Gesellschaft existieren und durch die Gesellschaft bestimmt werden, wird unser Wissen wohl auch bloß als ideologisch gedacht. Aber Geschichte ist uns gegenüber nicht bloß Gegenstand des Verstehens, sondern muss auch bedeuten, dass [sie] als Inhalt des Sollens uns bestimmt. Insofern für das, was als unsere Gesellschaft gedacht wird, die ‚persönliche Einheit' gedacht wird, muss so gedacht werden. Aber das, was als der äußerste Wurzelgrund unseres persönlichen Selbst als die gesellschaftliche Bestimmung gedacht wird, muss, wie oben gesagt, etwas sein wie das ‚Person[sein] Gottes' als absolute *agape*artige Bestimmung. Im Grund unseres persönlichen Selbst muss es bedeuten, dass wir durch den absoluten Tod leben. ‚Unser persönliches Selbst' muss durch die absolute Negation vermittelt werden, es muss bestimmt werden als Bestimmung ohne Bestimmendes. Dort hat unsere Person eine Bedeutung, die die sogenannte Gesellschaft oder Geschichte, in der bloß das Irrationale als Wurzelgrund gedacht wird, überschreitet. Das heißt, man kann eine überzeitliche, gemeinschaftliche Bestimmung denken. Wir können denken, dass wir durch unser Handeln die Idee sehen. Wenn dann so, wie gedacht wird, dass die Zeit als ewiges Jetzt bestimmt wird, die ‚Geschichte' als persönliche Bestimmung Gottes gedacht wird, kann man auch denken, dass wir durch das Handeln die Geschichte strukturieren. Die Umwelt bestimmt das Individuum und das Individuum bestimmt die Umwelt, und die Geschichte bewegt sich als wechselseitige Bestimmung von Umwelt und Individuum. Mit jedem dieser Schritte berühren [wir] die absolute Negation, und dort, wo wir aus dem absoluten Tod geboren werden, liegt die Bedeutung des geschichtlichen Prozesses. Es muss bedeuten, dass wir in jedem Moment [dieses Prozesses] die Idee sehen. Wenn man die geschichtliche Bestimmung bloß noematisch denkt, verfällt der Historismus wohl nichts anderem als einem Relativismus. Aber in seiner noetischen Bestimmung muss es stets die Bedeutung geben, dass man die Idee sieht. Wo man im absoluten Anderen das Selbst sieht, bedeutet dies auch, dass man die Idee sieht. Darauf baut die Objektivität der Werte. Die Objektivität der Werte wird fundiert durch die *agape*artige Bestimmung. Ohne die Bedeutung dieser noetischen Bestimmung wird die geschichtliche Bestimmung wohl nicht gedacht.

Was als unser begriffliches Wissen gedacht wird, muss gewöhnlich als eine Art ausdruckshafter Inhalt gedacht werden, es muss ein ‚*logos*artiger Inhalt' sein. In diesem Sinn kann man es als Inhalt des Verstehens denken. Aber bloß zu verstehen, ist kein Erkennen. Um zu ‚wissen' muss es die Bedeutung des Selbstgewahrens des transzendenten Selbst haben. Darin muss die Bedeutung liegen, dass wir im Selbst selber den absoluten Anderen sehen und zugleich im absoluten Anderen das Selbst sehen. Das heißt, es muss eine gesellschaftliche Bestimmung gedacht werden, die im Selbst selber das Zentrum hat, es muss die Bedeutung der Selbstbestimmung des gesellschaftlichen Selbst haben, das bestimmt worden ist. Wie oben gesagt, wird die ‚Selbstbestimmung unseres persönlichen Selbst' durch die Vermittlung der absoluten Negation gedacht, und am Standort der absoluten Negation muss etwas wie die ‚Selbstbestimmung des persönlichen Selbst', das die sogenannte Zeit überstiegen hat, gedacht werden. Diese Bestimmung wird im weiten Sinn als Vernunft gedacht, und dort auch etwas wie der Standort der theoretischen Vernunft gedacht, die unsere Individualität absolut negiert. Am Standort der gesellschaftlichen Bestimmung, die die Individualität negiert, mithin am Standort des persönlichen Selbst, das das Selbst selber negiert, wird der Standort des Wissens gedacht. Wenn an diesem Standort gedacht wird, dass man im Selbst den absoluten Anderen sieht, wird der Standort des Verstehens gedacht, und wenn gedacht wird, dass man im absoluten Anderen das Selbst sieht, wird etwas wie der ‚Standort des Wissens' gedacht. Im letzteren [Fall] wird das Einzelne als gänzlich durch das Allgemeine bestimmt gedacht, und die Gesellschaft wird als in der Gesellschaft das Selbst selber bestimmend gedacht, mithin wird die Bedeutung des Selbstgewahrens des handelnden Selbst sichtbar. Insofern die eine Seite unseres persönlichen Selbst diese Bedeutung besitzt, denken wir [es] als das Erkennen. Demgegenüber ist in der Bedeutung des Subjekts des Verstehens die Bedeutung dieses Selbstgewahrens nicht miteingeschlossen, es wird nur gedacht, dass man in jeder Richtung im Selbst den Anderen sieht. Daher kann man von diesem Standort her nicht den Wurzelgrund des gesetzmäßigen Wissens klären. Das heißt, als eine Seite der Selbstbestimmung des persönlichen Selbst wird vielleicht die Bedeutung des geschichtlichen Erkenntnissubjekts gedacht, aber das Bestimmen der Geschichte geht daraus nicht hervor. Aber auch der Verstehende kann nur in der Geschichte existieren und durch die Geschichte bestimmt werden. Auch ‚Verstehen' muss als Selbstbestimmung des handelnden Selbst die Bedeutung des in der Geschichte Handelns besitzen. In seinem Wurzelgrund muss es die Bedeutung der dialektischen Bestimmung geben. Wenn wir am Standort des persönlichen Selbst alles andere als Du sehen, und wenn wir denken, dass das Selbst außerhalb dieser gesellschaftlichen Bestimmung existiert, wird wohl etwas wie ein Subjekt des Verstehens gedacht. Aber in Wirklichkeit gibt es ein solches, transzendentes Subjekt des Verstehens gar nicht. ‚Verstehen' und ‚Erkennen' müssen wie die ‚beiden Seiten des intellektuellen Selbstgewahrens des handelnden Selbst' gedacht werden. In diesem Sinne kann man nicht umhin zu denken, dass die herkömmliche Lebensphilosophie, die das Subjekt des Verstehens zum Zentrum gemacht hat, einseitig ist.

III

In dem, was als persönliche Einheit unseres individuellen Selbst gedacht wird, muss gegenüber dem, was jeden Moment als das Ich gedacht wird, ein anderes Moment die Bedeutung des Du haben, d.h. seine [des individuellen Selbst] Einheit muss gesellschaftlich sein. Das heißt, dass das ‚individuelle Selbst' als eine Einheit gedacht wird, beruht darauf, dass in dieser Bestimmung das Ich das Du und das Du das Ich ist. Insofern gedacht wird, dass das Du Bestimmende das Ich Bestimmende ist und das Ich Bestimmende das Du Bestimmende ist, wird die ‚sich gewahrende Einheit des individuellen Selbst' gedacht. Darin muss die Bedeutung liegen, dass das Gemeinschaftliche das Selbst im Selbst bestimmt. Aber wenn das Ich und das Du bloß als eins gedacht werden, gibt es dort kein ‚Du' ohne ‚Ich', und damit verbunden wird das ‚Selbstgewahren des individuellen Selbst' nicht gedacht. ‚Ich' und ‚Du' müssen absolut Andere sein. Als Vereinigung dieser absolut Anderen, mithin als Kontinuität der Diskontinuität kommt unsere ‚sich selbst gewahrende Einheit' zustande. Das ist als Bestimmung ohne Bestimmendes die Bestimmung des Nichts zu nennen. Diese Bestimmung wird so gedacht, dass [das Nichts] im Grund des Selbst das absolute Andere umfasst und zugleich muss es so gedacht werden, dass das Selbst vom absoluten Anderen umfasst wird. Es muss eine dialektische Bewegung gedacht werden, in der das Einzelne das Allgemeine, das Allgemeine das Einzelne bestimmt. Innerhalb der persönlichen Einheit unseres Individuellen muss diese Bestimmung gedacht werden, das individuelle Selbstgewahren ist *ratio cognoscendi*, aber nicht *ratio essendi*. Von der geschichtlichen Bestimmung getrennt, gibt es kein persönliches Selbst. Dort, wo man vom absoluten Tod aufersteht, liegt das persönliche Leben des individuellen Selbst.

Was das ‚Wissen' als Selbstbestimmung des handelnden Selbst angeht, so muss, denke ich, die Beziehung zwischen dem Wissenden und dem Gewussten von der Beziehung zwischen dem Inhalt[17] 内容 der ganzen Person und dem je momentanen Ich her gedacht werden. Das Selbst ist absolut autonom und frei, ‚Subjekt' und ‚Objekt' werden als zu einander absolut gegensätzlich stehend gedacht und zugleich wird das Selbst gänzlich von der erkannten Welt 知られる世界, mithin vom Objekt her bestimmt und existiert darin. ‚Das Wissen kommt durch die Selbstbestimmung des Allgemeinen zustande' muss die Bedeutung der Selbstbestimmung der persönlichen Gesellschaft haben. Ich meine, dass innerhalb der Form dieser Bestimmung verschiedene [Gestalten von] Wissen gedacht werden. Wenn wir als ein Punkt der persönlichen Kontinuität am Standort der Selbstbestimmung des persönlichen Selbst stehen, muss alles dem Ich entgegenstehende die Bedeutung von Du besitzen. Der Inhalt dieser Welt muss insgesamt als ausdruckshaft gedacht werden. Wenn man innerhalb dieses Standorts im Selbst selber in jeder Richtung den Anderen sieht, kann man sagen, dass der ‚Standort des Verstehens' zustande kommt. Der ‚eine Punkt der persönlichen Kontinuität umfasst in jeder Richtung den Anderen', bedeutet, dass er eine ganze Person symbolisiert, es bedeutet, dass er die Gegenstandswelt persönlich sieht. Bei

---

17. Alias: Kern, Tiefe.

dieser Bedeutung der Selbstbestimmung des handelnden Selbst wird etwas wie das ‚Erkennen der Individualität', mithin das ‚geschichtliche Erkennen' zustande kommend gedacht. Demgegenüber liegt jeder Punkt der persönlichen Kontinuität in der persönlichen Einheit und wenn [jeder Punkt der persönlichen Kontinuität] durch sie ganz und gar bestimmt gedacht wird, mithin wenn das Selbst vom absoluten Anderen her bestimmt wird, kommt durch das selbstverneinende Moment dieses Selbstgewahrens etwas wie ‚das Erkennen der Universalgesetze' 一般的法則 zustande. Alles im Selbst Seiendes wird als durch das allgemeine Selbst bestimmt gedacht. Im Ersteren wird das ‚Zeitalter' oder die ‚Individualität' des Wissenden zum Zentrum, im Letzteren muss solcherlei gänzlich negiert werden. Als konkrete Form der handelnden Selbstbestimmung, die die Bedeutung von Verstehen und Selbstbestimmung beinhaltet, kann man wohl etwas wie einen ‚Typus' 類型 denken. Von diesem Standort her wird gedacht, dass alles Wissen die Bedeutung eines Typus besitzt. Das, was als intuitiv gedacht wird, ist der Inhalt des Selbstgewahrens des handelnden Selbst. Solange innerhalb der dialektischen Bestimmung des Selbstgewahrens das Bestimmende und das Bestimmte als eines gedacht werden, mithin solange eine unabhängige persönliche Einheit besteht, die sich selbst bestimmt, wird etwas wie ein ‚intuitiver Inhalt' sichtbar. Aber diese verschiedenen Fragen muss ich ein anderes Mal diskutieren.

# Book Reviews

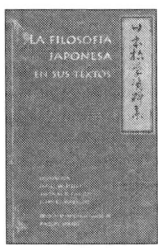

*La filosofía japonesa en sus textos.* Ed. por J. W. Heisig, T. P. Kasulis y J. C. Maraldo; edición española a cargo de Raquel Bouso García
Barcelona, Herder Editorial, 2016. 1.352 pág. €49,80. ISBN: 978-8425433191.

Hay obras que devuelven el sentido de la filosofía a sus orígenes, apuntando de nuevo al profundo sentido que la mueve, siendo ésta es una de ellas. Por fin disponemos de un volumen único fundamental para el estudio en castellano de la filosofía japonesa útil tanto para especialistas, como profesionales del pensamiento o estudiantes universitarios.

Encaramados en una tradición ciega y eurocéntrica, los filósofos occidentales han tanto sobrevalorado su aportación al pensamiento universal (o 'dominante') como despreciado la de las otras culturas. De hecho, desde la academia tan sólo se enseña autores y debates occidentales repitiéndose el manido y erróneo mantra del «la filosofía nació en Grecia». Lo que está claro es que cada pensadora o filosofía se ampara en una cultura que bajo una miríada de matices y elementos configura el espacio y los modos de lo pensable. Por ello, cada filosofía, en su proceso de transformar e identificar lo razonable de la realidad, bebe de una gran cantidad de fuentes que le otorgan un sello característico. En el caso de Japón, y bajo el objetivo de la liberación del «yo» y la reflexión sobre el modelo social, encontramos los aportes del sintoísmo, el confucianismo, el budismo o los estudios nacionales como elementos diferenciales que apuntan a una filosofía diferente (en relación a la occidental) pero necesaria en tanto que parte de las elaboradas formas de pensamiento que ha producido nuestra especie. Al fin y al cabo compartimos el ansia de la especie humana por saber, por poner en orden nuestra realidad bajo diversas categorías, ideas, o ritos, entre otros tantos elementos simbólicos. Pero la capacidad de acceso a otras culturas o tradiciones filosóficas tiene un problema: la barrera lingüística.

Por ello la traducción emerge como un proceso necesario que ya en el pasado permitió incluso a personas próximas geográficamente compartir ideas (pensemos en los académicos europeos intentando leerse entre ellos y la no siempre capacidad de dominar en la profundidad suficiente idiomas como el Castellano, Inglés, Italiano, Alemán, Francés o Danés, por mencionar algunos). Y no es un mal menor, puesto que la traducción pone de relieve los elementos fundamentales de una cultura a través no sólo de los elementos culturales que impregnan la semántica sino también de las peculiaridades que la sintaxis explicita acerca de cómo se captura y discretiza conceptualmente lo real.

A través de sus 1349 páginas, este libro nos presenta el trayecto de los pensamientos filosóficos en Japón, que se muestran como joyas ignotas de gran calado y valor para nuestra pśropia realidad actual. Sin duda alguna, por su calidad formal, temáticas cubiertas y traducciones hasta ahora no disponibles, esta obra es y será por mucho tiempo la referencia para cualquier lector interesado no sólo en el pensamiento japonés, sino en la revolución filosófica que aspira a la universalidad del proceso de pensar desde la diferencia cultural que delimita y permite establecer los límites o justifica la quiebra de las ideas anquilosadas, dadas como normales.

Además de las citadas 1349 páginas, la obra cuenta con 4 excelentes editores, un magnífico equipo de 77 traductores y colaboradores y una estructura formal que incluye tanto elementos de gran ayuda contextual e introductoria (Marco introductorio, los 5 Apéndices: Glosario, Bibliografía, Cronología, Índice temático, Índice analítico) como las propias traducciones de los textos ordenadas bajo una premisa temporal y conceptual pero siempre acompañados de una breve introducción al pensador o a la pensadora. Las traducciones se agrupan en las siguientes categorías: (a) Tradiciones (Preludio: la Constitución Shōtoku, Tradiciones budistas, Tradición Zen, Tradición de la Tierra Pura, Tradiciones confucianas, El sintoísmo y Estudios Nacionales, Filosofía académica moderna, Escuela de Kioto, Filosofía del siglo xx), y (b) Temas adicionales (Cultura e identidad, Pensamiento samurái, Filósofas, Estética, Bioética). Desde una perspectiva formal y estructural, el texto sigue en su totalidad la excelente y previa versión inglesa publicada en el año 2011: Heisig, James W.; Kasulis, Thomas P.; Maraldo, John C. (eds.) (2011) *Japanese Philosophy: A Sourcebook*, University of Hawai'i Press, excepto en el hecho que en la versión castellana se ha incorporado un apartado nuevo del pensador Yagi Seiichi, «El voto de la vida».

Si bien resulta imposible reunir en una única obra las totalidad de los pensamientos del Japón, este volumen aúna las grandes voces, las ideas fundamentales, los autores básicos que permiten comprender el desarrollo del pensamiento japonés, al tiempo que se apuntan debates de gran calado (pensemos en el apartado de Filósofas o Filosofías del siglo xx). Agradecemos al equipo editorial desde este lugar la ingente, ardua y magnífica tarea realizada, fuera de lo curricularmente rentable en nuestros días. Se nota que una obra como esta no persigue la fama o el beneficio (Herder de nuevo sacando un volumen espléndido que honra a la editorial y a la tarea que la orienta), antes bien el poner sobre el espacio de pensamiento unos recursos nuevos que de forma inexplicable nos habían sido silenciados.

Con todo, la visión sobre el *tetsugaku*, incluso desde los propios autores japoneses no es homogénea y el repaso de tales disensiones nos transporta a un debate más profundo sobre el objetivo y el contexto de lo pensable. Por ello, vemos en la crisis del *bakumatsu* la oportunidad para replantear la filosofía, algo que la era Meiji pondrá sobre la mesa: el debate entre lo tradicional y japonés en contra de lo moderno y occidental. En este debate se produce el apasionante momento de repensar desde los cimientos el significado del pensamiento. Seguramente el momento histórico más lúcido y honesto de la historia del pensamiento universal. Sin embargo, no se trató de un proceso unidireccional y globalmente aceptado, antes bien lo contrario: un proceso lleno de debates y diferencias. Para empezar, los tipos de análisis, argumentación, razonamiento o estilos de disputa habían bebido de otras formas y estilos en el Japón antiguo que en la filosofía de tradición europea. Inicialmente, para los críticos de la era Meiji, el término *tetsugaku* no designaba un pensamiento propio japonés, lo cual rechazaban de antemano (posición todavía en boga entre algunos sectores), sino más bien identificaba a los expertos japoneses que trabajaban el pensamiento occidental, a través de autores como Platón, Kant, Bergson o Heidegger, entre muchos otros. No se podía mezclar lo pre-filosófico autóctono con lo profesional europeo, y mucho menos en las citaciones. Tales autores tan sólo estudian el pensamiento occidental y no han sido incluidos en este libro Otra visión fue considerar el pensamiento japonés como aquel propio antes de la entrada del pensamiento europeo, especialmente en el pensamiento confuciano, como defendió Inoue Tetsujirō. Tal enfoque permitió una aproximación nueva al poso histórico pero al mismo tiempo difuminó la posibilidad de pastar una nueva forma de pensamiento japonés que se embebiera de las oportunidades conceptuales proporcionadas por el pensamiento occidental. Otra aproximación pasaría por considerar los métodos y temas filosóficos occidentales como los únicos correctos al tiempo que permiten sin embargo estudiar e iluminar los elementos autóctonos del pensamiento tradicional japonés. Kūkai y las investigaciones sobre las relaciones entre Dōgen y el ser y el tiempo o sobre la filosofía del lenguaje constituyen un ejemplo de tal aproximación. Siendo justos, debemos reconocer que tales autores defienden un abanico de camino de interacción entre las bidireccionalidad de los contactos entre la filosofía japonesa y europea, considerando el proyecto filosófico como algo inconcluso que requiere de la deconstrucción y reconstrucción sistemática, en un estado sísifico de cambio constante. Es este aspecto el considerado como más representativo por los autores del presente volumen. En cuarto y último lugar, lo filosófico japonés sería aquello originariamente y radicalmente original propio que constituiría un avance en el pensamiento universal. Es lo que pensaron sobre los logros de Nishida Kitarō autores como Takahashi Satomi o Shimomura Toratarō. Esto es, en cierto modo, un orientalismo invertido que trata de beber de las fuentes tradicionales para avanzar más allá del propio pensamiento occidental en pos de uno verdaderamente universal, emancipado de la mano de autores japoneses.

El volumen cumple con la tarea de recopilar las claves históricas del pensamiento japonés al tiempo que introduce amablemente al lector en los nuevos caminos filosóficos o teóricos de una tradición cultural distinta y, por lo tanto algo compleja de asimilar. Nos congratulamos por poder ampliar los límites de las filosofías a través del *tetsugaku* y los pensamientos que lo precedieron, puesto que de eso se trata: de pensar a través de los textos y no sobre los mismos. En resumen, este volumen es la bocanada de aire fresco que necesitaba el pensamiento occidental realizado en castellano, ya abotargado y consumido por sus propios laberintos académicos de pesada tradición.

Por todo lo expuesto es obvio decir, si bien insistiremos en ello, que es esta una obra fundamental para la biblioteca de cualquier personada con pasión por el pensar desacomplejado. No lo duden, es la mejor obra que podrán leer y comprar en décadas para estimular el pensamiento propio y genuino. «Un quilo de filosofía», como dijeron en la presentación realizada en Barcelona, el todo y la nada en un mismo lugar. Sean audaces y atrévanse a poner en duda todo lo que saben, pero en buena y japonesa compañía.

Jordi Vallverdú
*Universitat Autònoma de Barcelona*

**Itabashi Yūjin** 板橋勇仁『底なき意志の系譜』[Généalogie de la volonté sans fond]
Tokyo, Hōseidaigaku Shuppankyoku, 2016, 242 pages. ¥4,200. ISBN: 978-4588150753.

Itabashi Yūjin est un spécialiste de la philosophie de Nishida et de la philosophie allemande moderne. Il est aussi l'auteur des ouvrages suivants: Méthodologie logique de la philosophie de Nishida 『西田哲学の論理方法：徹底的批評主義とは何か』(2004, Hōseidaigaku Shuppankyoku), Livre sur Schopenhauer 『ショーペンハウアー読本』(2007, Hōseidaigaku Shuppankyoku), ainsi que Réalité historique et philosophie de Nishida 『歴史的現実と西田哲学：絶対的論理主義とは何か』

(2008, Hōseidaigaku Shuppankyoku). Selon moi, Itabashi a analysé soigneusement l'élaboration de la logique de la pensée chez Nishida, comme il l'a fait dans ses deux livres concernant cet auteur.

Cependant, ce dernier livre, Généalogie de la volonté sans fond, paru en 2016, est un ouvrage audacieux qui essaie de déployer les possibilités de la philosophie de Schopenhauer. À partir d'une analyse de la pensée schopenhauerienne, l'argumentation de l'auteur se centre sur une généalogie de la philosophie qui accorde de l'importance à « la volonté sans fond » et qui s'inspire de Böhme, de Schelling, de Nietzsche et de Nishida. Si vous avez déjà travaillé sur un ou plusieurs de ces philosophes, vous sentirez peut-être déjà que cette tentative n'est pas sans raison et qu'elle mérite d'être approfondie. Il existe déjà beaucoup de travaux sur Schopenhauer et les autres auteurs cités, mais je ne connais pas d'analyse qui, comme celle-ci, essaie d'englober ces philosophes au nom de « la volonté sans fond ». Je pense que ce livre a réussi à montrer, en apportant plusieurs preuves convaincantes, la ligne principale de cette généalogie.

Ce livre est organisé clairement, comme les autres livres de l'auteur. Il consiste en deux parties. La première contient deux chapitres dans lesquels émerge l'enjeu de la pensée de Schopenhauer, à savoir le sans-fond (*Grundlosigkeit*) de la volonté. Le monde comme représentation est une apparition objective de notre volonté, mais cette volonté n'a pas de fond. Ainsi, si le monde est un néant, c'est à cause de la volonté car il reflète la volonté qui est un néant. Ce sans-fond est une idée à double tranchant, selon Itabashi. Comme on le sait, la volonté schopenhauerienne tend vers la vie, ce qui nous cause des souffrances, car nous rencontrons inévitablement des obstacles à l'accomplissement de ce vouloir-vivre et donc des insatisfactions. Ainsi se manifeste le côté douloureux dû à l'absence de base de la volonté. D'un autre côté, Schopenhauer écrit qu'il faut nier la volonté de vivre pour pouvoir s'émanciper des souffrances et retrouver la liberté de la volonté. Ici se présente une autre face du sans-fond. Cependant, une question se pose, exactement ici, quand Schopenhauer décrit la négation de la volonté de vivre. Comment la volonté peut-elle gagner sa liberté, tout en étant niée dans sa composante centrale qu'est le vouloir-vivre? À cette question, Itabashi trouve une réponse en approfondissant la notion de sans-fond. Ce qu'on trouve après la négation de la volonté n'est pas le vide ou le rien; ce dont il s'agit relève plutôt d'une inapplicabilité du principe de raison. Itabashi nous rappelle que le mot allemand Grund signifie à la fois « raison d'être » et « fond ». S'il en est ainsi, la négation de la volonté nous incite à arrêter de chercher la raison d'être de notre volonté. Comme il n'y a plus de fond, cela nous permet de vivre le « maintenant » sans fond. Ainsi émerge la liberté de la volonté dans chaque moment du monde. Selon l'interprétation d'Itabashi, c'est à cause du sans-fond

(*Grundlosigkeit*) que la pensée de schopenhauer se trouve tantôt dans la souffrance, tantôt dans la liberté.

Dans la deuxième partie, Itabashi essaie de découvrir la généalogie de cette « volonté sans fond ». Les philosophes traités sont Hegel, Nietzche, Nishida, Schelling et Böhme. Hegel est évoqué à des fins de comparaison avec Schopenhauer. Il n'est donc pas compté dans la généalogie. Dans le cas des autres philosophes, Itabashi étudie d'abord la résonance entre eux et Schopenhauer. L'idée clé reste toujours la volonté sans fond. Mais la généalogie n'est pas une simple assemblée de philosophes qui se ressemblent. Il s'agit aussi des prolongements d'une pensée. Chaque fois qu'il ajoute un philosophe à la généalogie, l'auteur présente une des problématiques que Schopenhauer a omises, mais que l'autre philosophe peut contribuer à développer. Il s'agit de la relation entre la liberté de chaque individu et la liberté de la volonté sans fond (Nietzche), de la structure de reconnaissance simultanée du moi et de la volonté sans fond (Nishida) ou du caractère pratique de la volonté sans fond dans le monde réel (Nishida), de la coexistence du moi libre et d'autrui libre (Schelling), ou encore de la manière de relier le moi individuel aux autres (Böhme).

Ainsi, non seulement Itabashi découvre une résonance entre Schopenhauer et chaque philosophe, mais aussi il enrichit la généalogie en y ajoutant les fruits récoltés par d'autres philosophes. Dans ce cheminement, les lecteurs vont pouvoir témoigner d'une aventure dynamique et solide de la pensée d'Itabashi lui-même.

L'objectif de la création de la généalogie est chez lui de réfléchir sur la vie à partir de la vie, au lieu de spéculer sur la vie en y appliquant le principe de raison. Certainement, cet objectif a été aussi partagé par les philosophes cités, lesquels ont tenté de saisir la vie en tant que telle, sans l'expliquer. Il serait éventuellement possible, dans cette perspective, d'amplifier la généalogie en y ajoutant d'autres philosophes.

Je suis en réalité une des personnes qui sont fascinées par cette aventure de la pensée et il ne fait aucun doute que ce livre d'Itabashi est une des références importantes concernant le lien entre Schopenhauer et Nishida. Cependant, une question s'est imposée à moi lorsque j'ai lu l'étude portant sur la caractéristique pratique de la volonté sans fond dans le monde réel (chapitre 6). Itabashi superpose ici la volonté de vivre de Schopenhauer à l'attachement au moi (我執) de Nishida pour montrer que c'est en essayant d'échapper à cet attachement et en échouant dans cette tentative qu'on arrive à voir la réalisation de « la liberté sans fond ». Il les identifie car dans les deux cas, il s'agit d'un « état d'esclavage de notre âme », selon la terminologie de Nishida. Selon l'interprétation d'Itabashi, c'est parce que notre âme est forcée de chercher une identité autonome ayant sa raison en soi-même, alors que précisément celle-ci n'existe pas réellement. Cette recherche sans fin est bien la preuve de l'état d'esclavage de notre âme. Les écrits concernant l'attachement au moi chez Nishida ne sont ni très nombreux ni tout à fait clairs. Je n'ai donc pas encore une idée précise à propos de cette question dans sa pensée. À tout le moins, je suis d'accord avec le fait que Nishida ne se contente pas de chercher une identité autonome, car il admet volontiers la fluidité du monde réel. Pour lui aussi, le monde est certainement « sans fond ». Mais les écrits sur l'état d'esclavage de l'âme chez Nishida me semblent signifier un peu plus qu'une simple insistance à chercher une identité autonome. L'expression « esclavage de l'âme » est souvent utilisée par lui pour exposer la caractéristique principale de l'intuition (par exemple, NKZ 9: 201). Il écrit que les choses évoquent chez nous une action, que notre volonté est ainsi privée de décision et que, par conséquent, nous sommes en état d'esclavage. En ce sens, nous vivons avec les choses, en tant que chose (NKZ 9: 301). L'esclavage de l'âme n'est-il pas alors une preuve de notre dépendance à l'égard du monde plutôt que de l'attachement à l'identité autonome ?

L'intuition n'a pas simplement un côté troublant ; elle a aussi un aspect positif. Elle est même indispensable à notre accès à l'autoéveil car nous vivons au croisement de l'intuition et de l'agir (« l'intuition agissante »). Lorsque nous sommes déterminés par l'intuition en même temps que nous déterminons l'agir, nous nous trouvons dans l'auto-éveil.

Pour étudier le côté pratique de la volonté sans fond, je pense que la problématique de l'habitude peut être significative. Nishida établit différents degrés d'intuition agissante à la fin de sa vie en citant l'étude de Ravaisson portant sur l'habitude (NKZ 11: 366). Le monde historique est considéré comme « habituel » par Nishida, car l'activité obscure formée par l'habitude constitue la tonalité fondamentale de notre être, mais sans prendre jamais la forme d'un « fond ».

Les citations de Nishida (NKZ) sont tirées de 『西田幾多郎全集』 [Œuvres complètes de Nishida Kitarō], 19 tomes, (Tokyo: Iwanami Shoten) 1978–1980.

Imono Mika<br>Université de Strasbourg

**Yamazaki Nobuo** 山崎庸男 『安藤昌益の実像 : 近代的視点を超えて』 [**The Real Andō Shōeki: Looking beyond the Modern Perspective**]
Tokyo: Nōbunkyō, 2016. 285 pages. ¥1,944. ISBN: 978-4540152221.

Yamazaki Nobuo's *The Real Andō Shōeki's* is a rather ambitious book that tries to be a comprehensive compendium of the life and work of Andō Shōeki (1703–1762), the little known philosopher of Tokugawa Japan. I call it "ambitious" because it attempts not only to shed light on Shōeki's life, but also to present, synthetically yet comprehensively, the gist of his philosophical ideas, and the way in which his writings were discovered, read, and interpreted by Japanese and Western scholars.

But before I review the book, allow me a short digression. I have been conducting research on Andō Shōeki and his philosophical ideas for several years now, and I have in my office a rather extensive collection of books, articles, and other documents that have been published so far, both in Japanese and in other languages (mostly English and French). These include, of course, the excellent edition of the complete works 『安藤昌益全集』 published by Nōbunkyō, but also biographies of the philosopher, monographies about the Hachinohe area in the Tokugawa period, comparisons with other thinkers such as Miura Baien or Jean-Jacques Rousseau, and, last but not least, several works of fiction in which Shōeki is the protagonist. What I find surprising about all these books and materials is the fact that a significant proportion of them are actually written or prepared by non-specialists, i.e. people who are not necessarily involved in the academic world as researchers, but for some reason become interested in Shōeki and his works and embark on a personal journey to dissect and interpret them. This is not to say that I believe all research should be conducted exclusively by academics, quite the contrary—I think there are plenty of outstanding papers, articles and books produced by non-academics. However, in Shōeki's case, the high number of non-academics who engage with his work is intriguing to say the least. But why does this happen? Is it because so little is known about his life? Is it because his ideas appeal to the general public? Is it because the number of academics who study Shōeki's works is still relatively low? I believe these are important questions, and hopefully in the future there will be studies that can provide some answers.

To end this digression, let me just add that Yamazaki Nobuo is also part of the category of authors I mentioned above: according to his short bio, he is not a researcher, but a high school teacher somewhere in Chiba prefecture who is interested in local history and who, in his free time, conducts research on Shōeki's philosophy. Apart from contributions to volumes about the history of the city of Kimitsu, he also published several articles on Shōeki's ideas about medicine. That said, let me now go back on track.

The book consists of a preface, two parts, and an afterword. In the brief, two-page preface, Yamazaki announces the main ten points he wants to discuss in the book, which are as follows:

1. The true essence of Shōeki's thought as an amalgamation of old and new concepts, i.e., as a mixture of Daoist and Confucianist principles, and revolutionary ideas such as gender equality and the absence of hierarchy in human society;

2. The reevaluation of Kanō Kōkichi's role in forging the image of Andō Shōeki as a philosopher;
3. The reasons why a copy of the manuscript of 『自然真営道』 (*The True Way of the Functioning of Nature*), Shōeki's major work, was found in Kita Senjū;
4. An analysis of the so-called "Ōdate documents," a series of Shōeki-related materials discovered in the city of Ōdate in present-day Akita prefecture;
5. The need to discuss the proposition that the development of Shōeki's philosophical ideas was triggered by his firsthand experience of the Tōhoku famine and of the predicament of the farmers in the Hachinohe area;
6. The idea that Shōeki's understanding of medicine developed independently of the so-called "medical debate" of the Hōreki era (1751–1764), influenced by the publication of Rangaku anatomy treatises;
7. A detailed analysis of *shizen* (自然), *shin* (真) and other key concepts, in order to demonstrate that Shōeki's understanding of *shizen* is different from the modern intension of the notion, and from the meaning of the English word "nature";
8. The hypothesis that Shōeki's criticism of the four social classes (士農工商) is not directed at the hierarchy imposed by the Tokugawa régime, but at the "sages of old," i.e., the Chinese scholars responsible for the invention of the "laws" that have perverted human society by making it deviate from the "True Way of Nature";
9. The hypothesis that Shōeki's criticism of imported ideologies such as Daoism and Confucianism stems from his strong nationalism and the Shintoist background of his thought;
10. The need to reconsider the theory that Shōeki did indeed hold the so-called "Hachinohe symposium," where he allegedly exposed his philosophical ideas to a small gathering of disciples from all over Japan.

As can be seen from this list as well, Yamazaki's is indeed an ambitious project.

The first part of the book focuses on the discovery of Shōeki's manuscripts, the first researchers of his ideas (Kanō Kōkichi and E. Herbert Norman), and the small number of extant materials that document his life. In his effort to be as thorough as possible, Yamazaki takes an excursion to all the places that are associated with Shōeki, from Kyoto, where he received his Buddhist training, to Hachinohe, where he worked as a physician, and then to Ōdate, where he spent the final years of his life. Throughout this part, Yamazaki constantly refers to the ten points he laid out in the preface and attempts to provide answers to them. To give just an example, he dedicates a whole section to number (2) above, arguing that Shōeki never actually criticized Tokugawa Ieyasu (as Kanō Kōkichi had suggested), but in fact referred to him in a respectful, deferential manner. In his démarche, he quotes extensively from Shōeki's writings, including less known texts that are usually overlooked, such as 『私法神書巻』 (*Shinō as Private Law*).

The second part, the bulkiest, is dedicated to the development and evolution of Shōeki's thought. Thus, Yamazaki identifies three main stages—early, middle and late—in Shōeki's philosophy, and discusses them separately. He traces the evolution of two concepts (*shizen* 自然, and *shin* 真) throughout these stages and proposes that they constitute a sort of "core" (核心) of Shōeki's work, underpinning all other ideas and notions. Yamazaki implies that these concepts represent the main point of interest for Shōeki, and that his whole philosophy is in fact developed around them as a system of thought that is rather schematic and sometimes incoherent at first, but gradually becomes more and more consistent and convincing. Of course, he discusses other concepts as well (*ki* 気, *chokkō* 直耕, *tenchi* 転定 etc.), but suggests that they are subaltern to the two mentioned above, in that they are merely used to explain the intricacies of the world of Nature.

In most cases, Yamazaki's arguments and demonstrations are rigorous and meticulous and, as I have already said, he cites extensively from the original to prove his point. In some instances, however, he fails to make a convincing case; for example, when exploring the point mentioned at number (9) in the preface, he puts forth the idea that Shōeki's thought is fundamentally Shintoist, which is an idea that has already been debated and refuted in the literature, particularly by Terao in his commentaries to the Nōbunkyō edition of Shōeki's complete works. In this respect, Yamazaki's argument lacks clarity and power of persuasion.

Another aspect where I felt that Yamazaki pushes his interpretation too far is the idea that there is a nationalistic vein informing Shōeki's thought, which would explain his criticism of extraneous ideologies such as Daoism, Confucianism and Buddhism. In my view—and I am in agreement with most Shōeki scholars here—Shōeki perceives these ideologies more in terms of their potential to institute and regulate hierarchies within society, thus estranging the human being from the realm of Nature. He does not insist upon their origin, and in fact he includes Shintō in the same category of ideologies contrived by the "sages of old." To my mind, it is not nationalism that informs this view, but rather a deeply sympathetic, humanistic perspective of society and of the human being.

In conclusion, I would say that Yamazaki's book feels incomplete and unconvincing *precisely* because it is so ambitious: it attempts to be comprehensive and cover all the major concepts put forth by Shōeki but, in doing so, it is constrained in many instances to a superficial discussion, which ultimately produces very few new insights. For example, the section dedicated to Shōeki's vision of the human being is only three pages long, and extremely schematic—not to say simplistic—as it completely ignores the distinction that Shōeki makes between the World of Nature on the one hand, and human society on the other.

However, Yamazaki does raise some interesting questions that deserve a thorough examination, such as the idea that Shōeki's understanding of *shizen* differs from our modern interpretation of the notion of "nature" and that it should probably be rendered with a different term in English. On this point, I agree with him, as I believe this might be a topic relevant not only for Shōeki's thought but for Japanese philosophy in general. Therefore, I would recommend the book as a good starting point for a serious, rigorous debate about the status and role of philosophy in the intellectual landscape of Tokugawa Japan, and about the Japanese vision of Nature and its place within a wider, global context.

Roman Paşca
*Kanda University of International Studies, Japan*

**Takemura Makio 竹村牧男『ブッディスト・エコロジー：共生・環境・いのちの思想学』**[Buddhist Ecology: Symbiosis, Environment, and Ideas of Life]

Tokyo, Nonburusha, 2016, 312 pages. ¥3,000. ISBN: 978-4903470986.

2015年12月、気候変動抑制に関するパリ協定が採択された。しかし、その後アメリカのトランプ大統領が脱退の意を示しているように、この問題に対する国際的足並みは依然揃っていない。地球温暖化に限らず、大気・土壌・水質の汚染、生態系の破壊といった環境問題が騒がれるようになったのが1960年代であるとすると、それから既に半世紀以上の月日が流れたことになるが、我々は未だこの問題に対して態度を決めきれないでいるように思われる。そのような中、我々が意識的・強制的に生活を変えずとも問題を解決してくれる可能性として期待されてきたのは、"新たな"技術の開発である。具体的には代替エネルギーによる発電や浄化技術などが注目されている。しかしながら、日々世界中で進行する開発・工業化の規模とスピードを前にしては、これらの新技術は焼け石に水を注ぐような効果しかもたらさないのではないかという不安感は否めない。

新たなものを求める動きに対し、本書の著者が試みるのは真逆の方向、すなわち古代に誕生した宗教である仏教の思想に解決の糸口を探るというものである。まさに「温故知新」の実践によって、これからの世界のあるべき姿を構想しようとするのだ。

現在東洋大学の学長を務める著者は、日本を代表する仏教学者の一人であり、丁寧で明解な解説で定評の『入門 哲学としての仏教』(2009, 講談社現代新書) の著者でもある。2016年10月に刊行された本書は、これまで東洋大学の数々のプロジェクトで「共生」や「エコ・フィロソフィ」といったテーマに取り組んできた著者が、講演やエッセイといった形で発表してきた研究成果を一冊にまとめたものである。

著者自身が「やや刺激的」と呼ぶタイトルを持つ本書は、仏教思想研究としても環境思想研究としても得るものの多い"二重に美味しい"本となっている。ただし仏教の基礎的知識がない場合、読者は各時代の思想の配置が分からずやや苦労するかもしれない(その場合、前掲書『入門 哲学としての仏教』を読んでからこちらに進んでも良いだろう)。本書は「共生」・「環境」・「いのち」をテーマとした三部構成となっており、扱われるテクストは実に多岐にわたる。具体的には、著者が専門とする唯識思想に加え、原始仏典から空海、道元、大正時代の日本の共生思想まで、また一部ではあるが西田幾多郎や鈴木大拙も登場する(著者には『〈宗教〉の核心：西田幾多郎と鈴木大拙に学ぶ』(2012, 春秋社) など彼らの思想をめぐる著作もある)。

本全体を通じて一貫して見られる著者の態度は、そもそも我々はどのような存在なのかという本源的な問いから社会のあるべき姿を構想しようというものである。新技術の開発や個人の生の強制的抑制といった対策は、人間の生活と環境的条件との不適合の問題に対する根本的な解決となるとは言い難い。そうではなく、自己と環境・他者との関係を問い直し、「本来の人間のあり方・生き方が実はおのずから持続可能な未来を展望するのだとしたら、その道こそ追求されるべきである」(p. 44) と著者は主張する。このような主張の裏には、仏教の思想こそが環境や他者と不可分なかかわりの中にある我々のあり方を示すという著者の確信が見られる。「まず心 (識) があって、その中に身体と環境とが維持されて」(p. 144) いるという唯識思想の解釈などを通じて、著者は単に環境の捉え方ではなく、我々自身の自己了解の大きな転換を促す。

また本書では西洋に対して批判と協同両方の態度が見られる。著者は一方で、東洋の仏教を評価するという立場から、今日の環境問題の原因としての西洋近代化を批判する。しかし他方で、仏教とノルウェーのアルネ・ネスらのディープ・エコロジーの思想とに見られる共通点を挙げながら、「東洋と西洋の思想が一致して同じことを主張しうる状況を、深く考慮すべき」(p. 176) と今日の東西の協同可能性を指摘する。具体的には、本書では我々の行動指針として三聚浄戒という大乗仏教の戒律を現代の状況に合わせて改めた〈新三聚浄戒〉が提唱されるが、これを環境問題の具体的な取り組みにつなげていく際にはネスが示したライフスタイルが大いに参考になると著者は期待する (p. 224)。

このように射程の広い本書であるが、やや気になったのは、時に一つの論考の中で異なる仏教宗派の思想が連続的に論じられていることである。それこそ一つの思想に

縛られない自由な立場ともいえるが、素人目からは各論の整合性について判断することが難しい箇所があった。また、複数の場で発表された論文をまとめたものであることもあり、論考の間のつながりが見えにくかった。欲をいえば、各派の思想を踏まえた上で、著者自身の哲学、すなわち著者自身は人間・環境をどのように見ているのかをもっと知りたいと思われた。

しかし、対象とするテクストが広範囲に渡る本書が、読者に数々の時代の仏教思想への扉を開くことは確実である。また、思想研究を中心とした本書は環境問題に対する応用面でやや不足があると著者自身述べているが、〈新三聚浄戒〉という手がかりが提案されていることは今後の研究にも有用だろう。東洋大学のプログラムの成果は、同じノンブル社から『エコ・フィロソフィ入門：サステイナブルな知と行為の創出』（2010）、『サステイナビリティとエコ・フィロソフィ：西洋と東洋の対話から』（2010）、『自然と命の尊さについて考える：エコ・フィロソフィとサステイナビリティ学の展開』（2015）なども刊行されており、本書を読んで興味が湧いた人にはさらにこれらも参照することが薦められる。日本哲学に従事する研究者はもちろん、地球に生きる一人一人にかかわる問題として多くの人に本書が読まれることを望む。

INUTSUKA Yū 犬塚 悠
*The University of Tokyo*

Oleg Benesch, *Inventing the Way of the Samurai: Nationalism, Internationalism, and Bushido in Modern Japan*
New York, Oxford University Press, 2016, paperback, 284 pages. $31.60.
ISBN: 978-0198754251.

Most readers of this journal know that *bushidō*, whatever its claims to the contrary, is a twentieth-century creation. But if, like me, you are only knowledgeable about some of the major twists in its development, this book is the perfect fix for that lacuna. Benesch gives a thorough and balanced account of *bushidō*'s ideological development from the medieval period up to the present. In our contemporary historiographical context, we recognize the scent of historical reconstruction when we come across it. And in *bushidō* that scent is unmistakable.

Benesch follows that scent, tracking it to its sources. He traces the subterranean roots of *bushidō* to a time long before it became so visible in its modern form. Of course, going back to the roots of the tradition is exactly what the ideologues of the modern period purported to do, but Benesch digs up what was really there before it became so politicized. The reconstruction of the past seldom happens all at once, but is more often a complex event that surreptitiously starts in the margins of our collective consciousness, sneaking up on us until we cannot help but deal with it. By then, however, it is often too late to modify or mollify easily because some political group has already taken control of its articulation and put it to use in furthering its own agenda. If you want a balanced, sophisticated critique of how *bushidō* came to achieve such a powerful ideological presence in Japan, this book is again an excellent place to begin.

We can also can think of another way in which a reconstruction of the past influences societal developments, namely when a key idea gains enough legitimacy that, even when criticized, it is seldom rejected so fully that it is completely eradicated. Instead, it steps out of the spotlight for a while, waiting in the wings ready to come back on stage at a key moment, and then often in the guise of a new character or a least an old one with a costume change. Benesch appreciates this dynamic within the ideological history of *bushidō*, calling it "resilience." Once it establishes its presence in the Meiji period, *bushidō* sometimes recedes in its influence, but at other times returns in full force playing a key role in history.

I especially appreciate Benesch's avoiding the temptation to offer an essentialist, unequivocal characterization of *bushidō* as if it were a single idea interpreted from different perspectives through history. It is not that we change our view of it, but instead that *bushidō* itself transmutes into something different. Like a shape-shifting fox, *bushidō* assumes a variety of forms through its history, forms well documented by Benesch. He investigates the historical variations we might have expected: an array of pre-Tokugawa, Tokagawa, *bakumatsu*, Meiji, post-Meiji, wartime, and postwar appearances. Less predictably, though, he also takes us on a fascinating tour of a menagerie of Chinese-influenced species and anti-Chinese species, of Christian (including even Quaker!) variants and Buddhist anti-Christian variants, and of universalist permutations that actively sought western parallels alongside nativist constructions that used *bushidō* in support of its claim for Japanese uniqueness. I have nothing but admiration for Benesch's skill in unearthing so many forms of *bushidō* through history.

Now, as befits this journal, my review turns to making a few observations and comments of special relevance to philosophers. First, as a general principle, I suspect that the most resilient symbols and philosophical motifs are those, like *bushidō*, that elude a fixed definition and are pliable enough to assume new forms in new circumstances. When I teach American students about the context of twentieth-century Japanese philosophical discussions of such ideas as *kokutai* and the East Asian Co-prosperity sphere, I have used an analogy from their own culture, namely, the idea of "family values" as it is played out in American politics. At least from the time of Ronald Reagan, I cannot think of a single US politician who has taken a position *against* family values. Yet, I would be hard pressed to come up with the names of any two politicians who define family values in the same way. Are family values limited to two-parent families? Must the parents be a heterosexual couple? Do family values allow for medical interventions to limit family size or to avoid congenitally challenged offspring? And so forth. Although ordinary US citizens and politicians alike may answer such questions differently, they nonetheless all claim to be upholding "family values."

After reading Benesch, I wonder if at some point *bushidō* in modern Japan attained a similar status. Arguments about *bushidō* often seem more about how to define it than whether to advocate or reject it. That is, discussions often seem to shape the ideal to one's agenda rather than question its fundamental value. In his essay for *Rude Awakenings* concerning the Kyoto School relation to the political ideology of its time, Ueda Shizuteru called this phenomenon "a tug-of-war" over what politically charged words mean. In the history of philosophy, such tugs-of-war are more common than some purist philosophers might expect. As interpreters of Japanese philosophy, we should attune ourselves to the possibility that some philosophical discourse is not about justifying or refuting an idea, but instead an attempt to shape or re-shape what is accepted at the time as an unassailable ideal. In our contemporary political situation in both Europe and the United States, for example, the intellectual battle is not over whether patriotism is good or bad, but rather over what constitutes "true" patriotism.

Another philosophical issue I would like to raise is that of hybridity. As an historian Benesch seldom directly addresses the issue of how to locate *bushidō* within the cluster of Japanese philosophical traditions: Buddhist, Confucian, and Shintō. As a philosopher I would like to raise the following question: when a value, phrase, or idea historically connected with Confucianism becomes part of an account of *bushidō*, is it still "Confucian?" Or, once it has been assimilated into *bushidō*, has it become a *bushidō* phenomenon and no longer a Confucian one? For example, I maintain the Confucian values and the Buddhist values in the Shōtoku *Constitution* remain true to their origins. The *Constitution* allows Confucian values to remain Confucian, the Buddhist Buddhist. It does so by allocating them to distinctive domains, namely, Confucianism for social relations and political roles, Buddhism for psychological introspection and personal transformation. Does *bushidō* assimilate aspects of Confucianism (and Buddhism or Shintō) through such an algorithm of allocation or does it cross-breed them to create a new species of ideology? I believe *bushidō* has evolved into a true hybrid. First, I should explain what I mean by a hybrid because the term is often used by scholars in a loose fashion, making it almost a synonym for "syncretism." But both allocation and hybridization are syncretistic. Of philosophical importance is how they differ.

A hybrid is a cross-breeding of two species that creates *a new*, third species. Allocation leaves the two parents intact within its syncretizing and they can later be separated out if circumstances call for it. You can take the "Confucian" values out of the Shōtoku *Constitution* and still recognize them as Confucianism. By contrast, in a true hybrid you cannot go back in that way because the parents are absorbed into the DNA of the new species and can no longer be extracted. A mule is a cross-breeding of horse and donkey, but you cannot use a mule to be a parent of a horse or donkey. Or, according to the analysis of most genetic botanists, a loganberry is a hybrid of a raspberry and blackberry. In turn a boysenberry is a hybrid of a loganberry and a raspberry. Yet, you cannot cross-pollinate a raspberry and blackberry to create a boysenberry. So the practical issue behind my question about *bushidō* is whether the "Confucian values" within it can ever be extracted again into a Japanese Confucianism. I think not.

If I am right, that would help explain why we can identify the presence of "Confucian" values in Japanese society, but very little Confucianism *per se*, even as a philosophical tradition. There is certainly scholarship *about* Confucianism in modern Japan, but we do not find very much Confucian philosophizing (comparable to Soga Ryōjin's philosophizing in a Shin Buddhist tradition, Nishitani Keiji's in a Zen Buddhist one, or Ueda Kenji's in a Shintō one, for example). If Confucianism and its values are like the blackberry, the boysenberry of *bushidō* has gradually taken over the garden and pushed it out. In the genealogy of *bushidō*, we find values of Confucianism's parentage, but once the new species was established, Confucian values became *bushidō* values and truly Confucian no longer.

For example, although loyalty is certainly a major Confucian value (albeit admittedly not one of the cardinal five), Confucian loyalty evolved into a new species within Japan. The loyalty taught in, say, the National Morality system of the Japanese education system from the Taishō period up to the end of the War is not, I would argue, the loyalty of Confucianism. Once loyalty was bushidō-ized, it could no longer be extracted as Confucian. Starting from around the Akō Incident of the forty-seven *rōnin* up to 1945, the *bushidō* form of loyalty gradually flourished so much that it pushed out the Confucian sense.

In conclusion, I'd say Benesch's book is not only a classical work in Japanese history, but also one I would heartily recommend to anyone interested in the history of Japanese philosophy. It may not itself be philosophical, but it gives the detailed information about the historical development of an idea and an ideology that should provoke any philosopher interested in Japan. In general I would argue that scholars of Japanese philosophy can benefit from reading intellectual histories of Japan, at least ones of this caliber.

Thomas P. Kasulis
*Ohio State University (emeritus)*

Yuho Hisayama, *Erfahrungen des* ki. *Leibessphäre, Atmosphäre, Pansphäre*
Freiburg, Verlag Karl Alber, 2014, paperback, 136 pages. €24.00.
ISBN: 978-3495486344.

Yuho Hisayama legt mit seiner Monographie eine beachtenswerte Studie zum Begriff bzw. Phänomen des *ki* (氣 oder 気, chin. *qi*) vor, die das Forschungsfeld um neue methodische Ansätze bereichert.

Hisayama ist bisher durch seine Forschungen zu Goethe sowie Studien aus dem Umfeld der Leibphänomenologie Herrmann Schmitz' bekannt, die sich mit den japanischen Begriffen *kehai* („Stimmung", „Ahnung") und *kūki* („Luft") auseinandersetzen, d.h. Ausdrücken, die ebenfalls dem Bedeutungsfeld von *ki* entstammen.[1] Dabei spielt immer wieder das aus der Schmitz'schen Philosophie bekannte Phänomen der „Atmosphäre" eine zentrale Rolle, das im vorliegenden Buch durch die Ausdrücke „Leibessphäre" und „Pansphäre" weiter differenziert wird

Das Buch gliedert sich in zwei Teile. Der erste Teil widmet sich einer vorläufigen begrifflichen Annäherung an den Ausdruck *ki* sowie der methodischen Erschließung einer „Phänomenologie der Sphären" mit einer jeweiligen Behandlung der drei genannten Sphärentypen. Der zweite Teil behandelt einzelne Aspekte des Phänomens *ki* sowie der nominalen Komposita *kehai* („Stimmung", „Ahnung") und *keshiki* („Aussicht", „Landschaft"), die *ki* als semantisches Element enthalten. Zudem werden ästhetische und klimatische Phänomene sowie der Begriff des *kokoro* („Herz", „Geist", „Herzgeist") im Zusammenhang mit *ki* analysiert. Das methodische Vorgehen des zweiten Teils orientiert sich dabei an einer hermeneutischen Erschließung interkultureller Phänomene mittels der Übersetzung, wofür Hisayama Ausschnitte aus verschiedenen Romanen des japanischen Schriftstellers Natsume Sōseki (1867–1916) heranzieht, die diese Ausdrücke literarisch ausformulieren.

1. Hisayama 2011 und Hisayama 2015

Schon die Einleitung richtet sich vor allem gegen eine essentialistische bzw. substanzialistische Auffassung von *ki* als eines Urstoffes oder einer Lebenskraft im Sinne einer materialen Substanz gegenständlicher Art. Dem Diktum Humboldts folgend, „dass, so wie man von den Ausdrücken absieht die bloss körperliche Gegenstände bezeichnen, kein Wort Einer Sprache vollkommen einem in einer andren Sprache gleich ist", wird zudem eine einheitliche Übersetzung abgelehnt und ein hermeneutischer Umweg über plurale Übersetzungsweisen und phänomenologische Beschreibungen verschiedener *ki*-Erfahrungen eingeschlagen, die allerdings auf nicht ganz unproblematische Weise mit einer möglichen Lehre von kulturübergreifenden Archetypen bzw. Ur-Symbolen oder -Erfahrungen verbunden wird.

Die begriffliche Annäherung im ersten Teil zieht auf fruchtbare Weise sowohl japanische als auch westliche Literatur heran, um mögliche Unterscheidungspraktiken sowie alternative Schreibweisen und Interpretationsmöglichkeiten des *ki*-Begriffs aufzuzeigen. Die anschließende phänomenologische „Sphärentheorie" berücksichtigt neben Schriften von Hermann Schmitz auch Autoren wie Gernot Böhme, Thomas Fuchs und Hubertus Tellenbach, und wird als alternativer Weg zur Substanzontologie gedeutet, der eine Verdinglichung des *ki*-Phänomens und eine voreilige Spaltung in Subjekt und Objekt unterläuft, um das *zugleich* als „inneres Gefühl" *und* „äußere Atmosphäre" erscheinende Phänomen des *ki* ganzheitlich interpretieren zu können. Dabei werden die Leibessphäre, „die man als den eigenen Leib wahrnimmt", die Atmosphäre, „die man in seiner Umgebung wahrnimmt" und die Pansphäre, „in der die Kontinuität von Leibessphäre und Atmosphäre gespürt wird", unterschieden und die Atmosphäre wiederum in Homosphäre (der Leibessphäre gegenüber als ähnlich empfundene Atmosphäre) und Heterosphäre (der Leibessphäre gegenüber als fremd empfundene Atmosphäre) unterteilt. Fraglich bleibt dabei allerdings, ob die Unterscheidung von Leibessphäre und Atmosphäre nicht auf eine erneute Entgegensetzung von „Innen" und „Außen" hinausläuft und ob verschiedene Atmosphären (und Leibessphären) zu ihrer Vermittlung auf eine umfassende „Pansphäre" angewiesen sind und nicht schon von sich aus aufgrund ihres halb-dinglichen und vagen Charakters als Vermittlungsprozesse zu verstehen sind, die nicht wiederum in eine Totalität eingebettet zu werden brauchen.

Der zweite Teil des Buches beschäftigt sich wie bereits erwähnt hauptsächlich mit Ausschnitten aus dem literarischen Werk Natsume Sōsekis. Dabei werden verschiedene Phänomene behandelt, die in engem Zusammenhang zum Begriff des *ki* stehen. Der Ausdruck *kehai* (気配, „Verteilung des *ki*"), der im Deutschen eine mögliche Entsprechung in einer vagen „Ahnung" haben könnte, wird von Hisayama als „das Halbdingliche" im Sinne eines nicht eindeutig erfassbaren Gestaltungsprozesses interpretiert, auf den „nicht das rationale Ich, sondern die vordiskursive, synästhetische Leiblichkeit reagieren" muss, wodurch eine Objektivierung des *kehai* unmöglich erscheint und stattdessen ein „Wechselspiel zwischen der Leibessphäre und dem heterosphärischen *kehai*" einsetzt (S. 74f).

Im anschließenden Kapitel wird „Das fremde *ki*" als Thema einer „Xenologie der Sphären" behandelt. Interessant ist hierbei, das für Hisayama das Phänomen der Fremdheit – auf das er sich in Anlehnung an Schriften von Bernhard Waldenfels bezieht – stets der Heterosphäre zugerechnet und somit in ein Außerhalb des Leibes verlegt wird. Hierbei scheint die Fremdheit, die uns im Leib selbst begegnet und die wir als Leib selbst sind, unterschlagen zu werden, ein Kritikpunkt, der auch in Bezug auf die Leibphänomenologie Hermann Schmitz' geäußert wurde und den Hisayama zwar anspricht, aber letztlich nicht überzeugend ausräumen kann.

Dennoch sind die Analysen des zweiten Teils eine bereichernde Erweiterung der bisherigen Forschung zum Begriff des *ki* und verwandter Phänomene. Die Textstellen, die Hisayama aus den Werken Sōsekis heranzieht, bieten eine solide Quelle für konkrete Beispiele, an denen sich phänomenologische Bestimmungen ausweisen lassen. Mit Rückbezug auf den Ausdruck *kūki*, der wörtlich mit „Himmels-*ki*" bzw. „Leere-*ki*" wiedergegeben werden kann und sich auf die „Luft", aber auch „Atmosphären" und „Stimmungen" bezieht, stellt Hisayama den Zwischen-Charakter des *ki* anschaulich heraus. Die Gegenüberstellung der eng verwandten Begriffe *ki* und *kokoro* („Herz", „Herzgeist") gelingt teilweise mithilfe einer eindringlichen Textstelle aus dem Roman *Sanshirōs Wege*, in welcher die Wirkung eines wie Marmor erscheinenden, trüben Himmels beschrieben wird: „Unter einem solchen Himmel wird das *kokoro* schwer, aber das *ki* leicht." (S. 91) Das Zitat wirkt aufgrund der gewöhnlicherweise engen Verbindung von *ki* und *kokoro* in der japanischen Sprache zunächst befremdlich und ist gerade deshalb interessant für eine Analyse der unterschiedlichen Nuancen dieser Ausdrücke. Hisayama erklärt sich den Unterschied zwischen den beiden Begriffen mithilfe von Sphärendifferenzen: „[Es] ist festzustellen, dass hier mit dem *kokoro* die Ich-bezogene, d. h. reflektierte Wahrnehmung der Homosphäre bezeichnet wird, mit dem *ki* hingegen die leiblich unmittelbare, d. h. reflexionslose Erfahrung der Pansphäre." (S. 98) Leider wirkt die Annahme einer Pansphäre auch an dieser Stelle spekulativ und es wird nicht ganz ersichtlich, wie eine vollkommen reflexionslose Erfahrung bewusst zugänglich sein soll. Der Begriff bleibt im Vergleich zu denjenigen der „Leibesphäre" und der „Atmosphäre" zu blass und phänomenologisch unterdeterminiert.

Anhand des Ausdrucks *keshiki* („*ki*-Farbe", „Erscheinung des *ki*") wird das Phänomen der „Landschaft" im folgenden Abschnitt als „atmosphärischer Gesichtsausdruck" im Sinne eines physiognomischen Charakters geologischer Gegebenheiten interpretiert und mit einem „pansphärischen Spüren der Landschaft" verknüpft, bevor Hisayama im abschließenden Kapitel auf die Bedeutung des *ki* für die sino-japanische Tusch-Malerei im Stil des *ki in sei dō* (気韻生動) eingeht, wobei das *ki* hier als Ausdruck atmosphärisch-leiblicher Bewegungssuggestionen verstanden wird.

Trotz der möglicherweise problematischen Voraussetzung einer Pansphäre bleiben Hisayamas umfangreiche Analysen zu einer Vielzahl von Phänomenen im Umkreis des *ki* eine erfreuliche Bereicherung der Forschung zum Thema, auch aufgrund der relativ umfangreichen Einbindung japanischer Literatur. Die Monographie reiht sich neben den Arbeiten von Autoren wie Peter Pörtner[2], Kimura Bin[3], Ichirō Yamaguchi[4] und Rolf Elberfeld[5] in die wachsende Forschungsliteratur zum Phänomen des *ki* ein und zeigt damit, dass das Thema philosophisch noch lange nicht ausgeschöpft ist.

## Literatur

Elberfeld, Rolf
    2013    *Sprache und Sprachen. Eine philosophische Grundorientierung*. 2. Aufl., Freiburg im Breisgau, S. 303–11.

Hisayama, Yuho
    2011    *Ästhetik des kehai. Zur transkulturellen Phänomenologie der Atmosphäre*, Rostock.
    2015    „Individuum und Atmosphäre. Überlegungen zum Distanzproblem am Beispiel des japanischen Wortes *kûki*", in: Michael Großheim et al. (Hg.), *Leib, Ort, Gefühl: Perspektiven der räumlichen Erfahrung*, Freiburg.

Kimura, Bin
    1995    *Zwischen Mensch und Mensch. Strukturen japanischer Subjektivität*, übers. u. herausgegeben von Elmar Weinmayr, Darmstadt.

Pörtner, Peter
    1985    „Notizen zum Begriff des Ki", in: G. S. Dombrady und Franziska Ehmcke (Hg.): *Referate des vi. Deutschen Japanologentages in Köln, 12.–14. April 1984*, Hamburg, S. 215–54.

Yamaguchi, Ichiro
    1997    *Ki als leibhaftige Vernunft. Beitrag zur interkulturellen Phänomenologie der Leiblichkeit*, München.

Leon Krings
*Universität Hildesheim*

2. Pörtner 1985
3. Kimura 1995
4. Yamaguchi 1997
5. Elberfeld 2013, 303–11.

# Contributors

James W. Heisig is a permanent research fellow (emeritus) at the Nanzan Institute for Religion and Culture in Nagoya, Japan. In addition to his many volumes of writings and translations, he is the general editor of *Frontiers of Japanese Philosophy*. Recent recent works include *Nothingness and Desire* (2013) and *Much Ado about Nothingness: Essays on Nishida and Tanabe* (2015).

Quentin Hiernaux is an frs-fnrs research fellow and doctoral candidate in philosophy at the Université Libre de Bruxelles, Belgium. His main area of research is the history and philosophy of plant sciences.

Inutsuka Yū 犬塚 悠 is a doctoral student at the University of Tokyo and part-time lecturer at Dokkyō University. Since 2015 she has also been a visiting researcher of the Research Center for International Japanese Studies at Hōsei University. Her publications include the article "Sensation, Betweenness, Rhythms: Watsuji's Environmental Philosophy and Ethics in Conversation with Heidegger" (John Baird Callicott and James McRae, eds., *Japanese Environmental Philosophy*, 2017).

Imono Mika 鋳物美佳 currently teaches Japanese at the Université de Strasbourg. She received her doctorate from the Université de Toulouse II le Mirail in 2013 with a dissertation entitled "Sur le mouvement volontaire en tant que réflexion ou création." She is the author of various scholarly essays on Maine de Biran, Félix Ravaisson, and Nishida Kitarō. Her interests center on questions related to the body and expression.

Thomas P. Kasulis is is University Distinguished Scholar and Professor Emeritus in Comparative Studies at the Ohio State University, where he has taught in the departments of comparative studies, philosophy, and East Asian studies. His newest book, *Engaging Japanese Philosophy: A Short History*, is scheduled to appear this winter.

Katsumori Makoto 勝守 真 is Professor of philosophy at Akita University. After studying geophysics, he majored in the history and philosophy of science at the University of Tokyo. He holds a PhD in philosophy from the Vrije Universiteit, the Netherlands. His main fields of research are the philosophy of science, and contemporary European and Japanese philosophy. His publications include 『現代日本哲学への問い：「われわれ」とそのかなた』(2009) and *Niels Bohr's Complementarity: Its Structure, History, and Intersections with Hermeneutics and Deconstruction* (2011).

Leon Krings specialized in philosophy and Japanese studies at the University of Trier and Sophia University in Tokyo. He is currently preparing a doctoral thesis on "Theories of *Leiblichkeit* and Embodiment and the *Kata*-System in Japanese Practices of Self-Cultivation" at the University of Hildesheim, Germany. His research interests include Kyoto-School philosophy, Buddhism, phenomenology, and practices of embodiment and self-cultivation.

John W. M. Krummel is Associate Professor in Religious Studies at Hobart and William Smith Colleges, Geneva, NY; Assistant Editor of the *Journal of Japanese Philosophy*; Co-editor of *Social Imaginaries* (Zeta Books); and President of the International Association of Japanese Philosophy. He has a PhD in Philosophy from the New School for Social Research and a PhD in Religion from Temple University. His published work includes *Nishida Kitarō's Chiasmatic Chorology* (2015) and *Place of Dialectic, Dialectic of Place* (2011), in addition to numerous articles and translations on Japanese and continental philosophy.

Kuroda Akinobu, docteur en philosophie (l'Université de Strasbourg), maître de conférences à l'Université de Strasbourg où il enseigne l'histoire de la littérature et de la pensée japonaises. Thèse: *Enjeux, possibilités et limites d'une philosophie de la vie. Kitarô Nishida au miroir de quelques philosophes français*. Articles: « Une philosophie de la vie en train de se faire — la philosophie de Nishida au miroir de la phénoménologie française » (2004); « *Le Ciel vide et la terre saturée. Le néant médiateur, silencieux, ouvert et passible* » dans *Notions esthétiques. Résonances entre les arts et les cultures* (2013); « Le geste dans le théâtre *nô:* approche philosophique — réflexion phénoménologique sur la forme vivante, mise en scène dans le théâtre *nô* » (2015).

Rebeca Maldonado received her philosophical degrees at the Universidad Nacional Autónoma de México, where she has been teaching ontology and metaphysics since 1997. She has published on Nietzsche (*Metáforas del abismo Itinerarios de ascenso y descenso en Nietzsche*, 2008), Kant (*Kant: La razón estremecida*, 2010), and hermeneutics. These in turn interested her in the problem of nothingness in the mystics, Heidegger, and the Kyoto School along with its implications for the renounciation of anthropomorphism.

Ralf MÜLLER is currently a visiting research fellow at the Institute for Philosophy located in the University of Hildesheim. After completing a doctoral dissertation on "Dōgen's Idea of Language: Historical and Symbolic-Theory Perspectives" (Karl-Alber Verlag, 2013), he has been studying Nishida's idea of culture, particularly as it relates to the question of translating philosophy between cultures. For further details, see http://www.ralfmueller.eu.

Rossa Ó MUIREARTAIGH received his PhD in philosophy from the European Graduate School in Switzerland. He has also studied at Nagoya University (Japan), University College Dublin, Dublin City University, and the University of Limerick in Ireland. He taught at Dublin City University and Newcastle University (UK) before joining the staff of Aichi Prefectural University in Japan. In addition to his academic writings, he is also active as a translator of Japanese works into English.

ŌSAKI Harumi 大﨑晴美 received a PhD in contemporary French thought from Hitotsubashi University in 2003 and went on to complete a second doctorate on Japanese philosophy from McGill University in 2016. Her research interests include Japanese philosophy, twentieth-century French poststructuralism, and comparative philosophy. Among her articles in English are "Pure Experience in Question: William James in the Philosophies of Nishida Kitarō and Alfred North Whitehead" (2015) and "Killing Oneself, Killing the Father: On Deleuze's Suicide in Comparison with Blanchot's Notion of Death" (2008). She is currently completing work on the forthcoming publication of her second dissertation, *Nothingness in the Heart of Empire: The Moral and Political Philosophy of the Kyoto School in Imperial Japan*.

Roman PAŞCA received his PhD from the University of Bucharest in Romania and is currently a Lecturer at the Research Institute for Japanese Studies at Kanda University of International Studies in Chiba, Japan. His research interests include Tokugawa intellectual history, the concept of Nature in Japanese philosophy, and the relationship between philosophy and translation. He is currently working on a project attempting to redefine the place of thinkers such as Andō Shōeki and Yamagata Bantō within the socio-cultural context of Tokugawa Japan.

Marc PEETERS est professeur de logique et d'ontologie formelles à l'Université Libre de Bruxelles. Il est l'auteur de nombreux articles et ouvrages consacrés à Kant, Thomas d'Aquin, Descartes, Lesniewski. Son travail relève de la métaphysique spéculative conçue à partir de l'œuvre de Kant. Il s'est agi de proposer une fondation transcendantale des logiques développementales. Loin d'être détaché du réel, le travail de Marc Peeters se veut résolument politique dans le sens où faire de la métaphysique c'est affirmer une dissidence, inactuelle et intempestive. Ainsi la *philosophia perennis* dont se revendique l'auteur est-elle inscrite dans le concert actuel de la philosophie.

Jordančo SEKULOVSKI is Adjunct Professor in Humanities (Intellectual Heritage) at Temple University Japan; Associate Foreign Researcher at the East Asian Research Center, Kyoto University, and, general editor of *Studia Philosophica* (Chisokudō Publications). He received his PhD in philosophy from Paris West (x) University under the supervision of François Laruelle. He is the author of *Postures et pratiques de l'Homme. Libéralisme, philosophie non-standard et pensée japonaise* (2013). For more please visit: http://jsekulovski.wix.com/nonphi

Jordi VALLVERDÚ is a tenured Professor at the Autonomous University of Barcelona in Catalonia. His interests lies in epistemology and the cognitive sciences, especially in understanding the role of emotions in natural and artificial entities. Cross-cultural and historical themes play an important part in his work. In 2011 he received a grant from the Japan Society for the Promotion of Science to study human-robot interaction at Kyoto University. His books include *Bayesians Versus Frequentists: A Philosophical Debate on Statistical Reasoning* (2016), *Corporeidades* (2016, co-authored), and *Advanced Research on Biologically Inspired Cognitive Architectures* (2017, co-authored).

## Editors

Jan Gerrit STRALA, *Aichi Prefectural University*
MORISATO Takeshi, *Université Libre de Bruxelles*

## Editorial board

Hiroyuki AKATSUKA, *University of Hildesheim*
Laurentiu ANDREI, *Université Blaise Pascal*
Pierre BONNEELS, *Université Libre de Bruxelles*
Thorsten BOTZ-BORNSTEIN, *Gulf University for Science and Technology in Kuwait*
Raquel BOUSO, *Universitat Pompeu Fabra*
Emmanuel CATTIN, *Université Blaise Pascal*
Matteo CESTAIR, *Università Degli Studi di Torino*
Montserrat CRESPÍN PERALES, *Autonomous University of Barcelona*
Michel DALISSIER, *Université Blaise Pascal*
Alfonso FALERO FOLGOSO, *Universidad de Salamanca*
Felipe FERRARI GONÇALVES, *Nagoya University*
Enrico FONGARO, *Tōhoku University*
Alberto GARCIA SALGADO, *University Michoacana de San Nicolás de Hidalgo*
Marcello GHILARDI, *Università degli Studi di Padova*
GŌDO Wakako, *University of Tokyo*
INUTSUKA Yū, *University of Tokyo*
Romaric JANNEL, *École Pratique des Hautes Études*
David W. JOHNSON, *Boston College*
KUWANO Moe, *Ramon Llull University*
Michael LUCKEN, *Institut National des Langues et Civilisations Orientales*
Hanna MCGAUGHEY, *University of Trier*
Rebeca MALDONADO, *Universidad Nacional Autónoma de México*
Lucas dos Reis MARTINS, *University of Hildesheim*
Ramūnas MOTIEKAITIS, *Vilnius University*
Ralf MÜLLER, *University of Hildesheim*
ONO Jun'ichi, *Ghent University*
Tony PACYNA, *University of Heidelberg*
Ruben PFIZENMEIER, *Freie Universität Berlin*
Aingeru A. RAFAEL, *University of Tokyo*
Moritz SOMMET, *University of Fribourg*
Cody STATION, *Katholieke Universiteit Leuven*
Bernard STEVENS, *Université catholique de Louvain*
Jacynthe TREMBLAY, *Hokkaido University*

Made in the USA
San Bernardino, CA
26 March 2018